THE RIGHT TO SAY NO

Marital rape stands at the intersection of the socio-legal issues arising from both domestic violence and sexual assault. For centuries, women who suffered sexual assault perpetrated by their spouses had no legal recourse. A man's conjugal rights included his right to have sexual intercourse with his wife regardless of whether she consented. This right has been recognised in law, and still is in some jurisdictions today. This book emerges from the research undertaken by an innovative, multi-country, academic, collaborative project dedicated to comparatively analysing the legal treatment of sexual assault in intimate relationships, with a view to challenging the legal impunity for and inadequate legal responses to this form of gendered violence.

The Right to Say No

Marital Rape and Law Reform in Canada, Ghana, Kenya and Malawi

Edited by
Melanie Randall, Jennifer Koshan
and Patricia Nyaundi

•HART•
OXFORD • LONDON • NEW YORK • NEW DELHI • SYDNEY

HART PUBLISHING
Bloomsbury Publishing Plc
Kemp House, Chawley Park, Cumnor Hill, Oxford, OX2 9PH, UK

First published in Great Britain 2017

First published in hardback, 2017
Paperback edition, 2020

A catalogue record for this book is available from the British Library.

Library of Congress Cataloging-in-Publication Data

Names: Randall, Melanie, editor. | Koshan, Jennifer, editor. | Nyaundi, Patricia, editor.

Title: The right to say no : marital rape and law reform in Canada, Ghana, Kenya and Malawi / edited by Melanie Randall, Jennifer Koshan and Patricia Nyaundi.

Description: Portland, Oregon : Hart Publishing, 2017. | Includes bibliographical references and index.

Identifiers: LCCN 2017024447 (print) | LCCN 2017026544 (ebook) | ISBN 9781782258612 (Epub) | ISBN 9781782258605 (hardback)

Subjects: LCSH: Rape in marriage. | Human rights. | Law reform.

Classification: LCC K5197 (ebook) | LCC K5197 .R54 2017 (print) | DDC 344.03/28292—dc23

LC record available at https://lccn.loc.gov/2017024447

ISBN: HB: 978-1-78225-860-5
PB: 978-1-50993-669-4
ePDF: 978-1-78225-862-9
ePub: 978-1-78225-861-2

Typeset by Compuscript Ltd, Shannon

To find out more about our authors and books visit www.hartpublishing.co.uk. Here you will find extracts, author information, details of forthcoming events and the option to sign up for our newsletters.

FOREWORD

Marital rape is a gendered form of violence that is perpetrated across the globe. When the law fails to address marital rape effectively, it means that wives are denied their rights to equality, dignity, security of the person and access to justice. When the legal treatment of marital rape results in legally condoned violence, with the result that women and girls are treated as a form of property, it reinforces women's inequality in society and in other areas of the law. For example, it may be difficult to argue successfully that women are entitled to own property, when they are still treated as property themselves under the law. This allows for the devaluation of women in law, and allows for the reduction of their autonomy and independence in society.

In spite of the legal reality that marital rape is a violation of human rights protections against gender-based violence, the concept of marital rape is, for some, an idea that is challenging to conceive of. For example, in 1982, when Canadian Member of Parliament Margaret Mitchell raised the issue of domestic sexual assault for the first time in the House of Commons, some members laughed and called out to each other, making derisive gestures about beating their wives. One year later, in 1983, marital rape was criminalised in Canada, supporting the view that spousal sexual violence is an obvious violation of women's human rights that merits the same treatment by the justice system as other forms of sexual assault. Women should have an equal right to say no to unwanted sexual relations with their husbands and intimate partners as they have for other instances of unwanted sex.

Many of the analyses of marital rape in this book arise from an initiative undertaken by the Equality Effect. The Equality Effect is an international NGO that uses the law to make girls' and women's rights real.[1] The issue of marital rape presented the Equality Effect with an excellent opportunity to work collaboratively with human rights advocates and scholars from different jurisdictions, to analyse how the experience of sexual violence in marriage can be addressed to ensure that women are safe in their own homes. In 2009, Equality Effect team members from across Canada, Ghana, Kenya and Malawi met in Ottawa, Canada to compare their experiences of using the law to advance women's equality and improve women's lives. The team collectively identified the issue of rape in marriage as a priority issue because of a concern about how the institution of marriage can be used

[1] See the organisation's website at: http://theequalityeffect.org/.

as a legal loophole that leaves married women, including girls forced into early marriage, at risk of experiencing sexual violence. The team was interested in exploring how equality and human rights analyses could be applied to the issue, so that the law could be made to protect married women from harm.

As former colonies of Great Britain, the historical and present-day challenges with the criminalisation of marital rape in Canada, Ghana, Kenya and Malawi are derived from the same discriminatory rationales developed under British common law centuries ago. This shared colonial past forms a basis upon which to contextualise and understand women's experiences of discrimination, including sexual violence inside marriage. Comparing the different sexual violence laws in various countries allows for the examination of how different doctrinal approaches may lead to varying human rights violations in the marital rape context. A comparative approach also allows for the exploration of different options for reform, as well as the challenges that may be presented by legal pluralism and customary law, contributing to unique strategies for advancing girls' and women's human rights and securing their equal freedom from violence.

Extensive research, analysis, debate and critical thinking informed the discussions that helped to shape the contributions that make up some of the chapters in this book. Central to these discussions was a commitment to maintaining a positive and constructive approach to the work, and respectful communications that would allow Equality Effect team members to explore new and unique ideas with open-minded colleagues. Other chapters have been added to the book to round out the analysis, including chapters on the role of international and customary law that situate the legal treatment of marital rape within a truly global context.

Also central to the development of the Equality Effect's work on marital rape has been the exceptional generosity of the team members who dedicated their time on a pro bono basis, including: Dr Elizabeth Archampong, John Burke Baidoo, Kim Bernhardt, May Cheng, Andrea Dorfman, Mary Eberts, Pearl Eliadis, Sasha Hart, Marceline Kabir, Dr Winnie Kamau, Dr Ngeyi Kanyongolo, Jennifer Koshan, Tara MacDougall, June McCue, Sheila McIntyre, Patricia Nyaundi, Millie Odhiambo, Madame Justice Effie Owuor, Evelyn Palach, Margaret Parsons, Dr Melanie Randall, Jane Serwanga, Manprit Singh, Vasanthi Venkatesh and Seodi White. Special thanks are due to Sasha Hart and Vasanthi Venkatesh, who coordinated the work of many volunteer researchers who contributed to this book project. The Equality Effect is also grateful to the generous funders that made this work possible, including Fasken Martineau LLP, the International Development Research Council, Department of Justice Canada, the Stephen Lewis Foundation and private donors from across Canada.

The criminalisation of marital rape is not a panacea for the discriminatory legal treatment of marital rape claims, and criminalisation alone cannot bring an end to the experience of marital rape. Low reporting and prosecution rates for marital rape in Canada since its criminalisation in 1983 provide evidence of this reality, as do continuing problems with the judicial treatment of marital rape claims. Furthermore, the criminal justice system is by its very nature limited in its capacity to address the root causes of marital rape, and must be approached with caution because of its potential disproportionate use against the most marginalised members of society. However, the criminalisation of marital rape has important symbolic value, and can have a significant deterrent and educational effect that can contribute to a reduced incidence of marital rape. The criminalisation of marital rape and the legal treatment of marital rape victims consistent with domestic and international human rights norms are changes that could provide for real substantive equality for married women and girls.

Establishing legal and societal acknowledgement that rape can occur within a marriage may only evolve more fully over time and with the continued and applied efforts of equality seekers. The chapters in this book will hopefully contribute to the international conversation on the issue of marital rape, and help to advance women's rights so that all women are safe and equal in marriage.

Fiona A Sampson BA, MA, LLB, PhD, CM
CEO, the Equality Effect
July 2016

CONTENTS

DETAILED CONTENTS

LIST OF CONTRIBUTORS

Winifred Kamau is Associate Professor and Chair of the Private Law Department at the School of Law, University of Nairobi, Kenya.

Ngeyi Kanyongolo is a Senior Lecturer at the University of Malawi, Chancellor College, Zomba, Malawi.

Jennifer Koshan is a Professor in the Faculty of Law at the University of Calgary, Canada.

Renee Aku Sitsofe Morhe is a Senior Lecturer and Head of Private Law at the Kwame Nkrumah University of Science and Technology, Kumasi, Ghana.

Patricia Nyaundi is an Advocate of the High Court of Kenya and Secretary to the Kenya National Commission on Human Rights.

Melanie Randall is a full-time faculty member at the Faculty of Law, Western University, London, Ontario, Canada.

Fiona Sampson is the CEO of the equality effect.

Jane Serwanga is an Advocate of the High Court of Kenya and a Legal and Human Rights Consultant based in Nairobi, Kenya.

Vasanthi Venkatesh is an Assistant Professor in the Faculty of Law at the University of Windsor, Canada.

Seodi White is the Chief Director Responsible for Public Sector Reforms in the Malawi Government, Office of the President and Cabinet.

Part I

Marital Rape, Human Rights and the Law: Mapping the Issues

1

Introduction: Marital Rape and Law Reform: A Comparative Analysis of the Right to Say No

MELANIE RANDALL, JENNIFER KOSHAN AND PATRICIA NYAUNDI

A notable and important success of the women's movement and feminist organising over many decades, in many jurisdictions, has been bringing the significant problem of violence against women into public awareness and popular discourse. This awareness is evident in the now significant and expanding research literature on the topic, the network of shelters and victim services which have been established to assist women who have been assaulted, various state and international policy responses to the issue, educational initiatives, extensive law reform, media attention to the subject and the (still admittedly partial and limited) community recognition that violence against women exists as a social problem which requires public remedies.[1]

Yet within this broader story of success and social change, recognition of violence against women in the specific form of sexual assault in marriage (and other marriage-like intimate relationships) has lagged behind. The research and analyses in this book contribute to filling in this gap.[2] Our aspiration is for this

[1] This is not to deny the existence of major complexities and difficulties surrounding the results of feminist activism and analysis pertaining to gender violence and how it has been taken up at the policy level and in law reform. Instead, it is to draw attention to the efficacy of this work in achieving some very real and tangible shifts and improvements in women's lives. The partiality and implications of the results of feminist organising, and the massive amount of work still to be done require its own separate analysis. Some important feminist writing addresses these issues. See eg Sheila McIntyre, 'Tracking and Resisting Backlash against Equality Gains in Sexual Offence Law' (2000) 20(3) *Canadian Woman Studies* 72; Elizabeth Sheehy, Jane Doe, Carol Latchford and Rakhi Ruparelia (eds), 'Women Resisting Rape: Feminist Law, Practice, Activism' (2010) 28(11) *Canadian Woman Studies*, special issue; Clare McGlynn and Vanessa Munro (eds), *Rethinking Rape Law: International and Comparative Perspectives* (London, Routledge-Cavendish, 2010).

[2] It is encouraging that a recent shift is discernible towards a greater focus on marital rape. See eg Kersti Yllo and Gabriela Torres (eds), *Marital Rape: Consent, Marriage and Social Change in Global Context* (Oxford, Oxford University Press, 2016); Louise McOrmond-Plummer, Patricia Easteal and Jennifer Levy-Peck (eds), *Intimate Partner Sexual Violence: A Multidisciplinary Approach to Survivor Support and System Change* (London, Jessica Kingsley Publishers, 2013).

book to offer a critical perspective on some of the challenges and successes in the struggle to bring into view and ultimately work towards ending the problem of sexual assault of women in their most intimate relationships through ending legal impunity for marital rape.

This book originally emerged from a collaboration between African and Canadian feminist and human rights lawyers who participated in the work of the Equality Effect;[3] our work on the topic of marital rape then expanded further beyond its original starting point.[4] One of the ongoing ambitions of the Equality Effect is a project to challenge the legal impunity for marital rape, including demonstrating the ways in which this impunity undermines each partner country's constitutional guarantees of gender equality and of the rights to be free from discrimination along with other rights violations. The distinct nature of the partnership shaping the Equality Effect is also reflected in this book, which takes as its specific country case studies Canada, Ghana, Malawi and Kenya. These countries share a similar legacy of colonisation by Great Britain, resulting in the imposition of the common law in each jurisdiction along with the inheritance of legal thinking that led to husbands' impunity for marital rape. As chapter 3 makes clear, however, similar rationales for immunising spousal sexual violence from legal sanction existed (and continue to exist) in civil law countries as well, making the case studies pertinent in a global context.

Not surprisingly, one of the major themes running throughout the entire book is that marital rape must be understood deeply and centrally as an issue of gender inequality. This is consistent with the recognition by the major international institutions of the world that gender violence is an affront to women's equality rights, as well as their rights to autonomy, security of the person and access to justice.[5] As the World Health Organization has pointed out, because gender inequalities

[3] See Foreword to this volume, by Fiona Sampson. See also the Equality Effect's website, theequality-effect.org/papers/, which has several research papers and other resources on marital rape.

[4] Chapters 2, 3, 4, and 8 in this volume are all contributions going beyond the original project of the Equality Effect. For other research on this topic generated beyond our original collaboration on the Equality Effect, see eg M Randall and V Venkatesh, 'The Right to No: The Crime of Marital Rape, Women's Human Rights, and International Law' (2015) 41 *Brooklyn Journal of International Law* 153; M Randall and V Venkatesh, 'Criminalizing Sexual Violence against Women in Intimate Relationships: State Obligations under Human Rights Law' (2015) 109 *AJIL Unbound* 189; M Randall and V Venkatesh, 'Why Sexual Assault in Intimate Relationships Must Be Criminalized as Required by International Human Rights Law: A Response to the Symposium Comments' (2016) 109 *AJIL Unbound* 342; Jennifer Koshan, 'Marriage and Advance Consent to Sex: A Feminist Judgment in R v JA' (2016) 6(6) *Onati Socio-Legal Series* (online).

[5] See eg UN Committee on the Elimination of Discrimination Against Women, 'General Recommendation 19: Violence Against Women', adopted in the 11th Session of the CEDAW Committee, UN Doc A/47/38 1992; Y Ertürk (Special Rapporteur on Violence against Women, its causes and consequences), 'The Due Diligence Standard as a Tool for the Elimination of Violence against Women', UN Doc E/CN 4/2006/61 (20 January 2006); Inter-American Commission on Human Rights, *Access to Justice for Women Victims of Violence in Mesoamerica* (Washington, DC, Organization of American States 2011).

contribute to and increase the risk of acts of violence by men against women, 'promoting gender equality has been a critical part of violence prevention'.[6]

Another major theme pervading the book is that states are obliged to criminalise marital rape, both in terms of human rights norms and under international law, and in relation to countries' domestic constitutional guarantees of equality and other rights. This idea is explored throughout the first four overview chapters of the book, as well as in the specific country case studies in the book's latter five chapters. While criminalisation is certainly not seen to be a panacea for the problem of marital rape, it is viewed by the book's contributors as a crucial remedy that must be available to women who may wish to have access to the criminal justice system for responses to their experiences of sexual violence in intimate relationships. To deny this remedy is to provide unequal protection against sexual violence to married women (and women in other kinds of intimate relationships). At the same time, the country-specific chapters recognise that criminal remedies may need to be supplemented by civil remedies such as those available in domestic violence legislation, and discuss the ways in which various remedies for spousal sexual violence can intersect.

A third theme that resonates throughout the book is the role that feminist and anti-violence organisations have played in advocating for legal reforms in the area of sexual violence and marital rape. Although specific activities may differ amongst jurisdictions—for example, the extent to which legislative versus judicial reforms are pursued—it cannot be denied that women's rights and human rights organisations have played a leading role in spurring law reform efforts in the context of marital rape. In doing so, they often have had to overcome significant resistance from legislatures, the judiciary and some sectors of civil society, and reforms have not always been successfully implemented. Several chapters thus illuminate the possibilities and challenges of engaging with the law as a means of protecting women from sexual violence in their intimate relationships.

The book is divided into two parts. Part I, 'Marital Rape, Human Rights and the Law: Mapping the Issues', frames the issues and complexities surrounding spousal sexual assault. The chapters in this section address, in broad terms, the conceptual maps we think are critically important for thinking about and framing strategies for ending the problem of sexual violence against women in intimate relationships. The authors in this section of the book engage questions of how women experience, cope with and resist sexual assault in marriage, how this crime engages questions of human rights, what ideas have legitimised the impunity for marital rape historically and contemporarily around the world, and how the law and rights claims can be best engaged to end this form of violence against women. Part II, 'National Case Studies: Marital Rape and Law Reform in Canada, Malawi,

[6] World Health Organization, *Violence Prevention: The Evidence. Promoting Gender Equality to Prevent Violence against Women* (Geneva, WHO, 2009), www.who.int/violence_injury_prevention/violence/gender.pdf, 4.

Kenya and Ghana', is more applied, and offers national case studies of law reform (or attempts at law reform) in the context of spousal sexual violence. In these chapters, the authors critically analyse how law reform on marital rape has been undertaken and received in each of the countries in which they live and work, and assess the contemporary situation in each context, including opportunities for future law reform efforts. We provide a bit more detail on the focus of each of the chapters next.

In chapter 2, 'Marital Rape and Violence against Women in Intimate Relationships: The Hidden Form of Domestic Violence', Melanie Randall introduces the topic of sexual assault in the context of intimate relationships and situates this particular form of gendered violence in relation to the more recognised issue of domestic violence. Randall argues that 'much of the research and policy on domestic violence has not adequately addressed the fact that many women are also forced into sex by their physically abusive partners'. She calls for greater attention to be paid to the extent to which sexual assault can be a component of domestic violence as well as a distinct and separate form of violence against women in intimate relationships. The chapter also examines some of the harms and effects of sexual violence in intimate relationships, including the still relatively underappreciated phenomenon of revictimisation, which is the increased vulnerability to sexual victimisation later in life for those women sexually abused in childhood. The chapter also explores ways in which women often have difficulty naming this form of abuse in a victim-blaming society, how they cope with it, and, importantly, how they resist this form of violence. Randall also connects the ways in which social difficulties in apprehending the prevalence and nature of sexual violence in intimate relationships hinder the development of effective policy and legal responses to the problem.

Chapter 3, 'Normative and International Human Rights Law Mandates for Criminalising Intimate Partner Sexual Violence: The Marital Rape Impunity in Comparative and Historical Perspective', by Vasanthi Venkatesh and Melanie Randall, provides an overview of some of the consistent ways in which spousal sexual assault has been legitimised in life and law, the world over. The chapter offers 'a big-picture perspective on the long and bumpy road taken by many of the world's countries in moving towards legal recognition that sexual assault can occur in a marital relationship and in the provision of a criminal law remedy for this form of gendered violence'. It surveys the historical and normative justifications which have underpinned the marital rape exemption in countries around the world, including instrumentalist and proceduralist justifications, ideas about men's honour and women's shame, ideas about women as property and notions of privacy, the erasure of women's legal personhood, and the construction of marriage as a contractual sacrament in which women are not even viewed as parties to the contract. In arguing for the necessity of criminalisation as one of the strategies for ending marital rape, the authors point to the major sources of international human rights law which provide authority for the idea that the marital rape exemption is fundamentally incompatible with women's equal human rights.

In chapter 4, 'Pluralistic Legal Systems and Marital Rape: Cross-National Considerations', Vasanthi Venkatesh tackles the controversies and complexities surrounding the political and legal issues that arise when the call for criminalising marital rape takes place in nations with pluralistic legal systems. Arguing for the necessity of paying acute attention to the contextual specificities of the power structures in particular national formations, Venkatesh postulates that 'any inquiry into legal pluralistic systems and gender justice must address the specific colonial and imperialistic contexts in which Indigenous and subaltern groups have functioned, and must take into account the particular power structures that continue to subjugate these groups'. In assessing how the historical backgrounds of colonialism and national developments have shaped contemporary struggles, Venkatesh asks whether there really is a conflict of rights between culture and gender equality and argues that struggles for women's rights and cultural rights must not be seen as antagonistic but as similarly concerned with ending domination. As such, simplistic binaries pitting these rights in opposition must be transcended in favour of more contextualised approaches in a 'productive engagement with customary law'. Advancing a strong argument for the criminalisation of marital rape, Venkatesh argues that this strategy must form part of a broader and intersectional social justice movement attentive to the need for community-based solutions situated in specific contexts. Her chapter provides an important backdrop for discussions of the role of customary law in criminalisation struggles around spousal sexual violence in Malawi, Kenya and Ghana in the country case studies in Part II.

Part II of the book, 'National Case Studies: Marital Rape and Law Reform in Canada, Malawi, Kenya and Ghana', offers more in-depth examinations of what has taken place in these countries with regard to legislative reform and judicial developments aimed at recognising and interpreting the crime of sexual assault within marriage. While each chapter draws attention to the specificities of the unique history and challenges faced in each national context, similar themes emerge across the case studies. To take just one example, in each of the country case studies, the marital rape exemption was initially supported through political resistance to the idea that the government or state should interfere in the 'private' lives of married couples. The chapters in Part II also illustrate the role of feminist and anti-violence advocates in exposing and countering such discriminatory rationales for the marital rape impunity, with varying degrees of success.

In chapter 5, 'The Criminalisation of Marital Rape and Law Reform in Canada: A Modest Feminist Success Story in Combating Marital Rape Myths', Jennifer Koshan undertakes an historical review of the law reform process in Canada which led to the removal of the spousal rape immunity in 1983. After outlining a number of 'marital rape myths' that were used to prop up the immunity, Koshan describes the work undertaken in the 1970s and 1980s, pointing to the powerful and influential role feminist law reform and women's movement advocates played in shaping governmental action to change the laws governing sexual assault in Canada. Koshan reviews the post-1983 legal framework addressing marital rape in Canada, the laws governing consent, the new gender-neutral scheme of offences dealing with sexual assault in the Canadian Criminal Code, and the evidentiary and procedural rules as enacted and interpreted in some of the key Canadian case law. Her analysis reveals how 'sexual assault laws must be enacted, interpreted and applied in ways that repudiate marital rape myths and that are cognisant of the multiple inequalities faced by marginalised women', and explores strategies for undertaking this approach.

Ngeyi Ruth Kanyongolo and Seodi White analyse the legal treatment of marital rape in their chapter, 'Legislating Against the Odds: Lessons Learned from Efforts to Legislate against Marital Rape in Malawi', with a particular focus on the advocacy work of a national women's organisation, Women and Law in Southern Africa Research and Educational Trust (WLSA Malawi). The authors point out that despite some positive law reform efforts aimed at protecting victims of domestic violence, marital rape remains a common occurrence in Malawi, continues to be under-reported, and is 'generally deemed to be a private matter outside the realm of the state'. Kanyongolo and White examine the ways in which WLSA Malawi's efforts to advocate for explicit legal protection against marital rape became highly contentious, describing the basis for both support and resistance of such efforts by legislators, judges, faith and traditional leaders, and members of civil society. Their assessment of the current legal landscape in Malawi is that the 'Prevention of Domestic Violence Act does not give women power to obtain protection orders and other civil remedies in cases of marital rape since marital rape is not recognised under Malawi's penal law'. In the authors' view, a law is still needed in Malawi that explicitly criminalises or legislates against marital rape in order to achieve justice for women.

Chapter 7, 'Dismantling Barriers to Women's Equality: Making the Case for the Criminalisation of Marital Rape in Kenya', explores the legal treatment of marital rape in Kenya. The authors, Winnie Kamau, Patricia Nyaundi and Jane Serwanga, challenge Kenya's failure to criminalise marital rape in its sexual offences legislation, and make a strong case for the necessity of the criminalisation of this form of gendered violence. In arguing for criminalisation, the authors consider 'the possibilities offered by the Constitution of Kenya, 2010, and the recently enacted Protection of Domestic Violence Act, which for the first time recognises sexual violence within marriage'. Finding that the current law in Kenya is inadequate in terms of protecting women from sexual violence in marriage, Kamau, Nyaundi and Serwanga contend that the Kenyan state must live up to its obligations under international law and under the human rights obligations it has committed to at the regional level, as well as under the constitution, to 'enact or amend its legislation and take other measures to ensure protection against marital rape, including criminalisation of this practice'. They also argue for other 'measures to deal with underlying gender stereotypes and negative cultural attitudes and practices', including training of police and judges and public education.

Renee Aku Sitsofe Morhe echoes these themes in chapter 8, 'Marital Rape under Ghanaian Law'. Morhe takes the criminalisation argument further, stating that: '[C]ountries whose laws do not criminalise marital rape or effectively deal with it are permitting violence against women.' While marital rape is no longer explicitly exempted in Ghanaian law, it is not fully criminalised because, as Morhe points out, there is a force requirement built into the criminal law definition of the offence. Morhe also identifies the problems that persist in Ghana with the corroboration requirement for sexual offences, which, she argues, places a heavy burden on rape victims and must be eliminated. In this chapter, she outlines some of the social conditions of the lives of Ghanaian women, the challenges of the court system, the progress and obstacles in the law reform process and the strategies for ending marital rape. Morhe concludes by pointing out that Ghana's constitutional commitments to gender equality and human rights as well as its international obligations require more specific legislation criminalising marital rape to ensure that a woman's ability to consent to sex in marriage is protected.

The final chapter of the book, 'The Judicial Treatment of Marital Rape in Canada: A Post-Criminalisation Case Study', presents a critical examination by Jennifer Koshan of the reported Canadian case law on spousal sexual assault over a thirty-year period since the removal of the marital rape exemption from the Criminal Code in 1983. Koshan finds that despite some positive developments, there remain significant ongoing challenges with the judicial application of sexual assault laws in the spousal context, undermining protection of women's rights to equality before and under the law, as well as to security and freedom from sexual violence. Based on her extensive and in-depth analysis of this large body of cases, Koshan illustrates the ways in which, in too many cases, marital rape myths influence judicial decision-making as well as defence strategies, including the mistaken ideas that wives are likely to make false reports of rape in the context of family law disputes and that wives 'continuously consent' to sex in marital relationships. Koshan demonstrates that 'legislative abolition of the marital rape immunity alone is insufficient to provide women with legal recourse for sexual violence in spousal relationships free from the operation of discriminatory myths, stereotypes and rationalisations'.

This conclusion from the final chapter shows that law on the books criminalising marital rape, while important, is one aspect of the larger struggle to end this form of gendered violence in women's lives. This lesson from the Canadian experience—in addition to the insights offered from the other country case studies and from the framing chapters in Part I—can be used to inform criminalisation efforts elsewhere in terms of what law reform advocates can realistically expect to achieve, and how their strategies need to be multifaceted, responsive to local conditions, human-rights informed and ongoing. Only constant vigilance from women's advocacy organisations and civil society more broadly will ensure that a woman's right to say no is entrenched in law, implemented in practice and respected by all members of society.

2

Marital Rape and Sexual Violence against Women in Intimate Relationships: The Less Recognised Form of Domestic Violence[1]

MELANIE RANDALL

I. Introduction

> Sexual violence by husbands [or other male intimate partners] has been among the most hidden of all crimes of violence against women.[2]

Only in the last few decades has a significant recognition of sexual assault in the context of marriage (or marital-type relationships) emerged.[3] Previously the concept of rape in marriage was virtually unheard of, as men's control—sexual and otherwise—over their female spouses was historically understood to be part of a man's entitlement upon marriage.

Laws granting 'spousal immunity' in cases of sexual assault have been eliminated in many countries, yet remain firmly in place in a significant number of countries. This suggests that traditional and male-dominant ideas about men's rights of sexual access to their wives, and ideas about women as property of and subordinate to their husbands, retain legal sanction in a great many societies around the world.

[1] I am indebted to my co-editor Jennifer Koshan for her detailed and thoughtful feedback on this chapter, to Lori Haskell for her collaborations over many years, to Anna Bowness for her excellent and careful editing, and to Amanda Eston and Laura Snowdon, students at the Faculty of Law, Western University, London, Ontario for their excellent research assistance.

[2] Holly Johnson, *Dangerous Domains: Violence Against Women in Canada* (Toronto, Nelson Canada, 1996) 146.

[3] See Raquel Kennedy Bergen, 'Marital Rape', Violence Against Women Online Resources, Applied Research Forum: National Electronic Network on Violence Against Women, www.vaw.umn.edu, March 1999.

It is well recognised in much of the literature on the topic that the problem of sexual assault is deeply implicated in larger ideas about sexuality, gender roles, and what counts as 'normal' and expected with regard to traditional conceptions of heterosexual sex. Not surprisingly, then, the problem of sexual assault in intimate relationships is deeply shaped by prevailing attitudes, beliefs and practices surrounding heterosexual marital and dating relationships, which are in turn shaped by structured social gender roles and inequalities.[4] Social and legal responses to the problem of sexual violence in intimate relationships, therefore, cannot be understood, transformed or improved without acknowledging and addressing the broader contexts in which sexual violence takes place.

Ending sexual violence has been a major part of the struggle to achieve women's equality.[5] According to the World Health Organization, sexual violence is sexual contact without consent, including

> any sexual act, attempt to obtain a sexual act, unwanted sexual comments or advances, or acts to traffic, or otherwise directed, against a person's sexuality using coercion, by any person regardless of their relationship to the victim, in any setting, including but not limited to home and work.[6]

Despite advances in the separate spheres of domestic violence and sexual assault, the specific problem of marital rape and sexual violence in intimate relationships remains relatively under the radar both in society and in law.[7] The important work on improving awareness of and responses to domestic violence has not always recognised sexual violence in intimate relationships as a common or central component of this form of gendered violence.

In the North American context, as in other countries, for example, the distinct demarcation of funding and service delivery—such as the network of shelters for assaulted women and the separate network of sexual assault centres and crisis lines for victims of sexual assault—speaks to the ways in which these issues have too often been artificially separated, a separation that is also reflected and entrenched in law. Judith Berman observes that this is likely because 'advocacy for victims of domestic violence and sexual assault evolved along different timelines and involved different people and priorities'. Her point is 'to acknowledge

[4] The term 'intimate relationships' includes but is not limited only to legal and common law spousal relationships. It also includes dating relationships and ongoing intimate relationships which do not involve cohabitation. Note that the legal marital rape immunity does not necessarily apply to all such relationships, but some of the underlying attitudes and beliefs may nevertheless still pertain.

[5] See World Health Organization, 'Violence Against Women: Intimate Partner and Sexual Violence Against Women: Fact Sheet', www.who.int/mediacentre/factsheets/fs239/en/, September 2016.

[6] EG Krug et al (eds), *World Report on Violence and Health* (Geneva, WHO, 2002) www.who.int/violence_injury_prevention/violence/global_campaign/en/chap6.pdfChapter 6, 149.

[7] Sexual assault or rape in marriage (or marital-type relationships) is increasingly referred to as intimate partner sexual violence (IPSV) in the research literature, and domestic violence is often described as intimate partner violence (IPV).

ways in which victim advocacy as a movement has unintentionally contributed to a fractured system that makes it more rather than less difficult for victims to disclose their experience with [marital rape]'.[8] However, sexual violence in intimate relationships deserves more recognition as an issue and requires better social attention and more integrated services and resources, more prevention efforts and more effective legal responses.

In this chapter I address the context, dynamics and complexities of women's experiences of sexual violence in intimate relationships. I review some of the research on the problem of spousal sexual assault, and explore the interconnections between sexual violence in intimate relationships and other forms of domestic violence. I include a discussion of revictimisation, or women's increased vulnerability to sexual violence in intimate relationships if they have been sexually abused as children, and also include a qualitative analysis of some of the ways in which women cope with and resist violence from their male intimates. Finally, I point to the ways in which law has been implicated in upholding this form of gender inequality as well as the necessity of engaging law to end it.

II. Research Knowledge and Public Attitudes about Intimate Partner Sexual Violence

A. The Prevalent, Gendered and Relational Nature of Sexual Violence

Sexual assault, including sexual assault in intimate partner relationships, is a gendered crime. Men are overwhelmingly the perpetrators of sexual violence, and women and girls are overwhelmingly the victims. The gendered nature of sexual violence has been demonstrated by national and international studies. In 2008, Statistics Canada found that 92 per cent[9] of sexual assault victims are female and 99 per cent of perpetrators are men.[10] A subsequent Statistics Canada survey reported that 98 per cent of all persons charged with 'sexual assault level 1' (considered to be the least serious form of sexual assault in which little or no injury was

[8] See Judith Berman, 'Domestic Sexual Assault: A New Opportunity for Court Response' [Summer 2004] *Juvenile and Family Court Journal* 23, 27.

[9] Roxan Vaillancourt, Statistics Canada, *Gender Differences in Police-Reported Violent Crime in Canada*, Catalogue No 85F0033M (Ottawa, Statistics Canada, May 2010) 10.

[10] Maire Sinha (ed), Statistics Canada, *Measuring Violence Against Women: Statistical Trends*, Catalogue No 85-002-X (Ottawa, Statistics Canada, 25 February 2013) 31.

caused to the victim) were male.[11] This gendered pattern has also been demonstrated internationally.[12]

The Sex Information and Education Council of Canada examined the results from the Canadian 2013 Uniform Crime Reporting Survey (UCR) and the 2009 General Social Survey (GSS).[13] According to the GSS data from 2009, there were approximately 677,000 incidents of sexual assault in Canada. Of these incidents, 87 per cent of perpetrators were male. The victim was female in 472,000 incidents of sexual assault reported in the GSS, or 70 per cent of the total.[14]

In 2012, according to police-reported data on crime rates in Canada, over 90 per cent of the victims of the 21,900 incidents of sexual assault were women. This gender disparity holds true in every province and territory in the country. Data from the 2013 UCR reveals that the accused perpetrator was male in 99 per cent of the incidents of sexual violence against women.[15] The more recent 2014 GSS in Canada confirms that sexual assault is 'an offence mostly involving female victims'.[16]

According to the Centre for Disease Controls (CDC) National Intimate Partner and Sexual Violence Survey, 2011, conducted in the United States, an estimated 99 per cent of female rape victims had only male perpetrators. In addition, an estimated 94.7 per cent of female victims of sexual violence other than rape had only male perpetrators.[17]

The majority of sexual assaults are perpetrated against women by men who are known to them. In one of the most comprehensive Canadian surveys undertaken on the subject of intimate violence, 39 per cent of women randomly interviewed reported being sexually assaulted at some point in their lives since reaching sixteen years of age.[18] Of those women who were sexually assaulted, a clear majority of them—69 per cent—knew their assailant.

[11] Shannon Brennan, 'Police-Reported Crime Statistics in Canada, 2011', *Juristat* article, Component of Statistics Canada catalogue No 85-002-X (Ottawa, Statistics Canada, 24 July 2012).

[12] See eg data from the World Health Organization, 'Global and Regional Estimates of Violence Against Women: Prevalence and Health Effects of Intimate Partner Violence and Non-Partner Sexual Violence', www.who.int/reproductivehealth/publications/violence/9789241564625/en/ (2013).

[13] The UCR survey 'tracks the number of sexual assaults reported to and substantiated by Canadian police services, and the GSS asks Canadians 15 years of age and older to self-report whether they have been victims of sexual assault during the previous 12 months, including assaults they may not have reported to the police. The UCR and the GSS are limited to acts that reach the criminal threshold'. Sex Information and Education Council of Canada, *Sexual Health Issue Brief*, http://sieccan.org/wp/wp-content/uploads/2015/01/SIECCAN-Sexual-Health-Issue-Brief_Sexual-Assault.pdf (January 2015) 2.

[14] *Sexual Health Issue Brief*, ibid, 2.

[15] Cecilia Benoit et al, 'Issue Brief: Sexual Violence Against Women in Canada' (May 2014) commissioned by the Federal-Provincial-Territorial Senior Officials for the Status of Women www.gov.mb.ca/msw/publications/sexual_violence_brief.pdf, 15.

[16] Statistics Canada, 'Self-Reported Victimization, 2014', www.statcan.gc.ca/daily-quotidien/151123/dq151123a-eng.htm (released 11 November 2015).

[17] Matthew J Breiding et al, 'Prevalence and Characteristics of Sexual Violence, Stalking, and Intimate Partner Violence Victimization—National Intimate Partner and Sexual Violence Survey, United States, 2011' (5 September 2014) 63(SS08) *Centers for Disease Control and Prevention: Surveillance Summaries* 1–8.

[18] Johnson (n 2) 50.

Research suggests that in cases of sexual assault, the assailant is often someone in an intimate relationship with the victim (spouse, common-law partner or boyfriend). Other studies confirm this pattern of known assailants of sexual assault. Research conducted in the United States indicates that slightly more than half of female victims of rape reported being raped by an intimate partner. Data from the CDC indicates that many female victims of sexual assault identified their assailant as an intimate partner (51.1 per cent) or an acquaintance (40.8 per cent).[19] According to the 2014 Canadian GSS, one-quarter of spousal violence victims reported having been sexually assaulted, beaten, choked or threatened with a gun or a knife.[20]

The extensive body of research in this area confirms, therefore, that many if not most sexual assaults experienced by women are committed by male assailants known to them, and that within this category a significant proportion of sexual assaults are perpetrated by male intimates. In fact, a gradually expanding body of research is beginning more fully to document just how extensive the problem of spousal sexual assault actually is. Because the topics of sexual assault and unwanted sexual contact engage issues which are complicated and which often evoke controversy, it is not surprising that the subject has received relatively scant attention in many discussions of domestic violence. Yet this is not because it is a problem of great rarity.

To the contrary, the World Health Organization has found that lifetime prevalence of intimate partner sexual violence (IPSV) of women aged 15–49 years varies—from 6 per cent in Japan to 59 per cent in Ethiopia.[21] Earlier US research suggests that approximately 40–45 per cent of all assaulted women are forced into sex at one time or another by their male partners.[22] Research undertaken in Australia based on the 2012 Australian Bureau of Statistics' 2012 Personal Safety Survey (PSS) indicates that: 'Since the age of 15, 805,900 women were sexually assaulted by a male intimate partner: this is one out of every eleven women in Australia (9.2 per cent).'[23]

Sexual violence in intimate relationships may be the only form of abuse a woman experiences in that relationship, or it may be an element of other forms of ongoing violence. Recent research on global prevalence figures indicate that about

[19] MC Black et al, *The National Intimate Partner and Sexual Violence Survey (NISVS): 2010 summary report* (Atlanta, GA, National Center for Injury Prevention and Control Centers for Disease Control and Prevention, 2011) 21.

[20] Statistics Canada, 'Family Violence in Canada: A Statistical Profile, 2014', www.statcan.gc.ca/daily-quotidien/160121/dq160121b-eng.htm (released 21 January 2016).

[21] World Health Organization–Pan American Health Organization, 'Understanding and Addressing Violence Against Women: Sexual Violence', www.who.int/en/ (2012) 2.

[22] JC Campbell and P Alford, 'The Dark Consequences of Marital Rape' (1989) 89 *American Journal of Nursing* 946.

[23] Australia's National Research Organisation for Women's Safety Limited (ANROWS), 'Sexual Assault and Domestic Violence in the Context of Co-Occurrence and Re-Victimisation: State of Knowledge Paper', http://anrows.org.au/publications/landscapes/co-occurrence-and-re-victimisation, 11.

one in three (35 per cent) of women worldwide have experienced either physical and/or sexual intimate partner violence or non-partner sexual violence in their lifetime.[24] The majority of this violence is intimate partner violence. Around the globe, then, almost one-third (30 per cent) of women who have been in a relationship report that they have experienced some form of physical and/or sexual violence by their intimate partner.[25]

There are significant methodological challenges in carrying out research on a highly personal and stigmatised subject area such as unwanted, coerced or violent sexual experiences in an intimate relationship, whether opposite- or same-sex. As Holly Johnson notes, 'survey questions about sexual violence in marriage may be among the most difficult for women to disclose to interviewers'.[26]

Prevalence estimates vary as a result of methodological differences in research approaches. But they also vary due to the trend towards under-reporting, women's sense of shame, and some women's difficulty 'naming' or identifying their experiences of unwanted, forced or coerced sex in marital relationships in these terms. These factors suggest that the prevalence rates generated by even the most authoritative studies most likely still underestimate the extent of the problem of sexual violence in women's lives.

B. Sexual Assault in Intimate Relationships: Attitudes, Invisibility and Recognition

Early research on sexual assault and rape focused almost exclusively on 'stranger' or 'acquaintance' rape, leaving the issue of sexual assault in the context of intimate relationships virtually unexplored and unacknowledged. Yet research has also overwhelmingly documented that, contrary to the dominant myth of the stranger assailant, the vast majority of sexual assaults take place in the context of some kind of relationship, most often some kind of ongoing relationship. More specifically, 'sexual assaults committed in familiar settings by assailants known to the victim, including spouses, occur at a greater frequency than those committed in high risk situations by unknown assailants'.[27]

[24] World Health Organization, 'Violence against Women: Intimate Partner and Sexual Violence against Women', Fact Sheet No 239, www.who.int/mediacentre/factsheets/fs239/en/ (updated September 2016).

[25] World Health Organization, Department of Reproductive Health and Research, London School of Hygiene and Tropical Medicine, South African Medical Research Council, 'Global and Regional Estimates of Violence against Women: Prevalence and Health Effects of Intimate Partner Violence and Non-Partner Sexual Violence' (2013) 2. For individual country information, see 'The World's Women 2015, Trends and Statistics', ch 6 *Violence against Women* (United Nations Department of Economic and Social Affairs, 2015); see more at www.unwomen.org/en/what-we-do/ending-violence-against-women/facts-and-figures#notes.

[26] Johnson (n 2) 145.

[27] Lana Stermac, Giannetta Del Bove and Mary Addison, 'Violence, Injury, and Presentation Patterns in Spousal Sexual Assaults' (2001) 7 *Violence Against Women* 1218.

A number of researchers have been concerned about the relative lack of attention paid to the issue of spousal sexual violence in the areas of both research and public education. Kersti Yllo, a well-known domestic violence researcher in the United States, has observed that at 'the community level, as well as in the culture at large, efforts to challenge the taken-for-granted "right" of husbands to coerce their wives sexually lag at least two decades behind our work on physical violence'.[28]

Other research documenting popular perceptions about rape (depending on the relationship between the perpetrator and the victim) demonstrates a definite tendency to underplay the harm of sexual assault in the context of intimate relationships because of a tendency to fixate on 'stranger rapes' as the more serious problem. Related to this is the mistaken idea that sexual assault in a marriage is somehow less harmful due to the past or ongoing sexual relationship between the partners, such that the sexual assault is less of a violation or a wrong. Certainly this form of sexual violation between intimates is rarely recognised as criminal conduct, in many cases, even by those who are legally trained.[29]

In one study that assessed popular opinions about rape in the context of marriage, research participants were presented with a variety of scenarios depicting sexual contact and asked whether they defined any of these situations as constituting a rape. In each scenario, the perpetrator was a husband and the victim was his wife. When asked whether having vaginal intercourse with one's wife without her consent was rape, 74 per cent of those surveyed answered in the affirmative. However, when the same scenario was modified to include the husband's use of physical force, an overwhelming 93 per cent of respondents replied that the scenario constituted rape. Clearly, more people had difficulty recognising sexual assault in a spousal relationship in the absence of additional physical violence than they did when the sex was accompanied by physical assault.[30]

Other researchers have found that 'participants rated a rape between more closely acquainted people as less serious than stranger rape'.[31] Moreover, the same

[28] Kersti Yllo, 'The Silence Surrounding Sexual Violence: The Issue of Marital Rape and the Challenge it Poses for the Duluth Model' in M Shepard and E Pence (eds), *Coordinating Community Responses to Domestic Violence: Lessons from Duluth and Beyond* (Thousand Oaks, CA, Sage, 1999) 225. Increasing attention is now being paid to the issue of sexual assault in intimate relationships; see eg Vasanthi Venkatesh et al, 'Criminalizing Sexual Violence against Women in Intimate Relationships: State Obligations under Human Rights Law' (2016) 109 *AJIL Unbound* 189 and the other contributions to this symposium. See also Kersti Yllo and M Gabriela Torres (eds), *Marital Rape: Consent, Marriage, and Social Change in Global Context* (Oxford, Oxford University Press, 2016).

[29] See Melanie Randall, 'Sexual Assault in Spousal Relationships, "Continuous Consent", and the Law, Honest but Mistaken Judicial Beliefs' (2008) 32 *University of Manitoba Law Journal* 1; Ruthy Lazar, 'Negotiating Sex: The Legal Construct of Consent in Cases of Wife Rape in Ontario, Canada' (2010) 22 *Canadian Journal of Women and the Law* 329.

[30] Mary Kay Kirkwood and Dawn K Cecil, 'Marital Rape: Student Assessment of Rape Laws and the Marital Exemption' (2001) 7 *Violence Against Women* 1234, 1245.

[31] Kelly Simonson and Linda Mezydlo Subich, 'Rape Perceptions as a Function of Gender-Role Traditionality and Victim–Perpetrator Association' (1999) 7/8 *Sex Roles* 617, 629.

study concluded that '[marital rape] is minimized somewhat in terms of seriousness in contrast to other types of rape'.[32]

These studies demonstrate the common public perception of stranger-perpetrated sexual violence as more 'serious', more harmful and more deserving of criminal sanction than sexual violence perpetrated in intimate relationships. After reviewing the research in the area and conducting their own study, one set of researchers observed that 'knowing that the perpetrator and victim are spouses was shown to alter beliefs about both parties involved in conflictual interactions'.[33] They suggest that 'these findings imply that judges, jurors, and other individuals who hear reports of violence may also make different attributions about violence on the basis of the victim–perpetrator relationship'.[34] This underlines the point that popular misconceptions about what sexual assault involves, what it looks like and where it is most likely to happen tend to distort the subtleties and intricacies that characterise the crime of spousal sexual assault and contribute to a context in which disclosures are often inhibited and adequate remedies are often not provided.

C. The Interconnections Between Sexual and Physical Assaults in Intimate Relationships

Much of the research and policy on domestic violence has not adequately addressed the fact that many women are also forced into sex by their physically abusive partners. Similarly, public education and programmes addressing domestic violence typically focus on physical assaults, threats and even emotional abuse, while not drawing sufficient attention to the fact that in too many cases sexual violence is also a component of this violence.

A survey of community attitudes undertaken in Australia[35] demonstrated that very few of those surveyed

> spontaneously identified sexual assault or rape as an element of domestic violence. Even when the more obvious forms were nominated, such as physical violence or battering, sexual violence was only identified by 12 per cent of respondents when further pressed about what 'other forms' of domestic violence there might be. Ultimately, people surveyed were more inclined to describe domestic violence as being constituted by verbal abuse, mental abuse, and violence against children before they turned their minds to the possibility of sexual assault.[36]

[32] ibid, 630.

[33] J Langhinrichsen-Rohling et al, 'Attributions About Perpetrators and Victims of Interpersonal Abuse' (2004) 19 *Journal of Interpersonal Violence* 484, 496.

[34] ibid, 496.

[35] Office of the Status of Women, Department of the Prime Minister and Cabinet, *Community Attitudes to Violence Against Women: Detailed Report* (AGPS, Canberra, 1995).

[36] Melanie Heenan, 'Just "Keeping the Peace": A Reluctance to Respond to Male Partner Sexual Violence' (2004) 1 *Australian Centre for the Study of Sexual Assault* 2.

As Emily Sack explains, 'Rape and domestic violence traditionally have been conceptualised as separate forms of violence against women. While rape involves sexual violence, research and policy on domestic abuse has focused on non-sexual physical aggression, such as assaults or threats of violence.' However, in actuality 'the two forms of violence are intertwined. First, a significant percentage of rapes are perpetrated by an intimate partner of the victim'. Second, 'a substantial percentage of perpetrators who physically batter their intimate partners also sexually assault them'.[37]

In the same way that research on sexual assault and domestic violence is largely fragmented and separated, elaborate parallel service systems and legal responses divide domestic violence from sexual assault. A consequence of this division is the relative invisibility of domestic sexual assault. In her study of this issue in the United States, Judith Berman noted that neither the domestic violence response system nor the sexual assault response system has 'fully assumed responsibility for addressing the specific needs of perpetrators or victims of domestic sexual assault'.[38] Berman considered how this separation between domestic violence and IPSV affects the ability of the criminal and civil justice systems to respond appropriately to the problem of marital rape, and further maintained that this very separation of the issues of domestic violence and sexual assault has helped make marital rape invisible.

The US State Justice Institute supported the development of a survey sent to courts around the country to analyse the management of marital rape cases in the courts in 2003.[39] Many courts reported that they did not have the required information. One survey respondent answered: 'I don't believe anyone really has the information you are looking for.' Berman concluded that: 'These responses suggest that data on the overlapping phenomena of domestic violence and sexual assault are hidden by the separation of domestic violence and sexual assault cases in [the] court system, prosecutor's offices, and police departments.'[40]

Following her analysis of the factors influencing the invisibility of marital rape, Berman highlighted the potential consequences of this invisibility and the particular relevance for the legal system. As she explained:

> There are particular reasons to be concerned by the relative invisibility of domestic sexual assault to the criminal justice system. In a curriculum on intimate partner sexual abuse for batterer intervention program facilitators … the authors cite a number of studies that suggest that women who report sexual abuse by intimates experience more severe physical or emotional abuse. … Other studies suggest that men who physically and sexually abuse their partners are more likely to kill or severely injure their partners than men

[37] Emily J Sack, 'Is Domestic Violence a Crime? Intimate Partner Rape as Allegory' (2009) 24 *St John's J Legal Comment* 545–47.

[38] Berman (n 8) 23.

[39] Reported in Berman (n 8) 23.

[40] ibid, 25.

who perpetuate non-sexual physical abuse only. ... Another study found an association between intimate partner rape and perpetration of homicide by the victim.[41]

Clearly there is a significant amount of public education needed both to raise awareness of sexual violence as a form of domestic violence in intimate relationships, and to improve the criminal justice system and other legal responses to this form of gendered violence.

D. Prevalence of Intimate Partner Sexual Violence

Although domestic violence is often thought of largely in terms of physical violence, the extent to which women also experience sexual violence, either as an aspect of domestic violence more generally, or on its own, is becoming better documented. There is now a body of research documenting the prevalence of IPSV and demonstrating the link between physical violence perpetrated within an intimate relationship and a heightened risk of sexual assault within that same relationship.

Haskell and Randall found in their 1993 Canadian study that half (49.6 per cent) of the women in the random sample of respondents who reported physical assault in their intimate relationships with male partners were also forced to have sex by these same men.[42] This means that in roughly half of the cases of physical assault in intimate relationships (44 per cent),[43] women reported that they were also sexually assaulted. Moreover, some women in the study were sexually assaulted by their male intimates but not physically battered. More recent Canadian findings, from the 2014 GSS, indicate that 'among victims of spousal sexual assault, over half (59 per cent) reported non-consensual sexual activity that came as a result of being manipulated, drugged, or otherwise coerced, sometimes in combination with sexual assault through physical force'.[44]

In another North American study examining the prevalence and factors associated with sexual violence in intimate relationships among a sample of 432 women recruited at the scene of police-involved intimate-partner violence incidents, not quite half (43.98 per cent) of participants reported also experiencing sexual

[41] ibid, 28.

[42] Results of this study are reported in L Haskell and M Randall, '"The Women's Safety Project" Summary of Key Statistical Findings', *Appendix to Report of Canadian Panel on Violence Against Women* (Ottawa, 1993); M Randall and L Haskell, 'Sexual Violence in Women's Lives: Findings from the Women's Safety Project, a Community-Based Survey' (1995) 1 *Violence Against Women* 6.

[43] The number of women sexually assaulted in intimate relationships and the number of cases of physical assault in which women were also sexually assaulted are not identical due to some women's multiple experiences of these forms of sexual violence. For example, some women experienced physical assault and/or sexual assault in more than one of their intimate relationships with a man.

[44] Marta Burczycka, 'Trends in Self-Reported Spousal Violence in Canada, 2014,' part of Statistics Canada, *Family Violence in Canada: A Statistical Profile*, www.statcan.gc.ca/pub/85-002-x/2016001/article/14303/01-eng.htm (2014) text box 3.

violence.[45] This study suggests that many women in the sample who experienced what is generally recognised as domestic violence were also sexually assaulted in these same relationships.

Another Canadian study revealed that of women who had been physically abused in the context of an intimate relationship, roughly half (45.9 per cent) had also been sexually assaulted by their partners.[46] A similar study conducted in Mexico and the United States estimated that 40–52 per cent of women experiencing physical violence by an intimate partner have also been sexually coerced by that partner.[47] In Great Britain, a study found that of women who had been physically assaulted by their husbands, 35 per cent had also been sexually assaulted by them.[48] The 2005 multi-country study undertaken by the World Health Organization, mostly in low- and middle-income countries, found that, among women aged between 15-49 years, 'between 15% of women in Japan and 71% of women in Ethiopia reported physical and/or sexual violence by an intimate partner in their lifetimes.[49]

Research on IPSV undertaken in Sweden revealed that 'women sexually assaulted by their intimate partners … more frequently reported physical violence … than women assaulted by strangers and acquaintances'.[50] The research was based on medical and forensic records of 690 consecutive women attending a sexual assault centre in Stockholm, Sweden, resulting in a final research sample of 503 patients. The findings from this study suggest that sexual assaults committed by intimate partners are likely to involve more physical violence and result in injuries just as often as assaults committed by strangers.

This finding seems to be supported by some earlier Canadian research, results from which suggest a higher correlation still between physical and sexual assault in relationships in which domestic violence is present. The most comprehensive Canadian study, a national survey conducted by Statistics Canada in 1993, found that when sexual violence is perpetrated in marital relationships it is almost always accompanied by physical violence. Specifically, Statistics Canada reports that 92 per cent of women who were sexually assaulted in marital relationships were

[45] JT Messing, J Thaller and M Bagwell, 'Factors Related to Sexual Abuse and Forced Sex in a Sample of Women Experiencing Police-Involved Intimate Partner Violence' (2014) 39 *Health & Social Work* 181, 186.

[46] Stermac et al (n 27) 1219.

[47] M Granados Shiroma, *Salud reproductiva y violencia contra la mujer: un ana´lisis desde la perspectiva de ge´nero* [*Reproductive Health and Violence against Women: An Analysis from the Gender Perspective*] (Nuevo León, Asociación Mexicana de Población, Colegio de Mexico, 1996).

[48] Stermac et al (n 27) 1218–19.

[49] World Health Organization, 'Violence against Women: Intimate Partner and Sexual Violence against Women', Fact Sheet No 239, www.who.int/mediacentre/factsheets/fs239/en/ (updated November 2016).

[50] AS Moller, T Backstrom, HP Sondergaard and I Helstrom, 'Patterns of Injury and Reported Violence Depending on Relationship to Assailant in Female Swedish Sexual Assault Victims' (2012) 27 *Journal of Interpersonal Violence* 3131–32.

also hit, slapped, punched, choked, beaten up or threatened with guns or knives by the same perpetrator.[51]

Some studies have found that women who are both sexually and physically assaulted by their male partners are often subjected to even higher levels of physical violence than are women who are battered but not also raped. This is not simply the result of the compounding effects of these forms of violence; some research has shown that sexual assault in intimate relationships is actually often associated with more severe physical violence. American research conducted by Campbell and Alford indicated that half of the marital rape survivors in their sample were kicked, hit or burned during forced sex.[52] As one researcher concluded, based on her study of women's experiences of abuse by male intimates,

> the sexually abusing batterer [is] an extremely dangerous man. According to the female partner, these men were more tolerant of men hitting women, were more likely to have abused them during pregnancy, had inflicted more serious injuries, and were more likely to escalate the violence to a lethal situation than the other batterers in this study.[53]

It seems clear from the research that physical and sexual violence are very often intertwined in a battering relationship and that, although the sexual violence may remain undetected and/or unreported, women who are victims of domestic violence too often are subjected to both kinds of violence.

Overall, studies demonstrate that there is a strong correlation between physical violence and sexual violence often (though not always) going hand in hand in intimate partner relationships. Moreover, while it is the case that these forms of violence may exist in isolation from one another in particular relationships, research suggests that where one of these forms of abuse is present in the relationship, there is a higher likelihood that the other will be present as well.

E. Effects of Sexual Violence in Intimate Relationships

The effects of experiencing sexual assault(s) in the context of an intimate relationship can be profound and long lasting. Women who have been physically and sexually assaulted by their male intimates may suffer other physical consequences such as broken bones, black eyes, bloody noses and knife wounds that specifically occur during the sexual violence. The physical harm may include injuries to the vaginal and anal areas, lacerations, soreness, bruising, torn muscles, fatigue and vomiting.[54]

[51] Johnson (n 2) 145.

[52] Campbell and Alford (n 22).

[53] JC Campbell, 'Women's Responses to Sexual Abuse in Intimate Relationships' (1989) 10 *Health Care for Women International* 335, 343.

[54] Carol Adams, 'I Just Raped My Wife! What Are You Going to Do About it, Pastor?' in Emilie Buchwald, Pamela R Fletcher and Martha Roth (eds), *Transforming a Rape Culture* (Minneapolis, MN, Milkweed Editions, 1993) 57; Raquel Kennedy Bergen, *Wife Rape: Understanding the Response of Survivors and Service Providers* (Thousand Oaks, CA, Sage, 1996).

In addition to general physical harm, marital rape can cause gynaecological consequences such as vaginal tears and stretching, miscarriages, stillbirths, bladder infections, infertility and the potential contraction of sexually transmitted diseases, including HIV. Sexual violence in an intimate relationship can also put women at risk of unwanted pregnancies, especially when women are forced to have unprotected sex or are fearful of using contraception because of their partners' violent reactions.[55]

A recent study examined the factors associated with IPSV among a sample of women who had experienced domestic violence incidents requiring police involvement. The researchers were interested in understanding the specific factors related to women experiencing sexual violence in their intimate relationships as well as (non-sexual) physical violence. Regarding the particular effects of sexual violence in intimate relationships, they observe the following:

> Compared with women not reporting IPSV, women who were sexually abused or forced into sexual intercourse were significantly more likely to experience strangulation, feelings of shame, and posttraumatic stress disorder symptoms. Women whose partners had forced sex were more likely to report that they had a child in common with their abusive partner; and that their partner was sexually jealous, had threatened to kill them, had stalked or harassed them, or caused them to have a miscarriage due to abuse.[56]

The psychological effects of sexual assault in an intimate relationship can also be severe and long lasting. Like other kinds of sexual assault, survivors of spousal sexual assault report a variety of mental health consequences including depression, flashbacks, post-traumatic stress, difficulty sleeping and other psychosomatic disturbances. In fact, there is evidence to suggest that in some cases the mental health consequences of sexual assault perpetrated by a male intimate can be especially severe given the level of violation and betrayal which inheres in the experience. One expert in the field has observed that, 'compared to women raped by strangers and those whom they don't know well, marital rape survivors report even higher rates of anger and depression'.[57]

A fundamental element of the effects of IPSV must also be the sense of betrayal and hurt inflicted on women when someone with whom they are supposed to experience trust, safety and respect transgresses their boundaries and violates their bodily integrity. Clearly, then, the still under-reported and largely hidden problem of sexual assault in spousal and other intimate relationships carries a significant health and mental cost borne by its victims.

[55] Bergen (n 3); See also Campbell and Alford (n 22).

[56] Messing et al (n 45) 181.

[57] Bergen (n 3); see also Mary Koss et al, 'Stranger and Acquaintance Rape: Are There Differences in Victim's Experiences?' (1988) 12 *Psychology of Women Quarterly* 1.

F. Reporting Sexual Violence in Intimate Relationships

It is well established that sexual assault is an extremely under-reported crime. Reporting an experience of sexual violence presupposes a willingness to disclose the event, which may be experienced as shameful, and to seek some sort of help. These are internal barriers to reporting that many women may not be able or willing to overcome. Compounding these internal barriers are the external ones, including the stigma and shame imposed on survivors in a victim-blaming society, the tendency to minimise the harms of sexual violence, and the institutional failures and deficiencies in responding to the crime of sexual assault.

It is not an overstatement to suggest that only a very small fraction of sexual assaults ever get reported to the police or processed criminally. According to a crime victimisation survey by Statistics Canada of random respondents in which women were interviewed anonymously, an estimated 460,000 Canadian women were victims of sexual assault in 2004 and only 8 per cent reported the crime to the police, meaning that 92 per cent of sexual assaults in this sample were unreported.[58] In fact, all of the major victimisation surveys conducted in Canada between 1993 and 2014 indicate that fewer than 10 per cent of sexual assaults were reported to the police.[59]

In the context of this broader problem of the under-reporting of sexual assault, there is reason to assume that sexual assaults perpetrated against women by their spouses or other intimate partners are among those least frequently reported to police. Adherence to traditional gender roles and attitudes has been shown to decrease the likelihood that women will report experiences of violence and abuse by their partners.[60] The broader social context in which spousal sexual assault takes place, including dominant gender norms supporting a view of men's entitlement to sex with their female partners, can be highly influential in shaping women's own experiences and interpretations of this form of sexual violence in their lives. As Pease and Flood observe:

> Media portrayals and social norms teach women to 'self-silence', to place their partners' needs above their own. … Furthermore, stereotypical and narrow representations of violence inhibit women from even recognising and naming their experience as violence. One of the key reasons why women do not report incidents that meet the legal definition of sexual assault is that these do not fit common stereotypes of 'real rape'—they were

[58] M Gannon and K Mihorean, 'Criminal Victimization in Canada, 2004' (2005) 25 *Juristat* 85-002-XPE (Ottawa, Statistics Canada, 2005) 7, 23.

[59] Holly Johnson, 'Limits of a Criminal Justice Response: Trends in Police and Court Processing of Sexual Assault', *Sexual Assault in Canada* (2012) 613–34; see also Statistics Canada, 'Criminal Victimisation in Canada, 2014', reporting on findings from the General Social Survey, 2014, www.statcan.gc.ca/pub/85-002-x/2015001/article/14241-eng.htm.

[60] R Harris, J Firestone and W Vega, 'The Interaction of Country of Origin, Acculturation and Gender Role Ideology on Wife Abuse' (2005) 86 *Social Science Quarterly* 465.

> not by a stranger, did not take place outside and with a weapon, and did not involve injuries.[61]

Pease and Flood further note that:

> [V]ictims also do not report violence because of their perception of *others'* attitudes: their fear that they will be blamed by family and friends, stigmatised, and the criminal justice system will not provide redress ... there is an interrelationship between community attitudes, community services, and the psychological experience of the woman raped.[62]

Sexual violence in intimate relationships therefore can be safely assumed to be a highly under-reported form of gendered violence. Furthermore, research demonstrates that women whose lives are shaped by conditions of marginalisation and inequality are even less likely to report their experiences of sexual violence to the police. For example, Indigenous women are less likely to report to police, and women from other racialised groups,[63] impoverished women,[64] disabled women[65] and those in same-sex relationships[66] are less likely to report sexual assault experiences to police, particularly if perpetrated by intimate partners.

III. Social Norms, Gender Expectations and Women's Experiences of Intimate Sexual Violence

A. Revictimisation and Sexual Violence in Adult Intimate Relationships: How Sexual Abuse in Childhood Increases Women's Vulnerability to Rape in Marriage

A history of child sexual abuse can be a factor increasing a woman's likelihood of or vulnerability to further experiences in adulthood of sexual coercion, intrusion or violence, particularly in the context of intimate relationships. This increased vulnerability to repeat experiences of violence is described in the research literature as 'revictimisation'.

[61] B Pease and M Flood, 'Rethinking the Significance of Attitudes in Preventing Men's Violence against Women' (2008) 43 *Australian Journal of Social Issues* 549.

[62] ibid.

[63] Ottawa Rape Crisis Centre, *Sexual Assault Statistics*, www.orcc.net/sites/all/files/pdf/Sexual-Assault-Statistics-FS.pdf (2010) 1.

[64] ibid, 2.

[65] J Benedet and I Grant, 'Hearing the Sexual Assault Complaints of Women with Mental Disabilities: Consent, Capacity, and Mistaken Belief' (2007) 52 *McGill Law Journal* 243, 256.

[66] E F Rothman et al, 'The Prevalence of Sexual Assault against People who Identify as Gay, Lesbian, or Bisexual in the United States: A Systemic Review' [2010] *Trauma Violence and Abuse* 3.

One of the more comprehensive and sophisticated pieces of research on the topic of revictimisation was undertaken by Lori Haskell in her analysis of the experiences of a random sample of women who reported being sexually abused in childhood and who had experienced increased vulnerability to further sexual violence in adult intimate relationships.[67] Haskell undertook statistical analysis of a large and complex data set generated for the Women's Safety Project documenting the lifetime histories of gendered violence in a random sample of 420 women, in order to uncover any relationship between a history of child sexual abuse and experiences of sexual assault later in life.[68] Haskell found that a history of child sexual abuse in a woman's life increased the likelihood that she would experience sexual violence later in life, particularly in an intimate heterosexual relationship.

Haskell reports that of the 176 women who were sexually abused as children (including rape, attempted rape and fondling) from the randomly drawn sample of 420 women, 69 per cent reported that they were also sexually assaulted as adults. This compares with only 46 per cent of the women who were never sexually abused in childhood but who were sexually assaulted as adults, suggesting that women with histories of childhood sexual abuse experienced significantly higher rates of sexual assault as adults.

Developing a more comprehensive picture of the patterns of revictimisation requires an examination of different levels of the experience to elucidate what exactly accounts for this association. When the analysis of the data is narrowed to compare only experiences of rape or attempted rape in childhood and adulthood, the findings from this study were that 46 per cent of the women who had no childhood rape or attempted rape experiences experienced a rape or attempted rape in adult life. This compares with a significantly higher proportion of women who experienced rape or attempted rape in childhood and who then additionally had an experience of rape or attempted rape in their adult lives (73 per cent). This difference was found to be statistically significant ($p < 0.0001$).

However, when the data on sexual assault at the level of rape only (*excluding* all cases of attempted rape from the analysis) is analysed, an even greater disparity emerges between the two groups of women. Specifically, 33 per cent of the women in the sample who were never raped in childhood were raped as adults, compared to more than double the percentage—70 per cent—of the women who were raped in childhood and who were also raped after the age of 15 years.

This difference was also found to be statistically significant ($p < 0.0001$), confirming the association between sexual violence in childhood and increased likelihood of sexual violence again later in life. It appears that something about the

[67] Lori Haskell, *Revictimization in Women's Lives: An Empirical and Theoretical Account of the Links Between Child Sexual Abuse and Repeated Sexual Violence* (Dissertation, University of Toronto, 1999).

[68] Results of this study are reported in Haskell and Randall, 'The Women's Safety Project' (n 42); Randall and Haskell, 'Sexual Violence in Women's Lives' (n 42).

experience of sexual violation in childhood can potentially make women more vulnerable to further experiences of sexual violation in their adult lives, though how and why this might be the case is complex.

Subsequent data analysis from this study shed more light and showed that it is not just any perpetrator who poses the risk of further sexual violence to the women sexually violated as children; instead, the violence is relationally situated. More specifically, women sexually abused in childhood by male relatives were far more likely to be raped and/or physically abused in their adult intimate relationships by men who were their husbands or boyfriends. Again, Haskell's analysis of data from the Women's Safety Project suggests that a concept such as the normalisation of sexual violation in intimate relationships may explain this correlation.

As more attention has been paid to this issue of increased vulnerability in women's lives to abuse, a body of research has begun to further empirically document links between childhood sexual abuse and adult sexual revictimisation.[69] A number of other studies, not necessarily from random samples, have specifically shown the increased risk of sexual violence in intimate relationships borne by women who were sexually abused as children.

In a study of women who had recently obtained protection orders against their violent spouses, one in three had experienced threatened or forced sex by their partner as well as forced sex before the age of 14. In contrast, only one in five women in the research sample (19.8 per cent) had experienced child sexual abuse but not IPSV.[70] This study also demonstrated that women with histories of child sexual abuse had higher reported rates of sexual violence in their intimate relationships than did women without a history of child sexual abuse.

A 15-year prospective, longitudinal study of the experiences of young adult and adolescent females demonstrated a significantly increased risk of further sexual victimisation for those with child sexual abuse histories. As Barnes et al report from their research:

> Abused females were almost twice as likely to have experienced sexual revictimization and physical revictimization as compared to victimization rates reported by comparison

[69] CM Arata, 'From Child Victim to Adult Victim: A Model for Predicting Sexual Revictimization' (2000) 2(5) *Child Maltreatment* 28; EA Casey and PS Nurius, 'Trauma Exposure and Sexual Re-victimization Risk: Comparisons across Single, Multiple Incident, and Multiple Perpetrator Victimizations (2005) 4 *Violence Against Women* 505; CC Classen, OG Palesh and R Aggarwal, 'Sexual Re-victimization: A Review of the Empirical Literature' (2005) 4(6) *Trauma, Violence, and Abuse* 103; TL Messman-Moore, PJ Long and NJ Siegfried, 'The Revictimization of Child Sexual Abuse Survivors: An Examination of the Adjustment of College Women with Child Sexual Abuse, Adult Sexual Assault, and Adult Physical Abuse (2000) 2(5) *Child Maltreatment* 18; DA Neumann, BM Houskamp, V Pollock and J Briere, 'The Long Term Sequelae of Childhood Sexual Abuse in Women: A Meta-analytic Review (1996) 1(1) *Child Maltreatment* 6.

[70] J Cole, T Logan and L Shannon, 'Intimate Sexual Victimization among Women with Protective Orders: Types and Associations of Physical and Mental Health Problems' (2005) 20 *Violence & Victims* 705.

> females. Abused females' revictimizations were also more likely to have been perpetrated by older, non-peers and characterized by physical injury than were victimizations reported by comparison females.[71]

As another researcher explains:

> Given the wide disparity in findings, it is difficult to give specific estimates of the actual rates of revictimization, but a pattern of increased risk seems evident in the data. Despite the variability in definitions of abuse, the majority of studies indicate that women who are sexually abused as children are at an increased risk for sexual revictimization in adolescence or adulthood, or both. In examining these studies, a middle-ground estimate would be that approximately one-third of child sexual abuse victims are revictimized at some later point in time. In terms of risk, it appears that women sexually abused as children are at least two to three times more likely to be sexually assaulted as adolescents or adults than women without a history of child sexual abuse.[72]

The research and analyses in this important and still little understood area demonstrate that something about the vulnerability associated with being sexually violated and abused as girls increases the likelihood of further sexual and physical abuse later in life, especially in the context of intimate heterosexual relationships. This is an aspect of sexual violence in intimate relationships which warrants much greater recognition and understanding if we are to work towards breaking the cycle of violence in the lives of girls and women.

B. Unwanted Sex in Intimate Relationships with Violent Men and Women's Coping and Resistance

Sexual assault perpetrated by men with whom women have intimate relationships is a particularly painful and difficult form of sexual violence with which significant numbers of women have to contend. These sexual assaults are experienced by women in acutely complicated ways, given the intimate relational context in which they take place and the accentuated sense of shame, betrayal and violation that this kind of assault can engender.

This means that women who are both sexually and physically assaulted by their male partners are often at greater risk of physical harm and injury and are coping with more severe levels of physical assault. It is in this context that an analysis of the possibilities for and implications of women's resistance to forced sex must be understood. The qualitative data below comes from research conducted with a

[71] JE Barnes, JG Noll, FW Putnam and PK Trickett, 'Sexual and Physical Revictimization among Victims of Severe Childhood Sexual Abuse' (2009) 33 *Child Abuse and Neglect* 412.

[72] Catalina M Arata, 'Child Sexual Abuse and Sexual Revictimization' (2002) 9 *Clinical Psychology—Science and Practice* 135, 157.

random sample of women who consented to face-to-face, in-depth interviews for the Women's Safety Project.[73]

One of the most striking and complicated ways in which some of the women interviewed for this study reported avoiding the physical abuse and violence of their male intimates was through their conscious accommodation of unwanted sex, or their deliberate lack of resistance to forced sex. Some women flatly claimed that they saw having to endure this unwanted sex as an exchange; they tolerated their husbands' sexual invasion of their bodies in order to protect themselves from being beaten and further brutalised. In her interview, one woman referred to these sexual concessions as 'mercy fucks'.[74]

A number of women interviewed described their accommodation of this unwanted sex as necessary and/or inevitable, as the price that had to be paid for saving themselves from being beaten. In this way, not resisting unwanted sex was a conscious strategy they undertook in order to resist further physical assault. In one woman's words:

> Well he basically wanted to have sex and he was very insistent, so I thought it would be easier to comply. It was something I didn't want to do but I did it rather than say no. It would have caused a confrontation that I didn't want to get into.

Describing the ongoing nature of the unwanted sex in a previous relationship, another woman said:

> There is not a single incident, it was almost a normal pattern. I never had the option of saying no. The children shared our bedroom so I couldn't even talk properly. I always remember as a child trying to pretend I was asleep. He always pressured me for anal sex.

In the context of physical brutalisation by a male intimate, sexual assault often carries a further and intensified sense of stigmatisation and shame. Moreover, the very threat of further physical assault functions as a form of ongoing control, creating the conditions in which the choice to engage in sexual relations with a violent male partner is not really a choice at all.

For women who were living with or had lived with a violent man, determining what constitutes 'force' in relation to forced sex was often a fraught and difficult definitional problem. While some men did aggressively and violently force their female partners sexually, in other cases the simple knowledge that further violence could occur in the face of their sexual refusal sufficed to ensure the women's compliance. One woman's comments capture her struggle to define her experiences first by minimising them and downplaying that she had been 'forced' to have sex. She then immediately contradicts herself to acknowledge the ways in which her

[73] Haskell and Randall, 'The Women's Safety Project' (n 42); Randall and Haskell, 'Sexual Violence in Women's Lives' (n 42) 6–31; M Randall, *Agency and (in) Subordination: Victimization, Resistance and Sexual Violence in Women's Lives* (Doctoral Dissertation, Department of Political Science, York University, 1996).

[74] See Randall, *Agency and (in) Subordination*, ibid.

husband physically coerced her to submit to his sexual demands and states that she 'gave in' in order to spare herself from his temper and his violence. When asked by the interviewer about whether she had ever experienced forced sex with this man, she replied:

> It was never really forced. ... Well, he'd be very forceful, persistent, until I'd just give in. I really think it was because of his drinking. [How was he persistent?] Physically. He'd use his body to keep on at me. He would just sort of start doing it—he'd rub on me if he had a hard on. He'd just keep at it until I gave in. [What if you didn't give in?] He could have gotten violent. He's very violent tempered—especially when he's drinking.

When asked by her interviewer to describe the ways in which she was forced to have sex she did not want, she described a range of approaches from emotional manipulation to outright physical aggression.

> [How would he force you?] He'd beg. He'd threaten to leave me if I didn't have sex with him. He'd ask what was the matter with me. Sometimes he'd physically force me. He'd grab me, and push me down on the bed.

Still another woman's account captures the almost routine nature of unwanted sex in the final stages of her relationship with a violent man as well as the sense of resignation to and inevitability about this kind of experience in women's lives.

> We'd been living together for a while and you know when things aren't going well, and you don't want to have sex. But he does and he forces you to and he pins you down—you know, men are so strong. The relationship wasn't very good. [What happened?] He was pinning me down and I hate that feeling of being pinned down. But, the whole relationship was disintegrating by that point. You know, the guy thinks the problem is sexual and you don't. You're just angry. [You said he held you down?] Yah—he was pinning me and I guess there are times you have sex when you don't want to, but I mention it because it was scary. This time it really hurt.

Another theme which emerged in women's accounts of violence in intimate relationships was that they were often subjected to forced sex immediately after being physically beaten.

> He was often jealous, he always felt that I was seeing someone. If I was out with a friend he'd feel I was lying. He'd get angry and hit me. He'd throw me on the bed or against a wall. His anger would peak, and soon he'd just stop. [Did you ever fear that you'd be killed?] Yes ... [Then] he would, after he calmed down, want immediately to have sex with me. I hated the idea but after being assaulted I was too intimidated to think of refusing. It was so soon, I was still in fear. It really felt more like a rape. I just stayed passive. The real issue was the physical abuse, being overpowered, and thinking [whether] I could do something different to stop it.

Describing a pattern of repeated sexual assaults following physical assaults by her husband, another woman said that:

> All the times were upsetting. He would hit me and then want to make up using sex. He would just come and take it. [Did you say no?] No. [Were you afraid to say no?] Yes. [What did you think would happen if you said no?] He would hit me again.

A number of women described how their husbands used their bodies for their own sexual gratification while fully aware that the women did not consent to the sex, as is clear in the following accounts from two different women, both of whom had been repeatedly physically assaulted.

> I felt a little afraid, so I didn't want to add a spark to the flame. [What were you afraid he might do?] I don't know … I just didn't want to make trouble. I just lay there. He knew I wasn't into it.

> I was already in bed, he just starts his argument [for sex]. I took my nightie off and I say, go, do it. And he does it, even though he knows I'm not wanting it. I just lay there. I know that if I don't, we'll have a big argument, or I'll get beat up.

Another woman stated that when she tried to refuse sex with her husband 'he hit me in the face in anger, because of me not wanting to do what he wanted me to do'.

Yet some women did resist unwanted sex by their male intimates, including by explicitly saying that they did not want to be sexual and by physically struggling. But their protests were often to no avail, as is described in the accounts below, from three different women.

> It was New Year's Eve. We had people over at his apartment. I was staying over at his place. There'd been drinking. We went to bed. I was intending to go to sleep and he was intending to have sex. I said 'no'. I physically tried to push him away. He didn't see it as anything but a game of some sort. He didn't feel he was using force, he didn't hit me or use a weapon. But I was really afraid. I resisted but he forced me, successfully.

> I can just remember being adamant that I didn't want it and saying no. It didn't matter what I said. [What happened?] He held me down and did what he wanted to do. [What was that?] Anal sex. [And at other times?] He forced vaginal sex.

> [He] would come in after work, in the middle of the night. I would be sleeping and he would get into bed and start having sex with me. Saying no, or the fact that I was asleep carried no weight. He believed he shouldn't have to ask me for sex because I was his girlfriend.

Still another woman described how her physical resistance simply elicited greater physical force being used against her and appeared to excite her violent male partner even further.

> I was scared. [What were you afraid of exactly?] Him hurting me. It was awful. Physically I hurt, emotionally I hurt, and I felt betrayed and hopeless. [Was there any way in which you felt able to resist?] I tried struggling but that just made him more interested. He thought no meant yes.

Despite the fact that intimate relationships are the contexts in which women seem least likely to offer resistance to unwanted sex, it is not the case that women never do resist these kinds of assaults with success. In fact, despite the greater difficulties, some women are able successfully to resist sexual assaults by their male intimates, if not permanently then at least at specific times.

In the following account a woman describes how she would regularly avoid and escape her husband when he wanted to force her sexually.

> One day he locked me in the basement and my kids were upstairs. I didn't want to, it was summertime and he used to sleep in the basement. I was sick too. I didn't want to have sex, but he wanted to force me. I told him I wanted to go to the washroom. When I went upstairs I ran outside and hid in the garage. … He was a mechanic and had old cars in the garage so I would sleep in those old cars. Sometimes I couldn't get away from him. They have a law [in my home country] that when you are a man's wife, you have to do what he tells you.

Another woman describes how her repulsion was so strong that she stopped her husband from raping her after he beat her.

> After he really beat me up he wanted to have sex and I couldn't, it just made me sick. I never slept with him again. [What exactly did he force you to do?] He attempted intercourse. Finally, he tried to force me and I got sick. [You threw up?] Yes. He was so upset, he couldn't believe that this could happen. I thought he was going to kill me. But I just couldn't [do it]. Finally, we went to sleep.

Summarising the range of ways in which she resisted the sexual assaults of her violent husband, this woman gave a list of her techniques:

> I threw up. I took the baby to bed with me. I said I was sick. I said she [the baby] was sick. I said whatever I needed to.

Although some women do resist and are actually able to stop rapes by their male partners, the majority of women who lived with violent men indicated that they were not able to resist forced sex. The socially produced and legally enforced expectation that men have an 'entitlement' to pursue 'sex'—something women are seen to embody—plays a key role here, as does the often deeply felt social expectation that women should be sexually appealing to and accommodating of men's sexual desires and 'needs'.

What is interesting in this context is how many women tend to have the greatest difficulty resisting what they are taught and believe is 'expected' from them. For example, researchers David Finkelhor and Kersti Yllo found, in a survey of the experiences of women sexually assaulted by their husbands, that women were not often able to resist forced vaginal sexual intercourse from their husbands but were more likely to feel entitled to resist forced or demanded anal intercourse.[75] This, they speculate, is likely due to the view that vaginal heterosexual intercourse is the 'normal' and 'expected' form of sexual contact between men and women, whereas anal intercourse was seen by the women to be out of the ordinary and not something they should have to endure. In this way, social expectations surrounding sexuality shape and limit what and when women resist, especially in the context of intimate relationships.

It seems that women's resistance to sexual violence and intrusion is most fraught and most constrained within the context of intimate relationships. This is

[75] David Finkelhor and Kersti Yllo, *License to Rape: Sexual Abuse of Wives* (New York, Simon and Schuster, 1987) 113.

most likely attributable to the familial or chosen nature of the relationship, the difficulties in 'naming' and the confusion surrounding the abuse, the compounded sense of shame and betrayal which accompanies being assaulted by someone who is supposed to express care, not hostility, and the often conflicting but ongoing emotional and material ties to the abuser.

Moreover, built into the social and psychological structures of 'femininity' and 'masculinity' are relations of subordination and dominance, and these include the discourses and practices surrounding heterosexuality. These too, can and are being resisted and transformed—in fact, this is one of the explicit political aims of feminism. However, it is far too soon to claim that our lives are not still profoundly shaped by the dictates of these hierarchical structures or that these structures are not still deeply constitutive of the psyches of those people constructed and differentiated as 'men' and 'women' in our contemporary societies. Women's sexual agency, including the ability to choose to have sexual relations as well as *not* to have them, remains deeply circumscribed. The social expectation that men are 'entitled' to sex with the women who are their partners is still reinforced socially and expressed individually, as is evident in the narratives above.

Speaking pointedly to the complicated issues surrounding sexuality, power and control, especially for women who have known a lifetime of sexual violation, one woman I interviewed for the Women's Safety Project described repeated experiences of forced and unwanted sex from men she knew as boyfriends, common-law partners, dates or men she had just met, and explained how she negotiated (hetero)sexual relationships in order to 'save herself'.[76] Although she describes initially consenting to sex with the man she refers to below, what actually happened in sexual terms was, in her own words, 'way beyond' what she had expected or wanted sexually.

> I met him in a bar. … I sat and drank with him. He really shocked me … he was so intensively aggressive in bed. He didn't talk to me. He just arranged me and my body, moved me and did stuff to me. It was anal sex. Even with strangers there's a kind of courtesy in bed, but that was way beyond what I was prepared to offer. … It hurt me. It was like brutal sex without a sound. Suddenly he goes dead silent and does all this stuff to me. And then he left.
>
> I felt completely raped by him. I felt pummeled. I was sore and raw, my mouth, everything. … He'd gone in everywhere. He'd taken everything. [What did you do after he left?] I sat awake and watched the dawn. It's not like there was [a] part of me [that] was still mine. [I felt that] he'd taken everything.

Sex—which this woman described in the interview as 'the problem'—was in her experience something that men expected from her, as a form of service. As a woman who had been revictimised multiple times in her life, this sexual expectation had been imposed on her since her early childhood through repeated rapes

[76] See Randall, *Agency and (in) Subordination* (n 73).

and beatings by a male family member, and through a more insidious construction and shaping of her psyche in the context of these life experiences where sexual violation is routine and sexual agency is a mere abstraction. Without a sense of agency the realm of possibilities for women's resistance is very narrow indeed.

This is a crucial area in which the law can play a role. Where the law insists that without consent sexual contact is criminal, even in marriages or other intimate relationships, people learn that, contrary to the traditional view of men's entitlement to sexual access to their wives, there is instead an entitlement to autonomy and choice about sexual contact, even in our most intimate relationships.

C. Identifying and Naming Sexual Violence in Intimate Relationships

Larger patterns of social denial of men's violence against women shape women's own individual perceptions of their abuse experiences. In a society where the fact and extent of sexual violence against women in marital and other intimate heterosexual relationships is minimised or denied, it is not surprising that so many women have difficulty recognising or 'naming' unwanted sexual experiences with their spouses as sexual assaults.

As Pease and Flood observe:

> [W]omen's responses to their own subjection to violence are shaped by their own attitudes and those of others around them. To the extent that individual women agree with violence-supportive understandings of domestic violence or sexual assault, they are more likely to blame themselves for the assault, less likely to report it to the police or other authorities, and more likely to experience long-term negative psychological and emotional effects.[77]

Put differently, dominant and normative understandings of what constitutes a rape influence the ways in which victims, perpetrators, bystanders and legal actors understand sexual assault experiences. These dominant norms sharply influence women's recognition of their own experiences of sexual violence in intimate relationships.

Social paradigms also affect what behaviours are understood as rape or sexual assault. The normative understanding of what constitutes 'real rape' is defined in part as the belief that a rape is more 'real' if it is a physically violent assault by a stranger. For both men and women, support of heteronormative beliefs is associated with the acceptance and experience of being verbally pressured to have sex.[78] It is not surprising that these social attitudes and beliefs seep into and shape law.

[77] Pease and Flood (n 61) 549.

[78] For an analysis of this phenomenon, see DK Eaton and A Matamala, 'The Relationship between Heteronormative Beliefs and Verbal Sexual Coercion in College Students' (2014) 43 *Archives of Sexual Behavior* 1443.

As Heenan further explains:

> The reluctance of law, and of jurors, to criminalise men's sexually violent behaviour is further complicated by broader cultural conditions that allow for the majority of women's unwanted sexual experiences to be considered as *not* rape. The problem, as many commentators see it, is situated in our reluctance to apply a model of consent that is both communicative and mutually participatory. … According to Pineau (1989) and others … establishing the point at which rape should be distinguished from 'wifely acquiescence' has proved so difficult for the courts and for women, precisely because coercion, pressure, aggression and 'seduction' remain culturally acceptable expressions of male sexual behaviour.[79]

If naming unwanted experiences as sexual assaults is difficult for women in general when these assaults take place in an intimate relationship, then this difficulty is compounded for women whose childhood sexual abuse histories have already introduced them to traumatic sexualisation.

D. Intimate Partner Sexual Violence, Traditional Masculinities and Gender Inequality

No clear-cut 'profile' has been established to identify men who sexually assault their female intimate partners. But most of those working in the field concur that men who are sexually coercive and/or violent in their intimate relationships tend to be 'jealous, domineering individuals who feel a sense of entitlement to have sex with their "property"'.[80]

That gender inequality and sexual assault in intimate relationships are linked is also becoming increasingly well accepted. In an extensive review of research on violence prevention published in the highly respected medical journal, *The Lancet*, Rachel Jewkes, Michael Flood and James Lang identify an increasing recognition in the field 'that masculinity and gender-related social norms are implicated in violence'.[81] These researchers further explore the ways in which 'the relations, norms, and systems that sustain gender inequality and violence' must be transformed in order to make meaningful progress on preventing and ending gendered violence.[82]

Their review of research on the factors associated with men's use of violence towards women, including intimate partner violence and rape, shows that:

> [W]hen grouped together, many of these behaviours are rooted in expected practices or entitlements that flow from the hegemonic ideals that men should be strong, tough,

[79] *Just Keeping the Peace* (n 36) 9.

[80] Bergen (n 3) 4.

[81] Rachel Jewkes, Michael Flood and James Language, 'From Work with Men and Boys to Changes of Social Norms and Reduction of Inequities in Gender Relations: A Conceptual Shift in Prevention of Violence Against Women and Girls' (2014) www.thelancet.com, http://dx.doi.org/10.1016/S0140-6736(14)61683-4 (21 November 2014) 1.

[82] ibid, 1.

> in control over women and their bodies, heterosexual, and sexually dominant. … For example, key factors strongly associated with perpetration of intimate partner violence and non-partner rape include controlling behaviours towards women and inequitable gender attitudes, behaviours which emphasise (hetero)sexual prowess (transactional sex and having multiple sexual partners), and involvement in violence with men. … Other associated factors suggest that men who are violent are more likely to struggle to live up to a masculine ideal in other respects, for example by having depression, or alcohol and drug misuse, no high school education, and current food insecurity (the latter two being proxies for social marginalisation and poverty).[83]

These researchers further note that:

> [M]en's own history as victims of violence is visible in associations between perpetration and men's experiences of childhood victimisation, rape, and homophobic abuse. … These two groups of factors expose the other side of the coin: men struggling to live up to the ideals of manhood that are hard to reach, and men who have been traumatised through harsh childhoods and violence in adulthood.[84]

Traditional models of heterosexual relationships are built upon the patriarchal idea of men as the authority figures and the 'heads' of the household, whose decision-making power and needs are paramount. Indeed, historically, wives had no independent legal status or personhood apart from that of their husbands, expressed in the idea of coverture, a concept deeply implicated in legitimating marital rape.[85] This idea persists in many parts of the world, and even in those societies where norms of equality are ostensibly entrenched in law, remnants of these kinds of gender inequality continue to shape intimate relationships between men and women, including ideas about sexual relationships and consent, in ways that undermine women's autonomy and equality.

In contextualising her analysis of the defects in legal responses to sexual assault, MacKinnon points to the pervasiveness and 'normalcy' of sexual violence in women's lives, a point that applies perhaps even more sharply with regard to sexual violence in women's intimate relationships with men. While MacKinnon is not suggesting, as her critics have sometimes inaccurately claimed, that all men are rapists, or that all heterosexual sex is rape, she does point out that the frequency with which so many women experience sexual assault means that 'rape is indigenous, not exceptional, to women's social condition'.[86]

MacKinnon's analysis asks us to think critically about the nature of gendered relationships, of gender inequality, of dominance and submission in terms of sexual relations and about how these dynamics play themselves out in intimate life, including sexual life. This is very relevant and important with regard to marital rape.

[83] ibid, 5.

[84] ibid, 5.

[85] See Chapters 2 and 5 by Venkatesh and Randall, and Koshan, respectively, in this volume for discussions of this issue.

[86] Catharine MacKinnon, *Towards a Feminist Theory of the State* (Cambridge, Massachusetts, Harvard University Press, 1989) 172.

In social contexts where marriage is constructed as a hierarchy and where men's rights as head of the family and household are entrenched, and where sexual access to women is assumed as a male entitlement conferred by marriage, then the lines between consent and non-consent get very blurry indeed—if, in fact, they can even be said to exist meaningfully. These are the same social conditions, legally reinforced, which restrict or obliterate the space for women's choice, autonomy, freedom and consent to sexual relations within heterosexual marital relationships.

IV. Conclusion—Sexual Assault in Intimate Relationships, Mistaken Belief in Continuous Consent, Rape Myths and the Law

Many of the difficulties in finding appropriate and effective social, policy and legal responses to sexual assault and other forms of gender violence flow from restricted understanding of the problem of sexual assault and similarly restricted images of what 'real' victims 'look like'. This pertains to sexual violence in intimate relationships. The idea that there is an 'ideal victim' of a sexual assault limits social recognition that many victims of sexual assault are women who are married to (or intimately involved with) men who are their assailants. This is because one of the dominant ideas about an 'ideal victim' of sexual assault is that she is a woman who is attacked by a stranger or by someone she barely knows.[87] Exposing the reality and prevalence of sexual violence in women's marital and other intimate relationships with men challenges one of the most inaccurate and restricted features of the 'ideal victim' of sexual assault.

It is only in the last few decades that a significant understanding or recognition of sexual assault as a crime in the context of marriage (or marital-type relationships) has been developed.[88] Previously the concept of rape in marriage was almost unheard of as women were socially and legally thought of as property of their husbands.[89] It was considered an absurdity because sexual access to a woman was historically understood to be part of a man's entitlement upon marriage; indeed, this view still prevails today in many countries, societies and relationships. Related to this is the idea, still alive and well in the world, that a woman's consent to sex is presumed and continuous within a spousal relationship.

[87] See Jennifer Koshan's chapter, 'The Judicial Treatment of Marital Rape in Canada: A Post-Criminalisation Case Study', in this volume for some discussion of this; see also M Randall, 'Sexual Assault Law, Credibility, and "Ideal Victims": Consent, Resistance, and Victim Blaming' (2010) 22 *Canadian Journal of Women and the Law* 397.

[88] Bergen (n 3); See also Kersti Yllö and M. Gabriela Torres (eds), *Marital Rape: Consent, Marriage, and Social Change in Global Context* (New York, Oxford University Press, 2016).

[89] Mary Kay Kirkwood and Dawn K Cecil, 'Marital Rape: A Student Assessment of Rape Laws and the Marital Exemption' (2001) 7 *Violence Against Women* 1234, 1235.

Ideas about men's 'rights' to sex with their wives are sometimes entrenched in law explicitly, though more often implicitly by way of judicial attitudes and ideas which creep into legal reasons. This excerpt from a judgment by Justice Bollen of the South Australian Supreme Court in the 1992 rape case of *R v Johns* provides one example:

> There is, of course, nothing wrong with a husband, faced with his wife's initial refusal to engage in intercourse, in attempting, in an acceptable way, to persuade her to change her mind, and that may involve a measure of rougher than usual handling. It may be that handling and persuasion will persuade the wife to agree. Sometimes it is a fine line between not agreeing, then changing of the mind and consenting.[90]

In countries where a legal exemption for marital rape has been debated, traditional attitudes are often expressed to justify and legitimate why there should be no criminalisation of sexual assault in marriage, and no 'interference' in 'private life'.[91] There is much work to be done to criminalise sexual violence in intimate relationships along with challenging the ideologies that legitimise this violence in the first place.

As some human rights researchers on the topic of marital rape have noted:

> [L]egal systems in many countries continue to reflect the belief that rape within a marriage is not rape. Regardless of the extent to which marital rape is defined or recognized by law, in practice, it is rarely reported, prosecuted, or punished. Many women throughout the world do not know that marital rape is illegal and even when it is known, cultural norms and social stigmas discourage reporting. Law enforcement and prosecutors are often unwilling to respond to complaints and when they do, the burden is placed on the victim to prove the act was illegal, which generally requires visible physical injuries to prove lack of consent or resistance. In addition … marital rape is prosecuted and punished less often and less severely than are other crimes, in large part because of assumptions that women are complicit in or in some way provoked the assault.[92]

Criminalisation of marital rape and other forms of sexual violence in intimate relationships is a crucial component of ending the problem of sexual assault. But, as Eskow notes:

> Legislative and prosecutorial efforts to combat marital rape will not succeed until pervasive myths about sex, rape, and marriage are eradicated. … Legislatures must affirmatively negate the marital exemption from rape statutes, and prosecutors must become

[90] *R v Johns*, Supreme Court, SA No SCCRM/91/452, 26 August 1992, cited in PL Easteal et al, 'Language, Gender and "Reality": Violence against Women', www.researchgate.net/publication/255724783_Language_Gender_and_'Reality'_Violence_against_Women.

[91] See eg Jennifer Koshan's chapter, 'The Criminalisation of Marital Rape and Law Reform in Canada', in this volume.

[92] 'Stop Violence Against Women: A Project of the Advocates for Human Rights: Marital and Intimate Partner Sexual Violence', www.stopvaw.org/marital_and_intimate_partner_sexual_assault (2013).

> educators, not only in the courtroom, but also in society at large, communicating the realities of marital rape through effective use of the media.[93]

Criminalising marital rape contributes to creating the social conditions where equality, choice and autonomy surrounding sexual relations in marriage and other intimate relationships can become accepted norms. But establishing the legal recognition that sexual assault in a relationship is criminal is only a first and necessary step towards this larger goal.

The problem of sexual assault in intimate relationships is one that is both more widespread than had previously been realised, and yet—for a variety of reasons—one that still remains largely privatised. While domestic violence has been the subject of extensive law reform, has prompted the development of many services and a network of shelters and safe houses, and has commanded significant public attention, sexual violence within marriage and other intimate relationships has not been nearly so publicly scrutinised or acknowledged. Yet studies in Canada and internationally have documented both that far too many women are subjected to sexual assault by their male intimates and that sexual assault is very often a part of the experience of women who also experience ongoing domestic violence.

While the broader issues of sexual assault are still not adequately understood or remedied, socially or legally, the taboos which both militate against women disclosing sexual assault and limit their options for legal redress are exacerbated when the sexual assault takes place in a marital context. As Emily Sack observes: 'While the legacy of the rationales for condoning violence against women may be hidden from view and contemporary domestic violence policy generally it is alive and well in the treatment of marital and intimate partner rape.'[94]

Understanding the dynamics of sexual assault in intimate relationships is especially important given that public perceptions and misunderstanding of the phenomenon can too often render invisible the suffering of women who are sexually abused by their intimate partners. Research in the field has repeatedly documented that people's perceptions of the prevalence, seriousness and consequences of sexual violence are tied to the relational context in which it takes place. This is clearly tied to a normalisation of the idea that men are entitled to 'sex' in marriage along with gender norms and socialisation that teaches women that pleasing, accommodating and serving others is an expected part of traditional femininity.

Sack has also pointed out the interconnections between physical violence and sexual violence in intimate relationships, and the considerable amount of work still to be done to eradicate these social problems through law and policy. In her words:

> The historical legacy of unequal treatment of women remains present in the unfinished business of domestic violence law and policy. Just as marital rape is not truly considered

[93] LR Eskow, 'The Ultimate Weapon? Demythologizing Spousal Rape and Reconceptualizing its Prosecution' (1996) 48 *Stanford Law Review* 677.

[94] Sack (n 37) 538.

> 'real' rape, perhaps we do not think that domestic violence deserves to be considered a 'real' crime. This may help to explain our reluctance to fully implement domestic violence arrest and prosecution policies and to enforce protection orders. If domestic violence is ever to be fully addressed, we need to examine the unstated assumptions about women that we like to think we have long abandoned. We need to go back to thinking about women's equality.[95]

Recognition and understanding of the extent of and dynamics surrounding the problem of sexual violence in intimate relationships is necessary for formulating effective legal recognition of and responses to this same problem. The World Health Organization observes that: '[F]actors associated with increased risk of experiencing intimate partner and sexual violence include low education, exposure to violence between parents, abuse during childhood, and attitudes accepting violence and gender inequality.'[96] Ending sexual violence in intimate relationships, along with ending violence against women more generally, is crucial for the realisation of women's equality.

[95] Sack (n 37) 565.

[96] World Health Organization, 'Violence against Women: Intimate Partner and Sexual Violence against Women', Fact Sheet No 239, www.who.int/mediacentre/factsheets/fs239/en/ (updated November 2016).

3

Normative and International Human Rights Law Imperatives for Criminalising Intimate Partner Sexual Violence: The Marital Rape Impunity in Comparative and Historical Perspective

VASANTHI VENKATESH AND MELANIE RANDALL

I. Introduction

Marital rape (including other forms of sexual violence in intimate relationships) is a prevalent problem throughout the world. Some studies suggest that as many as one in three women has experienced sexual and/or physical violence perpetrated by a husband or other male intimate.[1] Yet many of the world's countries still fail to criminalise sexual assault in marital relationships (also described as intimate partner sexual violence, IPSV) or fail to criminalise it adequately.

The marital rape exemption has a long and varied social and legal history. Its entrenchment is inextricably linked to women's subordinate status in societies at large, and to women's subordination in marriage specifically. As entrenched as impunity for IPSV has been in so many jurisdictions, the marital rape exemption has not remained uncontested. On the contrary, it has been vigorously condemned by women's rights movements around the world. This condemnation has also been central to the repudiation of associated legal constructs of gender inequality, such as the doctrine of coverture, which obliterates married women's independent and autonomous separate legal existence, and constructs them as their husband's

[1] See eg World Health Organization, 'Violence against women: Intimate Parner and Sexual Violence against Women,' Fact Sheet, www.who.int/mediacentre/factsheets/fs239/en/ (November 2016).

property.[2] Yet so powerful and embedded are the taboos and privacy surrounding sexuality and marriage that even in some countries where extensive legal reforms have been made to end domestic and other forms of violence against women, the idea (and reality) persists that sexual assaults perpetrated by spouses should remain beyond the reach of the criminal law.

Human rights and women's groups in countries where marital rape retains its criminal immunity have been relying on international human rights law, inter alia, to demand its criminalisation in order to fulfil their state's obligations under international law.[3] The demand for an end to the marital rape exemption in criminal law is more than a demand for a penal remedy. It is fundamentally a demand for women's legal equality and autonomy, rights that centrally define international human rights law. The existence of a criminal remedy for sexual assault in marriage is a crucial form of state condemnation of and protection from gendered violence. But too many states still fail to provide it, either by retaining spousal immunity for sexual assault or by treating it as a less serious legal wrong. Criminalising sexual assault in marriage and providing legal remedies for this form of gendered violence is fundamental to achieving women's equality and other human rights. While this has been recognised by many of the world's states, too many others remain resistant and lag behind, insulating sexual violence against women by their spouses from legal sanction.

In this chapter we provide a big-picture perspective on the long and bumpy road taken by many of the world's countries in moving towards legal recognition that sexual assault can occur in a marital relationship and in the provision of a criminal law remedy for this form of gendered violence. We begin the chapter by articulating our arguments about why engaging the power of criminal remedies is necessary to the struggle to end sexual violence against women in marriage, particularly with reference to criminal law's importance in expressing fundamental social norms. Section II moves to a critical review of the historical origins and ideological justifications underpinning the marital rape exemption in diverse societies. We show how similar themes occur across very different social regimes.

This is followed in section III by a global, comparative analysis of the marital rape exemption and the criminalisation of marital rape in various countries of the world. We provide an overview of the historical and uneven progress towards

[2] See eg J Ross, *Making Marital Rape Visible: A History of American Legal and Social Movements Criminalizing Rape in Marriage* (PhD Dissertation, University of Nebraska–Lincoln, 2015) digitalcommons.unl.edu/historydiss/85; JE Hasday, 'Contest and Consent: A Legal History of Marital Rape' (2000) 88 *California Law Review* 1373; JS Mill, *The Subjection of Women* (London, Longmans, Green, Reader and Dyer, 1869).

[3] See eg Advocates for Human Rights, 'Marital and Intimate Partner Sexual Assault' [2013] Stop Violence Against Women—A Project of the Advocates for Human Rights, www.stopvaw.org/marital_and_intimate_partner_sexual_assault; M McWilliams and FD Ni Aolain, 'Moving Slowly to Regulate and Recognize: Human Rights Meets Intimate Partner Sexual Violence' Transitional Justice Institute Research Paper no 16-10 (2016), papers.ssrn.com/sol3/papers.cfm?abstract_id=2765432.

providing criminal legal remedies for women sexually assaulted by their husbands or intimate partners in different legal systems around the world. In this section we also analyse and critique the two most comprehensive and recent databases of marital rape legislation around the world, provided by the World Bank and the United Nations, respectively.

Section IV provides an overview of the major human rights instruments and sources of legal authority that require states to criminalise sexual assault in marriage, including the instruments aimed at securing women's equal rights and ending gendered violence.[4] We conclude the chapter by reiterating our argument that international human rights law and the due-diligence standard provide powerful normative bases on which women's movements and other social justice supporters can organise to end impunity for sexual violence in intimate relationships.

A. Why Are Criminal Remedies Essential for Ending Marital Rape?

A great deal of the advocacy undertaken by those seeking to end violence against women has focused on engaging state power to criminalise acts of physical and sexual abuse of women that had previously been seen to be 'normal' or legitimate. The appeal to criminal law represents a utilisation of both its expressive and remedial functions to put a stop to this kind of discrimination and inequality in women's lives, particularly in women's intimate lives.

Criminalising behaviour that has previously been condoned or considered acceptable in oppressing members of subordinated groups has long been a part of the struggle to achieve equality. As Cass Sunstein has pointed out, 'a large point of law may be to shift social norms and social meaning'.[5] This applies to law's changing grasp of various forms of what is now recognised as discrimination and harassment. For example, Sunstein notes that: 'Antidiscrimination law is often designed to change norms so as to ensure that people are treated with a kind of dignity and respect that discriminatory behaviour seems to deny.'[6]

Criminal law has an especially important role to play in shifting social norms towards equality and in condemning behaviours and actions, such as sexual

[4] A detailed exposition of these arguments is advanced in the following articles: M Randall and V Venkatesh, 'The Right to No: The Crime of Marital Rape, Women's Human Rights, and International Law' (2015) 41 *Brooklyn Journal of International Law* 153; M Randall and V Venkatesh, 'Criminalizing Sexual Violence against Women in Intimate Relationships: State Obligations under Human Rights Law' (2015) 109 *AJIL Unbound* 189; M Randall and V Venkatesh, 'Why Sexual Assault in Intimate Relationships Must Be Criminalized as Required by International Human Rights Law: A Response to the Symposium Comments' (2016) 109 *AJIL Unbound* 342.

[5] CR Sunstein, 'On the Expressive Function of Law' (1995) 144 *University of Pennsylvania Law Review* 2021, 2043.

[6] ibid, 2044.

assaults, which undermine equality, bodily integrity and dignity. As Sunstein elaborates: 'There are many areas in which law is used in an expressive way, largely in order to manage social norms. The criminal law is a prime arena for the expressive function of law.'[7]

Criminalising domestic violence, for example, has been a crucial dimension of the work to end this form of violence against women in intimate relationships. Criminalising the use of physical violence against wives provides, in theory at least, a way for individual women to seek state protection against this harm. It also simultaneously represents a rejection of traditional patriarchal ideas, which had previously legitimated men's use of force against their wives as a form of discipline and domination. Similarly, ending the marital immunity for sexual assault in criminal law is crucial both at the micro level, to give individual women the option of criminal remedies for their experiences of this form of violence, and at the macro level, to shift norms towards recognising women's full equality and autonomy rights in private relationships.

Criminalisation is, and should be, only one aspect of the multiple kinds of state and social responses to gendered violence which feminist human rights scholars and activists pursue. Calls for criminalisation are necessarily situated within a broader agenda for structural change and for an improvement in the social, economic and political conditions which allow for gendered violence in the first place. Julie Goldscheid has pointed to the range of responses which should be undertaken in order to require that states address gendered violence.[8] As she explains:

> International human rights laws' due diligence framework requires a range of responses that include the obligation to prevent, protect, and provide redress, along with the obligation to prosecute and punish. Explicitly framing states' obligations in terms of that more comprehensive approach would reach broadly to address the cultural and social barriers that allow marital rape to continue without sanction.[9]

Drawing on international human rights law as a source of authority for challenging the marital rape exception in criminal law allows feminist and other social justice organisations, working within their specific national and local contexts, to seek greater state action and accountability in ending this form of violence against women and violation of women's human rights.

The very fact that so much IPSV remains unreported and unremedied, and its victims unassisted, makes the law even more essential. Likewise, it further creates the need to intensify efforts to make the law more responsive, effective and just. Due diligence to criminalise marital rape does not stop at the level of statutory reform. It also requires proper and fair enforcement of the law. For example,

[7] ibid.

[8] J Goldscheid, 'Considering the Role of the State: Comment on "Criminalizing Sexual Violence against Women in Intimate Relationships"' (2015) 109 *AJIL Unbound* 202.

[9] ibid, 202.

there are multiple evidentiary difficulties in proving lack of consent in criminal proceedings and these are compounded in cases of spousal sexual assault.[10]

Struggles for women's human rights that engage criminal law as part of the strategy to eradicate gendered violence have been of central importance to the women's movement and to the move towards gender equality. This is not the same as suggesting criminal law is the *only* important strategy for challenging violence against women. Nor is it an unambivalent embrace of criminal law or the criminal justice system. Instead, it is a recognition that a state's criminal law power is an essentially important resource to be drawn upon, both conceptually and concretely, to shift social norms and practices such that sexual violence in intimate relationships is no longer seen to be acceptable. Engaging criminal law to end IPSV is especially critical at the normative level given the long-entrenched ideological and historical origins and justifications of it, a subject we address next.

II. Historical Origins and Ideological Underpinnings of the Marital Rape Exemption

Historically, in many societies, women have had no remedy against sexual coercion by their husbands.[11] Women's vulnerability to sexual violence in intimate relationships, and the lack of a legal remedy for it, has been inextricably connected to the social, economic and political subordination of women historically, and in most societies.

There have been exceptions. For example, there were (and there still are) matrilineal and polyandrous societies across the globe in which women had a much higher social status than they have had in patriarchal social formations, and in which violence against women was not condoned.[12] Women who were wealthy and privileged generally enjoyed some legal emancipation in certain periods and in certain societies and could take legal action against their husbands with

[10] For an analysis in the Canadian context, see M Randall, 'Sexual Assault in Spousal Relationships, "Continuous Consent", and the Law: Honest but Mistaken Judicial Beliefs' (2008) 32 *Manitoba Law Journal* 144; J Koshan, 'The Judicial Treatment of Marital Rape in Canada: A Post-Criminalisation Case Study', chapter 9 in this volume.

[11] MJ Anderson, 'Lawful Wife, Unlawful Sex—Examining the Effect of the Criminalisation of Marital Rape in England and the Republic of Ireland' (1998) 27 *Georgia Journal of International and Comparative Law* 139, 141–46.

[12] A Smith, *Conquest: Sexual Violence and American Indian Genocide* (Cambridge, MA, South End Press 2005) 18–21; M-B Watson-Franke, 'A World in which Women Move Freely without Fear of Men: An Anthropological Perspective on Rape' (2002) 25 *Women's Studies International Forum* 599; C Noble and C Bettman, 'Culture, Social Discourse and Domestic Violence: What Is the Connection?' [2003] *Women Against Violence: An Australian Feminist Journal* 42.

adequate support. This was the case, for example, in ancient Rome, medieval Europe and the Ottoman period.[13] Another notable example is found in the Brehon law in Ireland, based on ancient Celtic law, which offered more protection to women from spousal violence than the English common law or Christian ecclesiastical law.[14]

Additionally, the property, contractual and other rights that women possessed also played an important role in determining remedies for women facing domestic violence and marital rape. For example, Irish women under Brehon law and women in several Arab societies had inheritance rights and could independently hold property. They could also lawfully divorce or separate from their husbands on the basis of ill-treatment.[15]

Similarly, in many pre-colonial Namibian communities, women contributed to the bulk of subsistence agriculture and had access to property and the economy. Divorce was easily obtained, men had lesser control over their wives, and women played important roles as healers, leaders and rulers. Violence against women within the household was much more circumscribed by the laws in these places.[16]

Religious legal systems have also always had several interpretive lineages. For example, some Koranic and Talmudic interpretations have emphasised the legal equality of men and women in marriage, interpretations which have been used by courts and governments to provide legitimacy to gender justice claims.[17]

Nevertheless, and despite these exceptions, it is safe to say that for the most part sexual assault in marital relationships has been condoned throughout history and husbands have had enforceable 'rights' to sexual intercourse with their wives. While some customary legal systems insist that wives have a symmetrical expectation of sexual intercourse, this apparent equality has often only been used as a ground for divorce or compensation.[18] Furthermore, norms like these that

[13] Anderson (n 11) 143; F Zarinebaf-Shahr, 'Women, Law, and Imperial Justice in Ottoman Istanbul in the Late Seventeenth Century' in A El Azhary Sonbol (ed), *Women, the Family, and Divorce Laws in Islamic History*, 1st ed (Syracuse, NY, Syracuse University Press 1996) 87–89.

[14] Anderson (n 11) 160.

[15] ibid, 143; A El Azhary Sonbol, 'Law and Gender Violence in Ottoman and Modern Egypt', in *Women, the Family, and Divorce Laws in Islamic History* (n 13) 281.

[16] H Becker, 'A Concise History of Gender, "Tradition" and the State in Namibia' in C Keulder (ed), *State, Society, and Democracy: a Reader in Namibian Politics* (Windhoek, Namibia, Gamsberg Macmillan 2000) 177–78.

[17] Egypt Supreme Constitutional Court Case No 8 of Judicial Year 17 (18 May 1996) (holding that veiling is not mandatory under Islam and that a ban on a woman's right to wear a *niqab* was permissible); *Cohen v The State of Israel*, Criminal Appeal 91/80, 35 (3) PD (1980) 281 (holding that the criminal law exception for marital rape is incompatible with Jewish law). See also W Goldstein, *Defending the Human Spirit: Jewish Law's Vision for a Moral Society* (Jerusalem, Feldheim Publishers 2006) 166–75; CB Lombardi and NJ Brown, 'Do Constitutions Requiring Adherence to Shari'a Threaten Human Rights—How Egypt's Constitutional Court Reconciles Islamic Law with the Liberal Rule of Law' (2005) 21 *American University International Law Review* 379, 425–528; N Abiad, *Sharia, Muslim States and International Human Rights Treaty Obligations: A Comparative Study* (London, British Institute of International and Comparative Law 2008) 161–75.

[18] L Ahmed, *Women and Gender in Islam: Historical Roots of a Modern Debate* (New Haven, Yale University Press 1992) 91–93; K Ali, 'Progressive Muslims and Islamic Jurisprudence: The Necessity

suggest a formal mutuality between men and women in marriage must be read through the lens of the immense power that men carried as heads of household and as primary actors in the economic and political arenas. In patriarchal systems around the world and throughout history, the husband has been seen as the head of the household and to wield authority over it. Christian norms, for example, explicitly make men the authority in the family, and have reified patriarchal practices across the globe lasting for millennia.[19] The sections which follow articulate the thematic justifications which have been deployed in and through the various legal legitimations of men's rights to sexual access to their wives, consensual or forced.

Throughout history, the marital rape exemption has persisted through various legal doctrines that sought to uphold particular ideological constructs of women and marriage. While much has changed in the legal characterisations of women, their bodies and their degrees of autonomy across the world, it is important to understand the contingent and ideological nature of traditional patriarchal historical constructs and how these have ensured that vestiges from the past persist and maintain dominance structures that continue to inhibit women's rights today. Some of these fundamentally masculine-dominant ideas are outlined in the following sections.

A. Women as Private Property of Men

In general, rape laws were originally designed to protect male property interests in women and to protect the 'honour' of the family or social group from defilement by other men. In this way, women were constructed as the private property of their husbands and fathers. In Europe, for example, the father's interest in ensuring a virginal daughter for marriage, as opposed to justice for women victims, was the motivation for laws penalising rape.[20] After marriage, the woman became the property of the husband in accordance with common law doctrines such as coverture and the idea that women were chattels.

This socially construed legal framework made prosecuting a man for marital rape impossible as he had full legal rights over his own property, which included the body of his wife. Countries where marriage involves financial or commodity transactions such as bride-price or dowry continue to perpetrate the characterisation

for Critical Engagement with Marriage and Divorce Laws' in O Safi (ed), *Progressive Muslims: on Justice, Gender and Pluralism* (Oxford, Oneworld 2003) 171–72; P Caplan, *The Cultural Construction of Sexuality* (London, Tavistock, 1987) 222.

[19] Anderson (n 11) 143–46.

[20] MD Schwartz, 'The Spousal Exemption for Criminal Rape Prosecution' (1982) 7 *Vermont Law Review* 33; MDA Freeman, 'But If You Can't Rape Your Wife, Whom Can You Rape? The Marital Rape Exemption Reexamined' (1981) 15 *Family Law Quarterly* 1.

of women as chattels or property, ideas that continue to be upheld in criminal and family law in these countries.[21]

B. Coverture and the Erasure of a Woman's Legal Personhood

In various legal doctrines such as coverture, or *femme couverte* in English common law and 'marital power' in Roman-Dutch law, a woman had no legal identity outside of her husband's and was treated in law as a perpetual minor. This is a derivative of the Judaeo-Christian doctrine of the husband and wife constituting 'one flesh'.[22] William Blackstone justified this notion in his influential legal treatise, in which he stated: 'By marriage, the husband and wife are one person in law: that is, the very being or legal existence of the woman is suspended during the marriage, or at least is incorporated and consolidated into her husband's legal existence.'[23] On this view, once unified by marriage, the wife cannot enter into any independent legal transaction and her husband could not possibly be charged with rape of his wife as she and her husband were one; he could not rape himself.

Blackstone also used the coverture doctrine to legitimate a husband's 'chastisement' and physical violence towards his wife, as well as the perpetual 'minor' legal status of women.[24] In his words: '[A man could] give his wife moderate correction, for, as he is to answer for her misbehaviour, the law thought it reasonable to intrust [*sic*] him with this power of restraining her, by domestic chastisement, in the same moderation that a man is allowed to correct his apprentices or children.'[25] Blackstone's views remained influential through the eighteenth, nineteenth and even the twentieth century.

Reforms in both the United States and England in the 1800s led to the passage of several Married Woman's Property Acts that legally separated the identities of the spouses and abolished many of the common law restrictions on married women's rights. Husbands and wives could even sue one another over civil claims such as negligence, or petition the criminal law of assault.[26] Marital rape was nevertheless deemed an exemption, as is elaborated in the next section.

[21] F Banda, '"If You Buy a Cup, Why Would You Not Use It?" Marital Rape: The Acceptable Face of Gender Based Violence: Comment on "Criminalizing Sexual Violence against Women in Intimate Relationships"' (2016) 109 *AJIL Unbound* 321. See also chapters 6, 7 and 8 in this volume.

[22] NF Cott, *Public Vows: A History of Marriage and the Nation* (Cambridge, MA, Harvard University Press 2000) 11.

[23] W Blackstone, *Commentaries on the Laws of England* (Chicago, University of Chicago Press 1979) 430.

[24] ibid, 430–33.

[25] ibid, 432.

[26] KM Schelong, 'Domestic Violence and the State: Response to and Rationales for Spousal Battering, Marital Rape and Stalking' (1994) 78 *Marquette Law Review* 79, 91; MJ Anderson, 'Marital Immunity, Intimate Relationships, and Improper Inferences: A New Law on Sexual Offenses by Intimates' (2002) 54 *Hastings Law Journal* 1465, 1482; RB Siegel, 'The Rule of Love: Wife Beating as Prerogative and Privacy' (1995) 105 *Yale Law Journal* 2117, 2129–30.

Similarly, under the French *dotal* system, wives had no legal capacity and were considered to be under 'perpetual tutorship'. They could not even appear in any legal proceedings without permission from their husbands.[27] It was only in 1938 that the incapacity of married women was revoked in France, but property law changes took several more decades of reform.[28] In Spain, women had no legal capacity until reforms slowly began in 1958.[29]

England, France and Spain, as well as the Netherlands, were all colonising nations which imposed their laws through their colonial empires. In many postcolonial countries, these colonial-era laws and doctrines continue to exist without much progressive change and they continue to pose significant barriers for reforming sexual assault and other laws entrenching gender inequality.[30]

C. Privacy Rights over the Household

By the early nineteenth century, especially during the American Revolution, a nascent right to privacy within the family institution emerged in America. This right asserted an insulated private sphere which a government could not penetrate with its policies.[31] As Ruth Bloch explains, the household shrouded in a mantle of privacy rights 'worked to reinforce the unequal relationships between masters and slaves, parents and children, husbands and wives'.[32]

Before the Revolution, although 'reasonable chastisement' by husbands was legally allowed, women could get some protection against this violence by using criminal law to make a 'breach of peace' claim. Breach of peace was understood as an action against the sovereign as opposed to assault, which was a lesser, civil claim between individuals and which afforded women no reprieve.[33]

After the American Revolution, assault was reclassified as a crime, which could be used by wives as well. Several laws were passed to recognise divorce, thus desanctifying marriage. Nevertheless, despite the increase in available remedies for women, Bloch argues that the Revolution also brought about notions of privacy of the household, a concept ideologically favoured by judges and legislatures. As a result, marital violence, including marital rape, was delegated as a private act beyond the reach of the law.[34]

[27] A Tunc, 'Husband and Wife under French Law: Past, Present, Future' (1956) 104 *University of Pennsylvania Law Review* 1064.

[28] See L Neville Brown, 'The Reform of French Matrimonial Property Law' (1965) 14 *American Journal of Comparative Law* 308.

[29] LA Sponsler, 'The Status of Married Women under the Legal System of Spain' (1982) 3 *Journal of Legal History* 125.

[30] See eg V Venkatesh, 'Pluralistic Legal Systems and Marital Rape: Cross-National Considerations', chapter 5 in this volume.

[31] RH Bloch, 'The American Revolution, Wife Beating, and the Emergent Value of Privacy' (2007) 5 *Early American Studies: An Interdisciplinary Journal* 223.

[32] ibid, 226.

[33] ibid, 230–33.

[34] ibid, 244–49.

D. Protection of Men's Honour and the Attribution of Women's Shame

Male-dominant and misogynist concepts of 'honour' have often been used and continue to be used to justify acts of violence against women. Indeed, this has been captured by the term 'honour-based violence'.[35] Notions of honour in some patriarchal societies, as in some religious interpretations, are tied to the strict and oppressive regulation of women's lives, bodies and sexuality.

Historically and in some countries still today, if an unmarried woman is raped, marriage to her rapist is mandated to rescue her 'honour' and absolve her family of the loss of a virginal daughter.[36] One rationale is that the raped woman has been 'spoiled' for use by her future husband who is supposed to be entitled to exclusive sexual access to a woman.

In more than a dozen countries, including those in the Middle East–North Africa (eg Jordan and Tunisia) and in Africa (Angola, Cameroon, Equatorial Guinea and Eritrea), a rapist can still escape punishment if he marries his victim.[37] In the European Community, until September 2015, Bulgaria's penal code allowed a rapist to escape punishment, even when it was *statutory rape*, if it was followed by marriage.[38] Despite the changes made in 2015 to the law, spousal rape remains rarely prosecuted in Bulgaria, indicating the continued influence of the patriarchal values behind the repealed law. In many countries, such provisions were repealed only in the last two decades.[39] In Argentina, this legal doctrine, also

[35] See generally D Tokiharu Mayeda and R Vijaykumar, 'A Review of the Literature on Honor-Based Violence' (2016) 10 *Sociology Compass* 353; AK Gill, 'Introduction: "Honour" and "Honour"-Based Violence: Challenging Common Assumptions' in AK Gill, C Strange and K Anton Roberts (eds), *'Honour' Killing and Violence: Theory, Policy and Practice* (Basingstoke, Palgrave Macmillan, 2014); A Akpinar, 'The Honour/Shame Complex Revisited: Violence against Women in the Migration Context' (2003) 26 *Women's Studies International Forum* 425.

[36] See eg Tsun-Yin Luo, '"Marrying my Rapist?!" The Cultural Trauma among Chinese Rape Survivors' (2000) 14 *Gender & Society* 581; N Shalhoub-Kevorkian et al, 'Towards a Cultural Definition of Rape: Dilemmas in Dealing with Rape Victims in Palestinian Society' (1999) 22 *Women's Studies International Forum* 157; RA Van Cleave, 'Sex, Lies, and Honor in Italian Rape Law beyond Prosecution: Sexual Assault Victim's Rights in Theory and Practice Symposium' (2004) 38 *Suffolk University Law Review* 427, 433; CE Neumann, *Sexual Crime: A Reference Handbook* (Santa Barbara, ABC-CLIO, 2010) 94 (stating that in 2010, 19 states in Latin America allowed statutory rape charges to be dropped after marriage with the victim); C Sims, 'Justice in Peru: Victim Gets Rapist for a Husband', *New York Times*, 12 March 1997, www.nytimes.com/1997/03/12/world/justice-in-peru-victim-gets-rapist-for-a-husband.html.

[37] The World Bank Group, 'Women, Business, and the Law Indicator Data—Protecting Women from Violence', wbl.worldbank.org/data/exploretopics/protecting-women-from-violence.

[38] Penal Code, Bulgaria, amend SG 43/20 May 2005, Art 158; United States Department of State, '2015 Country Reports on Human Rights Practices—Bulgaria' (US Department of State 2016) 20 www.state.gov/j/drl/rls/hrrpt/humanrightsreport/index.htm?year=2015&dlid=252831.

[39] M McDaniel and Women Under Siege, 'From Morocco to Denmark: Rape Survivors around the World Are Forced to Marry Attackers—Women Under Siege Project' (2 May 2013) www.womenundersiegeproject.org/blog/entry/from-morocco-to-denmark-rape-survivors-around-the-world-are-forced-to-marry.

called *Avenimiento*, was removed from the penal code only in 2012.[40] Several other Latin American countries, such as Guatemala (2006),[41] Costa Rica (2007)[42] and Brazil (2005),[43] repealed their provisions only in the late 2000s.

E. Extension of Immunity for Sexual Assault to Any Male Intimate

Although many of the justifications for the marital rape exemption come from the patriarchal social construction of marriage, the exemption is often extended to all socially sanctioned relationships between men and women. For example, those US states that still maintain some form of marital rape exemption also extend it to other intimate partner relationships.[44] Intimate relationships for the purposes of the exemption are limited to cohabitants in some states, while others also include 'voluntary social companions'.[45] Delaware's code from 1986 to 1988 exempted from first-degree rape all perpetrators who were 'voluntary social companions' or who had sexual intercourse with the victim in the previous 12 months.[46] Rape shield laws and evidentiary requirements continue to codify implied consent in intimate relationships, even in countries which have long removed the marital rape exemption.[47]

In countries where extramarital relationships are not socially accepted, justifications to provide immunity to the perpetrators differ substantively from arguments in favour of the marital rape exemption, but are rooted in similar patriarchal constructions of a woman's lack of autonomy. In countries where only marital relationships are exempted from rape laws, one would logically expect extramarital relationships to be included within the definition of rape. Yet, women victims in such cases are constructed as promiscuous and without 'honour', and usually have even less access to justice than raped women who are spouses; the latter can at least rely on divorce and domestic violence civil protections, if not the criminal law.[48]

[40] 'Congress Pass Important Bills in First Session of the Year', *Argentina Independent*, 15 March 2012, www.argentinaindependent.com/currentaffairs/latest-news/newsfromargentina/congress-pass-important-bills-in-first-session-of-the-year/.

[41] US Department of State, '2006 Country Reports on Human Rights Practices—Guatemala' (US Department of State, 2007) Human Rights Report, www.state.gov/j/drl/rls/hrrpt/2006/78893.htm.

[42] Division for the Advancement of Women, 'Beijing at Ten and Beyond—Violence Against Women' (UN Women, 2005) 4, www.un.org/womenwatch/daw/beijing/beijingat10/D.%20Violence%20against%20women%20(Sep%2009).pdf.

[43] Organizing Committee of the CEDAW Shadow Report by Civil Society, 'Brazil and Compliance with CEDAW: Shadow Report of Civil Society to the Sixth National Report of Brazil on CEDAW, 2001–2005 Period' (Agende Action on Gender Citizenship and Development, 2007) 8, para 10, www.wunrn.com/wp-content/uploads/2007_5614271f1511c.pdf.

[44] Anderson (n 26) 1522–27.

[45] ibid, 1521–22.

[46] ibid.

[47] See eg Randall (n 10). For a discussion of these issues in Canadian law, see also Koshan (n 10).

[48] See eg N Shalhoub Kevorkian, 'Reexamining Femicide: Breaking the Silence and Crossing "Scientific" Borders' (2003) 28 *Signs* 581, 587–596.

Such social norms also seep into the decisions by the police and judiciary, making it almost impossible to pursue criminal action.[49]

F. Instrumentalist and Procedural Justifications for the Marital Rape Exception

One line of argument for maintaining the marital rape exemption in criminal law is based on the claim that criminal laws are themselves not the right forum for addressing marital rape. On this view, criminal law hinders possible reconciliation and needlessly permits state intervention into the privacy and sanctity of family life. The claim is further made that women sexually assaulted in marriage can use alternative remedies that are available in law such as assault and battery, or can pursue civil claims under domestic violence regulations.[50]

Along similar lines, arguments in favour of keeping a marital rape exemption are also based on the idea that it is necessary to protect men from malicious accusations or threats of criminal complaints by their wives and that protecting men from criminal liability for marital rape maintains peace and harmony in the household.[51] This viewpoint prioritises men's immunity over women's sexual safety in marital relationships and further entrenches the rape myth that women are likely to fabricate claims of sexual assault.

G. Marriage as a Contractual 'Sacrament'

The view of marriage as a contractual sacrament in which wives were, as part of the contract, to service husbands sexually, made marital rape impossible in some nations. Under Imperial Chinese law, for example, the fathers of the bride and groom were contracting parties to a marriage and marriage symbolised 'submission of maturing children to family roles and filial duty'.[52] The wife's consent played no role and no Chinese jurist even thought it necessary to ponder the concept of absence of consent and marital rape at any point.[53] In Western legal systems, consent of the wife may be required for a marriage to be legitimate, but

[49] For discussions of these dynamics, see Koshan (n 10). See also M Randall, 'Marital Rape and Violence against Women in Intimate Relationships: The Hidden Form of Domestic Violence', chapter 2 in this volume.

[50] Schwartz (n 20) 46–48, 54; L Weintraub Siegel, 'The Marital Rape Exemption: Evolution to Extinction' (1995) 43 *Cleveland State Law Review* 351, 362–64.

[51] For discussion of this argument in the Malawian, Kenyan and Ghanian contexts, see S White and N Kanyongolo, 'Sexual Violence in Intimate Relationships: The Case of Malawi', chapter 6 in this volume; W Kamau and others, 'Dismantling Barriers to Women's Equality: Making the Case for the Criminalisation of Marital Rape in Kenya", chapter 7 in this volume; R Aku Sitsofe Morhe, 'Marital Rape and the Law in Ghana', chapter 8 in this volume.

[52] M Harvey Sommer, *Sex, Law, and Society in Late Imperial China* (Redwood City, CA, Stanford University Press 2000) 39.

[53] ibid.

once a marriage is legitimated, the husband and wife were bound together in a sacrament 'before God', owing to each other a 'marital debt' of sexual service marked by 'continuous' consent.[54] These are paradigmatic examples of an underlying notion that marriage is a social institution where sexual intercourse is to be freely expected and available to husbands on demand, and one in which wives must have a lowered expectation of sexual autonomy. This viewpoint is often evident in the statements of media, legislators and the judiciary who oppose lifting the marital rape exemption.[55]

For example, when challenged by her government's reluctance to criminalise marital rape, the Indian Women and Child Development Minister recently opined that:

> The concept of marital rape, as understood internationally, cannot be suitably applied in the Indian context due to various factors, including levels of education, illiteracy, poverty, myriad social customs and values, religious beliefs, [and] the mindset of the society to treat the *marriage as sacrament* [emphasis added].[56]

In another example, a decade after South Africa criminalised marital rape, in an infamous case of marital rape which came before the High Court, the judge decided that the victim 'must have come knowing that this [sexual intercourse] was either likely to happen or was going to happen … given the nature of their relationship'. The judge further stated that 'this rape should therefore be treated differently from the rape of one stranger by another between whom consensual intercourse was almost unthinkable'.[57]

The recurring rationales legitimating men's rights to sexual access to their wives thematically relate to various expressions of gender inequality. As will be seen from the analysis below, the marital rape exemption has existed in law (and has also been contested) over many historical epochs, and in most of the world's nations.

III. Comparative Analysis of the Marital Rape Exemption around the World

Recent and increasing attention to the problem of gendered violence in general, and marital rape in particular, has led to attempts to document what countries around the world are doing, and still need to do, to remedy it. There is no accurate

[54] ibid.

[55] For a discussion of this phenomenon in the Malawian context, see White and Kanyongolo (n 51). See also Morhe (n 51) and Kamau et al (n 51) for discussion of marital rape and the law in Ghana and Kenya, respectively.

[56] '"Concept of Marital Rape Can't Be Applied in Indian Context": Maneka Gandhi', *Indian Express*, 11 March 2016, indianexpress.com/article/business/budget/imarital-rape-concept-maneka-gandhi-indian-context/.

[57] *S v Moipolai* (CA 53/2004) [2004] ZANWHC 19. See also *S v Modise* (113/06) [2007] ZANWHC 73.

international database on marital rape legislation, although the UN and the World Bank have each constructed helpful global databases on marital rape legislation.[58] These two databases provide essential information giving an international snapshot of law reform on gendered violence, but they are constructed around some methodological and definitional differences. Both the databases also have some limitations.

The definition of what constitutes criminalisation also appears to differ between reports and databases, leading to inconsistent statistics. For example, according to the UN Gender Statistics database, only 52 countries have laws on marital rape, which excludes several countries that are known to have criminalised marital rape such as the United Kingdom, Israel, Spain and the Netherlands.[59] The reason for this discrepancy is that the database only includes 'instances where the law explicitly criminalises marital rape, without qualifications', since explicit criminalisation is considered to be the 'best practice'.[60] Explicit criminalisation means that a country has legislated to state expressly that rape or sexual assault in a marriage is subject to criminal penalty; though not having this kind of 'explicit' criminalisation does not, in theory, preclude the prosecution of a husband for raping a spouse under the country's general rape laws. Explicit criminalisation includes countries such as Canada where the criminalisation of marital rape is stated in the amending legislative act or bill, if not in the penal code.[61]

Even while using the definition of *explicit* criminalisation, there are still many discrepancies between various reports on which countries prohibit marital rape. The UN Gender Statistics surprisingly includes Malaysia and the United States (where only some states explicitly criminalise marital rape), which are excluded in the explicit criminalisation category in the World Bank database. According to the World Bank database, there are 77 countries in which legislation has 'explicitly criminalised marital rape'.[62] This includes several countries, such as Bolivia,

[58] World Bank Group (n 37); UN Women and United Nations Statistics Division, 'Gender Statistics—Existence of Laws on Domestic Violence', unstats.un.org/unsd/gender/Data/Violence%20against%20women.xlsx.

[59] UN Women and UN Statistics Division, ibid.

[60] Examples of 'explicit' criminalisation include: providing that sexual assault provisions apply 'irrespective of the nature of the relationship' between the perpetrator and complainant, or stating that 'no marriage or other relationship shall constitute a defence to a charge of sexual assault under the legislation', or where 'a marital (or equivalent) relationship may be explicitly cited in the law as an aggravating factor'. ibid, fn iv.

[61] Bill C-127, 'Act to amend the Criminal Code in relation to sexual offences and other offences against the person and to amend certain other Acts in relation thereto or in consequence thereof', SC 1980-81-82-83, c 125 (1983) (Can), s 246(8); Criminal Code of Canada, RSC 1985, c C-46, s 278; Koshan (n 10).

[62] World Bank Group (n 37). Unlike the UN reports, the World Bank's determination of whether marital rape is criminalised or not is based on a more sophisticated questionnaire with four questions related to marital rape: (a) Does the legislation explicitly criminalise marital rape? (b) If not, can a woman otherwise file a criminal complaint against her husband for rape? (c) Is the husband exempt from facing criminal penalties for rape (marital rape exemption)? (d) Are perpetrators exempt from facing criminal charges for rape if they marry the victim? See methodology and data notes at World Bank Group, 'Women, Business and the Law 2016: Getting to Equal' (International Bank for Reconstruction and Development/The World Bank, 2015) wbl.worldbank.org/~/media/WBG/WBL/Documents/Reports/2016/Women-Business-and-the-Law-2016.pdf, 70.

Indonesia, Italy, Uzbekistan and Taiwan, which are not included in the UN Gender Statistics database. Also, the UN Secretary General's Violence against Women study declared in 2006 that marital rape was prosecutable in at least 104 states, evidently not limiting its analysis to just the 32 states where marital rape was explicitly deemed a 'specific criminal offence' at that time.[63]

Only 39 countries, according to the World Bank database, do not criminalise marital rape in any form. These countries, according to the methodology of the World Bank, do not have 'explicit' legislation criminalising spousal rape, nor do they allow women to file complaints against their spouses for rape, or they have explicit exemption for husbands from facing criminal penalties, or laws that exempt perpetrators from criminal penalties if they marry the victim. Most of these countries have an explicit marital rape exemption. There are 11 countries in this category from Sub-Saharan Africa, including Kenya and Malawi. However, Ghana is considered to have criminalised marital rape, albeit not explicitly.[64]

A. Limitations of the Data and Some Notes on Method

As useful as the World Bank data is, there are several concerns with the data (as well as with the data in the UN reports), which we outline below.

First, as noted above, there are errors in the 'explicit criminalisation' classifications. Additionally, the methodology claims that under 'explicit' criminalisation, the database only includes countries that (a) explicitly provide for penal punishment *and* (b) do not exclude spousal prosecution under any circumstances, even where there is no evidence of divorce or separation. Yet, there is no information on whether marital rape is criminalised as part of the penal code provision on rape or whether it is part of separate domestic violence legislation, with lesser penalties or civil remedies for sexual assault in a marital relationship.

One glaring example is that of Nigeria. The World Bank database states that marital rape is explicitly criminalised in Nigeria, pointing to a 2007 Domestic Violence regulation. But the regulation did not change the criminal law definition of rape. Marital rape continued to be exempted by the penal codes in the northern and southern regions as well as in the sharia criminal law-administered region.[65] It was only in 2015 that Nigeria passed the Violence Against Persons (Prohibition)

[63] UN Women and UN Secretary General, 'Ending Violence against Women: From Words to Action. Study of the Secretary-General' (United Nations, 2006) www.un.org/womenwatch/daw/vaw/publications/English%20Study.pdf.

[64] World Bank Group (n 37). See also chapters 6–8 in this volume.

[65] E Ekhator, 'Women and the Law in Nigeria: A Reappraisal' (2015) 16 *Journal of International Women's Studies* 285; T Monisola Ola and J Olusegun Ajayi, 'Values Clarification in Marital Rape: A Nigerian Situation' (2013) 9 *European Scientific Journal, ESJ* eujournal.org/index.php/esj/article/view/2199.

Act 2015, which significantly broadened the definition of rape. However, there still remain some doubts about whether marital rape is criminal, since the legislation did not explicitly remove the marital rape exemption. In any case, the World Bank does not rely on the new legislation to classify Nigeria.[66]

Indonesia is also included among the explicit criminalisation countries in the World Bank database. However, the marital rape exemption continues to exist in its penal code,[67] although the Domestic Violence Eradication Act of 2004 made marital rape an offence punishable with imprisonment for 4–12 years or a fine not exceeding 36 million rupiahs.[68] The World Bank database does not account for this inconsistency. Bhutan is included in both the UN and World Bank databases as having explicitly criminalised marital rape, which it did in its 2004 penal code, but it is classified as only a 'petty misdemeanour'.[69] The code thus still distinguishes rape based on one's marital status.

In other examples, neither database includes Israel or the United Kingdom, even though the judiciary explicitly ruled against and overturned the marital rape exemptions in these countries.[70] Judicial decisions thus appear as less significant compared to legislation, an approach that belies a contextual understanding of various legal systems.

Latin America (including Mexico) and the Caribbean (LAC) form the largest bloc with explicit criminalisation (around 62.5 per cent). Only about half of the Organisation for Economic Co-operation and Development (OECD) countries have explicitly criminalised marital rape (17 out of 32 countries). No Muslim or Arab country in the Middle East–North Africa has explicitly criminalised marital

[66] C Anarado, 'Why Nigeria's New Violence Against Persons (Prohibition) Act Is Only the Beginning' (15 June 2015) venturesafrica.com/why-nigerias-new-violence-against-persons-prohibition-act-is-only-the-beginning/.

[67] Penal Code of Indonesia (Amended by Law No 27 of 1999) 1982, Art 285: 'Any person who by using force or threat of force forces a woman to have sexual intercourse with him *out of marriage*, shall, being guilty of rape, be punished with a maximum imprisonment of twelve years' (emphasis added). See also Shaina Greiff, 'No Justice in Justifications: Violence against Women in the Name of Culture, Religion, and Tradition' (Women Living Under Muslim Laws (WLUML)—Violence is Not our Culture (VNC) Campaign, 2010) www.academia.edu/download/8810108/sksw%20policy%20briefing%20series%201_no%20justice%20in%20justifications_greiff.pdf, 18.

[68] Law of the Republic of Indonesia No 23 of Year 2004, Regarding Elimination of Violence in Household (2004) www.wcwonline.org/pdf/lawcompilation/Indonesia-Regarding-Elimination-of-Violence-in-Household.pdf, Arts 8(a) and 46. Art 8(a) defines sexual violence as 'forcing sexual intercourse carried out against an individual living within the scope of the household' where Art 2(1a) defines 'scope of household' as including the husband and the wife. Art 46 provides that: 'Anyone committing sexual violence act as referred to in Article 8(a) shall be punished with imprisonment of not longer than 12 (twelve) years or fine of not more than Rp36,000,000.00 (thirty-six million rupiah).'

[69] Penal Code of Bhutan 2004, s 199 (a defendant is guilty of marital rape where they engage in sexual intercourse with their spouse without consent or against the will of the other spouse). Under s 200, the offence is a petty misdemeanour.

[70] *R v R* [1992] 1 AC 599 (HL); *Cohen v The State of Israel*, Criminal Appeal 91/80, 35 (3) PD (1980).

rape, although eight countries in this region allow for criminal rape complaints to be filed by wives, according to the World Bank.[71] Only 14 out of 47 countries in Sub-Saharan Africa have explicit criminalisation, while 36 countries allow criminal complaints to be filed.[72]

Secondly, using data on whether a woman can otherwise file a criminal complaint against her husband as a proxy for non-explicit criminal prosecution can also lead to discrepancies. For example, the database claims marital rape is criminalised in China, albeit not explicitly, since China allegedly allows wives to file a complaint. However, other reports and news articles assert that marital rape is not illegal in China even though the penal code does not have an explicit exemption.[73] In fact, even China's most recent domestic violence bill does not include any mention of marital rape.[74]

Third, the World Bank database is unable to reconcile the multiple criminal law regimes that can exist in federal states such as the United States. The United States is rightly excluded from the countries that have explicitly declared marital rape to be a crime in their legislation because the treatment of marital rape differs significantly from state to state. In some states, marital rape is given a lesser penalty and has higher evidentiary requirements of proof.[75] However, this analysis is absent in the database and the report relies on the laws in New York State, which has one of the most equitable treatments of marital rape, thereby obscuring the inconsistencies throughout other jurisdictions in the country.

Lastly, in general, the World Bank's methodology (and that of the UN) appears limited to a plain reading of statutes and legislation. We are therefore left with no information as to how consent is actually interpreted, for example, or if or how the judiciary has actually ever applied the law.

[71] World Bank Group (n 37). The countries are Algeria, Dijibouti, Egypt, Kuwait, Morocco, Qatar, UAE and Yemen. Women can file a complaint in Iraq, Tunisia and Libya as well; however, the penal codes allow men to be exempt from criminal charges of rape if they marry their victims. The marital rape impunity thus exists in these three countries.

[72] World Bank Group (n 37).

[73] R de Silva de Alwis and J Klugman, 'Freedom from Violence and the Law: A Global Perspective in Light of the Chinese Domestic Violence Law, 2015' (2015) 37 *University of Pennsylvania Journal of International Law* 1.

[74] Al Jazeera Staff, 'China Makes Domestic Abuse a Crime', *Al Jazeera*, 1 March 2016, www.aljazeera.com/news/2016/03/china-outlaws-domestic-abuse-160301053424903.html; Joy Chia, 'How China's New Anti-Domestic Violence Law Could Save Lives', *Open Society Foundations*, 17 May 2016, www.opensocietyfoundations.org/voices/be-effective-china-s-new-anti-domestic-violence-law-needs-civil-society-s-support.

[75] Anderson (n 26) 1470–73; M Lee Woolley, 'Marital Rape: A Unique Blend of Domestic Violence and Non-Marital Rape Issues' (2007) 18 *Hastings Women's Law Journal* 269, 281–84; J Klarfeld, 'A Striking Disconnect: Marital Rape Law's Failure to Keep Up with Domestic Violence Law' (2011) 48 *American Criminal Law Review* 1819, 1833–36; M Held and J McLaughlin, 'Rape & Sexual Assault' (2013) 15 *Georgetown Journal of Gender and the Law* 155, 159–60.

B. Classifying Legal Systems

In our comparative analysis of the status of the marital rape exemption in the world's countries, we have grouped countries based in part on the structure of their legal systems (whether rooted in common law or civil law legal structures), and in part on their status as 'originating' common/civil law nations or as nations who have received these legal systems and traditions through colonial imposition.

The classification of legal systems created by the University of Ottawa's JuriGlobe project identifies countries and areas of the world as follows: civil law systems and mixed systems with civil law; common law systems and mixed systems with common law; customary law systems and mixed systems with customary law; Muslim law systems and mixed systems with Muslim law; and mixed systems. This classification shows that, except for five countries which have customary or Islamic law mono-systems, the rest of the world is governed by civil and/or common law systems or systems mixed with civil and/or common law.[76] The civil/common law distinction is important in classifying the trajectories towards criminalisation of marital rape and it can address the deficiencies in the databases that incorporate only a superficial understanding of marital rape laws.

However, a classification that differentiates only on the basis of civil or common law will also be deficient, as colonisation and regional contexts play an important role in how gender equality reforms are instituted.[77] Overseas colonies of European countries were given their civil or common law system 'exogenously' during the colonial period.[78] Many of these countries have mixed legal systems where their colonial occupier's legal system was mixed with local religious or customary legal systems; nevertheless, the meta-structure provided by the common law or civil law (as the case may be) plays a significant role in determining the conditions and development of legal reforms. To understand the development of marital rape and other laws, therefore, not only is the legal system relevant but so too is a country's colonial history.[79] Other recent studies have also incorporated colonial history to further classify legal systems.[80] Postcolonial countries are therefore classified as countries which 'received' a European civil or common law system. There are a few countries, such as Nepal, Thailand, Turkey and Japan, where the local ruling regime independently adopted foreign common law or civil legal systems; these countries are also included in the 'received' category.

[76] World Legal Systems Research Group, 'Customary Law Systems and Mixed Systems with a Customary Law Tradition' (University of Ottawa-JuriGlobe) www.juriglobe.ca/eng/sys-juri/class-poli/droit-coutumier.php.

[77] See Venkatesh, chapter 4 in this volume.

[78] DM Klerman et al, 'Legal Origin or Colonial History?' (2011) 3 *Journal of Legal Analysis* 379, 380.

[79] Venkatesh (n 30).

[80] Klerman et al (n 78).

Countries such as England, France, Germany and the Netherlands are classified as 'origin' countries, where the legal system arose endogenously.[81] Settler countries such as the United States, Canada, Australia and New Zealand are also included in this 'origin' legal system category, as the national legal system was developed and continues to be developed by settler colonial governments who were never replaced by Indigenous governments.

Recognising the limitations of the databases, in this chapter we organise our analysis around classifications of types of legal systems, and whether or not these legal systems have been borrowed or imposed through colonial histories. Within this classification we select a few representative countries to demonstrate how language in the penal code, structural aspects of the legal system, and colonial contexts matter to whether or not, and how, marital rape is criminalised, which allows for a more contextualised and in-depth analysis.

C. The Marital Rape Exemption in the Common Law

(i) Common Law 'Originating' Countries

Lord Matthew Hale published a famous dictum in 1736 on marital rape that still manifests itself in several common law jurisdictions to this day. Without citing any authority, Hale proclaimed that: 'The husband cannot be guilty of a rape committed by himself upon his lawful wife, for by their mutual matrimonial consent and contract, the wife hath given up herself in this kind unto her husband which she cannot retract.'[82] Although marital rape was largely condoned at that time, scholars have pointed out that Hale, even for his time, was a particularly misogynistic man whose decisions on the whole were 'strikingly antagonistic to the interests of women'.[83]

Hale's dicta on the marital rape exemption, and his assertion that women give continuous consent to their husbands upon marriage, became further solidified in the late nineteenth century.

Interestingly, in the first few cases when marital rape was raised as an issue in the courts, judges in both the United States and the United Kingdom expressed ambivalence about the persuasiveness of Hale's dicta.[84] For example, the 1888 case of *Regina v Clarence*, the first case in the UK where marital rape was properly addressed, involved the accused not revealing his venereal disease to his wife

[81] ibid, 380.

[82] M Hale, *Historia Placitorum Coronae: The History of the Pleas of the Crown*, vol I (London, E and R Nutt, and R Gosling 1736) 629.

[83] See eg G Geis, 'Rape-in-Marriage: Law and Law Reform in England, the United States, and Sweden' (1977) 6 *Adelaide Law Review* 284, 286.

[84] See SL Ryder and SA Kuzmenka, 'Legal Rape: The Marital Rape Exemption' (1990) 24 *John Marshall Law Review* 393; Freeman (n 20).

during sexual intercourse. Two judges criticised the lack of authority for the marital rape exemption and for Hale's dicta.[85] Judge Wills argued that there was no 'sufficient authority' and he was not 'prepared to assent' to the proposition that 'between married persons rape is impossible'.[86] He further stated: 'I cannot understand why, as a general rule, if intercourse be an assault, it should not be rape.'[87]

This time period presented a critical moment where the law could have avoided institutionalising impunity for marital rape. By the nineteenth century, wife-battering was already criminalised in several jurisdictions[88] and respected thinkers such as John Stuart Mill were condemning marital rape in strong words. Mill famously described a wife as someone who was forever 'chained' to her husband even if he was a brutal tyrant whom she loathed, and the husband as someone who 'can claim from her and enforce the lowest degradation of a human being, that of being made the instrument of an animal function contrary to her inclination'.[89]

Even as early as the nineteenth century, then, there were strong disagreements in legal and political forums in the Anglo-American common law jurisdictions about the marital rape exemption. By this time, women were no longer legally characterised as property or chattels and as having no legal existence outside of their husbands. In other non-criminal areas of law, such as family, property and matrimonial law, there was no presumption of implied consent between spouses.[90] There was no legal necessity, therefore, for a spousal exemption for rape in the criminal law; indeed, in some ways it was an anomaly at this time. But by the late nineteenth century, courts and legislatures had nevertheless uncritically and wholeheartedly accepted Hale's dicta that codified implied consent in criminal law.[91]

In 1976, South Australia claimed to be the first jurisdiction in the common law world to remove the marital rape exemption when it amended the presumption of consent in a marital relationship in its Criminal Code.[92] However, responding to objections in Parliament, the amendment also included a provision in section 73(5) that limited charges for rape and indecent assault in spousal relationships unless there was accompanying bodily injury, gross indecency, serious

[85] *Regina v Clarence*, 22 QB 23 (1888).

[86] ibid, 33.

[87] ibid.

[88] Bloch (n 31) 246.

[89] JS Mill, *On Liberty and The Subjection of Women* (New York, H Holt and Co, 1873) 263.

[90] Freeman (n 20) 14–15; Siegel (n 50) 355.

[91] Freeman (n 20) 11, 21–22.

[92] South Australia, An Act to amend the Criminal Law Consolidation Act 1935–1975, No 83 of 1976, s 12 (modifying s 73(3) of the Criminal Law Consolidation Act 1935–1976 to include: 'No person shall, by reason only of the fact that he is married to some other person, be presumed to have consented to sexual intercourse with that other person').

and substantial humiliation or threats of the same.[93] In the 1980s, all the other Australian jurisdictions amended their laws to end the marital rape immunity,[94] although it was only in 1992 that the section 73(5) qualifications for marital rape, that required threats or other harm, were removed.[95]

Interestingly, in 2012 the Australian High Court held that even if the marital rape exemption had ever been a part of the common law of the country, it was ended by 1935 when South Australia's Criminal Law Consolidation Act was enacted.[96] This ruling emerged in an appeal from a man's acquittal for raping his wife in 1963, a crime for which he was charged in 2010. The defendant contended that spousal rape was not an offence in South Australia in 1963. This argument, based on Hale's dicta on irrevocable consent, was soundly repudiated by a majority of Australia's High Court, which dismissed his appeal and found that he could, in fact, be tried and convicted for rape of his wife.[97]

New Zealand specifically and unequivocally abolished spousal immunity in 1985 following Canada in 1983.[98] Canada's 1892 Criminal Code had codified Lord Hale's conception of implied consent in marriage. The Code defined rape as 'the act of a man having carnal knowledge of a woman *who is not his wife* without her consent, or with consent, which has been extorted by threats or fear of bodily harm'.[99] Spousal immunity for rape was reiterated in the Canadian Criminal Code of 1970.[100] It was not until 1983 that amendments to the Canadian Criminal Code rejected the idea that marriage confers upon men presumed rights of sexual access to their wives, and removed spousal immunity in sexual assault law.[101] While this was a significant success in Canadian law reform, the transition from law on the books to law in practice has been less successful, as judges have, in too many cases, failed to apply the same legally required consent analysis to sexual assault cases between spouses.[102]

In the United Kingdom, the marital rape exemption was reaffirmed in 1976 in the statutory formulation of rape in the Sexual Offences (Amendment) Act,

[93] ibid, s 12 (modifying s 73(5) of the Criminal Law Consolidation Act 1935–1976). See also JA Scutt, 'Consent in Rape: The Problem of the Marriage Contract' (1976) 3 *Monash University Law Review* 255, 277–283.

[94] Australian Law Reform Commission and New South Wales Law Reform Commission, 'Family Violence: A National Legal Response' (ALRC and NSWLRC 2010) ALRC Report 114, para 24.59.

[95] Criminal Law Consolidation (Rape) Amendment Act 1992 (SA). See also Kellie Toole, 'Marital Rape in South Australia: R v P, GA' (2011) 35 *Criminal Law Journal* 237, 241.

[96] *PGA v The Queen* [2012] HCA 21; 245 CLR 355, 369.

[97] ibid, paras 58–66.

[98] New Zealand Rape Law Reform (No 2) Act of 1985, The Crimes Amendment Act (No 3) of 1985, NZ Stat. See also SA Adamo, 'The Injustice of the Marital Rape Exemption: A Survey of Common Law Countries' (1989) 4 *American University Journal of International Law and Policy* 555, 568–69.

[99] Criminal Code, 1892, c 29, s 266, 1892–93 Can Stat 107, 208 (emphasis added).

[100] An Act Respecting the Criminal Law, RSC, c C-34, s 143 (1970).

[101] Bill C-127, An Act to amend the Criminal Code in relation to sexual offences and other offences against the person and to amend certain other Acts in relation thereto or in consequence thereof, 1st Sess, 32nd Parl (assented to 4 August 1982).

[102] See eg Koshan (n 10); Randall (n 10).

which defined rape as 'unlawful sexual intercourse' without consent.[103] In an early amendment, the Bill in the House of Commons did carry an explicit inclusion of marital rape in the definition of rape, but it was removed in subsequent readings.[104]

Soon after the passage of the Sexual Offences (Amendment) Act, the English courts had to decide what constituted 'unlawful' in the definition of 'unlawful sexual intercourse' in a 'landmark series' of marital rape cases that culminated in the House of Lords decision in *R v R*.[105] By this time Scotland had already eliminated the marital rape exemption,[106] and even the English courts had allowed for penal remedies under conditions of marital separation. The House of Lords in *R v R* found that Parliament had not explicitly written a marital rape exemption into the Act and removed the exemption from British common law by dramatically declaring:

> [M]arriage is in modern times regarded as a partnership of equals and no longer one in which the wife must be the subservient chattel of the husband. Hale's proposition involves that by marriage a wife gives her irrevocable consent to sexual intercourse with her husband under all circumstances and irrespective of the state of her health or how she happens to be feeling at the time. In modern times any reasonable person must regard *that conception as quite unacceptable*.[107]

In the United States, statutory codification of Hale's dicta began in the early nineteenth century. American courts were much less critical of using Hale's formulation of the marital rape exemption than were British courts.[108] Legislative reform and judicial revocation of the marital rape exemption only began slowly in the 1970s.[109]

Many of the early law reforms in the United States merely removed the marital rape exemption for separated or divorced couples. However, some court decisions from various states in the 1980s were quick to abandon the marital rape exemption, which was deemed to have its source 'in a bare, extra-judicial declaration made some 300 years ago'.[110] The pivotal 1984 New York Court of Appeals decision in *People v Liberta* found the marital rape exemption to be unconstitutional and in

[103] T Fus, 'Criminalizing Marital Rape: A Comparison of Judicial and Legislative Approaches' (2006) 39 *Vanderbilt Journal of Transnational Law* 481, 486–87.

[104] Freeman (n 20) 27.

[105] Fus (n 103) 487–93. See *R v R* [1991] 3 WLR 767 House of Lords.

[106] *S v HM Advocate*, 1989 SCCR 248 (HCJ) (Scotland).

[107] *R v R* [1992] 1 AC 599 (HL), 616 (emphasis added).

[108] *Commonwealth v Fogerty*, 74 Mass 487, 491 (1847) (stating 'it would always be competent for a defendant to show a marriage to the victim as a defense to the charge of rape'); *Frazier v State*, 86 SW 754 (Tex 1905) ('[A] man cannot himself be guilty of actual rape upon his wife' and a wife cannot retract her consent').

[109] Freeman (n 20) 22–23.

[110] *State v Smith*, 85 NJ 193, 200 (1981). The phrase from *State v Smith* was also quoted in *Warren v State*, 255 Ga 151, 154 (1985).

violation of the Equal Protection Amendment; on this basis the court rejected the assumption that continuous consent existed in a marital relationship.[111]

Notwithstanding these cases, at least 26 US states still retain spousal immunity for sexual assault in one form or another.[112] In some states, marital immunity even exists for having sex with a wife who is incapacitated or unconscious. Astonishingly, this has been found to pertain even when it is the husband who has rendered his wife incapacitated without her consent and has then sexually used her body.[113]

In other US jurisdictions, there are separate regulations for marital rape with a lower sentence. In other states still, marriage provides cause for exemption from being charged with sexual offences of a higher degree. In several states, including Oklahoma, Arizona and Connecticut, for a sexual assault in marriage to be defined as such, it has to be accompanied by actual or threatened physical force or violence. In some states, there has to be proof of estrangement or separation, and in several states, there are higher evidentiary and reporting requirements.[114]

In each of these countries, Hale's pronouncement became accepted in the late eighteenth century as legal gospel. Despite some strong disagreements in legal and political fora, the spousal exemption persisted through most of the nineteenth century, demonstrating the strength of the marital rape exemption's anchor within a broader and deeply entrenched patriarchal ideology. Fidelity to precedent and other rule of law concepts were illusory in this regard, as illustrated by the reasoning of the Australian High Court in *PGA v The Queen*, which refused to accept Hale's dicta as reifying irrevocability of consent in common law, except perhaps during Hale's time.

The spousal rape exemption nevertheless continues to persist in some jurisdictions on the basis of a legal fiction that expresses misogynistic sociocultural norms obliterating women's right to say no to unwanted sex within marriage. Hale's pronouncement formed the basis and provided the language for the statutory law of rape throughout the British Commonwealth and protectorates from North America to Israel to Cyprus to countries across Asia, Africa and the Caribbean.

(ii) Received Common Law Countries

The colonial British government introduced codified criminal law across its colonies from the late eighteenth century onwards and included the Hale marital rape exemption in various ways. Even after independence, the colonial definitions of

[111] *People v Liberta*, 62 NY2d 651 (1984 NY).

[112] Anderson (n 26); Woolley (n 75) 281–84; Klarfeld (n 75) 1833–36; Held and McLaughlin (n 75) 159–60 ('35 states and the District of Columbia still provide some form of marital immunity in their legislation, typically for sexual assault that does not involve penetration, force, or great bodily harm').

[113] Anderson (n 26) 1487–88.

[114] ibid, 1491–96.

rape persisted in the postcolonial context without any change, as justifications began to intermingle with local patriarchal values around women's bodies and role of women in the family. Marital rape exemptions in common law countries generally fall into two categories, dealt with in the following sections: first, where marital rape is explicitly exempted from the rape laws; and second, where rape is defined as 'unlawful' sexual intercourse and the interpretation of the term 'unlawful' renders marital rape exempted or included in the criminal offence. Both kinds of codifications were initiated during the colonial period and the strategies for reforming the penal code have generally followed distinct paths.

(a) Wives not Included as Women Legally Protected from Rape

In many received common law countries, the codification of marital rape immunity took the form of an explicit exception, stating that only perpetrators other than husbands could be charged criminally. India's Penal Code, which was drafted by Lord Macaulay in 1860, has an exception to the definition of rape in section 135, stating: 'Sexual intercourse or sexual acts by a man with his own wife, the wife not being under ten years of age, is not rape.'[115] The Indian Penal Code was the model for the law in several countries in the British Empire, including Singapore, Sri Lanka, Malaysia, Kenya and Ghana.[116] The ten-year age limit was later increased to fifteen years, but the explicit exemption remains to this day in India, Singapore and Sri Lanka, even when the age of consent to marriage has increased.[117]

Singapore removed the explicit blanket spousal immunity in 2007 to add exceptions to the immunity, limited to when the husband was living apart from his wife and either formal separation proceedings had been initiated or there was a protection order against him.[118] Sri Lanka's law, which had Macaulay's explicit exemption until amendments in 1995, is currently similar to the Singapore law where marital rape immunity is removed for judicially separated spouses.[119]

115 Indian Penal Code (as modified up to 1 August 1860), Act No 45 of 1860, s 135, Exception 2 (1860).

116 KD Gaur, *Textbook on the Indian Penal Code* (Delhi, Universal Law Publishing Co, 2009) 9; JN Matson, 'The Common Law Abroad: English and Indigenous Laws in the British Commonwealth' (1993) 42 *International and Comparative Law Quarterly* 753, 758–59.

117 Indian Penal Code 1860 (Amended by the Criminal Law Amendment Act 2013), s 135, Exception 2; W Cheong Chan, 'Penal Code (Amendment) Act 2007: Rape within Marriage Legislation and Case Notes' (2009) 2009 *Singapore Journal of Legal Studies* 257, 257.

118 Chan, ibid, 257–60.

119 Sri Lanka Penal Code 1885 (as amended up to Act No 16 of 2006) Art 363(a); S Goonesekere, 'Family Law in a Multi Cultural Society with Plural Legal Traditions: The Sri Lanka Experience' (1996) *International Survey of Family Law* 461, 472; S Goonesekere, 'Overview: Reflections on Violence Against Women and Legal Systems in Some South Asian Countries' in S Goonesekere (ed), *Violence, Law, and Women's Rights in South Asia* (New Delhi, Sage, 2004) 60–61; K Pinto Jayawardane, 'Re-Visiting Our Right to Choice', *Sunday Times*, Sri Lanka, 29 August 2004, www.sundaytimes.lk/040829/columns/focus.html.

Except for a few countries, such as Trinidad and Tobago and Guyana, which have removed the marital rape exemption from their laws,[120] most countries in the Caribbean have similar explicit marital rape exemptions permitting prosecution only under conditions of separation or if the husband has a sexually transmitted disease (as is the case in Jamaica).[121] The existing Caribbean Committee (CARICOM) model legislation for sexual offences continues to demand criminalisation of marital rape only under specific conditions of divorce, separation or direct order, indicating a clear commitment to retaining criminal immunity for men who sexually assault women to whom they are still married and cohabiting.[122]

These jurisdictions are also similar to civil law jurisdictions which retain explicit marital rape exemptions in their penal codes. As will be discussed in the section on civil law and mixed countries, in such cases, the exemptions tend to have been judicially overruled on the basis of state obligations to fulfil constitutional and international human rights protections to women raped in marriages.

(b) 'Unlawful' Sexual Intercourse and Silent Exemptions

In many received common law countries, the penal code has been more ambiguous on the question of marital rape, resembling the UK Sexual Offences (Amendment) Act of 1976, which defined rape as 'unlawful' sexual intercourse without consent, where 'unlawful' was *interpreted* to exclude sexual intercourse between a husband and wife.[123] In Malawi, for example, the penal code on rape makes no reference to marital status. Section 132 defines rape as non-consensual 'unlawful carnal knowledge'.[124] It is, however, uniformly accepted as a matter of common legal knowledge that marital rape is not criminalised under common law or customary rules.[125]

In Kenya, rape is defined in section 3 of the Sexual Offences Act as an intentional act committed 'unlawfully' and which involves penetration without consent.[126] Section 3 has no explicit exemption; section 43 provides the meaning for 'intentional and unlawful' and contains an explicit exception clause, which states that 'the section shall not apply in respect of persons who are lawfully married to each other'.[127] Kenya falls somewhere in between the two categories with an

[120] Sexual Offences Act, Act 27 of 1986, ch 11:28 (2000) (as amended by Act 20 of 1994 and Act 31 of 2000) (Trin and Tobago), rgd.legalaffairs.gov.tt/Laws2/Alphabetical_List/lawspdfs/11.28.pdf; Sexual Offences Act, Act No 7 of 2010, Official Gazette (Legal Supp) 33 (2010) (Guy), scm.oas.org/pdfs/2010/CIM02920T-2.pdf.

[121] See eg Jamaica Sexual Offences Act 2009, Art 5; Bahamas Sexual Offences & Domestic Violence Act 2010, Arts 3 and 15(1). See generally SA Elvy, 'A Postcolonial Theory of Spousal Rape: The Caribbean and Beyond' (2015) 22 *Michigan Journal of Gender & Law* 89.

[122] CARICOM Model Legislation on Sexual Offences, para 4(4) (1997).

[123] Sexual Offences (Amendment) Act 1976 (UK).

[124] Malawi Penal Code, ch 7:01, Laws of Malawi, 1930, s 132.

[125] White and Kanyongolo (n 51).

[126] Sexual Offences Act, Act No 3 of 2006 (Kenya), s 3.

[127] ibid, s 43(5).

explicit exemption only in the interpretation clause for 'unlawful', which is not as unambiguous as the Macaulay codes.[128]

How has the term 'unlawful' been interpreted in other received common law jurisdictions? Since the marital rape exemption arose out of an exercise of judicial interpretation, it arguably leaves room for a different legal interpretation of what is 'unlawful', as is evidenced by the House of Lords decision in *R v R*.[129] This potential may be especially enhanced in countries with mixed legal systems, where the most progressive interpretation among the various systems can be selected as the interpretive source.

The Israeli legal system is based on a mixed common law, civil law and Jewish law system. The penal code on rape in 1977 was governed by the English common law definition where marital rape was deemed *lawful* sexual intercourse under all circumstances. The Israeli courts removed the marital exemption as early as 1979/1980.[130] In order to get around the English common law impunity for marital rape, the Supreme Court interpreted the word 'unlawful' in 'unlawful sexual intercourse' on the basis of Jewish religious law and principles, to argue that unlawful sexual intercourse includes marital rape.[131]

While South African law is mainly derived from Roman-Dutch civil law, it also contains influences of English common law.[132] By 1992, in *R v R*, the marital rape exemption had been rejected in English common law, but the exemption persisted in Roman-Dutch law. When a marital rape case came before a South African court that same year, the lower court convicted the husband, using the same argument as in *R v R*, that the marital rape impunity was obsolete and that the exemption had never been properly assimilated into African or Ciskei (part of South Africa) law.[133] However, unlike the Israeli Supreme Court, the South African Court of Appeal followed the conservative Roman-Dutch civil law interpretation in a 1993 ruling to maintain the marital rape exception, even though the common law had already changed in England.[134]

In general, once *R v R* was decided in England, it provided the much-needed impetus to change the law in other common law countries or countries with mixed common law. In 2002, the Hong Kong legislature decided to make its rape laws consistent with the British decision in *R v R* and its interpretation of 'unlawful'.[135]

[128] For further discussion, see Kamau et al (n 51).

[129] *R v R* (n 105).

[130] *Cohen v The State of Israel*, Criminal Appeal 91/80, 35 (3) PD (1979/1980) 281. The exception was removed in 1979 by the lower court and upheld in 1980.

[131] For a more detailed discussion of the case, see Goldstein (n 17) 166–75. See also Venkatesh, 'Pluralistic Legal Systems and Marital Rape: Cross-National Considerations' chapter 5 in this volume.

[132] J Campanella, 'The Marital-Rape Exemption Resurrected' (1994) 111 *South African Law Journal* 31.

[133] *S v Ncanywa*, 1992 (2) SA 182 (Ck). See also Campanella, ibid, 32.

[134] *S v Ncanywa*, 1993(1) SACR 297 (CkA). See Campanella, ibid, 33–35 and see discussion in the next section on civil law systems.

[135] R Emerton, 'Marital Rape and Related Sexual Offences: A Review of the Proposed Amendments to Part XII of the Crimes Ordinance' (2001) 31 *Hong Kong Law Journal* 415.

To explicitly bring marital rape into its criminal law legislation on rape, Hong Kong added a phrase in its criminal law stating that 'unlawful sexual intercourse does not exclude sexual intercourse that a man has with his wife'.[136]

In countries with common law influences, there exists some leeway to introduce cases from other common law countries for interpretive guidance. In addition to the House of Lords decision in *R v R*, which has strong persuasive authority, the New York Court of Appeal case in *People v Liberta* has also been influential, for example in the Philippines.

The Philippines has a mixed civil and common law system with many areas of law relying on a civil law style of codification. Nevertheless, since the American occupation, common law statutory interpretation has 'dominated' the Philippine legal system, especially with respect to their Supreme Court jurisprudence.[137] In 1997, the Philippine legislature passed an 'Anti-Rape Law', which was silent on marital rape but had a clause that allowed for the subsequent 'extinguishment' of the penalty for a husband if the wife forgave him.[138] In 2014, the Supreme Court of the Philippines was faced with having to interpret whether the legislation exempted or penalised marital rape.[139] The lengthy decision covered the history of the marital rape exemption from the medieval practice of 'bride-capture', to Hale's dicta, to the New York Court of Appeal decision in *People v Liberta*. The Court emphasised that the marital rape impunity is a violation of the Philippines' international law obligations. It elaborated at length on the state's commitments to the Convention on the Elimination of All Forms of Discrimination against Women and the UN Declaration on the Elimination of Violence Against Women, concluding 'marriage is not a license to rape' and that 'there exists no legal or rational reason for the Court to apply the law and the evidentiary rules on rape any differently if the aggressor is the woman's own legal husband'.[140]

D. The Marital Rape Exemption in 'Originating' European Civil Law Countries

(i) Originating Civil Law Countries

The European civil law countries have had similar laws to those of common law countries providing impunity for marital rape, which is not surprising given the

[136] Hong Kong Crimes Ordinance 1972, ss 117(1B), 118(3) (as modified in 2002); Man-chung Chiu, 'Contextualising the Rhetoric of Sexual Violence in Hong Kong' (2004) 2 *China: An International Journal* 83, 85.

[137] Petra Mahy and Jonathan P Sale, 'Classifying the Legal System of the Philippines: A Preliminary Analysis with Reference to Labor Law' (2012) 32 *Philippine Journal of Labor and Industrial Relations* 1, 3, 5–11.

[138] Republic Act No 8353, 1997 (or Anti-Rape Law of 1997), Arts 335, 226-C.

[139] *People v Jumawan*, GR No 187495, 722 SCRA 108 (21 April 2014) (Phil).

[140] ibid.

common religious and social lineage of gender practices across Europe. The penal code in some civil law countries was explicit about the exclusion. For example, the German code of 1871 was explicit in mandating *extramarital* sexual intercourse as one of the necessary elements of rape.[141] The exemption was only removed in 1997 during an overhaul of Germany's sexual violence laws.[142] Even after the changes in the late 1990s, German laws on sexual assault were considered inadequate to provide sufficient protection, especially because of a requirement that the victims should have defended themselves. The German parliament recently passed legislation to modify at least some of the problematic provisions in the sexual assault laws.[143]

In cases where the penal code was silent, the judiciary read impunity into the existing law if and when a marital rape case came before the courts. Since the 1970s, however, European courts have usually ruled in favour of criminalisation of sexual assault in marriage, as the following examples show.

In France, Italy and Spain, the definition of rape did not explicitly exclude marital rape. The French Cour de cassation in the early 1900s interpreted the definition of rape (*viol*) in the 1808 French penal code to explicitly exclude 'acts of violence' by a husband against his wife from constituting the crime of rape.[144] It was only in 1990 that the Cour de cassation removed the criminal exemption for husbands.[145]

The Italian Corte di cassazione decided earlier, in 1976, to interpret rape in the penal code as applying to marital relationships.[146] In 1992, the Spanish Tribunal Supremo ruled that there was no impunity for marital rape under the constitutional principle of freedom to make one's own decisions in sexual activities.[147]

The USSR was perhaps the first European country to remove the marital rape exemption. The tsarist criminal code in Russia had an explicit marital rape exemption, but the first criminal code of Soviet Russia in 1926 removed it.[148] At that time

[141] German Criminal Code 1871, Strafgesetzbuch für das Deutsche Reich vom 15 Mai 1871, s 177(1); E Livneh, 'On Rape and the Sanctity of Matrimony' (1967) 2 *Israeli Law Review* 415, 420.

[142] German Criminal Code, amended on 5 July 1997, s 177(1); C McNamee, 'Rape' in Rita J Simon (ed), *A Comparative Perspective on Major Social Problems* (Lanham, MD, Lexington Books, 2001) 20–21.

[143] See Bundesverband der Frauenberatungsstellen und Frauennotrufe in Deutschland (Federation of Women's Counselling Centres and Helplines in Germany), Campaign to Reform Section 177, *Report on Protection Gaps in the Sexual Assault Laws* (July 2014) www.frauen-gegen-gewalt.de/fallanalyse-zu-schutzluecken-im-sexualstrafrecht.html?file=tl_files/downloads/kampagnen/vergewaltigung-verurteilen/bff-Fallanalyse_Schutzluecken_Sexualstrafrecht.pdf; 'Germany Rape Law: "No Means No" Law Passed', *BBC News*, 7 July 2016, www.bbc.co.uk/news/world-europe-36726095.

[144] Cour de cassation, 19 March 1910, Bull Crim 1910 no 153, (France); Livneh (n 141) 419–20.

[145] Cour de cassation, Chambre criminelle, 5 September 1990, 90-83786, Bull Crim 1990 no 313; Cour de cassation, Chambre criminelle, 11 June 1992, 91-86346, Bull Crim 1992 no 232; McNamee (n 142) 20.

[146] Corte di cassazione, Sentenza 12857 del 1976 (Ita); Amy Jo Everhart, 'Predicting the Effect of Italy's Long-Awaited Rape Law Reform in the Land of Machismo Note' (1998) 31 *Vanderbilt Journal of Transnational Law* 671, 679.

[147] Spain, Tribunal Supremo, '[Judgment of 24 April 1992]' [1992] *Actualidad Jurídica Aranzadi* 1.

[148] Russian Soviet Federative Socialist Republic, Criminal Code of 1926 (Ugolovnyj kodeks 1926), Art 153; USSR Criminal Code, Art 117 (1960); Livneh (n 141) 420; D McBride Stetson, 'Law and Policy: Women's Human Rights in Russia' in W Rule and NC Noonan (eds), *Russian Women in Politics and Society* (Westport, CT, Greenwood Press, 1996) 160.

sexual freedom was considered to be an essential aspect of self-determination and socialism. Marriage was seen as a bourgeois institution, which should not impinge on the self-determination rights of women.[149] Other countries in the communist bloc which had no marital rape exemption included Czechoslovakia (1950) and Poland (1932).[150] Poland had removed its marital rape exemption even before it became a communist country.[151]

The Scandinavian countries are considered to be pioneers in criminalising marital rape because their penal codes have not had an explicit marital rape exemption since the 1960s. The 1962 Swedish penal code removed all references to relationship-based exemptions in its definition of rape.[152] It did, however, until amendments in 1984, permit for lighter sentencing if the 'woman's relationship to the man' or any other circumstances implied a 'less grave' crime.[153] Norway's laws also had no explicit marital rape exemption and the first conviction for marital rape occurred in 1974, which was upheld by the Supreme Court.[154] Denmark's penal code is also considered as lacking an explicit marital rape exemption. Denmark preceded Sweden by a few years in drafting a definition of rape without reference to marital status.[155] However, until 2013, the Danish Penal Code included several marital exemptions, applying many of its sexual assault provisions only to 'extra-marital sexual intercourse' and reducing or remitting punishment if the parties had had sexual relations before or were in a marital relationship.[156] These provisions reflected the stereotypes that have prevailed since the first Danish Penal Code in 1866, where rape was mainly punishable only when committed against married women by strangers.[157] Rape was seen a violation of women's honour because they had been forced into extramarital intercourse. In 2013, the Danish Penal Code was amended to remove all mentions of the marital status of the victim and offender from the provisions.[158]

[149] Livneh (n 141) 420; Geis (n 83) 296 n 82; McBride Stetson (n 148) 158–61.

[150] Czechoslovakia Criminal Code of 1950, s 238; Polish Criminal Code 1932, Art 204; Livneh (n 141) 421.

[151] Polish Criminal Code 1932, Art 204; Livneh (n 141) 421; Freeman (n 20) 26–27; Geis (n 83) 296.

[152] Geis (n 83) 297–300.

[153] Swedish Criminal Code 1962, ch 6, s 1(2); Livneh (n 141) 421; Amnesty International, 'Case Closed: Rape and Human Rights in the Nordic Countries' (Amnesty International Publications, 2008) amnesty.dk/media/1557/case-closed.pdf, 47; See also Geis (n 83) 297–98.

[154] Norway Supreme Court, Rt 1974 s 1121 (1974). See Freeman (n 20) 27; Norway, 'Information Provided by Norway in Follow-up to the Concluding Observations by the Committee on the Elimination of Discrimination against Women on the Eighth Periodic Report of Norway' (Committee on the Elimination of Discrimination against Women, 2014) CEDAW/C/NOR/CO/8/Add 1, 3.

[155] Geis (n 83) 297.

[156] Danish Criminal Code 2005 (as amended by Act Nos 1389 and 1400 of 21 December 2005), Arts 218, 220, 221, 227.

[157] Amnesty International (n 153) 16.

[158] Denmark, Act No 633 of 12 June 2013; Ministry of Gender Equality of Denmark, 'Report by Denmark on the Application of the Beijing Declaration and Platform for Action (1995) and the Results of the 23rd Special Session of the UN General Assembly (2000)' (Copenhagen 2014) www.unece.org/fileadmin/DAM/Gender/publication/Denmark__national_report_on_the_implementation_of_the_Beijing_Declaration_and_Platform_for_Action.pdf, 11.

(ii) Received Civil Law Countries

Just like the spread of British common law, civil law systems promulgated throughout the world as colonising countries introduced civil codes to their colonial subjects. Codification of criminal law usually resulted in explicit marital rape exemptions in the penal codes of colonised countries. When faced with such an explicitly codified exemption for marital rape, legal reform has required sustained, long-drawn legislative campaigns, sometimes over decades. The judiciary in civil law postcolonial countries with explicit marital rape exemptions has not always been the forum where marital rape has been successfully challenged. The courts have been reluctant unilaterally to overturn the marital rape exemption without the legislatures having taken the first step, as the following examples demonstrate.

South Africa was one of the first countries in Africa to criminalise rape in a spousal relationship, but through legislative reform. As discussed above, the South African appellate court had held that although English law had rejected the marital rape exemption, although the marital rape exemption in common law was based on a fiction created by Hale, and although it was possibly anachronistic and inconsistent with current standards, the exemption was nevertheless part of Roman-Dutch law, and therefore a part of South African law.[159] The decision led the South African legislature to enact the Prevention of Family Violence Act in 1993, even before the South African Constitution came into force. The Act removed the provision that exempted husbands from rape charges 'by reason of [a woman's] consent in marriage'.[160] It also incorporated an explicit marital rape criminalisation clause, which stated that 'a husband may be convicted of the rape of his wife'.[161]

Another example of successful legislative action from Africa is provided by Namibia, which like South Africa is also a mixed civil/common law jurisdiction. The Combating of Rape Act came into force in Namibia in June 2000 and was considered to be 'one of the most progressive laws on rape in the world'.[162] The Act overturned many of the colonial-era patriarchal laws around rape that had been present in the common and civil law, including the marital rape exemption. Marital rape was explicitly criminalised in section 2(3) by stipulating that 'no marriage or other relationship will be a defence to a charge of rape'.[163] The Act was tabled in 1999 and the inclusion of a marital rape clause was not without controversy as male parliamentarians used familiar arguments to oppose it, including that it would lead to the break-up of marriages and

[159] *S v Ncanywa* (n 134). See Campanella (n 132) 33–35.

[160] Prevention of Family Violence Act, No 133 of 1993.

[161] ibid, s 5.

[162] N Bohler-Muller, 'Valuable Lessons from Namibia on the Combating of Rape' (2001) 14 *South African Journal of Criminal Justice* 71, 74.

[163] Namibian Combating of Crime Act, Act No 8 of 2000 (2000), s 2(3).

vexatious, spurious claims by wives. Lobbying by very active women's groups, NGOs, high-ranking female politicians, civil servants and other supporters of the bill ensured that the clause remained.[164]

Once legislatures amended their countries' penal codes to include marital rape, the higher courts in at least a few countries helped in creating more progressive formulations of the code. The 1990s was a period of increased international activism among feminist groups in Latin America, where all countries have civil law systems.[165] Women's rights groups used a two-pronged approach combining intense participation in intergovernmental organisations and international policy arenas with grassroots mobilisation. Thus, the legislatures of several Latin American countries began to criminalise marital rape. But the judiciary played an important role in a few countries in articulating that the new marital rape criminalisation laws were essential for protecting human rights and in creating more progressive interpretation of the law.

For example, in 1996, marital rape was criminalised in Colombia. When this law was originally enacted, it provided for a lesser punishment for rape within the context of marriage than for rape generally.[166] However, the Constitutional Court of Colombia declared this difference in punishment unconstitutional.[167] The new Penal Code not only affirmed that sexual assault could take place in intimate relationships, but, as happened in Canada, it also made rape in spousal or intimate relationships *an aggravating factor to rape*, warranting a stricter punishment.[168]

In 1994, Mexico's Supreme Court of Justice ruled that forced sex within marriage is not rape but rather 'an undue exercise of conjugal rights'.[169] It also said that because the purpose of marriage is procreation, a man can force his wife to

[164] Becker (n 16) 188. Similar arguments were raised during parliamentary debates about criminalising marital rape in Ghana (see Morhe (n 51)), Kenya (see Kamau et al (n 51)) and Malawi (White and Kanyongolo (n 51)).

[165] SE Alvarez, 'Translating the Global Effects of Transnational Organizing on Local Feminist Discourses and Practices in Latin America' (2000) 1 *Meridians* 29. For a list of legal systems in Latin America, see World Legal Systems Research Group, 'Alphabetical Index of the Political Entities and Corresponding Legal Systems' (University of Ottawa-JuriGlobe) www.juriglobe.ca/eng/sys-juri/index-alpha.php.

[166] Colombia Ley 295 de 1996, Diario Oficial No 42.836, de 22 de Julio de 1996, Art 25; C Benninger-Budel and L O'Hanlon, 'Violence against Women in Colombia, Report Prepared for the Thirty-First Session of the Committee on Economic, Social and Cultural Rights', *Violence Against Women: 10 Reports/Year 2003* (World Organisation Against Torture (OMCT), 2004) 156.

[167] Colombia Constitutional Court, decision C-285 of 1997, Presiding Judge Carlos Gaviria Díaz (action for unconstitutionality of Article 25 of law 294 of 1996.) See also Center for Reproductive Rights, *Bodies on Trial: Reproductive Rights in Latin American Courts* (New York, Center for Reproductive Rights, 2003) 61.

[168] Colombia Ley 599 de 2000, Diario Oficial 44097 del 24 de julio de 2000, Art 211(5) (as amended by Art 30 de Ley 1257 de 2008); Benninger-Budel and O'Hanlon (n 166) 156. For the Canadian context, see Koshan (n10) and Canadian Criminal Code, RSC 1985, c C-46, s 718.2(a)(ii).

[169] Supreme Court of Mexico, Judgment 10/94, (1994); Human Rights Watch, 'The Second Assault: Obstructing Access to Legal Abortion after Rape in Mexico' (Human Rights Watch, 2006) www.hrw.org/sites/default/files/reports/mexico0306webwcover.pdf, 19.

have sex if the sex is for that purpose.[170] The case spurred Mexican women's rights groups to campaign for a legislative change removing the marital rape exemption and the Mexican government passed a new law criminalising marital rape in 1997.[171] In November 2005, when the next marital rape case came before the Mexican Supreme Court, it explicitly overturned the 1994 decision, asserted that forced sex within marriage is rape punishable by law, and affirmed the necessity of the legislation for protecting constitutional rights.[172] The Supreme Court of Mexico relied on several constitutional rights in its judgment, including the right to sexual and reproductive freedom.[173]

Nepal stands as a notable exception where the judiciary unilaterally overturned a marital exception in its penal code that was more than a century old. Nepal was not a British colony and remained at least semi-autonomous through the colonial era. In the late nineteenth century, the ruling monarchy embraced the codification programme that was taking place throughout Europe and its colonies.[174] Nepal's legal code, Muluki Ain, was inspired by the Napoleonic code and is an amalgam of European civil codes, common law doctrines, and Hindu tenets and scriptures.[175] When rape was codified, it was defined as sexual intercourse below the age of consent (sixteen years) or where there was threat, pressure, coercion or undue influence. It was, however, defined only in the specific contexts of a (unmarried) girl, widow or another person's wife, excluding spousal rape from the definition.[176] The marital rape exemption was continued in the 1963 code, when the country went through a period of legal reform. In 2006, the provision was declared constitutionally invalid by Nepal's Supreme Court. In a powerful judgment, the Court asserted that legal impunity for marital rape is a 'discriminatory practice … against the provisions of the Convention on the Elimination of All Forms of Discrimination against Women and [the letter] and spirit of Articles 11(1), (2) and (3) of the Constitution of the Kingdom of Nepal'.[177] The Court emphasised that women, like all human beings, have the right to equal protection of the law without discrimination, the right to live with self-respect (dignity), and rights of self-determination and independent existence, all of which were infringed by the marital rape

[170] A Madrazo and E Vela, 'The Mexican Supreme Court's (Sexual) Revolution Symposium: Latin American Constitutionalism: Section IV: Constitutional Review' (2010) 89 *Texas Law Review* 1863, 1872, fn 29.

[171] Neumann (n 36) 95.

[172] Judgment 9/2005-PS, First Chamber application for amendment of jurisprudence, 16 November 2005 (Supreme Court of Mexico); Madrazo (n 170) 1872.

[173] Madrazo (n 170) 1872.

[174] K Bikram Thapa, 'Religion and Law in Nepal' in J Martínez-Torrón, W Cole Durham and DD Thayer (eds), *Religion and the Secular State: National Reports Issued for the Occasion of the XVIIIth Congress of the International Academy of Comparative Law* (Madrid, Servicio de Publicaciones de la Facultad de Derecho de la Universidad Complutense de Madrid, 2015) 518; Nitya Ramakrishnan, *In Custody: Law, Impunity and Prisoner Abuse in South Asia* (Delhi, Sage Law, 2013) 295.

[175] Thapa (n 174) 518; Ramakrishnan (n 174) 295.

[176] Muluki Ain (Country Code) 1963, No 1 on the Chapter on Rape; See *Meera Dhungana v His Majesty's Government*, Writ No 55 of the year 2058 BS (2006) (Nepal).

[177] *Dhungana*, ibid.

exemption. In the same way that the Philippines Supreme Court used foreign case law such as *People v Liberta* in its decision, the Supreme Court of Nepal also referred to *R v R* and *People v Liberta* when it declared the marital rape exemption invalid.[178]

The recent higher court decisions in Nepal, Mexico and the Philippines show how international human rights norms and domestic constitutional rights provide the most formidable basis to challenge the marital rape immunity. The Nepal Supreme Court was forthright about how laws must be changed to conform to conceptions of 'universal values and traditions', where national level laws have to reconcile with 'globalisation' of values and 'reciprocal international relations' determined by treaties and conventions.[179]

E. Summary

In conclusion, originating countries with endogenous civil law codes were the first to remove the marital rape exemption. Originating common law countries began to criminalise marital rape only in the late 1970s, coinciding with the activism of their women's rights movements. Marital rape cases are rarely litigated and even more rarely reach the higher level of courts. Legal change has therefore more often happened in legislative institutions, not because of some intrinsic enlightened perspective of legislatures but because of the work and advocacy of feminist and other social justice grassroots organisations in pushing for this legal change.

Furthermore, in these countries before the 1970s, domestic courts supported legislatures in upholding the marital rape exemption. The trends in the United States, Israel and Italy show that after the 1970s, the courts shifted and have been responsive towards overturning the marital rape exemption so long as anti-gender discrimination laws were also recognised at that time.

Where penal codes are explicit in exempting sexual assault in marriage from the definition of rape, the judiciary has typically also been reluctant to step in where the legislature has not tread. Common law penal codes are unique in using the language of 'unlawful' to define rape, which has been somewhat easier to reinterpret as including marital rape than codes with stronger language. Common law courts in receiving countries with such ambiguous language have more leeway than other courts to rely on foreign and international human rights to resolve the ambiguity.

As constitutionalism, feminism and international human rights took root as global movements, legislatures began to respond, removing marital rape exemptions. The judiciary also played an important role in interpreting ambiguous codes and articulating the rights analysis underlying marital rape criminalisation.

178 *Dhungana*, ibid (Nepal), *Jumawan* (n 139) (Phil).

179 *Dhungana* (n 176) (Nepal).

The recent decisions by the Mexican, Nepalese, Philippines and other courts reveal expanded judicial understandings of how rights are intertwined, how marital rape expresses structural inequalities that women face in intimate relationships, and how extending rights in one area of law, such as sexual assault, reinforces and strengthens women's rights to equal benefit of the law in other areas, such as reproductive rights and anti-discrimination and procedural rights. In the next section of the chapter, we elaborate on the fundamental human rights norms and instruments making the criminalisation of marital rape imperative.

IV. Human Rights Law Requiring Criminalisation of Marital Rape

A. Introduction

More and more countries have criminalised marital rape over the last two decades, putting those countries that have failed to do so in the minority. Until 1997, only 17 states had criminalised marital rape.[180] By 2006, more than 50 states had followed suit[181] and now fewer than 50 states still entirely protect marital rape from penal prosecution. This trajectory has been lock-step with changes in the international human rights forums where women's rights, especially within the household, have slowly gained acceptance. Moreover, the public/private distinction that plagued international human rights law by focusing only on violations by state actors and privileging privacy in the family over gender justice has been slowly dismantled.[182]

As *People v Liberta* was being litigated in the United States and the marital rape amendment was being debated in Canada, the first international multilateral instrument against marital rape was adopted in the European Parliament. The 1986 Resolution of Violence Against Women called for the legal recognition of marital rape.[183] In the international human rights forum, a 1982 ECOSOC resolution labelled domestic violence and rape as offences against the dignity of the person, but it did not specifically address marital rape.[184]

[180] UNICEF, *The Progress of Nations 1997* (UNICEF, 1997) 48.

[181] UN Women and UN Secretary General (n 63) 113.

[182] D Sullivan, 'The Public/Private Distinction in International Human Rights Law' in JS Peters and A Wolper (eds), *Women's Rights, Human Rights: International Feminist Perspectives* (New York, Routledge, 1995).

[183] 1986 European Parliament Resolution on Violence Against Women, Doc A2-44/86, [1986] OJ C176, 73 (14 July 1986).

[184] UNESC Res 1982/22 1982.

The turning point came with the biggest milestone in international women's rights law, achieved by the passage of the Convention on the Elimination of All Forms of Discrimination against Women (CEDAW).[185] This was followed by two significant human rights instrument that directly addressed violence against women: General Recommendation 19 by the CEDAW Committee[186] and the Vienna Declaration on the Elimination of Violence against Women (DEVAW).[187]

Using these instruments as sources, regional and international human rights bodies, spurred on by the involvement of very active women's rights groups from across the globe, firmly institutionalised a due-diligence obligation on states to adequately prevent, combat and remedy marital rape, domestic violence and other acts of gender violence.

This was accomplished through a plethora of international and regional women's rights conferences specifically focusing on violence against women, the appointment of special committees, investigators and rapporteurs and the passage of multiple declarations. The due-diligence obligation was also influenced by cases brought before international and regional human rights adjudication bodies, the publication of reports, participation of NGOs in committee work, and affirmation of state and international responsibility to combat gender-based violence in all spheres by high-profile actors such as the UN Secretary General, combined with intense local activism by domestic women's rights groups.

The CEDAW Committee, UN Special Rapporteurs on violence against women, and several UN bodies have all recognised that criminalising sexual and physical violence against women in all its forms is essential for combating gender discrimination and for providing women with equal protection against violence under the law. At this point, the duty of states to criminalise marital rape can no longer be thought of as only an emergent norm. Instead, it is an established human rights obligation.[188] For these reasons, a state that fails to criminalise marital rape is also failing to live up to internationally recognised human rights obligations towards its citizens. The next sections will elaborate on the key international and regional instruments relevant to the criminalisation of marital rape.

[185] Convention on the Elimination of All Forms of Discrimination against Women (CEDAW) (18 December 1979) 1249 UNTS 13, 19 ILM 33 (1980), entered into force 3 September 1981.

[186] UN Committee on the Elimination of Discrimination Against Women, General Recommendation 19: Violence Against Women, adopted in the 11th Session of the CEDAW Committee, UN Doc A/47/38 1992.

[187] UN Declaration on the Elimination of Violence against Women (DEVAW), GA Res 48/104 1993.

[188] See Randall and Venkatesh, 'Right to No' (n 4); Randall and Venkatesh, 'Criminalizing Sexual Violence against Women in Intimate Relationships' (n 4); Randall and Venkatesh, 'Why Sexual Assault in Intimate Relationships Must Be Criminalized' (n 4).

B. Sources of International Human Rights Law Requiring an End to the Marital Rape Exemption

(i) The 1979 Convention on the Elimination of All Forms of Discrimination Against Women

CEDAW was adopted in 1979 by the UN General Assembly and came into force in 1981. Consisting of a preamble and 30 articles, the Convention is the primary international human rights instrument defining what constitutes discrimination against women and setting up an agenda for national action to end such discrimination. Marital status is specifically listed as a prohibited ground of 'distinction, exclusion or restriction'.[189]

However, this Convention contains a glaring omission: violence against women—unlike other issues such as the right to vote—was not explicitly addressed. CEDAW mentions 'discrimination' 22 times, 'equal' or 'equality' 34 times and 'human rights' five times, yet makes no mention of violence, rape, sexual assault, domestic violence and abuse, or battery.

The drafting of CEDAW took place in the 1970s, when the movement on violence against women in the family and society was still nascent and confined within states. It had yet to become an international movement. Within a few years, however, it became an issue for debate in international forums with increased reports on the widespread prevalence of violence against women and an emerging recognition of its human and economic impacts. Since it was not politically possible to create an entirely new convention addressing violence against women at that point, a 'two-pronged approach' was initiated by women's rights advocates.[190] First, the UN Commission on the Status of Women began drafting a non-binding declaration on violence against women, and second, the CEDAW Committee simultaneously began to draft General Recommendation 19, which would provide a binding obligation on state signatories to combat gender violence.

(ii) CEDAW's General Recommendation 19 (1992)

The CEDAW Committee attempted to fill the gap created by the lack of reference to violence against women in CEDAW by using an arguably retroactive 'creative interpretation' in drafting General Recommendation 19 (GR 19) in 1992.[191]

[189] CEDAW (n 185), Art 1.

[190] A Byrnes and E Bath, 'Violence against Women, the Obligation of Due Diligence, and the Optional Protocol to the Convention on the Elimination of All Forms of Discrimination against Women—Recent Developments' (2008) 8 *Human Rights Law Review* 517, 519.

[191] J Fitzpatrick, 'The Use of International Human Rights Norms to Combat Violence against Women' in RJ Cook (ed), *Human Rights of Women: National and International Perspectives* (Philadelphia, University of Pennsylvania Press, 1994) 534.

GR 19 explicitly extended the definition of discrimination in Article 1 of CEDAW to include gender-based violence, which 'is violence that is directed against a woman because she is a woman or violence that disproportionately affects women'.[192] It includes acts that inflict physical, mental or sexual harm or suffering, threats of such acts, coercion and other deprivations of liberty.

In a strongly worded section, GR 19 declares that domestic or family violence, including rape within the family, breaches Articles 16 and 5 of CEDAW:

> 23. Family violence is *one of the most insidious forms* of violence against women. It is prevalent in all societies. Within family relationships women of all ages are subjected to violence of all kinds, including battering, *rape*, other forms of sexual assault, mental and other forms of violence, which are perpetuated by traditional attitudes. Lack of economic independence forces many women to stay in violent relationships. The abrogation of their family responsibilities by men can be a form of violence, and coercion. These forms of violence put women's health at risk and impair their ability to participate in family life and public life on a basis of equality.[193]

GR 19 further recognised violence against women as 'a form of discrimination that seriously inhibits women's ability to enjoy rights and freedoms on a basis of equality with men', thus setting the stage to claim that the right to be free from gender violence is at least a derivative right based on fundamental and widely accepted rights, even though not explicitly stated in CEDAW.[194]

Other regional and international treaty bodies also firmly support this formulation, and following GR 19, they have demanded that their Member States fulfil their obligations to protect these fundamental rights by instituting measures and legislating laws specifically to combat violence against women. These general rights and freedoms include, inter alia, the right to equality in the family,[195] the right to liberty and security of person,[196] the right to equal protection under the law,[197]

[192] CEDAW Committee, General Recommendation 19 (n 186), para 6.

[193] ibid, para 23 (emphasis added).

[194] ibid, paras 1, 6.

[195] The UN Human Rights Committee has recognised that the gender-specific nature of domestic violence requires that it be classified as a violation of the human right to equality. See General Comment No 28, Art 3 (The Equality of Rights Between Men and Women), para 10, UN Doc CCPR/C/21/Rev 1/Add 10 (29 March 2000). Since intimate partner sexual assault and violence against women in general impair or nullify the enjoyment of economic, social and cultural rights, these forms of discrimination implicate the rights under the International Covenant on Economic, Social and Cultural Rights as well, see UN Comm on Econ & Soc Council, Comm On Econ, Soc & Cultural Rights, General Comment No 16, para 27, UN Doc E/C 12/2005/4 (11 August 2005).

[196] CEDAW Committee, Comm No 2/2003, *Ms A T v Hungary*, para 9.3, CEDAW/C/36/D/2/2003 (26 January 2005); Report of the CEDAW Committee on its Exceptional Session, transmitted by Letter Dated 15 September 2002 from the Chairperson of the CEDAW Committee to the General Assembly, paras 333–34, UN Doc No A/57/38 (2002); *S v Baloyi*, 2000 (2) SA 425 (CC), para 11 (S Afr); Inter-American Commission on Human Rights, *Access to Justice for Women Victims of Violence in Mesoamerica* (Washington, DC, Organization of American States, 2011) paras 48, 124.

[197] CEDAW Committee, General Recommendation 19 (n 186); Art 6, General Comment No 2 (n 195), paras 10, 20, 24; Y Ertürk (Special Rapporteur on Violence against Women, its causes and

the right to the highest standard attainable of physical and mental health,[198] and the right not to be subject to torture or to cruel, inhuman or degrading treatment or punishment.[199] Other rights violated by states' failure to address marital rape include the rights to life,[200] sexual self-determination, human dignity, humane treatment, individual privacy, effective judicial recourse, safety, physical and mental integrity, integrity of the person, and sexual and reproductive choice.[201]

GR 19 imposes a list of obligations that states must fulfil in order to protect women, which include penal sanctions along with preventative and protective measures. Specific to family violence, these measures should include criminal penalties where necessary and civil remedies in cases of domestic violence, legislation to remove any defence of 'honour', and the provision of services to ensure the safety and security of victims of family violence. GR 19 also places an obligation on states to report on the measures they have taken to combat each kind of violence and the impact of the measures.[202]

Despite a number of reservations, CEDAW is the second most widely accepted international human rights treaty after the Convention on the Rights of the Child (CRC). There are currently 189 state parties to the Convention.[203] The CEDAW Committee also has the largest membership of all the UN human rights treaty bodies with 23 members, making it the most representative of all the

consequences), *The Due Diligence Standard as a Tool for the Elimination of Violence against Women*, UN Doc E/CN 4/2006/61 (20 January 2006), para 35; R Manjoo, *Report of the Special Rapporteur on Violence against Women, its Causes and Consequences—Promotion and Protection of All Human Rights, Civil, Political, Economic, Social and Cultural Rights, Including the Right to Development*, UN Doc A/HRC/23/49 (2013) paras 50, 74.

198 See UN Comm on Econ & Soc Council, Comm on Econ, Soc & Cultural Rights, General Comment No 14, UN Comm on Econ & Soc Council, Comm on Econ, Soc & Cultural Rights, General Comment No 16, para 27, UN Doc E/C.12/2005/4 (11 August 2005).

199 See Comm against Torture, General Comment 2 to the Convention against Torture and Other Cruel, Inhuman or Degrading Treatment or Punishment on the Implementation of Article 2 by States Parties, UN Doc CAT/C/GC/2/CRP.1/Rev.4 (23 November 2007), paras 21, 18–22. See also *Aydin v Turkey* (No 50), 1996–VII 75 Eur Ct HR 1866, para 86 (1997); *Opuz v Turkey*, Eur Ct HR App No 33401/02 (2009).

200 See UN HR Comm, Concluding Observations on Colombia, UN Doc A/52/40 (1997), para 287; UN HR Comm, Concluding Observations on Peru, UN Doc A/52/40 (1997), para 167. The UN Human Rights Committee is drafting a General Comment 36 on Art 6 of the International Covenant on Civil and Political Rights that is expected to explicitly identify domestic and sexual violence as violations of women's right to life. See International Justice Resource Centre, *Human Rights Committee Developing New Right To Life General Comment* (28 July 2015) www.ijrcenter.org/2015/07/28/human-rights-committee-developing-new-right-to-life-general-comment/.

201 CEDAW Committee, General Recommendation 19 (n 186); Randall and Venkatesh, 'Right to No' (n 4) 177–95; Randall and Venkatesh, 'Criminalizing Sexual Violence against Women in Intimate Relationships' (n 4).

202 CEDAW Committee, General Recommendation 19 (n 186), para 24.

203 MR Bustelo, 'The Committee on the Elimination of Discrimination against Women at the Crossroads' in Philip Alston and James Crawford (eds), *The Future of UN Human Rights Treaty Monitoring* (Cambridge, Cambridge University Press, 2000) 79.

committees.[204] By ratifying CEDAW, states also accept the jurisdiction of the treaty body to monitor state compliance and to provide the substantive content for the rights and the nature of obligations through general comments and recommendations.[205] These factors militate against the claim that the CEDAW Committee invented a non-existing obligation, which was not assumed by states when they signed the Convention. Also, Member States have dutifully accepted the obligations imposed by CEDAW (even if they are imperfectly fulfilled), as evidenced in their periodic reports, not only to the CEDAW Committee but also to the UN Human Rights Committee. In these reports, states are required to present evidence on how they have addressed violence against women, including marital rape.[206]

GR 19, along with DEVAW, discussed next, seems to have been especially successful in diffusing a normative standard of due-diligence obligations of states to combat gender violence. A recent study on the impact of GR 19 finds that state parties to CEDAW were more likely to have anti-gender violence and domestic violence laws enacted since 1996 than non-state parties.[207] The number of pieces of legislation enacted and institutions built to combat domestic violence and violence against women increased drastically beginning in the late 1990s, and 'states rapidly conformed to General Recommendations 12 and 19, despite their rather loose basis in the treaty itself'.[208]

(iii) The 1993 UN Vienna Declaration on the Elimination of Violence against Women (DEVAW)

GR 19 must be read along with the 1993 DEVAW, which is an exceptional instrument that unambiguously spotlights gendered violence as an international human rights issue. Although it is non-binding, DEVAW clearly shows international

[204] Bustelo, ibid; Office of the United Nations High Commissioner for Human Rights (OHCHR), *Human Rights Bodies*, www.ohchr.org/EN/HRBodies/Pages/HumanRightsBodies.aspx.

[205] The United States is among the states that do not accept the opinions of treaty bodies as authoritative (see US Department of State, *Response of the United States to List of Issues to Be Taken Up in Connection With the Consideration of the Second and Third Periodic Reports of the United States of America* (27 July 2006)). However, courts in many jurisdictions, including several in the United States, have recognised that treaty bodies' 'interpretations deserve to be given *considerable weight* in determining the meaning of a relevant right and the existence of a violation' (emphasis added). See International Law Association, Committee on Human Rights Law and Practice, Final Report on the Impact of Findings of the United Nations Human Rights Treaty Bodies (2004) para 148.

[206] UN HR Comm, Concluding Observations on Colombia, UN Doc A/52/40 (1997), para 287; UN HR Comm, Concluding Observations on Peru, UN Doc A/52/40 (1997), para 167. In several concluding observations, the Human Rights Committee has specifically demanded that the member states criminalise marital rape. See eg UN HR Comm, Concluding Observations on Sri Lanka, UN Doc CCPR/CO/79/LKA, para 20 (2003).

[207] NA Englehart, 'CEDAW and Gender Violence: An Empirical Assessment' (2014) 2014 *Michigan State Law Review* 265, 268–74, 279–80.

[208] ibid, 275.

consensus and political commitment to combat violence against women in all its forms. DEVAW defines violence against women as:

> Any act of gender-based violence that results in, or is likely to result in, physical, *sexual* or psychological harm or suffering to women, including threats of such acts, coercion or arbitrary deprivation of liberty, whether occurring in public or *in private life*.[209]

Article 2 further elucidates the definition of violence against women, and specifically mentions marital rape and violence within the family:

> 2. Violence against women shall be … understood to encompass, but not be limited to, the following:
>
> (a) Physical, sexual and psychological violence occurring in the family, including battering, sexual abuse of female children in the household, dowry-related violence, *marital rape*, female genital mutilation and other traditional practices harmful to women, non-spousal violence and violence related to exploitation;
> (b) Physical, sexual and psychological violence occurring within the general community, including rape, sexual abuse, sexual harassment and intimidation at work, in educational institutions and elsewhere, trafficking in women and forced prostitution;
> (c) Physical, sexual and psychological violence perpetrated or condoned by the State, *wherever it occurs*.[210]

By prohibiting both state violence against women and private violence, DEVAW recognises the need to rethink boundaries between public and private life. The only aspect differentiating violence by private actors and violence perpetrated by the state is the location of the criminal act. Physical, sexual and psychological violence within the home is as condemnable in international law as is state-perpetrated violence. Gendered violence within private relationships was thereby proclaimed to be a matter of international concern in DEVAW.

Like GR 19, DEVAW affirms that violence against women constitutes a 'violation of the rights and fundamental freedoms of women and impairs or nullifies their enjoyment of those rights and freedoms'.[211] A state's obligations to punish acts of gender violence thus also derive from the state's obligation to prevent violations of fundamental freedoms recognised in international law.

DEVAW also has a programmatic component articulating a due-diligence obligation for states to protect women from violence. All UN Member States, not just signatories to CEDAW, have a duty to 'pursue by all appropriate means and without delay a policy of eliminating violence against women'.[212] This duty includes 'due diligence to prevent, investigate and, in accordance with national legislation,

[209] UN Declaration on the Elimination of Violence against Women (DEVAW) (n 187), Art 1 (emphasis added).
[210] ibid, Art 2 (emphasis added).
[211] ibid, preamble.
[212] ibid, Art 4.

punish acts of violence against women, whether those acts are perpetuated by the State *or by private persons*'.[213]

(iv) Other Major International Legal Initiatives to End Gendered Violence

The Fourth World Conference on Women in Beijing in 1995 and the resulting Beijing Declaration and Platform for Action reiterated that violence against women is recognised under international law as including 'physical, sexual and psychological violence occurring *in the family*, including battering … *marital rape* … and violence related to exploitation' as well as gender violence condoned by the state.[214] The due-diligence standard was reiterated in the Beijing Declaration and Platform for Action, which was adopted by 189 UN Member States.[215] The Beijing Declaration further recognised that violence against women, including marital rape, 'is a manifestation of the historically unequal power relations between men and women' and demanded that states enact or reinforce sanctions that punish perpetrators and provide women with access to justice.[216]

Numerous women's rights advocates from across the globe participated in the Beijing Conference and other UN summits.[217] The participation of these women's rights groups played a critical role in bringing equality-based and feminist legal conceptions of gender violence into international, regional and domestic legal institutions.[218] This role of women's rights groups at the grassroots and transnational levels must be given particular emphasis, as without their involvement, the norms in GR 19 and DEVAW would not have the binding import and international consensus they have now.

In 1994 the UN Economic and Social Council adopted Resolution 1994/45 of the UN Commission on Human Rights, and established the mandate of the Special Rapporteur on Violence against Women to recommend measures to eliminate violence against women and its causes and to remedy its consequences.[219] The Resolution emphasised that it is

> the duty of Governments to refrain from engaging in violence against women and to *exercise due diligence* to prevent, investigate and, in accordance with national legislation, *to punish acts of violence against women* and to take appropriate and effective action

[213] ibid, Art 4(c) (emphasis added).

[214] World Conference on Women, Rep of the Fourth World Conference on Women, UN Doc A/CONF177/20/Rev1 1996 48, para 113(a) (emphasis added).

[215] ibid 51, para 124(b).

[216] ibid, paras 118, 124.

[217] Alvarez (n 165) 29–31.

[218] ibid; SE Merry, 'Transnational Human Rights and Local Activism: Mapping the Middle', *Dialogues on Human Rights and Legal Pluralism* (New York, Springer, 2013); SE Merry, *Human Rights and Gender Violence: Translating International Law into Local Justice* (Chicago, University of Chicago Press, 2006).

[219] Commission on Human Rights, Res 1995/86, UN Doc E/CN 4/1995/176 1995, preamble.

> concerning acts of violence against women, whether those acts are perpetrated by the State or by private persons, and to provide access to *just and effective remedies* and specialised assistance to victims.[220]

The current UN Special Rapporteur on Violence against Women, Rashida Manjoo, notes the discriminatory treatment of spousal violence in many Member States.[221] Even in countries where spousal violence is a criminal offence, it is often minimised by being categorised as a minor offence, prosecuted as only a misdemeanour, with reports of spousal violence not being taken seriously by the police.[222] The due-diligence standard, however, requires that states impose 'severe' and effective sanctions against spousal violence to prevent future conduct 'because of the on-going nature of the relationship between victim and perpetrator'.[223] The previous Special Rapporteur confirmed that the criminalisation of domestic and intimate partner violence is a specific requirement under the Beijing Platform and was a 'minimum standard'.[224]

In 2006, the United Nations established the Task Force on Violence Against Women, and the UN Secretary-General released an 'in-depth study on all forms of violence against women'.[225] The study points out that '[t]he most common form of violence experienced by women globally is intimate partner violence', which includes 'a range of *sexually*, psychologically and physically coercive acts'.[226] It reiterates the Beijing Platform's exhortation 'to treat all forms of violence against women and girls as "criminal offences"', explaining why criminalisation is an important and essential response:

> State inaction with regard to the proper functioning of the *criminal justice system* has particularly corrosive effects as impunity for acts of violence against women encourages further violence and reinforces women's subordination. Such inaction by the State *to address the causes of violence against women constitutes lack of compliance with human rights obligations*.[227]

(v) Regional Instruments and the Criminalisation of Marital Rape

Regional human rights systems also make spousal rape a high priority for legislative action. The Inter-American Convention to Prevent, Punish and Eradicate Violence against Women (the Convention of Belém do Parà), which has been

220 ibid, para 2 (emphasis added).
221 Manjoo (n 197).
222 ibid, para 50.
223 ibid, para 74.
224 Y Ertürk, *Report of the Special Rapporteur on Violence against Women, Its Causes and Consequences, Indicators on Violence against Women and State Response* (2008) UN Doc A/HRC/7/6, paras 71, 78, 81.
225 UN Women and UN Secretary General (n 63) ix.
226 ibid, 43 (emphasis added).
227 ibid, 12, 37 (emphasis added).

ratified by 32 states,[228] recognises all gender-based violence as an abuse of human rights and fundamental freedoms.[229] This Convention's definition of violence against women includes 'physical, sexual and psychological violence' that occurs 'within the family or domestic unit or within any other interpersonal relationship', covering IPSV.[230]

The Inter-American Commission on Human Rights (IACHR) has consistently demanded that states adopt '*criminal*, civil and administrative laws to prevent, punish and eradicate violence against women' and demands that states make no distinctions based on the marital status of victim or perpetrator.[231] A recent IACHR report also points out that while 'honour' and other patriarchal cultural values used to be the core interests at stake in sexual violence crimes, it is no longer condoned in many states.[232] The report also asserts that under all circumstances rape is a crime against society and has to be prosecuted by the state as a crime even when the victim 'forgives' the perpetrator.[233]

The Council of Europe and the European Union have consistently reiterated that violence against women, including intimate partner sexual assault, is a form of discrimination that requires adequate criminal remedies.[234] The European Union has expressly called for the criminalisation of marital rape for several decades, beginning with the European Parliament's Resolution on Violence Against Women of 1986.[235]

The 2009 European Parliament's Resolution on the Elimination of Violence against Women states that:

> [M]en's violence against women represents a violation of human rights, and in particular: the right to life, the right to safety, the right to dignity, the right to physical and mental integrity, and the right to sexual and reproductive choice and health.[236]

The Resolution further notes that gendered violence 'is an obstacle to the participation of women in social activities, in political and public life and in

[228] Inter-American Convention on the Prevention, Punishment and Eradication of Violence Against Women, 9 June 1994, 33 ILM 1534, preamble; see also *List of Countries that Signed, Ratified and Acceded to the Convention of Belém do Pará*, Organization of American States, www.oas.org/juridico/english/sigs/a-61.html.

[229] ibid, preamble, Art 7.

[230] ibid, Art 2.

[231] *Access to Justice for Women Victims of Sexual Violence in Mesoamerica* (n 196) ix. See also *Maria Da Penha v Brazil*, Case 12.051, Inter-Am Comm'n HR, Report No 54/01, OEA/Ser L/V/II.111, doc 20 rev 704 (2001) (emphasis added).

[232] *Access to Justice for Women Victims of Sexual Violence in Mesoamerica* (n 231) para 48.

[233] ibid, 35–40.

[234] Council of Europe Comm of Ministers, Recommendation Rec (2002)5 on the Protection of Women Against Violence, 794th Sess, para 34 (30 April 2002); [2010] OJ C285E, 53 preamble, Art 1 (26 November 2009) (Eur Parl Resolution on the Elimination of Violence against Women).

[235] 1986 European Parliament Resolution on Violence against Women (n 183).

[236] European Parliament Resolution on the Elimination of Violence against Women, Doc P7_TA(2009)0098, [2010] OJ C285E, 53 (26 November 2009), preamble, para E.

the labour market, and can lead to marginalisation and poverty for women'.[237] Member States must recognise sexual violence and rape against women, including within marriage and intimate informal relationships and/or where committed by male relatives, as a *crime*, and must ensure that such offences result in '*automatic prosecution*'.[238]

The Resolution repeats the language of the 1986 European Parliament's Resolution on Violence Against Women and also urges states to reject any reference to cultural, traditional or religious practices or traditions as a mitigating factor in cases of violence against women.[239] Resolutions by the European Parliament are not legally binding, but the European Parliament's call for the criminalisation of sexual violence in the domestic sphere in several resolutions illustrates the importance given to the need to criminalise sexual violence in intimate relationships.[240]

Furthermore, a 2012 EU directive establishing mandatory minimum standards and safeguards to protect victims of crime *assumes* that IPSV is criminalised in the Member States.[241] Unlike resolutions of the European Parliament, directives are legal acts of the EU imposing obligations on Member States to achieve a specific result through the implementation of domestic legislative procedures.[242] The 2012 EU directive called for effective imposition of criminal sanctions in cases of IPSV, inter alia, that must be implemented by Member States within two years of its enactment, and required that within three years Member States must show the Commission data on how victims have accessed the rights in the directive. The directive furthermore explicitly recognises the particular dynamics of violence in intimate relationships and the need for states to adopt special protection measures:

> *Where violence is committed in a close relationship, it is committed by a person who is a current or former spouse, or partner or other family member of the victim, whether or not the offender shares or has shared the same household with the victim.* Such violence could cover physical, sexual, psychological, or economic violence and could result in physical, mental or emotional harm or economic loss. *Violence in close relationships is a serious and often hidden social problem, which could cause systematic psychological and physical trauma with severe consequences because the offender is a person whom the victim should be able to trust.*

[237] ibid, preamble, para F.

[238] ibid, Art 24 (emphasis added).

[239] ibid.

[240] See Resolution with Recommendations to the Commission on Combating Violence Against Women, pmbl; Eur Parl Doc P7_TA-PROV (2014) 0126, preamble.

[241] Directive 2012/29/EU of the European Parliament and of the Council of 25 October 2012 Establishing Minimum Standards on the Rights, Support and Protection of Victims of Crime, and replacing Framework Decision 2001/220/JHA, [2012] OJ L315, 57.

[242] R Folsom, 'European Union Law Making Machine' in RH Folsom, RB Lake and VP Nanda (eds), *European Union Law after Maastricht: A Practical Guide for Lawyers Outside the Common Market* (The Hague, Kluwer Law International, 1996) 5.

> Victims of violence in close relationships may therefore be in need of special protection measures. Women are affected disproportionately by this type of violence and the situation can be worse if the woman is dependent on the offender economically, socially or as regards her right to residence.[243]

One of the most comprehensive instruments against gender violence, the Council of Europe Convention on Preventing and Combating Violence against Women and Domestic Violence (the Istanbul Convention), which came into effect in August 2014, explicitly obliges its parties to *criminalise* sexual violence when committed against former or current spouses or partners (whether or not they were living in the same residence).[244] The Council of Europe currently includes 47 countries extending all the way to the Russian Federation.[245] The fact that the Istanbul Convention, a binding instrument, was accepted by such a wide swath of countries provides further evidence of the existence of an international consensus that marital rape must be criminalised.

In 2003, the African Union adopted the Protocol on the Rights of Women in Africa, which defines violence against women as including 'all acts perpetrated against women which cause or could cause them physical, *sexual*, psychological, and economic harm, including the threat to take such acts … in *private* or public life'.[246] Sub-regional instruments such as the Southern African Development Community (SADC)'s Declaration on Gender and Development on Prevention and Eradication of Violence against Women and Children specifically mentions marital rape as an expression of violence against women and a 'serious violation of fundamental human rights'.[247]

The multilateral Arab Charter on Human Rights explicitly prohibits all forms of violence or abuse against women.[248] However, marital rape is not explicitly mentioned and none of the 14 ratifying Arab states have criminalised marital rape.[249]

[243] Directive 2012/29/EU of the European Parliament at para 18 (n 241) (emphasis added).

[244] Council of Europe, Convention on Preventing and Combating Violence against Women and Domestic Violence, Art 36, para 36, 11 May 2011, CETS No 210.

[245] *Our Member States*, Council of Europe, www.coe.int/en/web/about-us/our-member-states.

[246] African Commission on Human and Peoples' Rights, Protocol to the African Charter on Human and People's Rights on the Rights of Women in Africa, Art 1(i) (11 July 2003) (emphasis added). As of December 2015, only 3 out of 54 African countries have not signed the Protocol and 38 states, including Kenya, Ghana and Malawi have ratified it. See African Commission on Human and Peoples' Rights, Ratification Table, www.achpr.org/instruments/women-protocol/ratification/.

[247] Heads of States or Government of Southern African Development Community, *Prevention and Eradication of Violence against Women and Children (Addendum to the 1997 Southern African Development Community Declaration on Gender and Development)* (1998) Arts 4, 5(1).

[248] League of Arab States, *Arab Charter on Human Rights*, 22 May 2004, entered into force 15 March 2008. Commission of Human Rights–League of Arab States, *Member States*, www.lasportal.org/ar/humanrights/Committee/Pages/MemberCountries.aspx.

[249] World Bank Group (n 37).

Asia lacks an effective regional human rights system. However, at least 11 Asian countries, including Nepal, Thailand and Indonesia, explicitly criminalise marital rape.[250]

C. Summary of Human Rights Law Requiring the Criminalisation of Marital Rape

As this overview of international human rights law has shown, marital rape exceptions to the criminalisation of sexual assault impinge on international human rights instruments and binding principles, as courts and states across the world have affirmed.[251] Many state constitutions now include similar rights protections that add another layer of obligation on states to ensure women's equality and protect them from violence in all its forms. The due-diligence obligation further expresses the legal requirement that states take action to prevent and remedy sexual violence, including sexual violence in intimate relationships. Criminalising sexual violence against women in intimate relationships is clearly necessary for the protection of women's full and equal human rights.

Most of the world's countries now criminalise sexual assault by spouses, even if imperfectly in terms of implementation, and those countries that do not are outliers. However, only a minority of countries explicitly state in their penal code or statutes that marital rape is not to be distinguished from other forms of rape. The risks of implicit criminalisation are evident in the experiences of the Scandinavian countries and the erstwhile communist bloc. For example, the legislation in all the Scandinavian countries did not explicitly immunise marital rape from prosecution, but until recently, their ambiguous provisions allowed for differences in charges and sentencing, as described in the preceding section on the laws in Denmark and Sweden. These countries have had very low rates of prosecution and even lower rates of conviction even though surveys show that stranger rapes are less common than IPSV.[252] In Poland and Russia, the first two countries to remove the marital rape exemption, marital rape continues to be a serious social problem that is under-reported and unacknowledged by the courts and police.[253] Explicit criminalisation removes ambiguity in the law, sends a strong message of

[250] ibid. See also *Dhungana* (n 176) (Nepal), *Jumawan* (n 139) (Phil).

[251] *Dhungana*, ibid (Nepal); *Jumawan*, ibid (Phil).

[252] K Bennhold, 'In Norway, Gender Equality Does Not Extend to the Bedroom', *New York Times*, 24 October 2011, www.nytimes.com/2011/10/25/world/europe/in-norway-gender-equality-does-not-extend-to-the-bedroom.html; Amnesty International (n 153).

[253] K Aberg et al, 'Domestic Violence in Poland' (Minnesota Advocates for Human Rights, Warsaw Women's Rights Center and New York International Women's Human Rights Clinic, 2002) www.theadvocatesforhumanrights.org/uploads/poland_domestic_violence_2002_10-18-2002_2.PDF, 34–35; C Benninger-Budel and LO'Hanlon, 'Violence against Women in Russia, Report Prepared for the Thirty-First Session of the Committee on Economic, Social and Cultural Rights', *Violence Against Women: 10 Reports/Year 2003* (World Organisation Against Torture (OMCT), 2004).

condemnation, and creates the conditions for social change. This approach is espoused by human rights groups, the Council of Europe and the United Nations. The UN model legislation for violence against women, for example, states:

> The legislation should specifically criminalise sexual assault within a relationship (ie, 'marital rape'), either by:
>
> — providing that sexual assault provisions apply 'irrespective of the nature of the relationship' between the perpetrator and complainant;
> — or stating that 'no marriage or other relationship shall constitute a defence to a charge of sexual assault under the legislation'.[254]

International human rights law and the due-diligence standard clearly require that states no longer exempt married women from legal protections against rape by their spouse, and that marital rape, like rape generally, must be subject to criminal sanctions.

V. Conclusion: Why Criminalising Sexual Violence in Intimate Relationships is Essential for the Protection of Women's Equal Rights

Intimate partner sexual violence is a form of gendered violence which breaches women's fundamental human rights. Criminalisation of IPSV is one use of state power necessary to the protection of women's human rights, including, most importantly, rights to equality, autonomy and bodily integrity.

Engaging criminal law to bolster the protection of human rights and to empower local and international struggles to end gendered violence is not a new strategy. On the contrary, it has been and remains a crucial plank of the struggle to seek state accountability and end impunity for a range of rights violations. Engaging the power of criminal law is only one important, but by no means exclusive, component of feminist strategies to remedy and end gendered violence in women's lives. Furthermore, an insistence on the criminalisation of marital rape can, and necessarily does, coexist with robust critiques of the practices and effects of the criminal justice system and the many deficiencies in criminal law responses.

Many of the criticisms of those feminists who believe that the criminal justice system should play a role in remedying gendered violence miss the fact that feminist work in the area of criminalisation has largely been cognisant of the perils of engaging this very system. Indeed, alongside calls for criminalisation of gendered violence, feminist scholars and activists have worked vigorously for criminal law

[254] United Nations Division for the Advancement of Women, *Handbook for Legislation on Violence against Women* (New York, United Nations, 2010) 26.

reform to improve criminal law responses and this remains a fundamental component of criminalisation strategies.[255]

Law and human rights movements such as feminism exist in dynamic interplay. The World Bank Report of 2016 identifies the link between law reform and the social movements seeking equality and human rights. The Report observes that: '[O]ver the past 25 years, the number of economies introducing laws addressing domestic violence has risen precipitously from close to zero, to 118. This increase has been driven by international and regional human rights conventions and campaigns.'[256] This finding speaks to the importance of engaging the language and protections offered by human rights law, domestically and internationally. There has been a sea change in reconfiguring social relationships of gender, at both the structural and the micro levels, in the direction of more full and equal protection of women's human rights.

Criminalisation of marital rape articulates, at the social level and in the public sphere, the message that sexual violence in the domestic and private sphere is not to be tolerated. Criminalising spousal sexual assault repudiates the view that a woman becomes a man's property upon marriage, and fundamentally challenges traditional and patriarchal social norms that confer upon men unlimited rights of sexual access to the women who are their spouses. Eradicating legal immunity for men who sexually violate their wives or other intimates is predicated on principles of equality and signals a significant move towards establishing new social norms of gender equality, consent, autonomy and sexual personhood for women. This is one crucial element of the broader structural social change sought by those concerned with human rights and equality for women.

The United Nations, the World Health Organization and the World Bank describe gender-based violence, including that in marriage, as a global pandemic. While a majority of the world's countries recognise, in theory at least, that gendered violence in the form of marital rape requires criminal legal remedies, too many countries fail to protect married women, and fail to observe their due-diligence obligations by persisting in inadequately criminalising, or not criminalising at all, this form of violence against women. These are legal gaps that must be closed as a crucial step towards protecting all women from gendered violence.

[255] See eg United Nations Office on Drugs and Crime, *Strengthening Crime Prevention and Criminal Justice Responses to Violence against Women*, (New York, United Nations, 2014); ES Buzawa, CG Buzawa and ED Stark, *Responding to Domestic Violence: The Integration of Criminal Justice and Human Services* (Thousand Oaks, CA, Sage, 2015); KA Lonsway, and J Archambault, 'The "Justice Gap" for Sexual Assault Cases Future Directions for Research and Reform' (2012) 18 *Violence Against Women* 145; L Kelly, *Promising Practices Addressing Sexual Violence—Expert Report* (New York, UN Division for the Advancement of Women, 2005) www.un.org/womenwatch/daw/egm/vaw-gp-2005/docs/experts/kelly.sexualviolence.pdf.

[256] World Bank Group (n 62) 22.

4

Pluralistic Legal Systems and Marital Rape: Cross-National Considerations

VASANTHI VENKATESH

I. Introduction

There are several kinds of legal frameworks arising from the practices of specific communities that exist pluralistically with state-centric civil or common law legal systems. In many African countries, for example, 'customary' legal systems—legal frameworks stemming from the practices of specific tribes—have been officially recognised by the state as having jurisdictional authority over certain areas of law. In many countries, religious codes provide the basis for family laws and sometimes even criminal laws—not only for the adherents of that religion but also, sometimes, for everyone in the jurisdiction. In settler countries such as Canada Indigenous law has almost no official recognition as a sovereign source of law by the Canadian state. But despite decades of oppression, Indigenous legal knowledge constitutes an essential source of norm making and a source of law for Indigenous peoples and, in many territories such as Nisga'a and Gikstan lands in Canada, for everybody who resides in the Indigenous territory.[1] In some states in the United States, jurisdiction in specific areas of law is ceded to native tribal authorities.[2] Generally, in all contexts, even when a self-proclaimed secular state has assumed complete and total jurisdiction over all legal matters, custom and cultural practices can play an important role in the interpretation of law, especially as it applies to women.

Group-based cultural and traditional institutions, especially legal systems based on non-Western philosophies, have often been a source of particular controversy in the women's rights arena. Can women's substantive equality rights be protected

[1] Douglas Sanders, 'We Intend to Live Here Forever: A Primer on the Nisga'a Treaty' (1999) 33 *University of British Columbia Law Review* 103, 117; Patricia Dawn Mills, *For Future Generations: Reconciling Gitxsan and Canadian Law* (Saskatoon, SK, Purich, 2008).

[2] Sarah Deer, 'Toward an Indigenous Jurisprudence of Rape'(2004) 14 *Kansas Journal of Law & Public Policy* 127–28; DE Wilkins and K Tsianina Lomawaima, *Uneven Ground: American Indian Sovereignty and Federal Law* (University of Oklahoma Press 2001); RN Clinton, 'Criminal Jurisdiction over Indian Lands: A Journey through a Jurisdictional Maze' (1976) 18 *Arizona Law Review* 503.

and enhanced *within* other legal systems? Is the violation of women's rights inherent in legal systems such as African customary law systems? The demand for criminalising marital rape in particular raises these concerns as criminalising marital rape demands intervention into the family and marriage, the basic social institutions around which community systems are often structured.

On the other hand, advocates for women's rights face critical challenges when using international law or frameworks rooted in Western liberalism to argue for the criminalisation of marital rape. These challenges are especially significant in relation to communities with different ideas of ethical philosophies of living and social well-being, who have experienced and continue to experience geopolitical and historical inequities and oppression. The universalist human rights frameworks are often resisted as being essentialist, illegitimate and foreign, and are challenged on the grounds that they impose imperialistic domination and ignore the particular social realities of women in these communities. Moreover, the general state system in these nations itself often presents an obstacle to challenging patriarchal values that have been ossified into the system.

This chapter focuses on political issues that arise when claims for gender justice, such as the call for criminalising marital rape, are made in societies or states with pluralistic legal systems, especially with customary and Indigenous law systems. To this end, the chapter offers three arguments. First, any inquiry into legal pluralistic systems and gender justice must address the specific colonial and imperialistic contexts in which Indigenous and subaltern groups have functioned, and must take into account the particular power structures that continue to subjugate these groups. Calls for legal reform and the criminalisation of marital rape have to pay particular attention to the contextual factors in each country, including how proposed law reforms will interact with the political claims for self-determination and alternative legal frameworks. The chapter provides snapshots from a few African countries on the development of customary legal systems. These examples show how the historical background of European colonialism and specific nationalistic developments are extremely important for understanding challenges to combating domestic sexual assault in these contexts.

Second, the arguments for and against the criminalisation of marital rape reflect the broader dynamic in the international human rights arena, often described as a conflict between women's rights and rights to cultural self-determination. These are exemplified by the juxtaposition of the provisions demanding cultural change to protect women's rights in the Convention against Elimination of Discrimination against Women (CEDAW),[3] with the reservations by states to CEDAW on the basis of 'cultural defence'. I argue that the purported 'conflict' in the global human rights regime between women's rights and group-based cultural rights or Indigenous or 'customary' laws is an inadequate and erroneous framing which does not illuminate the political and intersectional nature of either type

[3] Convention on the Elimination of All Forms of Discrimination against Women (CEDAW) (New York, 18 December 1979) 1249 UNTS 13, 19 ILM 33 (1980), entered into force 3 September 1981.

of claim. The international human rights agenda to combat gender violence and criminalise marital rape can and should have a synergistic relationship with local activism and respect for cultural autonomy. Group identities and ideologies are constantly evolving and responding to social, economic and political changes at local, regional and global levels. As new sociopolitical spaces are being created, no longer do the issues of women's liberty and equality present a simplistic binary choice between Western liberalism and cultural parochialism.

Lastly, in this chapter I argue that particularised claims to culture to defend marital rape cannot be defended. Law reform to criminalise marital rape is an important step to protect *all* women. Critical race feminists have pointed out that women's experiences of subordination and violence cannot be monolithically or universally described, nor can they be homogenised into those of women from Western or racially or economically privileged groups.[4] But neither can the experiences of women be homogenised *within* a social category, such as race, tribe or class, by resorting to essentialist descriptions to ascribe cultural and social attributes to the entire social category.[5] Unlike practices that are *unique* to particular groups and cultures and that have differing significance for different communities, marital rape was or continues to be condoned by diverse and most states and societies across the globe.[6] In many cases, the state uses 'culture' and tradition as a convenient fig-leaf to cover its commitment to retaining patriarchy and protecting special and dominant political interests.

The cultural and gender identities of women in many contexts are so intertwined that one cannot create neat boundaries without problematic trade-offs. Addressing rights issues through discrete dichotomies such as women's rights versus group rights ignores the multiplicity and overlap of these 'dichotomies' and the broader social justice context. A context-driven approach to the human rights of women, which avoids generalisations and the perpetuation of other inequalities, can protect women from intimate partner sexual violence (IPSV) without women having to relinquish communal identities and rights.

II. Situating 'Customary Law' within the Colonial Context

Legal pluralism exists in various forms in virtually all societies. In many countries, a positivistic general legal system based on common or civil law, where laws

[4] Kimberle Crenshaw, 'Mapping the Margins: Intersectionality, Identity Politics, and Violence against Women of Color' (1990) 43 *Stanford Law Review* 1241.

[5] Nira Yuval-Davis, 'Intersectionality and Feminist Politics' (2006) 13 *European Journal of Women's Studies* 193.

[6] V Venkatesh and M Randall, 'Normative and International Human Rights Law Imperatives for Criminalizing Intimate Partner Sexual Violence: The Marital Rape Impunity in Comparative and Historical Perspective', chapter 3 in this volume.

are promulgated as part of state governance, coexists with religious systems and other legal systems that apply to specific communities, such as tribal, Indigenous and cultural minority groups. According to the World Legal Systems Research Group at the University of Ottawa, about 56.6 per cent of the world population is governed by either customary law or customary law mixed with civil or common law, where 'customary law' includes Aboriginal/Indigenous law and other religious laws but does not include Islamic law.[7] Including Islamic law, the number rises to around 67–69 per cent.[8] Such pluralistic legal systems are often a product of colonial histories and state modernisation projects. In countries in Africa the tribal or community-based systems are officially called 'customary legal systems' and the law that emerges from communities is termed 'customary law'.

However, in other contexts, the term 'customary law' is a controversial one, as it assumes a teleological distinction between laws of certain 'cultures' versus laws emerging from European governing orders.[9] As Eberts and Monture have pointed out in the Canadian context, the very nature of an inquiry into how 'customary' legal systems can or cannot protect women's rights 'automatically situates Indigenous knowledges and practices as subjugated to Canadian law'.[10] Classifications of legal systems, however, continue to subsume Indigenous and Aboriginal legal systems and any legal system not based on civil, common or Islamic law into a broad category of 'customary law'.[11]

In terms of gender justice, the presumption of the progressive and civilisational superiority of Eurocentric and state-centred laws is especially ironic, in light of the fact that marital rape was explicitly condoned in Anglo-European legal systems until very recently.[12] Moreover, the Anglo-European legal systems legitimated marital rape using arbitrary, extra-legal justifications that sought to uphold patriarchal, social and religious traditions in European societies, a fact that belies any claims to European societies being based on progressive, rational, Enlightenment-based laws.

Every colonial experience has differed remarkably, even within the same country/state, due to the different motivations of specific colonial actors and the unique sociopolitical and economic contexts in each place. Nonetheless, it is safe to say that colonisation resulted in violent ruptures of the pre-existing legal

[7] World Legal Systems Research Group, 'Customary Law Systems and Mixed Systems with a Customary Law Tradition' (University of Ottawa-JuriGlobe) www.juriglobe.ca/eng/sys-juri/class-poli/droit-coutumier.php.

[8] World Legal Systems Research Group, 'Muslim Law Systems and Mixed Systems with a Muslim Law Tradition' (University of Ottawa-JuriGlobe) www.juriglobe.ca/eng/sys-juri/class-poli/droit-musulman.php.

[9] See M Eberts and PA Monture, 'Is "Customary Law" a Solution or a Continuing Problem of Colonial Oppression of Aboriginal Women in Canada?' (Equality Effect—formerly African Canadian Women's Human Rights Project (ACWHRP), 2010).

[10] ibid, 2.

[11] See eg World Legal Systems Research Group, 'Introductory Remarks' (University of Ottawa-JuriGlobe) www.juriglobe.ca/eng/sys-juri/intro.php.

[12] See Venkatesh and Randall (n 6).

and social fabrics, and that these ruptures have implications for gender justice in three broad ways.

First, European colonialisation was marked by the dissemination of Anglo-European cultural norms of patriarchy, including the marital rape exception, into the laws of the various colonies, which continues to persist in the postcolonial states, even as legal reforms have been made in the erstwhile colonising states. Second, colonialism also caused irrevocable changes to the local legal systems (or 'customary' systems) as well as to the socioeconomic and political structures. As a result, customary law today is not even the 'debris' of precolonial tribal law.[13] Instead, it is essentially the constructed after-effect of the interplay between official state law and what has remained of customary law.[14] The colonial changes reified patriarchy within the legal system and changed family, kinship and community relations in a manner that increased women's economic vulnerability, commodified the personhood of the 'wife', diminished any community mechanisms that empower women, and increased the vulnerability of women to household violence, including sexual violence. Third, colonialism was marked by the state's extreme violence towards colonised women along with the violent rupture of the political equilibrium between various communities.[15] In settler countries, such as Canada, the state continues to inflict violence and ruptures on Indigenous communities. This renders the settler state an inadequate and illegitimate recourse as a forum for Indigenous women to assert their rights to be free from violence inflicted from members within their household and communities and also by those outside their communities.[16]

In postcolonial countries, to this day, changes to power structures continue to shape the debates around any women's rights law reform, including combating marital rape, as can be seen in the public debates in Kenya, India and other countries.[17] Historical and continued oppressions have engendered a politics where women's rights, especially those protecting women from violence, are used as weapons in a discourse that ignores intersectionalities and political contexts. The following section illustrates these dynamics by describing the historical trajectory seen in the example of a few African countries.

[13] JB Ojwang, 'The Meaning, Content and Significance of Tribal Law in an Emergent Nation: The Kenya Case' in GR Woodman and A Olusegun Obilade (eds), *African law and Legal Theory* (New York, New York University Press, 1995) 49.

[14] F Banda, *Women, Law and Human Rights: An African Perspective* (Oxford, Hart Publishing, 2005) 49; W Kamau, 'Customary Law and Women's Rights in Kenya' (Toronto, Equality Effect, 2011).

[15] A Smith, *Conquest: Sexual Violence and American Indian Genocide* (Brooklyn, South End Press, 2005).

[16] A Davis, 'The Color of Violence against Women', *Colorlines*, 10 October 2000, www.colorlines.com/articles/color-violence-against-women; Roe Bubar and Pamela Jumper Thurman, 'Violence against Native Women' (2004) 31 *Social Justice* 70.

[17] W Kamau, P Nyaundi and Serwanga, 'The Legal Impunity for Marital Rape in Kenya: A Women's Equality Issue' (Toronto, Equality Effect, 2013) theequalityeffect.org/wp-content/uploads/2013/04/Marital-Rape-Paper-Winnie-Kamau-Final-edited-July-18.pdf, 9–10; S Mandal, 'The Impossibility of Marital Rape' (2014) 29 *Australian Feminist Studies* 255, 259–63.

A. Colonisation and its Destructions

In precolonial times, before nation-state governance, authority was distributed among various tribes or kingdoms, which had territorial and/or personal jurisdiction over their members. Community leaders administered the laws through various processes of deliberation.[18] The most basic disputes related to property, wrongdoings (torts) and the family, and these were settled in accordance with the norms or laws of that particular community.[19] While authority rested on a male head in the majority of societal organisations, a number of matrilineal systems and female tribal leadership structures existed globally,[20] some notable examples being the Ashanti in West Africa and Iroquois in North America, which are also associated with being 'low-rape cultures'.[21]

In the process of colonisation, colonial states were gradually carved out and the colonising power assumed sovereignty and appropriated the ultimate authority to make and enforce laws. Indigenous governance structures were either replaced or subsumed in various ways by the colonial governments.[22] In Malawi, colonial courts applied English common law as well as customary and religious laws for specific tribes and religions.[23] Native courts were later established where chiefs and headmen were given judicial power to adjudicate civil disputes. Kenya was also subject to a racially stratified system where native tribunals applied native law *and* custom to Africans while English courts applied English law to non-Africans.[24] Criminal law, contract and torts were governed by English common law and statute law.

In the Gold Coast countries, such as Ghana, the colonised countries also followed a dual-court system along with appellate review of native court decisions.[25] The Supreme Court in Ghana, administered by the British, had the legal authority to veto any law by the native courts that was found to be 'repugnant to natural justice, equity, and good conscience' or to any other enacted statute, where repugnance depended on the subjective views of the colonial administrators.[26] Rules of customary law were treated as questions of fact, not law, and could be subject to relitigation in each case.

[18] GR Woodman, 'Introduction' in Woodman and Olusegun Obilade (n 13) xvi–xvii.

[19] B Sam, 'The Relationship between Customary Law and Women's Rights in Ghana' (Toronto, Equality Effect, 2011) 5.

[20] PE Peters, 'Introduction (Special Issue on Matriliny)' (1997) 17 *Critique of Anthropology* 125; M-B Watson-Franke, 'A World in Which Women Move Freely without Fear of Men: An Anthropological Perspective on Rape' (2002) 25 *Women's Studies International Forum* 599.

[21] Watson-Franke (n 20).

[22] See M Mamdani, *Citizen and Subject: Contemporary Africa and the Legacy of Late Colonialism* (Princeton, Princeton University Press, 1996) 109–28; M Chanock, *Law, Custom, and Social Order: The Colonial Experience in Malawi and Zambia* (Cambridge, Cambridge University Press, 1985).

[23] N Kanyongolo and N Nweso, 'Customary Law and Women's Rights: A Case of Malawi' (Toronto, Equality Effect, 2011) 8.

[24] Kamau (n 14) 7.

[25] JA Davies and D Dagbanja, 'The Role and Future of Customary Tort Law in Ghana: A Cross-Cultural Perspective' (2009) 26 *Arizona Journal of International and Comparative Law* 303, 305.

[26] ibid, 306.

In general, the colonial governments had a patronising and condescending attitude towards native norms and used concepts such as 'rule of law' to construct a mythical discourse representing local amoral primitives who were in need of rescue by the morally and culturally superior, 'civilised' and 'modern' West. As Sally Merry puts it: '[T]he rule of law was viewed as a "gift" to people who were typically envisioned by nineteenth-century European imperialists in the eloquent metaphors of The Heart of Darkness: chaotic and bestial, wholly unregulated, and without morals or rules.'[27] This discourse persisted through most of the twentieth century. The colonial authorities imposed regulations arbitrarily and capriciously, to reflect their puritanical, conservative, patriarchal values. Numerous religious and ritual practices around drinking, festivals, sexuality, attire, and forms of habitation and family, as well as forms of resistance within the communities, were criminalised.[28] Civilising intrusions, based on European moral values, sought to sculpt the 'unrestrained, dangerous Indigenous subject'. In Zanzibar, for example, Africans were even arrested for 'idleness' and dancing, and were characterised as 'childish savages' described as dissipating their 'small stock of energy in a demoralizing dance'.[29]

If a particular Indigenous norm was deemed 'repugnant' to a European or Christian value-system (which was by no means a gender-egalitarian system), the custom was usually arbitrarily banned or modified. These often prejudiced and short-sighted top-down colonial acts resulted in a breakdown of community institutions and in the dismantling of mechanisms that protected the rights of women while supporting deep-rooted patriarchal structures in the community and colonial state. In Kenya, the levirate system, which gave a widow the opportunity to marry her deceased husband's brother, often in polygamy, was condemned as an anti-Christian act and was coercively curtailed.[30] Levirate (which was practised by many other cultures including Judaic and Asian cultures) is rooted in patriarchal notions where marital bonds determine financial and physical security and under this system women had no safe, independent existence outside marriage.[31]

[27] As quoted in S Engle Merry, 'Colonial and Postcolonial Law' in A Sarat (ed), *The Blackwell Companion to Law and Society* (Hoboken, NJ, Blackwell, 2004) 571.

[28] J Comaroff and JL Comaroff, *Of Revelation and Revolution* (Chicago, University of Chicago Press, 1991); F Cooper, *From Slaves to Squatters: Plantation Labor and Agriculture in Zanzibar and Coastal Kenya, 1890–1925* (New Haven, CT, Yale University Press, 1980); F Cooper and AL Stoler (eds), *Tensions of Empire: Colonial Cultures in a Bourgeois World* (Oakland, University of California Press, 1997); P Fitzpatrick, *The Mythology of Modern Law* (London, Routledge, 1992); Merry, 'Colonial and Postcolonial Law' (n 27); AL Stoler, 'Making Empire Respectable: The Politics of Race and Sexual Morality in 20th-Century Colonial Cultures' (1989) 16 *American Ethnologist* 634; AL Stoler, *Race and the Education of Desire: Foucault's History of Sexuality and the Colonial Order of Things* (Durham, NC, Duke University Press 1995).

[29] Cooper (n 28) 114.

[30] Kamau (n 14) 9.

[31] Banda (n 14) 119; SO Olanisebe and OA Oladosu, 'Levirate Marriage amongst the Hebrews and Widow's Inheritance amongst the Yoruba: A Comparative Investigation' (2014) 35 *Verbum et Ecclesia* 1; E Westreich, 'Levirate Marriage in the State of Israel: Ethnic Encounter and the Challenge of a Jewish State' (2004) 37 *Israel Law Review* 426, 428–29.

Furthermore, it also made widows vulnerable to coercive marriages. It was, however, also a means for the widow to get access to her deceased husband's property and to ensure the inheritance claims of her children.[32] If a woman did not accept levirate, she could return to her family of origin and cultivate her father's land for her own nutrition, but she would only have usufruct rights to her father's land and was often left destitute.[33] The levirate system was curtailed and banned; however, there were no changes made to succession laws until much later.

The colonial system also further entrenched and legitimated existing patriarchies. In South Africa, the Boer and British authorities condemned bride-price as 'purchase in women' but legislated customary laws by constituting women as 'perpetual minors' under the patriarchal authority of the chiefs.[34] In another example, the land tenure system was changed to make the male household head the title deed-holder. This resulted in the dispossession of widows from their land and increased their vulnerability to economic, social and cultural marginalisation.[35] Martin Chanock captures the ineffectiveness of gender 'reforms' by the colonial state, when he states:

> The introduction of Western legal modes in the form of the colonial legal order had the effect that women were not able to take advantage of a period of redefinition of relationships because it was male claims, which were legitimated as 'customary law'. Because recognition as custom was virtually the only way in which Africans could impose their social aims upon the colonial order, women's claims were almost by definition non-traditional, and could not be made effective.[36]

In other instances, criminal reforms meant to 'save' the colonised women were used by colonial states to persecute Indigenous and colonised groups. For example, in Canada, polygamy was criminalised by the settler state, and was used as a basis for prosecuting Indigenous families.[37] On the other hand, the Canadian state did not recognise divorce under customary law, which curtailed the freedom to marry among women and led to many women losing their tribal status and rights, as subsequent remarriages were not recognised.[38]

[32] Kamau (n 14) 9; R Smith Oboler, 'Nandi Widows' in B Potash (ed), *Widows in African Societies: Choices and Constraints* (Redwood City, CA, Stanford University Press 1986) 77–83.

[33] Kamau (n 14) 9, 33.

[34] Mamdani (n 22) 117.

[35] MJ Hay, 'Women as Owners, Occupants, and Managers of Property in Colonial Western Kenya' in MJ Hay and M Wright (eds), *African Women and the Law: Historical Perspectives* (Boston University, African Studies Center, 1982) 120; F Akiiki Asiimwe and O Crankshaw, 'The Impact of Customary Laws on Inheritance: A Case Study of Widows in Urban Uganda' (2011) 3 *Journal of Law and Conflict Resolution* 7, 8; A Oba, 'The Future of Customary Law in Africa' in J Fenrich, P Galizzi and TE Higgins (eds), *The Future of African Customary Law* (Cambridge, Cambridge University Press, 2011) 71.

[36] M Chanock, 'Making Customary Law: Men, Women, and Courts in Colonial Northern Rhodesia' in MJ Hay and M Wright (eds), *African Women and the Law: Historical Perspectives* (Boston University, African Studies Center, 1982) 66.

[37] S Carter, *The Importance of Being Monogamous: Marriage and Nation Building in Western Canada to 1915* (Edmonton, University of Alberta Press, 2008) www.deslibris.ca/ID/423013, 10–11, 134–43; Eberts and Monture (n 9) 43.

[38] Carter (n 37) 167–69; Eberts and Monture (n 9) 43.

Customary law mechanisms that upheld social and communal harmony were subject to various attempts at 'civilising' by the European powers, through the imposition of European cultural standards. It is therefore not surprising that impunity for marital rape became codified and entrenched in the colonial law. This occurred even in regions with matrilineal systems and traditional beliefs that had empowered women, and where community dynamics could offer women protection from domestic and sexual violence.

Family and kinship structures were deeply affected by socioeconomic disruptions during the colonial (and postcolonial) period that changed the foundations of the customary systems and made women more disempowered.[39] For example, in many countries, property was earlier held communally or through complex kinship structures.[40] With the advent of market systems and colonial property law, communities were compelled to adopt defined ownership structures with individual power to alienate. New kinds of capitalism-based markets and monetary systems and the ensuing increased rural labour migration led to a severing of the kinship system, the nucleation of families and individual male ownership of property; women, especially in rural households, struggled financially to maintain themselves and their families, even as they became primary care-takers of the rural land (that was owned exclusively by their husbands).[41] *Lobola* or bridewealth marriage became monetised where men 'paid' for the reproductive and domestic labour of their wives with cash (replacing communal cattle), leading to further commodification of women as their husband's property.[42] These changes made women more vulnerable to poverty and domestic violence and facilitated conditions for a social system that condoned marital rape.

It should also be noted that while colonial court proceedings often reinforced patriarchal control and tribal power structures, in some instances, the colonial laws provided means of resistance to women to challenge oppressive, misogynistic conditions and abusive husbands. Studies show how several women used colonial divorce courts to obtain divorces that would not have been sanctioned by their own traditional laws.[43] Victims of domestic violence also approached colonial

[39] Mamdani (n 22) 120, 119–22, 144–47; M Chanock, 'Neither Customary nor Legal: African Customary Law in an Era of Family Law Reform' (1989) 3 *International Journal of Law and the Family* 72, 83–85; Hay (n 35).

[40] Mamdani (n 22) 66, 139–44.

[41] ibid, 66, 119–21, 139–44; Hay (n 35) 123.

[42] Kamau (n 14) 9.

[43] The colonial courts in some places, at least initially, granted divorces. But that soon changed in places like French Soudan where 'women seeking divorce were seen as a threat to social stability': Marie Rodet, 'The Colonial Invention of Female Desertion as a Customary Criminal Offense, French Soudan, 1900–1949' in E Burrill, RL Roberts and E Thornberry (eds), *Domestic Violence and the Law in Colonial and Postcolonial Africa* (Athens, Ohio University Press, 2010) 78–82. See also B Ibhawoh, *Imperialism and Human Rights: Colonial Discourses of Rights and Liberties in African History* (Albany, State University of New York Press, 2007) 119–120. In India, many Hindu women were prevented from divorcing but women often converted to other religions to use the colonial courts to divorce under grounds of cruelty (or desertion or adultery): M Sharafi, 'The Marital Patchwork of Colonial South Asia: Forum Shopping from Britain to Baroda' (2010) 28 *Law and History Review* 979.

courts for protection, as they constituted new alternative venues to challenge family violence. However, the women faced several challenges as colonial, racialised subjects and as women. In India, for example, rape victims were subject to colonial ideas about Indian culture, prejudices about the unreliability of native witnesses and presumptions of false charges by Indian women.[44] The sexual history of the victim and physical evidence of resistance, which had reduced in importance in Britain, remained crucial in trials in India. As Elizabeth Kolsky puts it: 'Indian rape victims were doubly suspect suspects.'[45] In other instances, laws were soon changed in many colonial and postcolonial states to prevent women from approaching the court.[46]

In many cases, colonialism relied on violence as an important tool to ensure compliance and subordination, violence that included rampant sexual violence against and exploitation of women.[47] In settler colonial states, research shows how continued colonisations created conditions that have resulted in the high rates of intimate partner rape and other violence experienced by Indigenous women within their households.[48] The conditions include continued social and economic injustice, cultural oppression, political and legal alienation, colonial destruction of traditional kinship patterns and entrenchment of colonial patriarchy, the epistemic violence that has caused the erasure of Indigenous knowledge forms, and state-sanctioned violence experienced by Indigenous populations.[49]

Furthermore, the colonial political economy also changed the power structures in African countries; customary arbitration became less democratic and chiefs and colonial administrators became more autocratic.[50] Local patriarchal privileges and powers were filtered through colonial patriarchal standards and ossified into relatively immutable state laws and regulation. The colonial courts were also unable to reconcile the diversity of groups and customary law systems that existed within one country.[51] As a result, the customs of the numerically or politically

[44] E Kolsky, '"The Body Evidencing the Crime": Rape on Trial in Colonial India, 1860–1947' (2010) 22 *Gender & History* 109.

[45] ibid, 111.

[46] E Burrill, RL Roberts and E Thornberry, 'Domestic Violence and the Law in Africa' in Burrill et al (n 43) 2–3. See also Ibhawoh (n 43) 124–125.

[47] AI Castañeda, 'Sexual Violence in the Politics and Policies of Conquest: Amerindian Women and the Spanish Conquest of Alta California' in A de la Torre and B M Pesquera (eds), *Building With Our Hands: New Directions in Chicana Studies* (Oakland, University of California Press, 1993).

[48] S Maddison and E Partridge, 'Agonism and Intersectionality: Indigenous Women, Violence and Feminist Collective Identity' (2014) 37 *Intersectionality and Social Change*, www.emeraldinsight.com/doi/full/10.1108/S0163-786X20140000037000; P Moffitt et al, 'Intimate Partner Violence in the Canadian Territorial North: Perspectives from a Literature Review and a Media Watch' (2013) 72 *International Journal of Circumpolar Health* www.circumpolarhealthjournal.net/index.php/ijch/article/view/21209; Bubar and Thurman (n 16); Deer (n 2).

[49] Bubar and Thurman (n 16); M-E Kelm, *Colonizing Bodies: Aboriginal Health and Healing in British Columbia, 1900–1950* (Vancouver, UBC Press, 1998) public.eblib.com/choice/publicfullrecord.aspx?p=3412353; J-A Fiske, 'Political Status of Native Indian Women: Contradictory Implications of Canadian State Policy' (1995) 19 *American Indian Culture and Research Journal* 1.

[50] Mamdani (n 22) 43, 47, 56–57, 119.

[51] Sam (n 19) 6.

dominant ethnic groups ended up being imposed on others.[52] This further exacerbated intercommunal conflicts and the general confusion about the content and scope of customary law. These factors directly influenced how the postcolonial states treated women's rights and customary legal systems after independence.

B. The Postcolonial Modernisation Period and the Entrenchment of Patriarchy

In the newly independent countries, colonial patriarchal practices and laws continued to be entrenched while, simultaneously, customary legal systems became subject to state-induced reconstructions. As many commentators have observed, the customary law as applied by the state is just an artificially invented institution, which does not reflect the actual, diverse legal culture that exists in communities.[53] Also, protests against reforms for gender equality and combating marital rape and domestic violence were often politicised proclamations by government and groups, clothed as claims for cultural sovereignty.

After independence in many of the previously colonised nations in Africa, native courts were not seen positively by the new ruling elites. In Malawi and in South Africa, for example, native courts were seen as instruments through which colonialism and apartheid were legally imposed.[54] In the early stages of independence and state building in several African countries, tradition was seen as inimical to the development and the creation of a modern state.[55] However, women's rights were not necessarily prioritised during this phase, with many constitutions failing to include gender among the enumerated grounds for non-discrimination.[56]

At the same time, legal pluralism and cultural self-determination also gained currency as elements of an anti-apartheid, anti-Eurocentric, Indigenous legal philosophy. The two main objectives of the nation-state, modernisation *and* indigeneity (an anti-colonial political objective), were expectedly at odds with each other in several political instances. For example, repugnancy clauses from the colonial era continue to be maintained[57] but cultural rights, including rights to a traditional or tribal culture, became instituted in many of the constitutions.[58]

[52] Banda (n 14) 22.

[53] Chanock (n 22); Chanock (n 39); Mamdani (n 22) 111–22; Woodman (n 18); Ojwang (n 13).

[54] TW Bennett, 'Re-introducing African Customary Law to the South African Legal System' (2009) 57 *American Journal of Comparative Law* 1. See also Woodman (n 18).

[55] Woodman (n 18) xxiv.

[56] Banda (n 14) 33.

[57] For example, the Kenyan 1967 Judicature Act asserts that customary law should be applied in certain civil cases but only so long as it is 'not repugnant to justice and morality', Judicature Act (1967) Cap 8 (Kenya). See also G Otieno Ochich, 'The Withering Province of Customary Law in Kenya' in Fenrich et al (n 35) 116–18; L Juma, 'Putting Old Wine in New Wine Skins: The Customary Code of Lerotholi and Justice Administration in Lesotho' in Fenrich et al (n 35) 148.

[58] For example, Art 26 of the Ghanaian constitution provides for cultural rights. Art 39(1) encourages 'the integration of appropriate customary values into the fabric of national life through formal and informal education and the conscious introduction of cultural dimensions to relevant aspects of

In the fray, it was not surprising that gender equality was an afterthought that was sacrificed by the modernising state in a superficial show of support for indigeneity and nationalism. Family violence was not an issue requiring attention for many countries.

There is great variance in how customary or traditional legal systems are incorporated in the national legal systems even within Africa, which is relevant for understanding how marital rape and gender inequality reforms can be initiated in environments of legal pluralism. In terms of adjudication, some countries, such as Kenya and South Africa, have separate adjudicatory bodies such as tribal councils (South Africa) or Islamic *qadi* courts (Kenya) that exert jurisdiction over their specific communities, at least in family or property matters and sometimes even in criminal and other civil claims.[59] The appellate courts of the state legal system review the decisions of the traditional courts on appeal. However, Ghana, Kenya and Malawi have disbanded traditional customary law courts, although they recognise traditional justice systems for dispute resolution.

The jurisdiction of the traditional courts and purview of judicial review, as expected, varies between jurisdictions. In South Africa, for example, traditional courts have extensive jurisdiction, extending to even criminal matters (except for certain offences and the punishments these courts can deliver are limited).[60] The traditional courts are recognised in policy and law; they have their own resources and built-in legal mechanisms. In Ghana, in contrast, the courts of the state legal system themselves apply customary laws in most areas of law although the traditional form of arbitration is recognised by courts in certain matters.[61] The state courts are obliged to apply customary law in the state system and they rely on the chiefs and their councils for their expert opinions on customary law interpretation. The Kenyan Judicature Act specifies that the High Court and all subordinate courts are to be 'guided' by African customary law in civil cases where a customary law affects one or more of the parties.[62] Such civil cases include matters dealing with customary land tenure; intestate succession and estate management; marriage and divorce; matters affecting the status of women, widows and children, such as guardianship, custody, adoption and legitimacy; and intriguingly, matters dealing with 'seduction or pregnancy of an unmarried woman or girl' and 'enticement of or adultery with a married woman'.[63]

national planning'. Art 39 also requires the government to 'ensure that appropriate customary and cultural values are adapted and developed as an integral part of the growing needs of the society as a whole' and to 'foster the development of Ghanaian languages and pride in Ghanaian culture'. Constitution of the Republic of Ghana 1992, Arts 26, 39.

[59] Ochich (n 57).

[60] D Sqhelo Koyana, 'Traditional Courts in South Africa in the Twenty-First Century' in Fenrich et al (n 35) 229–30.

[61] B Akamba and I Kwadwo Tufuor, 'The Future of Customary Law in Ghana' in Fenrich et al (n 35); Sam (n 19).

[62] Judicature Act (1967) Cap 8 (Kenya).

[63] Ochich (n 57) 109.

Across the different kinds of legal pluralistic systems in Africa, there are certain common historical trajectories that have led to the strengthening of gendered policies and practices, which pose barriers for groups fighting for gender equality and against gender violence in these countries. The governments' treatment of customary legal systems is marked by arbitrary interference and reformulations and is prejudicial against women's interests.

In Kenya, for example, native courts were dismantled in 1967 soon after independence because the Indigenous justice systems were deemed inimical to socioeconomic development by the ruling elites. Instead, a single, unitary legal system was deemed the appropriate system for the incipient nation-state.[64] Nonetheless, the replacement of traditional legal systems did not take place as envisioned. For example, the Kenyan government was unable to institute a unitary, uniform marriage and divorce code for all Kenyans.[65] In matters of inheritance, the Kenyan state was largely successful in creating a uniform Succession Act with only a few exceptions for particular communities. However, the new law also extinguished customary community rights to land tenure and created an individualised land ownership system.[66] The Kenyan government thus continued to follow colonial-era policies that had serious and negative implications for women's rights. Land title, which had earlier belonged to the family or to the entire community, including the women, continued to be conferred onto the male head of the household. As the masculine individualisation of property rights continued, so did the commodification of bride-price and dowry and the subjection of women to violence and objectification.[67] The post-independence state not only replicated colonial practices but also adopted most of the colonial laws, including criminal laws around gender and sexuality, such as the marital rape immunity for husbands.

Kenya restricts the influence of customary law by codifying and limiting its jurisdiction. In terms of constitutional recognition of customary law, the Kenyan Constitution subsumes customary systems into a more general right to 'culture' and mandates customary law to be subordinate to the Constitution.[68] The Kenyan

[64] Kamau (n 14) 7.

[65] ibid, 7–8.

[66] ibid.

[67] In many other countries, land reform and changes to succession law, even where well intentioned, worked to the detriment of women as they lost customary rights without gaining any new protections. For example, the Ghanaian Intestate Succession Law, enacted to unify succession rules, resulted in disintegrating traditional family structures and separating widowed women and their children from the family of the deceased, so that they ended up in their losing customary access to their late husband's property. The new laws also did not recognise customary marital-type relationships and reified the position of the husband as head of household. Sam (n 19) 8.

[68] The Constitution of Kenya, 2010, Published by the National Council for Law Reporting with the Authority of the Attorney General, Art 11. Culture is articulated in Art 11(1) of the Kenyan Constitution as 'the foundation of the nation and as the cumulative civilisation of the Kenyan people and nation'. Article 2(4) states that: 'Any law, including customary law, that is inconsistent with this Constitution is void to the extent of the inconsistency, and any act or omission in contravention of this Constitution is invalid.'

Constitution only contains generic cultural rights and circumspect references to customary laws, in contrast to Ghana and other countries, which expressly recognise customary law.[69] In civil matters, the litigating parties can call on chiefs or traditional office-holders, usually elderly males, in disputes.[70] But the court is not bound to seek independent advice in civil litigation, and there is no method to ensure that the experts on traditional law are not misleading the court to support their own party.[71] Since the experts are usually men, this system reinforces patriarchal privilege and there is no process to ensure that voices of the women in the community are heard. When the Kenyan state courts apply customary law, they rely on codified authoritative textbooks or Restatements.[72] The Restatements were created in 1968 and customary law as codified at that time continues to apply to this day. In several cases in Kenya, where the courts relied on the codified Restatements, there was reliable, cogent evidence showing that the Restatement was contrary to current custom.[73] In other cases, courts have applied erroneous precedents from previous cases or derived their own interpretation by drawing from precedents dealing with different customary groups, thus perpetuating the legal errors.

The Kenyan Restatement included specific laws on the rights and duties of a husband (which included being the guardian of his wife and his wife's property, providing for the wife and enjoying the right to discipline his wife) as well as of a wife (the right to maintenance, the duty to cultivate fields and prepare food, and a duty in respect of her husband's 'reasonable demands for sexual intercourse').[74] The Restatements ended up cementing the demarcated and unequal gender roles that existed in the local culture in 1968, when the Restatements were created.[75] The Kenyan system prioritised neither women's rights nor the rights of traditional communities for self-determination and cultural freedom. The marriage laws were changed only recently, in 2014.[76]

Native courts were maintained in some African nations albeit after reforms—such as removing punitive remedies and criminal adjudication from the jurisdiction of native courts, and subjecting the tribal courts both to constitutional rights strictures and to appellate review by the state courts.[77] In South Africa, for

[69] ibid, Art 44(3). The Constitution also requires the promotion of all forms of national and cultural expression (Art 11) and protects linguistic rights as well as the to right to participate in the cultural life of his or her choice (Art 44). The same Art 44 also unambiguously enjoins any person from compelling another person to perform, observe or undergo any cultural practice or rite.

[70] Kamau (n 14) 11, 16; J Ubink, 'The Quest for Customary Law in African State Courts' in Fenrich et al (n 35) 97.

[71] Ubink (n 70).

[72] The first edition of the Kenyan restatements codifying customary law was published in 1968.

[73] Kamau (n 14) 10.

[74] Ojwang (n 13) 47.

[75] Kamau (n 14) 10.

[76] Marriage Act, Act No 4 of 2014.

[77] Bennett (n 54); Kanyongolo and Nweso (n 23) 9. The Kenyan 1967 Judicature Act states that customary law should be applied in certain civil cases but only so long as it is 'not repugnant to justice and morality' or 'inconsistent with any written law': Kenya Judicature Act, (1967) Cap 8 (Kenya).

example, the post-apartheid government was supportive of traditional leadership, and passed legislative and policy initiatives aimed at developing customary legal systems, but only ensured their compatibility with governmental socioeconomic and legal practices.[78] The process is still ongoing, as evidenced by the public debates and legislative bills for changes to the traditional courts. Moreover, the so-called 'mainstream' legal practice continues to arbitrarily apply customary law and excuse marital rape, even after marital rape has been officially criminalised, as seen in several cases which are further discussed in subsequent sections of this chapter.[79]

The newly formed independent State of Ghana, in contrast, embraced customary law as an essential aspect of the state. The 'repugnancy' clause was eliminated. Customary law issues were designated as questions of law, not merely questions of fact. The law would be ascertained after consultation with persons in the community possessing specialised knowledge.[80] The colonial legislature had introduced the dual system of law in the Ghanaian Supreme Court Ordinance of 1876. It was adopted by the independent Ghanaian state. Each citizen has the 'right to be governed by his or her own native law' and the Supreme Court is '*obliged* to observe and enforce the observance of any law or custom existing in the colony'.[81]

The 1992 Ghanaian Constitution explicitly includes customary law as part of the common law, defining customary law as 'the rules of law, which by custom are applicable to particular communities in Ghana'.[82] The scope and content of customary law is given a broad berth to include practices relating to the history of the 'founding fathers of the community', to the 'marriage and puberty rights of the women' and to the 'day-to-day life of the community'.[83] Customary tribunals[84] and the institution of chieftaincy and traditional councils as established by customary law and their usage is constitutionally protected.[85] Special chieftaincy courts decide on all matters related to the selection of chiefs, and chiefs adjudicate over local arbitration.[86] Chiefs and the traditional councils can adjudicate disputes within their communities; land disputes constitute a significant portion of the disputes.[87] The chiefs also adjudicate customary arbitration, the results of which are enforced by the state so long as both parties have voluntarily consented

[78] Koyana (n 60) 243.

[79] For example: *S v Moipolai* (CA 53/2004) [2004] ZANWHC 19, *S v Modise* (113/06) [2007] ZANWHC 73, *S v Mvamvu* (350/2003) [2004] ZASCA 90, [2005] 1 AU SA 435 (SCA).

[80] Davies and Dagbanja (n 25) 306. Note that Ghanaian courts continue to use the word 'repugnancy' to overrule customary law norms: see *Abangana v Akogo* [1977] GLR 382.

[81] Akamba and Tufuor (n 61) 206.

[82] Constitution of the Republic of Ghana (n 58) Art 11(1)–(3). See also ibid, Art 26 (laws that are dehumanising or injurious to the physical and mental well-being of the person are prohibited).

[83] Davies and Dagbanja (n 25) 307.

[84] Constitution of the Republic of Ghana (n 58) Art 125(2).

[85] ibid, ch 22, specifically Arts 270–77.

[86] Akamba and Tufuor (n 61) 206.

[87] ibid, 204, 207, 222.

to the arbitration and specific procedures are followed.[88] National and Regional Houses of Chiefs are constitutionally entrusted with undertaking 'the progressive study, interpretation, and codification of customary law' and 'an evaluation of traditional customs and usages with a view to eliminating those customs and usages that are outmoded and socially harmful'.[89] The legal system thus at least nominally acknowledges the 'unwritten' nature of customary law and promotes its adaptability and dynamism, unlike in countries such as Kenya, which relies on codified customary law.

A large percentage of Ghanaians claim allegiance to one chief or the other. Ghana also has matrilineal tribes where queen mothers act as paramount decision-makers.[90] The jurisdictional and proprietary authority of Ghanaian chiefs differs between ethnic groups. However, courts are known to apply precedent across ethnic groups and across countries, and often apply the laws of the dominant ethnic group.[91] Furthermore, constituting customary law as questions of law (not fact) in Ghana created new problems, specifically in the application of the common law principle of *stare decisis* to the natural dynamism of customary law, and discounted the variation in customary law from region to region and within groups.[92] The state and its courts have also regularly overlooked the differences in chieftaincy rules in different parts of the country.[93]

In general, the legal pluralistic structures that have subsumed customary law into the state system have reified entrenched patriarchal norms since there is limited room for change and dynamism in the architecture of customary law formation. Discriminatory inheritance and divorce laws restrict ownership of property by women and have serious repercussions for deepening the impoverishment of women, which in turn leads to further perpetuation of gender inequality.

In Malawi, despite constitutional and statutory guarantees against gender discrimination, the customary law system continues to perpetuate gender inequality, especially in the areas of inheritance,[94] marriage and land.[95] Customary marriages support early and even child marriages.[96] The current Malawian Constitution allows for a child of 15 years of age to contract a marriage with parental consent and does not outright forbid child marriages. Even children who have not attained

[88] ibid, 207.

[89] Constitution of the Republic of Ghana (n 58) Art 272.

[90] See eg M Steegstra, 'Krobo Queen Mothers: Gender, Power, and Contemporary Female Traditional Authority in Ghana' (2009) 55 *Africa Today* 105; L Brydon, 'Women Chiefs and Power in the Volta Region of Ghana' (1996) 28 *The Journal of Legal Pluralism and Unofficial Law* 227.

[91] Sam (n 19) 6.

[92] ibid, 6–7.

[93] ibid, 6.

[94] See Kanyongolo and Nweso (n 23) 16. Kanyongolo has described how the Wills and Inheritance Act of 1967 reflects traditional, patriarchal, customary norms, which serve to diminish the rights of women. Even where the statute tries to be egalitarian, it has not translated into practice.

[95] ibid, 15–21.

[96] ibid, 19.

puberty may be forcibly contracted into marriage by their parents.[97] Certain customary practices encourage boys who have reached puberty to have sex as part of their initiation, while young girls are taught to be obedient and submissive and accede to coercive sexual initiations. Marital rape is not subject to any sanctions. Under customary law, only sickness, menstruation, lactation and funerals are allowed as excuses for a woman to refuse sexual intercourse within a marriage.[98] Dowry and bride-price (*lobola*) are accepted customary practices that subordinate women and serve to treat a woman as property to be owned either by her husband or by her father. Under Ghanaian customary law, marriage confers the husband with complete and exclusive sexual rights to his wife and to his wife's domestic labour. However, it is interesting to note that in several customary law cases the courts in Ghana have applied non-discrimination principles.[99]

This enumeration of practices does not in any way imply that there is no contestation within the communities, that the meaning of the practice is homogeneous or that such oppressive practices are uniform. However, it shows that state control of customary laws has not diminished gender inequality. In fact, the adoption of a static view of customary law only reinforced male privilege by ossifying patriarchal norms into written law and preventing progressive change.[100]

Additionally, in countries with such customary legal systems, there are no sharp boundaries between state law and the customary law. The lines get blurrier still as political changes shift and challenge existing privileges.[101] It is erroneous and pejorative to consider the two systems as lying on either side of a modern/primitive divide. If demarcated at all, the two systems are usually demarcated by racial and privilege fractures, where subordinated groups are separated from the ruling class, their practices and norms sidelined from those of the state and main polity, and where the practices of the privileged groups are imposed on others.[102] Marital rape and the legal acceptance of gender inequality in marital relationships cannot therefore be attributed solely to customary norms; the state and other actors play a critical role in maintaining impunity for gender violence and gender injustice.

The examples above testify to contradictory attitudes to customary law expressed by the governments of these countries. On the one hand, the governments exalt customary law as an essential aspect of the 'African' and national identity. On the other hand, state actions are geared towards severely curtailing the jurisdiction

[97] ibid, 15–21.

[98] ibid, 20.

[99] J Fenrich, 'Promise Unfulfilled: Law, Culture, and Women's Inheritance Rights in Ghana' (2001) 25 *Fordham International Law Journal* 259; M Ndulo, 'African Customary Law, Customs, and Women's Rights' (2011) 18 *Indiana Journal of Global Legal Studies* 87, 108.

[100] Banda (n 14) 33.

[101] S Falk Moore, 'Certainties Undone: Fifty Turbulent Years of Legal Anthropology, 1949–1999' (2001) 7 *Journal of the Royal Anthropological Institute* 95.

[102] ibid; Laurence Juma, 'Reconciling African Customary Law and Human Rights in Kenya: Making a Case for Institutional Reformation and Revitalisation of Customary Adjudication Processes' (2001) 14 *St Thomas Law Review* 459; L Amede Obiora, 'Reconsidering African Customary Law' (1993) 17 *Legal Studies Forum* 217.

and independence of customary legal systems and breaking the very foundational social dynamics of customary law. The capriciousness with which certain groups and practices have been accepted and others rejected in the guise of nationalist and modernist ideologies reflects the differences in political privilege or lack thereof between various political groups. Arguments by national governments that gender justice reforms cannot be made and marital rape cannot be criminalised because it interferes with a continuous, historically unchanged customary culture are therefore fundamentally suspect.

In addition to colonialism, modernisation-based development practices, Christian missionary activities, labour migration and socioeconomic changes wrought by capitalist development have all resulted in fundamental changes in tribal kinship and community practices and created new social dependencies and changes in power structures.[103] This has led not only to internecine political fights but also to actions to further control women's sexuality and freedoms in the name of cultural protection. Additionally, women politicians and activists also struggle between ensuring the political representation of their community in a divided society and fighting for gender equality.

For example, in Kenya, ethnicity in the form of tribal allegiance plays a critical role in politics as politicians vie for political supremacy.[104] In a famous case, when a prominent women and Mau Mau freedom fighter, Wambui Otieno, tried to claim a right to the remains of her husband, who was from a different tribe, she was faced with having to deal with inter-clan (Luo–Kikuyu) political rivalry and patriarchal resistance.[105] Ethnicity-based electoral politics have played an extraordinary role in Kenya (and in other countries) in limiting legal reforms for gender equality and in discounting claims to criminalise marital rape.[106]

To summarise, in the context of postcolonial countries with diverse ethnic communities and legal systems, Thompson and Erez's succinct conclusion from their research on spousal abuse in Sierra Leone is on point. As they explain: '[B]oth legal systems (customary and general law) condone male violence and permit it as one way of preserving tribal social cohesion and economic welfare through marriages and families.'[107] Since domestic violence, including marital rape, does not

[103] See generally Mamdani (n 22).

[104] J Lonsdale, 'Soil, Work, Civilisation, and Citizenship in Kenya' (2008) 2 *Journal of Eastern African Studies* 305; P Mwangi Kagwanja, 'Facing Mount Kenya or Facing Mecca? The Mungiki, Ethnic Violence and the Politics of the Moi Succession in Kenya, 1987–2002' (2003) 102 *African Affairs* 25.

[105] P Stamp, 'Burying Otieno: The Politics of Gender and Ethnicity in Kenya' (1991) 16 *Signs* 808.

[106] Mandal (n 17) 259–61; Z Pathak and R Sunder Rajan, 'Shahbano' (1989) 14 *Signs* 558; AM Goetz, 'The Problem with Patronage: Constraints on Women's Political Effectiveness in Uganda' in AM Goetz and S Hassim (eds), *No Shortcuts to Power: African Women in Politics and Policy Making* (London, Zed Books/David Philip, 2003); H Britton, 'Organising against Gender Violence in South Africa' (2006) 32 *Journal of Southern African Studies* 145; Y Tambiah, 'Realizing Women's Sexual Rights: Challenges in South Asia' (1998) 67 *Nordic Journal of International Law* 97; M Bosmans et al, 'Palestinian Women's Sexual and Reproductive Health Rights in a Longstanding Humanitarian Crisis' (2008) 16 *Reproductive Health Matters* 103.

[107] R Bankole Thomson and E Erez, 'Wife Abuse in Sierra Leone: Polygamous Marriages in a Dual Legal System' (1994) 18 *International Journal of Comparative and Applied Criminal Justice* 27, 37.

threaten the social order, while its criminalisation might upset powerful leaders and communities, legal reform is often not a priority at any level of legal system.

Furthermore, postcolonial states such as Kenya, Ghana and Malawi also differ markedly from settler countries such as Canada and the United States, which have had their own distinct history of colonialism and where decolonisation is considered to be ongoing. Customary law in the form of Aboriginal law has been entirely marginalised and is assumed to have a much lower legal status, if indeed it has any status at all within the state's legal system.[108] In Canada, opinions of Indigenous community members may play a role in sentencing decisions but the court is not obliged to consider such opinions.[109]

Settler states such as Canada are also marked by other unique factors. First, the history of many countries, including Canada, the United States and a number of Latin America states, is marked by extreme sexual violence and dehumanisation of Indigenous women where rape was a pervasive, important tool of conquest, and where there was forced imposition of colonial sexual mores and control over the Indigenous body.[110] Moreover, sexual violence laws were not legislated to protect Indigenous (and other racialised) women.[111] Early discussions about rape law when law reforms were first being instituted, focused mainly on the experiences of white women.[112] In fact, the law in some states in the United States initially only criminalised sexual assault when the victim was a 'white woman'.[113]

Second, marital rape is already criminalised in most settler countries, such as Canada and Australia, and this law applies to all Indigenous peoples within the state. The United States is an exception because it has a complicated jurisdictional arrangement between tribes and the federal government whereby tribal governments retain criminal jurisdiction under certain conditions and the marital rape exemption persists in various forms in many tribal nations.[114] However, Indigenous

[108] Eberts and Monture (n 9) 2–4, 36–48; K Anker, 'Law, Culture and Fact in Indigenous Claims: Legal Pluralism as a Problem of Recognition' in R Provost (ed), *Centaur Jurisprudence* (Cambridge, Cambridge University Press, 2016) papers.ssrn.com/abstract=2750066> (forthcoming).

[109] J Koshan, 'The Legal Treatment of Marital Rape and Women's Equality: An Analysis of the Canadian Experience', theequalityeffect.org/pdfs/maritalrapecanadexperience.pdf.

[110] Castañeda (n 47); S Deer, 'Sovereignty of the Soul: Exploring the Intersection of Rape Law Reform and Federal Indian Law' (2004) 38 *Suffolk University Law Review* 455; Smith (n 15); ME Turpel, 'Patriarchy and Paternalism: The Legacy of the Canadian State for First Nations Women' (1993) 6 *Canadian Journal of Women and the Law* 174. For recent examples of how state military in Latin America, Africa, Asia have used rape to subjugate Indigenous peoples see International Indigenous Women's Forum (FIMI/IIWF), 'Mairin Iwanka Raya, Indigenous Women Stand Against Violence—A Companion Report to the United Nations Secretary-General's Study on Violence Against Women' (FIMI, 2006) 29–30.

[111] See S Razack, 'What Is to Be Gained by Looking White People in the Eye? Culture, Race, and Gender in Cases of Sexual Violence' (1994) 19 *Signs* 894.

[112] Deer (n 2) 125.

[113] ibid. Deer points out that: 'The colonialist mindset could not conceive of a legal wrong in raping a Native woman.'

[114] Deer (n 2).

women are subject to high rates of domestic and sexual violence, including spousal sexual violence. Despite the criminalisation of violence against women (including marital rape), the criminal justice system is widely considered as having failed to protect Indigenous women from violence.[115] Furthermore, Indigenous persons are greatly overrepresented in the Canadian state's criminal system.[116] Aboriginal women in custody represent 35.5 per cent of all in-custody women, with 73.5 per cent serving a sentence for a violent offence (as compared to 47.2 per cent)[117] and Aboriginal men and women were more likely than non-Aboriginal persons to receive imprisonment rather than a non-custodial sentence.[118] The operating question in settler states is therefore not one of whether and how marital rape should be criminalised by the state. Instead, the key question is how to incorporate a legitimate system of justice that has an emancipatory potential, and that Indigenous women can meaningfully and freely engage.

III. Culture versus Women's Rights in International Human Rights Law

Recognition of women's rights is a relatively new development in international human rights law, and it has created a universal framework and an entire transnational culture of organisations, actors and discourses that have affected state posturing and local dynamics. Criminalisation of marital rape is now considered an obligation for states as it impinges many fundamental rights protected under international human rights treaties.[119] Hence, states cannot rely on their internal domestic laws, including customary laws, or make any culture-based excuse to escape their obligations. The international human rights framework sets universal

[115] R Kuokkanen, 'Self-Determination and Indigenous Women's Rights at the Intersection of International Human Rights' (2012) 34 *Human Rights Quarterly* 225; J Borrows, 'Aboriginal and Treaty Rights and Violence against Women' (2012) 50 *Osgoode Hall Law Journal* 699.

[116] 'Prison Watchdog Shocked at Number of Aboriginal Inmates', *CBC News*, 14 January 2016, www.cbc.ca/news/Aboriginal/Aboriginal-inmates-1.3403647 ('more than a quarter of inmates in Canadian prisons are Aboriginal people').

[117] Public Safety Canada Portfolio Corrections Statistics Committee, '2015 Corrections and Conditional Release Statistical Overview' (Public Safety Canada, 2016) www.publicsafety.gc.ca/cnt/rsrcs/pblctns/ccrso-2015/ccrso-2015-en.pdf, 53, 61.

[118] G Balfour, 'Do Law Reforms Matter? Exploring the Victimization–Criminalization Continuum in the Sentencing of Aboriginal Women in Canada' (2013) 19 *International Review of Victimology* 85, 91. Also see C Murdocca, *To Right Historical Wrongs: Race, Gender, and Sentencing in Canada* (Vancouver, UBC Press, 2013).

[119] See M Randall and V Venkatesh, 'Criminalizing Sexual Violence against Women in Intimate Relationships: State Obligations under Human Rights Law' (2015) 109 *AJIL Unbound* 189; M Randall and V Venkatesh, 'The Right to No: The Crime of Marital Rape, Women's Human Rights, and International Law' (2015) 41 *Brooklyn Journal of International Law* 153.

standards for women's rights, utilising institutions and procedures. This approach lends itself to several criticisms. These include accusations of imposing rights imperialism, supporting a patronising ideology bolstering a Eurocentric saviour complex, ignoring intersectional issues important to women in other contexts (such as historical subordination, globalisation impacts and rights to cultural and political self-determination), and being unable to respond to the tailoring that is needed in every cultural, political and social setting.[120]

The culture-versus-gender debate is particularly illustrated in the discourse around CEDAW,[121] the chief UN instrument that codifies women's rights and articulates state responsibility to counter gender discrimination in all its forms, including domestic sexual violence, and its associated treaty body committee (the CEDAW Committee). CEDAW forms a core instrument for imposing due-diligence obligations on states to combat violence against women and to criminalise marital rape.[122]

However, the CEDAW Committee has been accused by some of being deeply suspicious of culture, lacking in an intersectionality approach and exemplifying the paradigm of prioritising women's rights over 'culture'.[123] The accusations are not surprising just from judging the language of CEDAW and examining the published work of the Committee. For example, Article 2(f) of CEDAW requires changes in existing, discriminatory 'customs and practices'.[124] Article 5 further emphasises prioritising gender rights over the protection of local, collective practices: 'States Parties shall take *all* appropriate measures to modify the social and cultural patterns of conduct.'[125] Religious institutions, personal state laws and tribal traditions that discriminate against women all qualify for potential change based on the articles.

[120] SE Merry, *Human Rights and Gender Violence: Translating International Law into Local Justice* (Chicago, University of Chicago Press, 2006); K Engle, 'International Human Rights and Feminisms: When Discourses Keep Meeting' in D Buss and AS Manji (eds), *International Law: Modern Feminist Approaches* (Oxford, Hart Publishing, 2005); M Mutua, 'Savages, Victims, and Saviors: The Metaphor of Human Rights' (2001) 42 *Harvard International Law Journal* 201; Banda (n 14) 28–33, 44–45; David W Kennedy, 'The International Human Rights Regime: Still Part of the Problem?' (2002) 14 *Harvard Human Rights Journal* 101; R Coomaraswamy, 'To Bellow like a Cow: Women, Ethnicity, and the Discourse of Rights' in RJ Cook (ed), *Human Rights of Women: National and International Perspectives* (North York, ON, Scholarly Book Services Inc, 2002) 39–41, 44, 46–47; N Kim, 'Toward a Feminist Theory of Human Rights: Straddling the Fence between Western Imperialism and Uncritical Absolutism' (1993) 25 *Columbia Human Rights Law Review* 49, 56–63.

[121] CEDAW (n 3).

[122] See Randall and Venkatesh, 'Right to No' (n 119); Randall and Venkatesh, 'Criminalizing Sexual Violence against Women in Intimate Relationships' (n 119).

[123] See AE Mayer, 'Cultural Pluralism as a Bar to Women's Rights: Reflections on the Middle Eastern Experience' in J Peters and A Wolper (eds), *Women's Rights, Human Rights: International Feminist Perspectives* (London, Routledge, 1995) 178; Kim (n 120) 58. Also see 'Declarations, Reservations and Objections to CEDAW' (UN Women) www.un.org/womenwatch/daw/cedaw/reservations-country.htm#N38.

[124] CEDAW (n 3) Art 2(f).

[125] ibid, Art 5 (emphasis added).

The CEDAW Committee also supports dramatic rights-based interventions (including criminalisation) over slow and unpredictable strategies of embedding reforms within existing religious and customary structures.[126] This is reflected in the General Recommendations (GRs) and Committee reports.

GR 21 addresses equality between men and women in marriage and family relations and covers a large breadth, from equal rights to choices in marriage and nationality to equality in the legal system.[127] It specifically states that 'there can be no justification for applying different and discriminatory laws or customs' to activities in the public or private sphere.[128] It underscores that 'culture and tradition' play a significant part 'in restricting the exercise of basic rights by women'.[129] It criticises a list of cultural practices that support patriarchy, such as polygamy, forced marriages, and customary inheritance and property laws.[130] Similarly, GR 19 criticises 'traditional practices perpetuated by culture and tradition that are harmful to the health of women and children'.[131] GR 23 states that in all nations, cultural traditions and religious beliefs have played a part in confining women to the private spheres of activity and excluding them from active participation in public life.[132]

It is perhaps not surprising that CEDAW has the dubious distinction of having the largest number of reservations.[133] Article 16, which provides for equality in marriage and family relations, has the greatest number of reservations.[134] About 75 per cent of all the reservations to CEDAW are substantive in nature and contradict the object and purpose of CEDAW. Most of the reservations are linked to conflict with domestic family law, local legislative autonomy, traditional cultural rights, and local custom or practice of dominant or state religion.[135] These reservations are incompatible with the object and purpose of the treaty,

[126] Merry (n 120) 98.

[127] UN Committee on the Elimination of Discrimination Against Women, 'General Recommendation 21: Equality in Marriage and Family Relations, Adopted in the 13th Session of the CEDAW Committee, UN Doc A/49/38' (1994). General recommendations of the CEDAW Committee, like the general comments by the Human Rights Committee, are not binding on states. They are nevertheless significant as progressive development of international norms and are an important source of interpretive guidelines.

[128] ibid, para 12.

[129] ibid, para 3.

[130] ibid, paras 14, 16, 28, 33, 35.

[131] UN Committee on the Elimination of Discrimination Against Women, General Recommendation 19: Violence Against Women, adopted in the 11th Session of the CEDAW Committee, UN Doc A/47/38 1992.

[132] UN Committee on the Elimination of Discrimination Against Women, General Recommendation 23: Women in Political and Public Life, adopted in the 16th Session of the CEDAW Committee, UN Doc A/52/38 1997, para 10.

[133] Economic and Social Commission for Asia and the Pacific, *Combating Human Trafficking in Asia: A Resource Guide to International and Regional Legal Instruments, Political Commitments and Recommended Practices* (New York, United Nations, 2003) 217.

[134] 'Declarations, Reservations and Objections to CEDAW' (n 123).

[135] See eg reservations by Algeria, Oman, Bangladesh, Israel, Singapore, Niger; declaration by Mexico in ibid.

yet they exist. Moreover, many of the reservations provide such broad latitude for non-compliance that they restrict the applicability of CEDAW in the very cases for which it was created. These 'culture'-based reservations that prohibit any interference in marriage relationships are rooted in the same arguments that are used to justify retaining the marital rape exemption in law.

However, the reservations perhaps belie a deeper issue, which may not necessarily be rooted in a blanket support for gender inequality amongst the reserving countries. That Lesotho has a reservation on the basis that its customary laws are exempt from CEDAW, when it was one of the *first* few countries to ratify the Draft Maputo Protocol of the African Charter[136] (which has more substantive gender protections) suggests something deeper and political about some strands of the resistance to CEDAW.[137] With the exception of Somalia and Sudan, every African nation has ratified the Convention. Regional instruments in Latin America, Africa and Europe contain stronger entitlements to gender equality and freedom from intimate partner violence.[138] The reservations to CEDAW by African states and the use of cultural self-determination to resist law reforms, including criminalising marital rape, appear to be just polemical grandstands against 'Western' imposition of values and sovereignty.

The African regional system reflects the intersectionalities and multiplicity of claims of African women, which include the rights to gender equality and also to self-determination in all its forms. While the right to be free from cultural imperialism is strongly asserted in African human rights instruments, so is gender equality, and not just in nominal language but also in practice and in legally justiciable provisions. The African Charter on Human and *Peoples'* Rights (emphasis added) is the foundational normative instrument for the protection and promotion of human rights in Africa, and reflects the history, values, traditions and economic needs of the continent.[139] Although there is no specific definition of 'peoples', the Charter recognises several collective rights, including an assertion of the importance of the African 'historical tradition and the values of African civilisation' in defining the concept behind human peoples' rights, an 'unquestionable and inalienable' right to self-determination as well as the right of a group to be free from domination by another group, and a right of peoples to economic, social and cultural development which respects their freedom and identity.[140]

However, the Charter also has a strong anti-discrimination provision (Article 2) and Article 18, which deals with the family context, obliges the state party to 'ensure the elimination of *every* discrimination against women and also ensure the

[136] Protocol to the African Charter on Human and Peoples' Rights on the Rights of Women in Africa 2003 (Maputo Protocol).

[137] Banda (n 14) 63–66.

[138] Randall and Venkatesh 'Right to No' (n 119) 171–76; Randall and Venkatesh, 'The Marital Rape Impunity in Comparative and Historical Perspective' (n 6).

[139] African [Banjul] Charter on Human and Peoples' Rights, adopted 27 June 1981, OAU Doc CAB/LEG/67/3 rev 5, 21 ILM 58 (1982), entered into force 21 October 1986.

[140] See ibid, Arts 19, 20, 22.

protection of the rights of the woman and the child as stipulated in *international declarations and conventions*'.[141] The Charter has been relied upon by courts, committees and organisations to make their claim for gender equality. For example, the High Court of Botswana relied on the Charter to affirm that women have the right to non-discrimination and equal protection before the law.[142] The African Charter thus constitutes an essential and important regional source, which cannot be considered an international or Eurocentric imposition that ignores the collective and cultural aspect of human well-being, to demand that states remove the marital rape exemption that permits unequal protection before the law for women in spousal and intimate relationships.

Gender mainstreaming in general is a 'key plank in the African Union policy'.[143] Sub-regional instruments such as the Southern African Development Community (SADC)'s founding treaty prohibits Member States from gender discrimination and has listed gender mainstreaming as a specific objective.[144] Malawi is a member of SADC. SADC's Addendum on Violence specifically highlights marital rape as a type of violence against women that Member States have to prevent and eradicate.[145] The founding treaty of the East African Community (EAC), in Chapter 22, also mainstreams gender issues in the development process and requires that states 'abolish legislation and discourage customs that are discriminatory against women' and take measures to 'eliminate prejudices against women and promote the equality of the female gender with that of the male gender in *every respect*'.[146] Numerous other instruments, such as the Grand Bay (Mauritius) Declaration of 1999,[147] the Constitutive Act of the African Union[148] and the Kigali Declaration of 2003,[149] illustrate the emphasis on gender equality and the need to combat violence against women in all its forms, culminating in the Maputo Protocol and the Declaration on Gender.[150]

The Protocol to the African Charter on Human and Peoples' Rights on the Rights of Women in Africa, also known as the Maputo Protocol or the African

141 ibid, Arts 2 and 18 (emphasis added).

142 *Attorney General v Unity Dow* (2001) AHRLR 99 (BwCA 1992). The court ruled that non-discrimination as protected by the Charter required the government to change its citizenship structure to allow children of Botswanian women to claim citizenship even if Botswana was 'culturally' patrilineal.

143 Banda (n 14) 49.

144 Treaty of the Southern African Development Community (1992) Art 6(2), Art 5(1k).

145 Southern African Development Community, 'Prevention and Eradication of Violence against Women and Children (Addendum to the SADC Declaration on Gender and Development)' (1998) Art 5(1).

146 Treaty Establishing the East African Community (1999) Art 121 (emphasis added).

147 Organisation of African Unity, 'Grand Bay (Mauritius) Declaration and Plan of Action' (1999) para 6.

148 Organisation of African Unity, 'Constitutive Act of the African Union', adopted in 2000 at the Lome Summit (Togo), entered into force in 2001 preamble, Arts 3(g), 3(h), 4(m).

149 Kigali Declaration of 2003, adopted in the 1st African Union (AU) Ministerial Conference on Human Rights in Africa meeting on 8 May 2003 preamble, Arts 16, 25.

150 African Union Solemn Declaration on Gender Equality in Africa (2004) preamble, ss 1–10, 12; Maputo Protocol (n 136).

Women's Protocol, entered into force in 2005 and has been ratified by Kenya, Ghana, Malawi and most other African nations.[151] It offers one of the most powerful articulations of women's rights in an international instrument.[152] It obligates states to prevent, punish and eradicate all forms of violence against women, including marital rape.[153]

The Protocol prohibits states from making cultural excuses by demanding that 'any practice that hinders or endangers the normal growth and affects the physical and psychological development of women and girls should be *condemned and eliminated*'.[154] The protocol not only guarantees equal rights of women in marriage,[155] but Article 2 of the Protocol specifically obligates states parties to commit themselves

> to modify the social and cultural patterns of conduct of women and men through public education, information, education and communication strategies, with a view to achieving the elimination of harmful *cultural and traditional practices and all other practices which are based on the idea of the inferiority or the superiority of either of the sexes, or on stereotyped roles for women and men*.[156]

Article 4 reiterates the obligation of Member States to take all measures to prevent and eliminate gender violence, including measures 'to eradicate elements in traditional and cultural beliefs, practices and stereotypes which legitimise and exacerbate the persistence and tolerance of violence against women'.[157] Article 5 deals with the prohibition of harmful practices where 'harmful practices' includes 'all behaviour, attitudes and/or practices which negatively affect the fundamental rights of women and girls'.[158]

Yet, the Protocol simultaneously acknowledges women's multiple identities. It entitles women to extensive participatory and socioeconomic rights and provides that 'women shall have the right to *live in a positive cultural context* and to participate at all levels in the determination of cultural policies'.[159] The regional African instruments thus unequivocally support gender equality and the need to take all measures, including combating social and cultural practices that condone and facilitate private acts of violence against women.

[151] African Commission on Human and Peoples' Rights, 'Ratification Table—Protocol to the African Charter on Human and Peoples' Rights on the Rights of Women in Africa' (African Commission on Human and Peoples' Rights (ACHPR)) www.achpr.org/instruments/women-protocol/ratification/.

[152] Incidentally, it is the first international human rights instrument that has explicitly articulated a woman's right to abortion, at least under certain circumstance. See Maputo Protocol (n 136) Art 8(f).

[153] ibid, Art 4(b), (e).Violence against women is defined as including 'all acts perpetrated against women which cause or could cause them physical, *sexual*, psychological, and economic harm, including the threat to take such acts … in *private* or public life' (emphasis added). Marital rape is a form of sexual harm in private life and can therefore be deemed to be included. Also, Art 2(a) specifically mandates prohibition of unwanted or forced sex in the private sphere.

[154] Maputo Protocol (n 136) preamble (emphasis added).

[155] ibid, Arts 6,7,21.

[156] ibid, Art 2(2) (emphasis added).

[157] ibid, Art 4(a), (c), (d).

[158] ibid, Arts 5, 1(g).

[159] ibid, Art 17 (emphasis added).

In the context of Indigenous and Aboriginal peoples, the UN Declaration on the Rights of Indigenous Peoples also affirms that the rights and special needs of Indigenous women should be given 'particular attention'.[160] Indeed, Indigenous women are at the forefront in demanding self-determination and independence for their people[161] while also fighting for equality and gender justice within their various nations.[162] The International Indigenous Women's Forum affirms how crucial collective rights and self-determination are to Indigenous women. This forum aims 'to chart a third way between the one-size-fits-all notion of global sisterhood that denies crucial power differences between women, and a relativist stance that stresses differences over potential points of connection between women'.[163]

Women's equality within the family and society, and their right to be free from violence, cannot therefore be characterised as if they are Western and colonial impositions. Changes in the past two decades have also altered discourse and practice to such a large extent that binaries dividing (Western) rights affirming liberalism from (African or Indigenous) cultural affirmation can no longer be sustained. Even the autochthonous constitutions of the African countries have declarations protecting 'custom' and traditions, but, at the same time, they constitutionally guarantee rights for women to be free from discrimination and violence. Of course, the degree to which custom and traditions are subject to anti-discrimination laws and other human rights laws varies from country to country; nevertheless, women's equality before the law and their right to be free from violence is an accepted state obligation.[164]

For example, the Malawian Constitution not only has a specific, elaborate section on women's rights which includes equal protection and right not to be discriminated against on the basis of marital status,[165] but the Fundamental Principles of the Constitution also specifically obligates the government to adopt policies and legislation to obtain 'gender equality for women with men' and implement measures to address *domestic violence*.[166] Further, the Constitution mandates legislation to eliminate customs and practices that discriminate against women, particularly sexual abuse and violence.[167]

[160] Declaration on the Rights of Indigenous Peoples, GA Res 61/295, adopted 13 September 2007, UN GAOR, 61st Sess, 107th plen mtg, UN Doc A/RES/61/295 (2007) Art 22.

[161] See PA Monture, *Journeying Forward: Dreaming First Nations' Independence* (Nova Scotia, Fernwood, 1999) (arguing for the recognition of full sovereignty and independence of First Nations in Canada).

[162] A Smith, 'Native American Feminism, Sovereignty, and Social Change' (2005) 31 *Feminist Studies* 116; Deer (n 2); R Kuokkanen, 'Self-Determination and Indigenous Women—"Whose Voice Is It We Hear in the Sámi Parliament?"' (2011) 18 *International Journal on Minority and Group Rights* 39.

[163] International Indigenous Women's Forum (FIMI/IIWF) (n 110) 4.

[164] For a convenient topography that classifies countries into 'strong cultural relativism', 'weak relativism', 'universal', see Banda (n 14) 35.

[165] Kanyongolo and Nweso (n 23) 7. Constitution of the Republic of Malawi (1994) s 24.

[166] Constitution of the Republic of Malawi (1994) Art 13(a).

[167] ibid, Art 24(2a).

The Kenyan Constitution similarly enshrines women's right to equal treatment and prohibits discrimination on the basis of gender and marital status.[168] Although, unlike the Malawi constitution, it only prescribes a general right (not gender-specific) to be free from violence by private sources.[169] However, as mentioned above, customary laws have to be consistent with the Constitution.[170] The Ghanaian Constitution also prohibits discrimination *and prejudice* on the basis of gender and mandates equal protection before the law.[171] However, it does not mention marital status as a specific ground for non-discrimination or a specific right to be free from private sexual violence. The governments, which are bound by their countries' constitutions, cannot therefore simply rely on anti-imperialistic or protectionist arguments to deny recourse to the criminal law for women who face sexual and physical violence from their husbands.

State constitutions and regional treaties place the same, if not stronger, obligations on states to protect women's rights, including the right to be free from violence by all actors, equal treatment before the law, and non-discrimination on the basis of their gender or marital status. Lastly, the actors in CEDAW and other international proceedings are no longer predominantly from Western nations but also extensively represent the global South and Indigenous groups.

It is important to acknowledge the criticisms of NGO participation in international forums, such as their lack of accountability and legitimacy, their problematic funding environment, their Eurocentric orientation (even of those from the global South), and the fact that several of the NGO actors still constitute the urban elite of their countries, who may be incapable of addressing deep-rooted structural problems as they are far removed from traditional or rural societies and the daily realities faced by the women they claim to represent.[172] Nevertheless, it is a reality that these actors constitute important intermediaries between international bodies, the state and local communities. Additionally, they play a significant role in indigenising and creating new meaning of rights that have resonance in particular local context. This process, which has been termed as 'vernacularising', helps in mainstreaming human rights of women and changing the discourse at the local level.[173]

Furthermore, not all participants can be accused of being elites[174] and 'thousands of women's rights advocates' from across the globe have participated

[168] Constitution of Kenya, 2010, Arts 27(3,4).

[169] ibid, Art 29(c).

[170] ibid, Art 2(4). Also see ibid, art 159(3) which affirms that traditional dispute resolution mechanisms cannot contravene the Bill of Rights, be repugnant to justice and morality, or inconsistent with the Constitution or any written law.

[171] Constitution of the Republic of Ghana (n 59) Arts 12(2), 17(1)–(3), 35(5).

[172] Banda (n 14) 78, 289–94; Merry (n 120) 3, 10–11, 15–16, 101–02, 164–65; M Mutua, 'Standard Setting in Human Rights: Critique and Prognosis' (2007) 29 *Human Rights Quarterly* 547, 593, 604–19; M Mutua, *Human Rights: A Political and Cultural Critique* (Philadelphia, University of Pennsylvania, 2002) 36–37.

[173] The term 'vernacularisation' is taken from SE Merry's work. SE Merry, 'Transnational Human Rights and Local Activism: Mapping the Middle' (2009) 108 *American Anthropologist* 38; Merry (n 120); Banda (n 14) 286–88, 294.

[174] Merry (n 120) 174–76.

and continue to participate in transnational forums and UN summits.[175] There is extensive 'bottom-up' activism by women from rural and subordinated groups across the globe fighting for their rights to equality and freedom from violence.[176] The activism of these women plays a critical role in bringing equality-based legal conceptions of gender violence into international, regional and domestic legal institutions and in creating a feminist legal meaning of the right to self-determination, culture and other human rights.

Yet, despite the activism by women from all backgrounds claiming human rights to be free from violence, and despite mandates by regional instruments and national constitutions, some states continue to claim protection of national or traditional culture as an excuse to avoid legislative and other reforms criminalising marital rape and protecting women's rights to equality.[177] Oppressive legal institutions, and patriarchal laws, including marital rape impunity and criminalising homosexuality, for example, are deemed to be a part of national culture even when they are, in fact, the product of colonial policy and are anachronous with current cultural practice.

'Culture' and 'othering' stereotypes (especially of politically disempowered and Indigenous communities) are also used to justify apathy and inaction by states. State representatives are quick to blame 'culture' as the cause for gender inequality and violence against women, even in the face of evidence of feminised poverty and female unemployment, socioeconomic and political subordination of minority and Indigenous communities, and other political and economic conditions that present a clear dereliction of state duty in addressing root causes of inequality and

[175] SE Alvarez, 'Translating the Global Effects of Transnational Organizing on Local Feminist Discourses and Practices in Latin America' (2000) 1 *Meridians* 29.

[176] S Grabe, A Dutt and SL Dworkin, 'Women's Community Mobilization and Well-Being: Local Resistance to Gendered Social Inequities in Nicaragua and Tanzania' (2014) 42 *Journal of Community Psychology* 379; G Huiskamp, 'Identity Politics and Democratic Transitions in Latin America: (Re) organizing Women's Strategic Interests through Community Activism' 29 *Theory and Society* 385; S González Montes, 'Violence against Women, Rights and Citizenship in Rural and Indigenous Contexts of Mexico' [2009] *Convergencia Revista de Ciencias Sociales*, convergencia.uaemex.mx/article/view/1212; L Stephen, *Women and Social Movements in Latin America: Power from Below* (Austin, University of Texas Press, 1997) 29–85, 158–234; A Mari Tripp, 'Women in Movement Transformations in African Political Landscapes' (2003) 5 *International Feminist Journal of Politics* 233, 240–44, 248–49; MR Vanegas and LR Pruitt, 'CEDAW and Rural Development: Empowering Women with Law from the Top Down, Activism from the Bottom Up' (2011) 41 *University of Baltimore Law Review* 263; M Kishwar, 'Nature of Women's Mobilisation in Rural India: An Exploratory Essay' (1988) 23 *Economic and Political Weekly* 2754; Merry (n 173).

[177] See PTI, 'Government Says Concept of Marital Rape Cannot Be Applied in India', *Financial Express*, 30 April 2015, financialexpress.com/article/miscellaneous/concept-of-marital-rape-cannot-be-applied-in-india-says-government-cpi-m-reacts/68147/; V Arora, 'Maldives President Vetoes Marital Rape Bill as "un-Islamic"', *Washington Post*, 16 January 2014, www.washingtonpost.com/national/religion/maldives-president-vetoes-marital-rape-bill-as-un-islamic/2014/01/16/d8f50b8a-7ed3-11e3-97d3-b9925ce2c57b_story.html; Sally Armstrong, 'Marital Rape in Africa: The Right to Say No', *The Globe and Mail*, 11 June 2010, theglobeandmail.com/news/world/marital-rape-in-africa-the-right-to-say-no/article4328673/; F Banda, '"If You Buy a Cup, Why Would You Not Use It?" Marital Rape: The Acceptable Face of Gender Based Violence: Comment on "Criminalizing Sexual Violence against Women in Intimate Relationships"' (2016) 109 *AJIL Unbound* 321.

gendered violence. It is therefore important to interrogate closely the claims of imperialism and cultural protectionism that are used to deny women rights and to permit marital rape, just as it is also necessary to situate these claims within the broader political contexts.

IV. Is There Really a Conflict of Rights Between Culture and Gender Equality?

A. Criticisms of Eurocentric, Decontextualised Approaches to Gender Violence

Women's rights issues in general, and the use of criminal law to achieve gender justice specifically, have generated numerous antagonistic, contentious debates. The use of human rights and international law paradigms to espouse universal women's rights globally has traditionally pitted liberal feminists on one end against cultural feminists, cultural relativists, and postcolonial and critical race scholars at the other end.[178] Similarly, the issue of using criminalisation to combat gender violence has caused antagonistic positions amongst feminists and race scholars alike. The emphasis on criminalising domestic sexual and physical violence as a remedy for gender injustice has been particularly lambasted as reinforcing state coercion of racialised and subordinated groups, and as reinforcing colonial oppression in the case of Indigenous groups. Criminalisation strategies have also been criticised for distracting the women's movement from considering other intersectional strategies, and as presenting the experience of the 'white woman' as the universal standard.[179]

Western, liberal feminists have often essentialised women from other cultures and constructed them as unwitting participants in their own and other women's oppression. On this view, women from 'other' cultures are seen as needing to be convinced tactfully and strategically to adopt women's rights.[180] Global politics and the human rights discourse have been fraught with often-justifiable accusations of Eurocentrism and stereotypical 'othering' where violence against women and patriarchal traditions are considered particularly endemic to traditional, religious, or non-Anglo-European cultures.[181]

[178] Coomaraswamy (n 120).

[179] Crenshaw (n 4); KW Crenshaw, 'From Private Violence to Mass Incarceration: Thinking Intersectionally about Women, Race, and Social Control' (2011) 59 *UCLA Law Review* 1418; Davis (n 16); Turpel (n 110).

[180] Engle (n 120) 57.

[181] See eg S Moller Okin's article and the responses to her article in J Cohen, M Howard and M Craven Nussbaum (eds), *Is Multiculturalism Bad for Women? (Susan Moller Okin with Respondents)* (Princeton, Princeton University Press, 1999).

Intersectional and critical race scholars and 'third-world' and postcolonial feminists have illuminated the differences between different groups of women, the importance of cultural practices for women in subordinated (globally or domestically) cultural groups, and the multiplicity of identities that women inhabit.[182] They point out the imperialistic and patriarchal legacies of international law. They also highlight the failures of Western liberal feminists to see similar modalities of oppression in Western cultures and the salience of religion and culture in Western legal systems and the problems in advancing individualistic legal norms.

Women in cultural groups in which customary law operates straddle two areas of subordination: first, as women asserting equality *within* their group; and second, as group *members* seeking to assert cultural equality in the broader political system. These contexts are informed by three centuries of colonisation followed by decades of Western economic and political supremacy during which colonised nations have fought to assert their identities as independent, postcolonial, developing nations.

The condemnation of customary laws by international and foreign interests on the basis that they impinge upon women's equality is not recent. During the colonial period, there were many so-called reforms coercively imposed under the rubric of the emancipation of colonised women, but the cultural ignorance and the paternalistic, prejudiced attitude on which the reforms were founded only served to reinforce disenfranchisement of women, as described above. The subjugation and forced assimilation of Indigenous people, and the marginalisation and destruction of their cultures, are phenomena present in almost every nation's history and which actively continue to this day.

Within the context of a relentless history of ethnic oppression and colonisation, self-determination and cultural rights are necessary remedies not only to address the claims of historically oppressed peoples, but also to protect against further ethnic, cultural and religious oppression. It is not surprising that after centuries of colonialism, anti-colonialist movements grounded their claims in a 'genuine national culture' liberated from Western philosophical, social and political domination.[183] During the postcolonial era, nations of the global South strengthened their claims to sovereign equality by claiming the prerogative to define one's own culture, definitions which had been denied to them over centuries of colonisation. The identity and cultural claims of subordinated groups must therefore be understood *not as deifications of their culture* but as claims for rights and challenges to existing power structures.

Indigenous women's movements for legal reform have shown how state laws have institutionalised patriarchy in tribal structures, essentialised and subordinated

[182] Crenshaw (n 4); Yuval-Davis (n 5); Banda (n 14); Mary Sillett, 'Ensuring Indigenous Women's Voices Are Heard: The Beijing Declaration of Indigenous Women' (1996) 16 *Canadian Woman Studies* 62; International Indigenous Women's Forum (FIMI/IIWF) (n 110) 9–11.

[183] M Ishay, *The History of Human Rights: From Ancient Times to the Globalization Era* (Oakland, University of California Press 2004) 196.

the experiences of Indigenous women and continued to colonise and violate Indigenous women in the present day.[184] Indigenous women leaders assert that Indigenous women cannot rely on 'external' systems of justice to protect their rights and that decolonisation necessarily involves rejections of all kinds of violation of the Indigenous woman's body.[185]

Fareda Banda, among other feminist scholars from the global South, has convincingly articulated the view that the Eurocentric approach to women's equality has been counterproductive for asserting gender rights.[186] The Eurocentric approach, on this view, uses problematic, unsupported assumptions about the kind of societal organisation that a priori is assumed to be gender oppressive. These scholars further criticise the assumption that individualistic secular societies which protect privacy and autonomous property rights, and which favour conflict over consensus for resolving disputes, are automatically perceived as providing space for advancing gender equality.

These Eurocentric assumptions are ironic considering that the struggle for gender equality is very nascent even in the West and that it faces tremendous hurdles to this day. Many of these hurdles are also associated with liberalism's emphasis on privacy and individualism.[187] 'Male life patterns' (in the formal economy, business and warfare) are traditionally associated with the public sphere, and 'female life patterns' (in the family, religion and informal economy) are associated with a devalued private sphere. The public–private distinction that continues to pervade Western liberalism effectively provides immunity to perpetuate gender inequality and violence within private spaces.[188] The removal of the marital rape exception in criminal law is only a recent development in most Anglo-European countries. Furthermore, there still exist numerous hurdles in these countries to creating lasting social change where marital rape is uniformly condemned and can be successfully prosecuted.[189]

African and Indigenous feminists, along with other feminists from the global South, have further argued that a context-blind anti-discrimination analysis ignores the unique ways in which women's lives are affected by factors such as poverty and a lack of education, representation and resources, which are independent

[184] Deer (n 110); International Indigenous Women's Forum (FIMI/IIWF) (n 110); Kuokkanen (n 162).

[185] Deer (n 2); Kuokkanen (n 115); Bonita Lawrence and Enakshi Dua, 'Decolonizing Antiracism' (2005) 32 *Social Justice* 120; International Indigenous Women's Forum (FIMI/IIWF) (n 110).

[186] Banda (n 14); Engle (n 120); Coomaraswamy (n 120).

[187] CA MacKinnon, 'Reflections on Sex Equality under Law' (1990) 100 *Yale Law Journal* 1281; J Fudge, 'The Public/Private Distinction: The Possibilities of and the Limits to the Use of Charter Litigation to Further Feminist Struggles' (1987) 25 *Osgoode Hall Law Journal* 485.

[188] H Charlesworth, 'Worlds Apart: Public/Private Distinctions in International Law' in M Thornton (ed), *Public and Private: Feminist Legal Debates* (Oxford, Oxford University Press, 1995); C Chinkin, 'Gender, Inequality and Human Rights Law' in A Hurrell and N Woods (eds), *Inequality, Globalization, and World Politics* (Oxford, Oxford University Press, 1999).

[189] Randall and Venkatesh, 'The Marital Rape Impunity in Comparative and Historical Perspective' (n 6).

of cultural claims.[190] Third world feminist scholars emphasise that various forms of Western imperialism, including colonialism and economic globalisation, have undermined women's autonomy and that the focus on 'culture' and traditions ignores the critical impact of other political and economic forces on the disempowerment of women. For example, Mitra Channa, in her study of globalisation in India, describes how repressive practices such as dowry have been rejuvenated under the aegis of 'modernisation and technological advancement'.[191] Both Winnie Kamau and Bernice Sam have pointed out how unfettered capitalistic economic policies in Kenya and Ghana have resulted in the dismantling of communal land over which women also had rights, and the commoditisation and escalation of traditional practices such as bride-price.[192] These complexities form the crucial background against which all forms of violence against women, including marital rape, operate and have to be simultaneously addressed.

B. The Case for Criminalising Marital Rape

At the outset, it must be acknowledged that criminalisation of IPSV alone is indisputably insufficient to solve the problem. As an extension of existing rape laws, the evidentiary requirements for proving an act of sexual assault in an intimate relationship to a criminal standard may be too hard to satisfy except in the most egregious cases of domestic violence or in divorce proceedings.[193]

Furthermore, marital life is such a fundamental aspect of many women's economic and social worlds that initiating a criminal action would be unfathomable for them, except possibly during a divorce. Women often accede to sex to avoid being subject to physical and emotional violence.[194] Even the initiation of

[190] Banda (n 14) 31; Yuval-Davis (n 5); Coomaraswamy (n 120).

[191] S Mitra Channa, 'Globalization and Modernity in India: A Gendered Critique' (2004) 33 *Urban Anthropology and Studies of Cultural Systems and World Economic Development* 37.

[192] Kamau (n 14); Sam (n 19).

[193] For example, a woman judge in Hungary told Amnesty International for their report on spousal rape in Hungary: 'I have worked as a judge for 20 years, but to tell you the truth, I myself would not report rape. It is very difficult because of the procedures, the attitudes, and social conventions. It is the victim who has to defend and prove everything.' Amnesty International, 'Hungary: Cries Unheard: The Failure to Protect Women from Rape and Sexual Violence in the Home' (Amnesty International, 2007) EUR 27/002/2007.

[194] *R v MacFie*, [2001] AJ No 152, 2001 ABCA 34 [Alberta Court of Appeal, Canada]; see Table 7: Women's Reasons for Having Sexual Intercourse Against Their Will, in Kate Painter, 'Wife Rape in the United Kingdom' (1991) www.crim.cam.ac.uk/people/academic_research/kate_painter/wiferape.pdf. 'The difference between rape in films and marital rape is that we cannot scream, as our child might wake up in the other room. Or that our child is right there, next to us, her or his face distorted with terror. And another difference is that the person who does this to us is someone we used to love, someone we once trusted more than anyone else. And there's another difference, too: that others say that we invented the whole thing. That we tell lies. Or if this can really happen, it is not such a big deal.' 'I knew that if I said no and resisted, he went on the rampage. I could not do this to my children, so in order not to cause them trouble, I closed my eyes and waited until it was over.' Interviews in Amnesty International (n 193).

marital life for many women in the world begins as an act of rape, as a researcher observed in her interviews of Indian women:

> And in an uncharacteristic move, they began to discuss their very first sexual encounters. I was shocked, not by the unexpectedly liberated manner of these women, but by the acts that they described on their wedding night, where their husbands had pounced on them in hormone and alcohol-fuelled frenzies. Their initiation into conjugal life was through an act that can only be described as rape. They did not know the word for rape, but from what they described, they hated the encounter, which turned into a lifelong abhorrence for their husbands.[195]

Marital rape is an accepted part of life for women in many societies. Women are in such a vulnerable position, dependent on their husbands, kin and community for their social and economic well-being, that criminal law will always remain a last resort. Furthermore, criminal law enforcement mechanisms are known for using tactics that further produce racialised and gendered violence.[196] Many women, especially those whose communities are subordinated by the state, would prefer solutions arising from within their groups. Hence, intersectionality scholars insist on framing gender violence, including marital rape, within a larger set of demands that includes concerns about poverty, incarceration, colonialism, exploitation and root cause conditions.[197]

Recognising all of these concerns, it is nevertheless important to support criminalisation initiatives addressing marital rape for many significant reasons. First, criminalisation has a powerful symbolic value that identifies marital rape as a blameworthy act.[198] It demonstrates state support for combating gender violence in all its forms and sends a strong message of condemnation of the act.[199] A World Bank report that surveyed responses to combat gender violence in several countries across the world articulated that multiple interventions at different

[195] V Sirnate, 'When Marriage Is Less than Sacred', *The Hindu*, 24 June 2015, www.thehindu.com/opinion/op-ed/when-marriage-is-less-than-sacred/article7315485.ece.

[196] Crenshaw (n 4); NJ Sokoloff and I Dupont, 'Domestic Violence at the Intersections of Race, Class, and Gender Challenges and Contributions to Understanding Violence against Marginalized Women in Diverse Communities' (2005) 11 *Violence Against Women* 38.

[197] D Spade, 'Intersectional Resistance and Law Reform' (2013) 38 *Signs* 1031; S Cho, K Williams Crenshaw and L McCall, 'Toward a Field of Intersectionality Studies: Theory, Applications, and Praxis' (2013) 38 *Signs* 785; Yuval-Davis (n 5).

[198] MD Schwartz, 'The Spousal Exemption for Criminal Rape Prosecution' (1982) 7 *Vermont Law Review* 33, 50–51.

[199] EJ Sack, 'Is Domestic Violence a Crime: Intimate Partner Rape as Allegory' (2009) 24 *St John's Journal of Legal Commentary* 557; Schwartz (n 198) 50–51. 'Removing the marital exemption would make an important statement about the relative position of married women in society. If the continuation of the marital rape exemption protects male property interests, removal of the exemption asserts the right of married women to the physical integrity of their bodies, and of the right to choose what uses their bodies will be put to. It is unlikely that spousal rape differs in intent from any other rape in that it is not a crime of sex, but one of humiliation and degradation. As an educational tool for both men and women, removing the spousal exemption from rape laws is a powerful statement about the rights of partners in a marital relationship' (ibid, 51).

levels (individual, community, institutional, legal and policy) are necessary.[200] The report maps out a table of risk factors at the individual level, relationship level (eg male control of decision-making and wealth; polygamy), community level and societal level, including norms, laws and policies that support male dominance over women and that require women's obedience and sexual availability. The report points out that criminal justice system implementation problems aside, the mere presence of criminal laws have advanced efforts to strengthen women's rights and to combat violence against women.[201]

Criminalisation moves marital rape from being constructed as an individual wrong that happens within the confines of the private sphere, to a systemic, societal concern that affects the entire public. Given the pervasiveness of marital rape across all societies globally,[202] criminalisation is necessary to indicate the strictest public condemnation of IPSV and to point out that there is no 'legitimate' rape. In countries where legal rules have been successful in deterring conduct, criminalisation may also provide direct relief and may *initiate* the process of changing mind-sets. Sociolegal research illustrates the everyday influence of law as it is embedded in everyday social practices and '[shapes] the rules people carry in their heads'.[203] Also, the state legal system provides an important avenue for those women who are able and willing to go against their families and communities, but who would otherwise have no other recourse.[204]

Second, a refusal to intervene with the state law and an abandonment of the demand for legal reform that protects women in all their identities means that advocates for women's rights as well as for Indigenous rights and cultural self-determination cede territory to state patriarchy and colonial practices.[205] As postcolonial scholars have pointed out, the marital rape exception is rooted in colonial laws.[206] Matthew Hale's infamous treatise on marital rape was codified across the British Empire and was used as the source for legalising marital rape

200 Andrew Morrison, Mary Ellsberg and Sarah Bott, 'Addressing Gender-Based Violence: A Critical Review of Interventions' (2007) 22 *World Bank Research Observer* 25.

201 ibid, 35.

202 Randall and Venkatesh, 'Right to No' (n 119) 157–64.

203 S Engle Merry, 'Human Rights and Transnational Culture: Regulating Gender Violence through Global Law' (2006) 44 *Osgoode Hall Law Journal* 53, 57; P Ewick and SS Silbey, *The Common Place of Law: Stories from Everyday Life* (Chicago, University of Chicago Press, 1998).

204 This argument has often been framed as 'exit rights'. See M Craven Nussbaum, *Sex & Social Justice* (Oxford, Oxford University Press, 1999) 30.

205 With respect to feminists ceding the territory, see V Munro, 'Violence against Women, "Victimhood" and the (Neo)Liberal State' in M Davies and V Munro (eds), *The Ashgate Research companion to Feminist Legal Theory* (London, Ashgate, 2013) 242.

206 M Sinha, *Colonial Masculinity: The 'Manly Englishman' and the 'Effeminate Bengali' in the Late Nineteenth Century* (Manchester, Manchester University Press, 1995) 161–62; JE Hasday, 'Contest and Consent: A Legal History of Marital Rape' (2000) 88 *California Law Review* 1373; S-A Elvy, 'A Postcolonial Theory of Spousal Rape: The Caribbean and Beyond' (2015) 22 *Michigan Journal of Gender & Law* 89; SA Adamo, 'The Injustice of the Marital Rape Exemption: A Survey of Common Law Countries' (1989) 4 *American University Journal of International Law and Policy* 555.

in many jurisdictions.[207] Removing the marital rape exception is therefore necessary to dismantle the existing colonial structures that subordinate Indigenous and other groups.

Third, the purported ineffectuality of criminalisation cannot be a reason for a state to abdicate its responsibilities to protect women from gendered violence and to offer them legal remedies. The fact that most of the African countries are all signatories to CEDAW and the African Charter Draft Protocol, and that most have constitutionalised gender equality, shows that these states themselves have acceded to the substantive content of equality. States are therefore obligated to show due diligence in changing their laws to reflect substantive gender equality. The due-diligence standard includes criminalisation of marital rape.[208] Criminalisation, undoubtedly, cannot be the *only* step taken to combat marital rape. It has to be part of a broader initiative towards gender equality.

Lastly and importantly, concerns about criminalisation are also countered by the benefits that can be accrued from the symbolic benefits of criminalisation and the radiating effects from the legal mobilisation for criminalisation. From a mobilisation perspective, advocating the criminalisation of marital rape serves several purposes. The demand for criminalisation has now become a part of a broader gender-equality social movement led by women activists in several countries.[209] In the few instances where local women's rights groups have been successful in criminalising marital rape legislatively or through the judicial process, the law has provided a precedent to challenge specious claims of cultural protection and has opened up space for a progressive interpretation of cultural norms. For example, the Nepal Supreme Court recently found that there could be no criminal impunity for marital rape.[210] The litigation was preceded by a decade of judicial legal education after surveys by civil society groups in South Asia confirmed an entrenched gender bias within the predominantly male-dominated judiciary.[211] Importantly, the numerous decisions in the Nepal Supreme Court in the last decade reveal a contestation for the contemporary meaning of cultural values and practices, where

[207] M Hale et al, *Historia Placitorum Coronae. The History of the Pleas of the Crown*, 1st US edn (Robert H Small, 1847) 629. According to Hale: '[T]he husband cannot be guilty of a rape committed by himself upon his lawful wife, for by their mutual matrimonial consent and contract the wife hath given up herself in this kind unto her husband, which she cannot retract.'

[208] Randall and Venkatesh, 'Right to No' (n 119) 165–70.

[209] Mandal (n 17); C Cruise, 'Making Spousal Rape a Crime', *VOA (Voice of America)*, 18 November 2013, learningenglish.voanews.com/a/spousal-rape-marital-rape-femnet-malawi-kenya-liberia-nigeria-uganda-burundi-zimbabwe/1790823.html; T Suan Chian and S Sudderuddin, 'Singapore: Proposed Marital Rape Law Welcomed', *Straits Times*, 18 February 2012; BBC News–Africa, 'Anger at Kenya's Diluted Rape Law', *BBC*, 1 June 2006, news.bbc.co.uk/2/hi/africa/5036398.stm; International Indigenous Women's Forum (FIMI/IIWF) (n 110).

[210] *Meera Dhungana v His Majesty's Government et al*, Writ No 55 of the year 2058 BS (2006 AD).

[211] Kabita Pandey, 'Judicial Education on the Convention on Elimination of Discrimination against Women in Nepal', *Women's Human Rights: CEDAW in International, Regional, and National Law* (Cambridge, Cambridge University Press, 2013).

the Court relies on Hindu norms and 'Nepali culture', alongside international law and constitutional sources, to justify its decisions.[212]

With consistent mobilisation, legal (and legislative) institutions can be compelled to adopt a multicultural, legal pluralistic approach that simultaneously takes into account the intersectional nature of identity and power to protect women's equality. Courts and legislatures can provide essential sites for contesting culture, traditions and rights. Criminalisation initiatives specifically have the capacity to generate public debate and awareness of the issue of sexual violence in marriage.

Support for criminalisation of marital rape also allows women's rights groups to challenge the state's institutionalisation of patriarchy in other significant ways. In Kenya, during parliamentary debates on the Marriage Bill, Members of Parliament had, on various occasions, rejected drafts of the bill on the basis that the legislation was un-African and represented an imposition of Western values.[213] The provisions criminalising marital rape in the Sexual Offences Act 2006 were rejected on the basis that they went against 'African culture'.[214] The report on the resistance of male parliamentarians to the passage of the Domestic Violence Legislation in Rwanda showed that such sentiments prevail in governments in many places.[215] However, all the legislative efforts were marked by the extraordinary efforts of *local* women's rights groups and women parliamentarians in campaigning for the bill, creating male allies for the bill, and holding the legislature accountable for gender justice.

The judicial mobilising in Nepal and the legislative mobilising in other countries by local women's rights groups is part of a legitimate 'internalisation' or 'vernacularisation' process led by human rights groups, a process that cannot be discounted as Western, Eurocentric imperialism.[216] Seen from a social movement perspective, the marital rape criminalisation initiative offers an opportunity to align with racialised, Indigenous or ethnic women's groups and to rely on their organising methods to mobilise women to create safety from sexual violence within their marriages.

[212] R Pradhan, 'Legal Pluralism, Cultural Contestation and Gender (In)justice: An Interpretation of Women's Rights Cases in the Supreme Court of Nepal', www.repository.cam.ac.uk/handle/1810/226699. Also see *People v Jumawan*, GR No 187495, 722 SCRA 108 (21 April 2014) (Phil).

[213] Kamau (n 14) 37.

[214] ibid.

[215] E Pearson, *Demonstrating Legislative Leadership: The Introduction to Rwanda's Gender-Based Violence Bill*, ed Elizabeth Powley (Initiative for Inclusive Security, 2008). Also see the Indian government refusing to criminalise marital rape because marriage is 'sacrosanct': PTI (n 177). The Minister of State for Home, Haribhai Parathibhai Chaudhary, said: 'It is considered that the concept of marital rape, as understood internationally, cannot be suitably applied in the Indian context due to various factors, including level of education, illiteracy, poverty, myriad social customs and values, religious beliefs, mindset of the society to treat the marriage as a sacrament, etc.'

[216] See Merry (n 120); Merry (n 203); P Levitt and S Merry, 'Vernacularization on the Ground: Local Uses of Global Women's Rights in Peru, China, India and the United States' (2009) 9 *Global Networks* 441.

V. Intersectional Strategies for Combating Marital Rape

A. Criminalisation as Part of a Broader Community-Based Social Justice Movement

Intersectional strategies for engaging law to end the problem of marital rape need to be bottom-up, not top-down. Supporting meaningful egalitarian pluralism in a country, while recognising the sovereignty and self-determination claims of Indigenous groups and the cultural and political rights of other subordinated groups, involves not just providing access to multiple voices in legal institutions. It also requires reconstituting courts and law, as these are crucial sites of contestation of norms and values.

Radhika Coomaraswamy illustrates the problems with top-down approaches to legal reform by analysing a notorious Indian case in which a university student self-immolated on the funeral pyre of her dead husband following the traditional dicta of *sati* (which had been banned in India since colonial times).[217] Members of the ethnic group that espoused *sati* marched in thousands *against* the horrified urban, progressive groups, who pushed successfully for even tougher legal reforms, reforms that did not have any resonance amongst the ethnic groups who desired to practice *sati*. Yet, in India, there are also other numerous instances of women in traditional and/or rural groups fighting for their empowerment and emancipation against the patriarchal powers within their group. Coomaraswamy points out that it is essential to create a solidarity movement across all levels by including women embedded within the traditional cultural group.

Indigenous women's groups in various national contexts have been affirming the need to take an Indigenous approach to domestic and sexual violence that takes into account their claims for independence and Indigenous self-determination while asserting their rights to be free from violence and sexism within the community.[218] Many Indigenous scholars have demanded that Indigenous legal knowledge and traditions be used to engender what Sarah Deer calls an 'Indigenous jurisprudence of rape'.[219] The International Indigenous Women's Forum endorses criminalisation of domestic violence as a 'potentially effective strategy', while emphasising that criminalisation strategies 'must be undertaken with critical regard for physical and structural violence perpetrated by States themselves'.[220]

[217] Coomaraswamy (n 120).

[218] Deer (n 2); International Indigenous Women's Forum (FIMI/IIWF) (n 110); E Snyder, V Napoleon and J Borrows, 'Gender and Violence: Drawing on Indigenous Legal Resources' (2015) 48 *UBC Law Review* 593.

[219] Deer (n 2); International Indigenous Women's Forum (FIMI/IIWF) (n 110); Snyder et al (n 218).

[220] International Indigenous Women's Forum (FIMI/IIWF) (n 110) 26.

In Kenya, after decades of dictatorship, there is now an extraordinarily active women's movement that is seeking to ride the wave of political change and bring about gender justice on the ground, even when there are large and powerful sections in the country that oppose the changes. Groups that advocate criminalisation of marital rape could easily align with the broader women's rights movement in Kenya.

It is evident that any struggle for progressive change from the dictates of a religion or a cultural group has to be initiated and won from within the communities themselves. Coomaraswamy exhorts scholars to avoid the 'Orientalist Trap' by not dividing the world into bipolar categories. She urges that scholars and advocates recognise that legal strategies need to allow women to use traditional bases for empowerment and must collaborate with local social movements. Many local women's rights groups in Africa centre their strategies for addressing gender inequality in traditional systems with an emphasis on process; that is, by ensuring that women's voices are heard, that their participation is emphasised, and that the states as well as local justice systems are democratised.[221] An example of a successful participatory strategy is cited by Winnie Kamau, who describes how women in the Turkana region in Kenya were provided with paralegal training and then obtained positions in local councils convened by administrative chiefs.[222] Women's groups have used the discursive processes inherent in traditional cultures to bring about a debate on gender violence and to contest norms internally. These processes are important to initiate a 'vernacularisation' of women's rights norms, where even 'imported' institutions and symbols can be made to resonate locally using community frames and practices.[223]

There are many traditional and Indigenous communities throughout the world where women play a major role in cultural practices and wield official power within their communities as creators and transmitters of culture. Such roles include queen mothers in Ghana,[224] headwomen and traditional councillors in

[221] Kamau (n 14) 40–41; Banda (n 14) 278–85; UN Women, 'Role of Traditional Leaders and Customary Justice Mechanisms' (End VAW Now, 2012) www.endvawnow.org/en/articles/1684-role-of-traditional-leaders-and-customary-justice-mechanisms.html; Kishwar (n 176); Levitt and Merry (n 216); Vanegas and Pruitt (n 176).

[222] Kamau (n 14) 41; UN Women (n 221). ('The Turkana Women in Development Organization (TWADO) runs a paralegal program specifically focused on monitoring cases that involve violence against women and children in the remote Turkana region of Kenya. Women paralegals are trained on human rights, gender equity, and relevant Kenyan laws. They are then seconded to customary dispute resolution processes in Turkana, where they provide input to cases that relate to women's rights. They also monitor the system for cases that should be referred to the formal courts and encourage families to use that process.') For other examples, see UN Women (n 221); Gender and Development Network, 'How to Note: A Practical Guide on Community Programming on Violence against Women and Girls' (Department for International Development, 2012) www.gov.uk/government/uploads/system/uploads/attachment_data/file/67335/How-to-note-VAWG-2-community-prog.pdf.

[223] Merry (n 120) 44.

[224] BJ Stoeltje, 'Asante Queen Mothers: Precolonial Authority in a Postcolonial Society' (2003) 19 *Research Review/Institute of African Studies* 1.

Namibia,[225] and first-nation chiefs and leaders in settler countries.[226] Women's cultural status in certain cases can be used to mutually reinforce cultural rights and women's rights.[227] In many such places, women leaders and Indigenous women's groups have forcefully demanded that they want to be the instruments of change and fight domestic and sexual violence on their terms.[228]

In contrast, in communities where there is systemic and deep-rooted gender inequality, the woman's position may be so subordinated that she may have no power to negotiate her status—not only within her community, but also with legal institutions.[229] Support from the male members of her community may be crucial for her to access substantive as well as procedural equality.[230] As Anne Griffiths notes, in the context of the Kwena community in Botswana, even where women have access to the law, they may opt not to use the law for fear of severing their kin-based networks.[231] Transforming these power relations requires not only women's empowerment but also support from other members of the community. There is no doubt that, in such contexts, women face tremendous barriers, especially if there is no support from within the community, and transformative change would be a slow process. Nevertheless, in such contexts, working within the community becomes even more essential. It also makes it more crucial to remove other barriers through economic empowerment, providing alternative institutional mechanisms which are closer to the community, have easier procedures, and use the same language, mandating women's participation in local institutions, and supporting all mobilising initiatives by women.

In general, the capacity for women to resist violence is also usually limited by other *external factors*, such as economic deprivation, limited education and employment opportunities, diminished nutritional capacity, inter alia, and many of these factors may be a result of inequalities between various groups. For example, many postcolonial states have been left with the vestiges of colonial divide-and-rule where a particular community has established political dominance; both women and men belonging to the subordinated groups are disenfranchised. In such cases, advocating for rights for the entire community, especially relating to

[225] He Becker, 'A Concise History of Gender, "Tradition" and the State in Namibia' in C Keulder (ed), *State, Society, and Democracy: a Reader in Namibian Politics* (Windhoek, Namibia, Gamsberg Macmillan, 2000) 193–94.

[226] HK Aikau et al, 'Indigenous Feminisms Roundtable' (2015) 36 *Frontiers: A Journal of Women Studies* 84; Cora Jane Voyageur, *Firekeepers of the Twenty-First Century: First Nations Women Chiefs* (Montreal/Kingston, McGill-Queen's University Press 2008).

[227] Secretariat of the Permanent Forum of Indigenous People (SPFII), 'Gender and Indigenous People's Culture' (United Nations 2007) Briefing Note 4.

[228] Aikau et al (n 226); International Indigenous Women's Forum (FIMI/IIWF) (n 110); Tripp (n 176); Becker (n 225).

[229] A Griffiths, 'Gender, Power, and Difference: Reconfiguring Law from Bakwena Women's Perspectives' (2000) 23 *PoLAR: Political and Legal Anthropology Review* 89.

[230] ibid.

[231] A Griffiths, *In the Shadow of Marriage: Gender and Justice in an African Community* (Chicago, University of Chicago Press 1997) 43.

poverty, access and opportunity, is an essential element of advocating for gender equality *within* that group.

B. Working Within Customary Systems

In many, but not all, contexts, women seeking remedies for spousal oppressions often prefer to go through customary arbitration systems rather than state-based legal systems.[232] In South Africa, for example, traditional courts play an important role in the adjudication of justice.[233] Customary law courts are accessible, inexpensive, have simplified procedures and are conducted in the same language as the litigants. Traditional courts may therefore be best placed to provide some recourse to women suffering marital rape. Anne Griffiths, in her in-depth ten-year-long study of the Tswana-speaking people in Botswana, shows how women are disadvantaged in both the formal state legal system and the customary legal system.[234] Her research demonstrates how kinship and economic patterns can work in complex ways in hindering women's access to justice. However, Griffiths also shows how the customary legal system, gendered as it may be, provides resources for women seeking justice in their family relationships. Women in her study moved between both the state and customary systems in making claims. The Swahili *qadi* courts in Kenya have also been found to offer women a forum to negotiate their marriage relationships.[235]

This engagement with customary legal systems may warrant essential structural changes within the traditional courts. The South African traditional courts, for example, have received much criticism because the chiefs are usually illiterate men, who have limited knowledge or experience, and have no expertise to balance common law and constitutional law concerns.[236] Women have limited avenues to participate. Reforms to the traditional courts have been proposed in the South African legislature, but the proposed bills have been very controversial and not

[232] ibid. In recent surveys in Somaliland, Puntland, Timor-Leste, Afghanistan, Liberia, and Indonesia, large majorities preferred the customary systems, as described in Erica Harper, 'Customary Justice: From Program Design to Impact Evaluation' (International Development Law Organization, 2011) 26–27; Mark Tran, 'Why We Need to Make Customary Laws Work for Women', *The Guardian*, 6 February 2013, www.theguardian.com/global-development/poverty-matters/2013/feb/06/make-customary-laws-work-for-women. 86% of Muslim women in India, who belong to a beleaguered minority group, preferred religious *qazis* to administer family law. However, when it came to domestic violence, the women overwhelmingly report to their families (44.7% in the survey), police (24%) or NGOs (15%). Only 1.4% approached their religious *qazis*. See Noorjehan Safia Niaz and Zakia Soman, 'Seeking Justice Within Family: A National Study on Muslim Women's Views on Reforms in Muslim Personal Law' (Bharatiya Muslim Mahila Andolan, 2015) 91, 107.

[233] Koyana (n 60) 246.

[234] Griffiths (n 231).

[235] SF Hirsch, *Pronouncing & Persevering: Gender and the Discourses of Disputing in an African Islamic Court* (Chicago, University of Chicago Press 1998) 129–37.

[236] Koyana (n 60) 232–33.

sufficiently protective of women's rights.[237] Corruption and influence are serious problems affecting the delivery of justice. Courts in Lesotho and South Africa also do not allow legal representation and therefore do not permit trained lawyers or human rights specialists to participate in the adjudication.

Nevertheless, it cannot be assumed that the state appellate courts offer any recourse for women. South Africa was one of the first African nations to criminalise marital rape.[238] However, the South African courts continue to ignore the legislation and rely on stereotypes and patriarchal assumptions to provide impunity to husbands for raping their wives.[239] One recent South African case raised the question of customary law, when a man kidnapped and raped his separated wife.[240] The judge found that since the complainant had not reimbursed her husband for the *lobola* (bride-price) when she decided to leave him, the husband believed that they were still married and that he was entitled to 'conjugal benefits'. The judge further found that this belief, as well as the likelihood that they were still married according to customary law, was sufficient to legally condone the defendant's rape of the complainant. The judge stated that 'his actions, though totally unacceptable in law … were shaped and moulded by the norms, beliefs and customary practices by which he lived his life'. The judge further stated that his court was entitled to depart from the mandatory minimum life sentence when faced with such cases.[241]

In Ghana, even though cohabitation (*mpena aware*) is recognised as akin to a marital relationship by local customary law, the state courts only endorse relationships 'sanctified' by marriage and have ruled that a cohabitation relationship is 'mere concubinage' and is not recognised by either the statutory law or the state-sanctioned customary law.[242] After separation from such a union, the parties cannot bring a claim for property distribution or maintenance or any of the other rights given to state-sanctioned married persons. This decision ignores the realities of women living in other kinds of intimate relationships. The decision also provides a compelling reason to ensure that any criminalisation of marital rape legislation extends to all intimate relationships.

There are several examples where customary laws have changed to embrace gender equality and where the local customary law has offered more protection for women than the state law. For example, as early as 1979, the Traditional Appeal

[237] S Mnisi Weeks, 'South Africans Braced for New Confrontation with Government over Controversial Law', *The Conversation*, 8 June 2015, theconversation.com/south-africans-braced-for-new-confrontation-with-government-over-controversial-law-42829.

[238] Prevention of Family Violence Act, No 133 of 1993 (South Africa) s 5.

[239] In *S v Moipolai* (CA 53/2004) [2004] ZANWHC 19, the judge decided that the victim 'must have come knowing that this [sexual intercourse] was either likely to happen or was going to happen … given the nature of their relationship'. The judge further stated that 'this rape should therefore be treated differently from the rape of one stranger by another between whom consensual intercourse was almost unthinkable'. Also see *S v Modise* (113/06) [2007] ZANWHC 73.

[240] *S v Mvamvu* (350/2003) [2004] ZASCA 90, [2005] 1 AU SA 435 (SCA).

[241] ibid.

[242] Sam (n 19) 13–14 quoting *Badu v Boakye* [1975] 1 GLR 283.

Court of Malawi ruled in one case that a woman cannot be forced into polygamous marriage without her consent and, in another case, ruled that a husband cannot treat his wife as property simply because he has paid a dowry for her.[243]

In Kenya, the customary norms relating to trusts have been used to enable women to hold land on behalf of the family and to make decisions about apportionment and use.[244] Customs have also responded to local campaigns by women's groups and health groups to change practices such as widow-cleansing[245] and female genital cutting.[246] Customary marriage laws in Ghana also recognise many more factors that can serve as a basis for divorce than do statutory laws and, as stated above, Ghanaian queen mothers have been an important resource for empowering women within their communities.[247]

In a context of a staunchly resilient patriarchal state and where much of the life of the average woman is lived outside the purview and jurisdiction of the state's legal system, it may be possible to find 'a repository of customary values which provide better building blocks [for ensuring gender justice]' outside of even the state-sponsored juridical customary legal system.[248] Strategies to criminalise marital rape can also tap into the dynamism in traditional systems. In fact, perpetuating monolithic, static understanding of traditional systems plays into the hands of the power brokers within the systems who use the same discourse to resist change to prevent any dilution of their power.

Aboriginal rights movements have used Indigenous frames to campaign for the emancipation of women in their communities against state and communal oppression, thereby showing a path for non-Eurocentric, non-patronising models of law reform within communities.[249] Winnie Kamau describes an 'internal adjustment' model in Kenya, where existing cultural structures are used to modify discriminatory cultural practices.[250] Changes to the practice of female genital cutting in Kenya and widow-cleansing in Ghana are examples where traditional structures were used to modify local custom. Another example can be found in Senegal, where a grassroots human rights group, Tostan, effectively mobilised within and with local communities a consensus-building education programme to rethink and collectively abandon the ancient and widely practised cutting of the genitals

[243] *Poya v Poya*, NTAC Civil Appeal Case No 38 of 1979, *Wasili Mpaweni v Wasili Mary*, NTAC Civil Appeal Case No 86 of 1979, *Msikawa v Msowaya* NTAC Civil Appeal Case No 40 of 1979. See Kanyongolo and Nweso (n 23) 14–15.

[244] Kamau (n 14) 11.

[245] Widow 'cleansing' is a practice in which a widow must have sex with a brother to her husband or other relative, or with a village cleanser, ostensibly to release her husband's spirit into the afterlife and protect herself and her village from his spirit. This is done before she can marry anyone else. See Robyn Curnow and Jenni Watts, 'Lawyer Fights "Widow Cleansing" Tradition in Malawi', *CNN*, 21 March 2013, www.cnn.com/2013/03/21/world/africa/seodi-white-women-malawi/index.html.

[246] Kamau (n 14) 11.

[247] Sam (n 19) 21–22, 10.

[248] Chanock (n 39) 87.

[249] Deer (n 2); Turpel (n 110); Kuokkanen (n 115).

[250] Kamau (n 14) 41.

of female children.[251] These successful initiatives are remarkable in particular because they engaged the very community and family ties which had embedded the harmful tradition in order to end it. They also demonstrate the possibilities for using traditional frames and customary arbitration to combat marital rape.

Sometimes, religious and traditional laws can be used for progressive interpretation when state laws display entrenched patriarchal norms and state legislatures have been apathetic in advancing women's rights or upholding the state laws. In one of the earliest cases of judicial overruling of the marital exemption, the Supreme Court of Israel used religious Jewish law to advance Israeli sexual assault law.[252] Israeli state law has sole jurisdiction over criminal cases and is governed by legislation enacted by the parliament (Knesset) and common law, which is composed of English common law and Turkish law.[253] But the religious laws (of various communities) have full jurisdiction over many aspects of family law, especially marriage and divorce.

The penal code on rape in 1977 in Israel was governed by the English common law definition, which deemed marital rape to be lawful sexual intercourse under all circumstances. In order to get around the English common law impunity for marital rape, the Court decided to interpret 'unlawful' sexual intercourse on the basis of Jewish religious law.[254] It used expert evidence to interpret Jewish religious law, which is governed by the Bible and the Talmud and associated religious commentaries, as not permitting sexual intercourse without consent within a marriage. Under the court's interpretation of Jewish law, marriage was based on reciprocal conjugal obligations; the Bible permitted the wife to refuse intercourse during menstruation and other circumstances, and the Talmud explicitly prohibited a man from compelling his wife to have sex with him. Judge Bechor also said that the British common law was 'primitive' and observed that even 'so-called enlightened and progressive nations' had laws that did not recognise the 'fundamental notion of the dignity of a woman as a free person'.[255]

However, in 1987, in a marital rape case involving a Bedouin, instead of supporting a progressive community-based interpretation of Islamic Bedouin law, the Court ruled that Israeli state law on women's rights took precedence over Islamic

[251] CW Dugger, 'Movement to End Genital Cutting Spreads in Senegal', *New York Times*, 15 October 2011, www.nytimes.com/2011/10/16/world/africa/movement-to-end-genital-cutting-spreads-in-senegal.html.

[252] *Cohen v The State of Israel*, Criminal Appeal 91/80, P.D. 35 (3) 281.

[253] The territory around Israel was Ottoman Turkish territory until it became a protectorate of the British kingdom, first upon conquest and then later on by UN mandate. The British followed the Turkish practice and instituted an amalgam of British, Turkish, and religious law (Christian, Jewish and Islamic). When Israel became an independent state in 1948, it adopted the system after it made some modifications to it. See JJ Gross, 'Marital Rape—A Crime? A Comparative Law Study of the Laws of the United States and the State of Israel' (1991) 15 *International Journal of Comparative and Applied Criminal Justice* 207; Warren Goldstein, *Defending the Human Spirit: Jewish Law's Vision for a Moral Society* (Spring Valley, NY, Feldheim Publishers, 2006).

[254] Goldstein (n 253) 168–74.

[255] ibid.

law and as such, all women 'have the right to refuse sex to any man, including her husband'.[256] The case reveals how legal adjudication, especially in women's rights issues, reflects and is constructed by complex and shifting political power structures.

In a recent example, the Supreme Court in Nepal engaged in a progressive interpretation of Hindu religious law and found that marital rape is not legitimated by religion or traditional norms:

> The learned government advocate appearing on behalf of the respondents pleaded that it is not in conformity with Hindu religion and tradition to say that consent is required to have sexual intercourse with one's own wife. … Sexual intercourse in conjugal life is a normal course of behaviour, which must be based on consent. *No religion may ever take it as lawful because the aim of a good religion is not to hate or cause loss to anyone.* Thus, the pleading of the learned government attorney appearing on behalf of the respondent can not be accepted.[257]

Legal anthropological work shows how plural legal orders engage in continuous processes of adaptation and transformation and how coexisting legal orders influence each other.[258] Recognising all the different legal norms that affect an individual's life, including the transnational and customary legal systems, can allow for the emergence of 'new, hybrid, or syncretic legal forms'.[259] International women's rights activism needs to engage this pluralism strategically to promote productive cross-fertilisations instead of perceived rights conflicts.

Lastly, instead of adopting a paternalistic strategy towards customary law, Indigenous law and other legal systems that are not based on European civil/common law, one can also envisage a legal-political context where groups have self-determination rights and the jurisdiction to administer a different legal system, but also responsibilities and obligations. If non-state actors, such as tribes and communities, are given authority and state-like autonomy, then it stands to reason that they could have state-like duties too. Several Indigenous rights groups have been more than willing to accept the responsibilities associated with human rights treaties provided they maintain autonomy to fulfil those responsibilities.[260]

[256] C McNamee, 'Rape' in Rita J Simon (ed), *A Comparative Perspective on Major Social Problems* (Lanham, MD, Lexington Books, 2001) 29.

[257] *Meera Dhungana v His Majesty's Government et al*, Writ No 55 of the year 2058 BS (2006 Nepal Supreme Court) (emphasis added).

[258] Merry (n 173); René Provost and Colleen Sheppard, 'Introduction: Human Rights Through Legal Pluralism' in René Provost and Colleen Sheppard (eds), *Dialogues on Human Rights and Legal Pluralism* (Dordrecht, Springer Netherlands, 2013) link.springer.com/chapter/10.1007/978-94-007-4710-4_1; Gad Barzilai, 'Legal Categorizations and Religion: On Politics of Modernity, Practices, Faith, and Power' in Austin Sarat (ed), *The Blackwell Companion to Law and Society* (Oxford, Blackwell, 2004); Franz von Benda-Beckmann and Keebet von Benda-Beckmann, 'The Dynamics of Change and Continuity in Plural Legal Orders' (2006) 38(53–54) *Journal of Legal Pluralism and Unofficial Law*, http://dx.doi.org/10.1080/07329113.2006.10756597.

[259] von Benda-Beckmann and von Benda-Beckmann (n 258).

[260] Deer (n 2); Aikau et al (n 226); Kuokkanen (n 162); International Indigenous Women's Forum (FIMI/IIWF) (n 110).

Accepting cultural freedoms and opening the discourse to non-state actors will only help the international law and international human rights frameworks gain wider credibility and legitimacy.

VI. Conclusion

Human rights are 'imperatives arising in response to experiences falling collectively under the rubric of domination'.[261] As such, struggles for women's rights and cultural rights are joined in principle by the same concern of ending domination. This insight needs to be centrally foregrounded and vigorously applied to struggles to end marital rape by criminalising it, particularly in contexts with pluralist legal systems. Addressing rights issues as if there were discrete dichotomies—such as women's rights versus cultural rights—ignores the multiplicity and overlap of these categories. The cultural and gender identities of women in many concrete community contexts are so intertwined that one cannot create neat essentialist boundaries delineating these identities.

The tired debates about the universal-versus-particularist nature of human rights are traditionally framed in extremes. This simplistic frame, which dichotomises universal and particular rights, fails to acknowledge that human rights contain both characteristics simultaneously.[262] The inability to perceive and acknowledge the social and communal dimensions along with the individual dimension of human rights is particularly detrimental to the project of protecting the rights of women in specific cultural groups.

Cultural essentialism cannot be used as an excuse to permit violence against women or violence against other groups. Nevertheless, to combat marital rape, the human rights framework must be informed by a context-driven approach. The point of an intersectionality-based strategy is 'to analyse the differential ways in which different social divisions are concretely enmeshed and constructed by each other and how they relate to political and subjective constructions of identities'.[263]

Both gender justice as well as rights claims of subordinated groups are responses to marginalisation and discrimination. Women and the cultural groups in which they live seek the genuine capacity to influence the broader political and socio-economic agendas shaping their lives. Women in Indigenous groups and other groups who challenge the legitimacy of the state and of state coercion in their lives are seeking not only the right to be free from violence inflicted by individuals within their families and communities, but also the right to be free from violence perpetrated by the state and by racist individuals outside of their community.

[261] W Barbieri, 'Group Rights and the Muslim Diaspora' (1999) 21 *Human Rights Quarterly* 907, 914.

[262] C Chinkin, 'Cultural Relativism and International Law' in CW Howland (ed), *Religious Fundamentalism and the Human Rights of Women* (New York, St Martin's Press, 1999).

[263] Yuval-Davis (n 5) 205.

Gendered sexual violence is deeply linked with racialised political violence.[264] Women from within marginalised groups and communities do not see a hierarchical relationship between rights but an intersection of their collective and individual rights. The core of an intersectional approach towards criminalising marital rape is to ensure the centrality of women's experiences and interests in every context.

Modernisation, globalisation and democratisation have not resulted in gender justice in postcolonial states, as can be seen in the entrenchment of patriarchy within their state systems. Likewise, religious, Indigenous and customary systems (as experienced on the ground) do not always necessarily and unambiguously favour patriarchy—and as a result these systems can offer forums for women to challenge gender injustice from within.

Throughout the world, gender justice advocates have strategically drawn on different levels of law—customary, local, national and international. Contrary to the view that they are only sources of domination for women, customary and Indigenous legal systems can hold the potential for lasting societal change. First, customary and Indigenous mechanisms can be used to bring legitimacy to the condemnation of rape of women in intimate relationships, which in turn can be used to pressure the state to change its laws or enforce existing laws. Second, even if the state criminalises marital rape, local, community-based mechanisms are essential for providing access to justice, enforcing the laws taking into account the particular context of the community, obtaining community support and changing mind-sets.

Under these circumstances, it is essential to advocate for the criminalisation of marital rape while also supporting Indigenous women's rights movements, seizing opportunities within customary legal systems and engaging in broader social justice reforms. Despite the valid concerns about bolstering state coercion that inhere in criminalisation initiatives, it is short-sighted to allow the state to continue upholding colonial laws around marital rape exceptions. As Catherine Mackinnon states: 'One of the most effective strategies for maintaining a system of dominance is to convince those who seek to end it that the tools of domination must be left in the hands of the dominant.'[265]

Kenya, Malawi and Ghana, among others, are examples of countries where the state has proactively sought to limit the power of customary law as a competing source of authority through various processes such as codification, dismantling of traditional courts, or limiting the jurisdiction and application of customary law. The juridical version of state-accepted customary law is thereby ossified and shorn of its inherent capacity for dynamism and change.[266] State-adopted customary

[264] Castañeda (n 47); Bubar and Thurman (n 16); Maddison and Partridge (n 48); Moffitt et al (n 48); Davis (n 16); Crenshaw (n 4).

[265] CA MacKinnon, *Women's Lives, Men's Laws* (Cambridge, MA, Belknap Press of Harvard University Press, 2005) 42.

[266] Chanock (n 39).

law also does not reflect the disputes within each community about the scope and content of a particular law. At the same time, these states remain resistant to challenges to patriarchal and discriminatory laws, including the rape exception, by asserting a cultural 'African' identity. The state's use of invocations to culture to justify the marital rape exception in law and to endorse other gender inequities is often simply an intimidation tactic to avoid dealing with the issues and to protect the status quo. States often resort to discourses of cultural or religious freedoms to maintain gender inequality in their legal and political institutions as a means to placate powerful (patriarchal) groups and as a way to allow racist or colonial gendered policies to persist.

Strategies for criminalising marital rape do not need to trade on simplistic binaries, which sever women's rights from cultural rights or pit them in opposition to each other. Nor do these strategies need to marginalise customary or Indigenous law. Indeed, the strategy of ending marital rape through criminalisation is best launched in dynamic relationship to customary and Indigenous law in its specific, national and local contexts, and is most effectively pursued on the ground, through a productive engagement with customary law. Criminalising sexual assault within intimate relationships forces the recognition that marital rape is not just a private 'woman's problem' nor is it only a problem of particular cultural groups.

Criminalising marital rape through state law offers mobilising opportunities for women's rights groups to change the mind-sets of people in their communities. Criminalising marital rape also provides an essential recourse for those women who are able and willing to use the state system to seek protection from this form of gendered violence. Criminalisation transforms marital rape into a publicly stigmatised wrong.

Marital rape is ubiquitous across all societies and is indicative of generalised patriarchy, not community-specific patriarchy. The very universality of marital rape defies claims about cultural protection. Challenging the marital rape exception in criminal law brings into stark focus how culture-based excuses for gender injustice are, more often than not, used by male politicians and state actors merely to protect their patriarchal power. When women from Indigenous and subordinated groups are excluded from protection on the basis of cultural protection, it not only compounds the already-existing invisibility and official indifference towards their claims, it also denies women the right to act as 'culture-creating' agents who define their culture as much as men.[267] However, if criminalisation is the *only* step taken to combat marital rape, there is no doubt that the victimisation of women will persist and women who do not wish to use the coercive force of the law will be left without recourse. It is essential that criminalisation efforts coexist with community solutions to combat marital rape.[268]

[267] R Sylvain, 'At the Intersections: San Women and the Rights of Indigenous Peoples in Africa' (2011) 15 *International Journal of Human Rights* 89, 102–03. Sylvain's anthropological study on domestic violence in the San Indigenous community in Namibia shows the importance of ensuring state protection for women from violence.

[268] Spade (n 197).

Part II

National Case Studies: Marital Rape and Law Reform in Canada, Malawi, Kenya and Ghana

5

The Criminalisation of Marital Rape and Law Reform in Canada: A Modest Feminist Success Story in Combating Marital Rape Myths

JENNIFER KOSHAN*

I. Introduction

Marital rape is both a product of and a contributing factor to women's inequality in Canadian society and internationally. Before 1983 in Canada it was legally permissible for a man to rape his wife without criminal sanction.[1] This chapter reviews the struggles surrounding the criminalisation of marital rape[2] in Canada with a view to identifying the arguments, processes and ongoing challenges that may be relevant to other jurisdictions contemplating the shift to criminalising sexual assault in spousal relationships.

Section II provides the factual context for the legal analysis, including the prevalence and harms of sexual violence in spousal relationships. Section III outlines the historic rationales for the marital rape immunity, and how these marital rape myths were disputed and dispelled in the law reform efforts that lead to the criminalisation of marital rape in Canada. Sections IV and V examine the legal frameworks applying to marital rape following criminalisation, illustrating the broader doctrinal changes which have been necessary for criminalisation to

* Earlier excerpts of this chapter were published in Jennifer Koshan, *The Legal Treatment of Marital Rape and Women's Equality: An Analysis of the Canadian Experience* (Equality Effect, 2010), online: theequalityeffect.org/pdfs/maritalrapecanadexperience.pdf. The author wishes to thank Sheila McIntyre, Melanie Randall and Elizabeth Sheehy for their feedback on the original report.

[1] Criminal Code of Canada, RSC 1970, c C-34.

[2] The term 'marital rape' is used in this chapter even though rape is no longer an explicit offence under Canadian law, and is intended to describe conduct that was subject to immunity prior to 1983 and other sexual assaults occurring in spousal relationships, regardless of whether the parties are (or were) legally married.

be implemented in a meaningful way. Despite these reforms, however, marital rape continues to be subject to problematic state (in)action in Canada. Section VI considers arguments and strategies that aim to hold the state to account for ensuring that the criminalisation of marital rape is fully implemented. Section VII concludes with lessons learned from Canada that may be relevant to criminalisation efforts in other jurisdictions.

II. Women's Human Rights and the Prevalence of Spousal Sexual Violence in Canada

Sexual violence is a strong indicator of women's inequality. Statistics Canada reports that women are 8–10 times more likely to be victims of sexual assault than men.[3] Victims of sexual violence know their abusers over 80 per cent of the time,[4] and over 15 per cent of women experiencing spousal abuse are sexually assaulted.[5]

Sexual violence is a serious breach of women's sexual and reproductive autonomy, bodily and psychological integrity, and, when it occurs in intimate relationships, a breach of trust and serious risk factor for domestic femicide.[6] The consequences of intimate violence (including sexual violence) for women include physical injury, emotional harm, unwanted pregnancy and exacerbation of other health conditions.[7]

Women experiencing spousal violence are far more likely than men to be fearful, depressed or suffer anxiety attacks.[8] For Indigenous women, sexual violence may also be 'a threat to health and security of the entire community'.[9] Poverty, social inequalities and the lack of available services may make it difficult for women to leave violent relationships, putting them at risk of further violence and harm. Conversely, intimate sexual violence may displace women from their homes and communities when they do leave violent spouses. Statistics Canada biannually

[3] T Hotton Mahony, *Women and the Criminal Justice System* (Ottawa, Statistics Canada, 2011) 7; R Vaillancourt, *Gender Differences in Police-Reported Violent Crime in Canada, 2008* (Ottawa, Statistics Canada, 2010) 10; M Sinha, *Measuring Violence against Women: Statistical Trends* (Ottawa, Statistics Canada, 2013) 11.

[4] S Brennan and A Taylor-Butts, *Sexual Assault in Canada, 2004 and 2007* (Ottawa, Statistics Canada, 2008) 13.

[5] Statistics Canada, *Women in Canada. A Gender-Based Statistical Report*, 5th edn (Ottawa, Statistics Canada, 2006) 15, 161.

[6] AJC O'Marra, *Domestic Violence Death Review Committee Annual Report to the Chief Coroner* (Ontario, 2005) 86.

[7] Health Canada, *The Family Violence Initiative: Year five report* (Ottawa, Health Canada, 2002) 10–12.

[8] Statistics Canada, *Women in Canada* (n 5) 163.

[9] Native Women's Association of Canada, *Proposed Amendments to the Criminal Code under Bill C-49: The Perspective of Aboriginal Women* (Ontario, NWAC, 1992) 3.

documents the usage of shelters in Canada on 'snapshot days', and a typical report shows that close to 80 per cent of women in shelters on these days were fleeing spousal abuse of some form,[10] with 23 per cent[11] to 30 per cent[12] escaping sexual violence.

There are few specific statistics available on the extent of sexual violence in intimate relationships in Canada.[13] The Canadian Panel on Violence Against Women (1993) included data from the Women's Safety Project, a survey finding that 81 per cent of sexual assaults were perpetrated by men who knew their victims, with 38 per cent committed by husbands, common law partners or boyfriends.[14] The most recent Statistics Canada General Social Survey (GSS) from 2014 found that spousal sexual assault was self-reported by 7 per cent of victims, and within this group, 'over half (59%) reported non-consensual sexual activity that came a result of being manipulated, drugged or otherwise coerced, sometimes in combination with sexual assault through physical force'.[15] Other Statistics Canada research confirms that intimate partners are the most common perpetrators of violent crime against women.[16] Moreover, while the overall rate of police-reported intimate partner violence decreased between 2009 and 2014, the rate of spousal sexual assaults rose 19 per cent for female victims during this same period.[17]

Women are more likely than men to report multiple victimisations and more serious forms of domestic violence, including sexual assault.[18] This is true both during the spousal relationship and after separation.[19] One Canadian study found that following separation, 35 per cent of women who were assaulted by their ex-partners were sexually assaulted.[20] Moreover, a recent Statistics Canada

[10] See eg J Sauvé and M Burns, *Residents of Canada's Shelters for Abused Women, 2008* (Ottawa, Statistics Canada, 2009) 8.

[11] B Mazowita and M Burczycka, *Shelters for Abused Women in Canada, 2012* (Ottawa, Statistics Canada, 2014).

[12] D Locke and R Code, *Canada's Shelters for Abused Women, 1999/2000* (Ottawa, Statistics Canada, 2001) 6.

[13] In the United States, studies estimate that 10–14% of women are raped by their husbands, increasing to 40–50% for battered women. See KM Edwards et al, 'Rape Myths: History, Individual and Institutional-Level Presence, and Implications for Change' (2011) 65 *Sex Roles* 761, 764.

[14] Canadian Panel on Violence against Women, *Changing the Landscape: Ending Violence–Achieving Equality* (Ottawa, Minister of Supply and Services, 1993) 30, citing L Haskell and M Randall, *The Women's Safety Project: A Community Based Study of Sexual Violence in Women's Lives* (Toronto, 1993).

[15] Statistics Canada, *Family Violence in Canada: A Statistical Profile, 2014* (Ottawa, Statistics Canada, 21 January 2016), 3. The General Social Survey (GSS) on victimisation is conducted every five years by Statistics Canada, based on a random sample of Canadian women and men. The 2014 GSS is the first time that respondents were asked whether they had been forced into sexual activity through non-physical means (ibid, 8). See also Sinha (n 3) 30, reporting that 17% of police-reported sexual offences are committed by intimate partners.

[16] Sinha (n 3) 14, 49.

[17] *Family Violence in Canada, 2014* (n 15) 24.

[18] R Kong et al, *Sexual Offences in Canada* (Ottawa, Statistics Canada, 2003) 6; see also Statistics Canada, *Family Violence in Canada, 2014* (n 15) 7; Sinha (n 3) 26–27.

[19] M Lindsay, *Violence Perpetrated by Ex-Spouses in Canada* (Ottawa, Department of Justice Canada, 2014) 12.

[20] T Hotton, *Spousal Violence after Marital Separation* (Ottawa, Statistics Canada, 2001) 5.

report indicated that the 'vast majority of victims of police-reported intimate partner sexual offences (98%) were female'.[21] Female victims of spousal sexual violence are also more likely to experience injury than women sexually assaulted by non-spouses.[22]

Spousal sexual violence also occurs in same-sex relationships, although there is little research available on the prevalence of this form of violence in Canada.[23] The 2014 GSS reported that 'individuals who described themselves as gay, lesbian or bisexual were twice as likely as heterosexuals to report having been the victim of spousal violence during the previous 5 years', but did not include specific statistics on sexual violence.[24] A review of American studies on sexual violence against lesbian, gay and bisexual (LGB) men and women found that the median prevalence rates of intimate partner sexual violence were similar for LGB men and women (12.1 and 12.6 per cent), but lesbian and bisexual women were more likely to report this form of violence than gay and bisexual men. Given the methodology of the studies, however, the perpetrator could not be assumed to have been a same-sex or bisexual partner.[25] The authors noted the lack of statistics available for sexual violence against transgender persons, and the same is true in Canada. Spousal sexual violence is most often reported and prosecuted in a heterosexual context, committed by men against women.[26]

Statistics on sexual violence are generally not disaggregated, but the particular vulnerability of some women to this violence—poor women, racialised women, Aboriginal women, immigrant women, lesbian women, women with disabilities, older women and rural women—has been documented.[27] This increased vulnerability is tied to marginalised women's systemic inequality and devalued humanity, in addition to greater dependency on men and isolation.[28] Marginalised women are more vulnerable to domestic violence as well, including Aboriginal women, women living in rural and remote communities, women with disabilities and racialised women.[29] Aboriginal women are three times more likely to be victims of spousal abuse than non-Aboriginal women, and are more likely to experience serious forms of spousal violence, including sexual assault.[30] Aboriginal

[21] Statistics Canada, *Family Violence in Canada: A Statistical Profile, 2013* (Ottawa, Statistics Canada, 2015) 25. See also *Family Violence in Canada, 2014* (n 15) 23 (reporting that sexual offences are ten times more common among female victims of intimate partner violence than male victims).

[22] Sinha (n 3) 85.

[23] See ibid, 59.

[24] *Family Violence in Canada, 2014* (n 15) 14.

[25] EF Rothman et al, 'The Prevalence of Sexual Assault against People who Identify as Gay, Lesbian, or Bisexual in the United States: A Systematic Review' (2011) 12 *Trauma Violence and Abuse* 55.

[26] See chapter 9 of this volume, which shows that in over 400 reported cases of marital rape in Canada since 1983, all but one involved women reporting sexual violence by men.

[27] *Changing the Landscape* (n 14) 59.

[28] ibid.

[29] Family Violence Initiative (n 7) 10–12.

[30] *Women in Canada* (n 5) 163. See also NWAC, *Perspective of Aboriginal Women* (n 9) 3; Sinha (n 3) 19.

people also are more likely to report having been abused as children, which—as Randall discusses in chapter 2—is a factor associated with increased likelihood of victimisation in adulthood.[31]

While there are few specific statistics on reporting rates available for marital rape in Canada, general studies on spousal and sexual violence suggest that marital rape is largely underreported to police. For example, the 2014 GSS found that only 19 per cent of spousal violence was reported to the police by the victims themselves.[32] Even more markedly, the 2009 GSS found that 88 per cent of sexual assaults were not reported to police.[33] Other research suggests that sexual assault may be one of the forms of spousal violence more likely to come to the attention of police.[34] However, reporting rates for marital rape may be lower for some groups of women. The Native Women's Association of Canada indicates that fewer Aboriginal women report sexual violence to the police because of a lack of trust in and alienation from the Canadian justice system.[35] Other racialised women,[36] women with disabilities,[37] poor women[38] and lesbian women[39] may also underreport sexual violence, including that perpetrated by spouses.

A survey conducted by the Department of Justice in 2000 provides some context for whether sexual assault survivors choose to report sexual violence.[40] Women indicated their reasons *for* reporting the sexual violence to the police, including a desire to expose or punish the perpetrator, to protect themselves, their children or other women, and for personal healing. The women's reasons for *not* reporting included fear of or previous negative experiences with the criminal justice system, fear of disclosure of their personal records, pressure from family and fear of the perpetrator.[41] Studies in the United States indicate that an ongoing belief that husbands cannot rape their wives may also lead to underreporting.[42]

[31] *Family Violence in Canada, 2014* (n 15) 3; see also M Randall, this volume, chapter 2.

[32] *Family Violence in Canada, 2014* (n 15) 10.

[33] S Perreault and S Brennan, *Criminal Victimization in Canada, 2009* (Ottawa, Statistics Canada, 2010) 14.

[34] Sinha (n 3) 10, 95 (indicating a 53% reporting rate for spousal sexual assault).

[35] NWAC (n 9) 4. But see Sinha (n 3) 97, indicating similar reporting rates for spousal violence for Aboriginal and non-Aboriginal women.

[36] Ottawa Rape Crisis Centre, *Sexual Assault Statistics* (2010), online: www.orcc.net/sites/all/files/pdf/Sexual-Assault-Statistics-FS.pdf, 1.

[37] J Benedet and I Grant, 'Hearing the Sexual Assault Complaints of Women with Mental Disabilities: Consent, Capacity, and Mistaken Belief' (2007) 52 *McGill Law Journal* 243, 256.

[38] Ottawa Rape Crisis Centre, *Sexual Assault Statistics* (n 36) 2.

[39] Rothman et al (n 25) 8.

[40] T Hattem, *Survey of Sexual Assault Survivors* (Ottawa, Department of Justice Canada, 2002) 9–10. See also Sinha (n 3) 98–99.

[41] Hattem, ibid, 13, 15, 19. See also Kong et al (n 18) 6, where reasons for not reporting sexual offences included 'because the incident was dealt with another way' (61%); 'it wasn't important enough' (50%); 'it was a personal matter' (50%); 'they didn't want the police involved' (47%); 'the police could [not] do anything' (33%); 'the police would not help them' (18%); fear of revenge (19%) and avoidance of publicity (14%). Similar reasons are given by women for not reporting spousal violence. See Statistics Canada, *Family Violence in Canada*, 2014 (n 15) 10.

[42] Edwards et al (n 13) 763.

Those sexual offences that are reported are less likely than other violent offences to be considered 'founded' and to result in charges, prosecutions or convictions. According to the most recent Statistics Canada report examining unfounded sexual offences from 2007, charges were laid in only one-third of police-reported sexual offences, compared to almost half of other types of violent offences.[43] Statistics Canada has not tracked data on unfounded rates since 2007, but a 2017 investigative report determined an average unfounded rate of almost 20 per cent in Canada, with rates over 50% in some cities.[44] Conviction rates are also lower for sexual offences as compared to other violent crimes.[45]

Overall, the factual context highlighted in this section indicates that Canadian women continue to experience vulnerability to sexual violence in spousal relationships. Furthermore, this form of gendered violence is beset by very low reporting rates, although reforms to the law on sexual offences have had some impact, as the next section will describe.

III. Criminalisation of Marital Rape in Canada: History and Law Reform

From 1892, the time of Canada's first Criminal Code, until 1983, men were immune from criminal consequences for raping their wives.[46] The last codification of the common law immunity for marital rape appeared in Canada's 1970 Criminal Code, and provided that: 'A male person commits rape when he has sexual intercourse with a *female person who is not his wife* … without her consent.'[47]

Several rationales existed for men's historical criminal immunity for marital rape, most having their genesis in British colonial laws and attitudes. These rationales can now be seen as marital rape myths. They are based on unfounded assumptions about women and their assailants similar to those underlying more general myths and stereotypes about women and sexual violence.[48]

[43] Brennan and Taylor-Butts (n 4) 10. See also T DuBois, 'A Critical Analysis of Police Investigation: The "Wrongful Unfounding" of Sexual Assault Complaints' in E Sheehy (ed), *Sexual Assault in Canada: Law, Legal Practice & Women's Activism* (Ottawa, University of Ottawa Press, 2012) 196.

[44] R Doolittle, "Unfounded: Why Police Dismiss 1 in 5 Sexual Assault Claims as Baseless" (3 February 2017), *The Globe and Mail*.

[45] H Johnson, 'Limits of a Criminal Justice Response: Trends in Police and Court Processing of Sexual Assault' in Sheehy (n 43).

[46] For early histories of the law of sexual assault in Canada, see C Backhouse, 'Nineteenth-Century Canadian Rape Law 1800–92', in DH Flaherty (ed), *Essays in the History of Canadian Law*, vol II (Toronto, Osgoode Society/University of Toronto Press, 1983); C Boyle, *Sexual Assault* (Toronto, Carswell, 1984). For a history of the legal treatment of marital rape, see RM Ryan, 'The Sex Right: A Legal History of the Marital Rape Exemption' (1996) 20 *Law & Social Inquiry* 941.

[47] Criminal Code of Canada, 1970 (n 1) s 143 (emphasis added).

[48] The first discussion of rape myths by the Supreme Court of Canada occurred in *R v Seaboyer; R v Gayme* [1991] 2 SCR 577. The Court has not yet discussed marital rape myths specifically. See chapter 9 of this volume.

Under the implied consent theory, women gave up their entitlement to resist unwanted sexual relations with their husbands upon marriage. According to Sir Matthew Hale: '[T]he husband cannot be guilty of a rape committed by himself, upon his lawful wife, for by their mutual matrimonial consent and contract the wife hath given up herself in this kind unto her husband, which she cannot retract.'[49] The theory of coverture, articulated by William Blackstone, provided that after marriage, a woman was incorporated into the person of her husband, making marital rape impossible.[50] Wives were also seen as the property of their husbands, conferring an entitlement on husbands to rape their wives with impunity.[51] As Snider put it, rape was seen as 'a crime committed by men against men'.[52] Other rationales focused on the evidentiary problems inherent in proving lack of consent in an ongoing marriage relationship;[53] the alleged propensity of women to lie about rape to gain an advantage in divorce, matrimonial property or child custody proceedings;[54] the importance of maintaining marital privacy and harmony;[55] the argument that marital rape was less serious than rape outside of marriage as the parties had previously had sex;[56] and the desirability of protecting husbands (who could alternatively be convicted of assault in appropriate cases) from the stigma of rape.[57] Religious institutions also played a role in perpetuating the idea that husbands could not rape their wives.[58]

Australia was the first common law jurisdiction to criminalise marital rape, which it accomplished by statutory repeal of the common law immunity in 1976 in South Australia.[59] In Britain, the marital rape immunity was not codified, but

[49] M Hale, *The History of the Pleas of the Crown*, vol I (1763) 629. See also C Boyle, 'Married Women: Beyond the Pale of the Law of Rape' (1981) 1 *Windsor Yearbook of Access to Justice* 192, 195–96; C Backhouse and L Schoenroth, 'A Comparative Survey of Canadian and American Rape Law' (1983) 6 *Canadian–US Law Journal* 48, 49; EJ Sack, 'From the Right of Chastisement to the Criminalization of Domestic Violence: A Study in Resistance to Effective Policy Reform' (2009–10) 32 *Thomas Jefferson Law Review* 31, 49; K Lesses, '*PGA v the Queen*: Marital Rape in Australia: The Role of Repetition, Reputation and Fiction in the Common Law' (2014) 37 *Melbourne University Law Review* 786, 787.

[50] Sir William Blackstone, *Commentaries on the Laws of England*, vol 1 (Oxford, Clarendon Press, 1765–69) 430. See also Lesses (n 49) 809–10; N Naffine and J Neoh, 'Fictions and Myths in *PGA v The Queen*' (2013) 38 *Australian Journal of Legal Philosophy* 32, 36–37.

[51] Boyle (n 49) 202; Backhouse and Schoenroth (n 49) 48; S McIntyre, 'Tracking and Resisting Backlash against Equality Gains in Sexual Offence Law' (2000) 20(3) *Canadian Woman Studies* 72, 73; E Sheehy, 'Legal Responses to Violence against Women' (1999) 19(1) *Canadian Woman Studies* 62.

[52] L Snider, 'Legal Reform and Social Control: The Dangers of Abolishing Rape' (1985) 13 *International Journal of the Sociology of Law* 337, 339.

[53] Boyle (n 49) 201–02; Backhouse and Schoenroth (n 49) 54–55; T Fus, 'Criminalizing Marital Rape: A Comparison of Judicial and Legislative Approaches' (2006) 39 *Vanderbilt Journal of Transnational Law* 481, 484.

[54] Backhouse and Schoenroth (n 49) 53; Fus (n 53).

[55] Backhouse and Schoenroth, ibid, 52; Fus, ibid.

[56] Backhouse and Schoenroth, ibid, 53–54; Sack (n 49) 49–50.

[57] Naffine and Neoh (n 50) 37, 42.

[58] ibid, 37, n 16; Edwards et al (n 13) 764.

[59] Naffine and Neoh (n 50) 40; W Larcombe and M Heath, 'Developing the Common Law and Rewriting the History of Rape in Marriage in Australia: *PGA v The Queen*' (2012) 34 *Sydney Law Review* 785, n 4.

was softened over time by judicial interpretation—for example, in cases where the parties were separated or divorced—until the abolition of the immunity was eventually codified in 1994.[60] In the United States, a successful constitutional challenge to the immunity in New York in 1984 spurred statutory reform in other states, and by 1993 all states had repealed the full exemption, although some states continue to provide some immunity for certain kinds of sexual offences.[61]

In Canada, the statutory marital rape immunity was treated strictly; there are no cases where the courts read down the immunity so as to reduce its impact.[62] It seemed to be well accepted amongst commentators at the time that the immunity could only be abolished by legislative amendment in Canada.[63]

Reform efforts around sexual violence were led by feminist organisers and groups in Canada in the 1970s and 1980s.[64] Women were mobilised by studies showing police 'suspicion and hostility' towards rape victims, as well as 'relatively light sentences' for rape.[65] Women sought not only the abolition of the marital rape immunity, but also the repeal of laws requiring corroboration and recent complaint in the case of sexual offence prosecutions, protections against being questioned on their sexual history and reputation, and overall, a stronger response to sexual violence against women.

The Advisory Council on the Status of Women (ACSW) issued a report in 1976 recommending that 'laws against sexual assault should apply to all persons regardless of their sex, age, marital status or previous sexual conduct'.[66] Similarly, in 1977 the National Action Committee on the Status of Women (NAC) released a position paper on rape which, amongst other recommendations, called for rape to be treated as an offence against the person rather than a property offence, and to be 'prohibited and punished regardless of the age, marital status or socio-economic position of the victim'.[67] The National Association of Women and the Law (NAWL) argued that the marital rape immunity was 'one of the most serious deficiencies in the present offence of rape', and that procedural difficulties in prosecuting marital rape should not be permitted to justify the continued

[60] Fus (n 53) 485–96, citing *R v Clarke* [1949] 2 All ER 448. The abolition of the immunity was codified in the Criminal Justice and Public Order Act, 1994 (Fus, ibid, n 264).

[61] See Ryan (n 46) 988–90; Sack (n 49) 50–51, discussing *People v Liberta*, 474 NE 2d 567 (NY 1984). See also JF Decker and PG Baroni, '"No" Still Means "Yes": The Failure of the "Non-Consent" Reform Movement in American Rape and Sexual Assault Law' (2012) 101 *Journal of Criminal Law & Criminology* 1081, 1155–66 for a discussion of current laws on marital rape in each state.

[62] Boyle (n 49) 196; Backhouse and Schoenroth (n 49) 50.

[63] Backhouse and Schoenroth (n 49) 51; Fus (n 53) 497.

[64] See L Clark and D Lewis, *Rape: The Coercive Price of Sexuality* (Toronto, Women's Educational Press, 1977); D Kinnon, *Report on Sexual Assault in Canada* (Ottawa, Canadian Advisory Council on the Status of Women, 1980); M Stanley, *The Experience of the Rape Victim with the Criminal Justice System Prior to Bill C-127. Report No 1* (Ottawa, Department of Justice, 1985).

[65] Snider (n 52) 340.

[66] Advisory Council on the Status of Women, *Rationalization of Sexual Offences in the Criminal Code* (Ottawa, ACSW, 1976) 5.

[67] National Action Committee on the Status of Women, *Status of Women News* (November 1977) 14. A resolution recommending repeal of the marital rape exemption was passed by NAC in March 1978 (*Status of Women News* (June 1978) 24).

immunity.[68] Rape crisis centres across the country were key players in advocating for systemic change to rape laws and their enforcement.[69]

Although these efforts began before the Canadian Charter of Rights and Freedoms came into effect in 1982,[70] arguments for reform were often framed in terms of women's equality, sexual autonomy, self-determination, dignity and physical integrity.[71] In the particular context of marital rape, women contended that 'the subordination of women as wives to their husbands' sexual demands [was] a perpetuation of sex-role dependency relationships'.[72] At the same time, views of women as 'sexually passive' and men as 'sexually aggressive' were said to be based on stereotypes that were harmful to women as well as men.[73] This thinking informed not only the argument for abolishing the marital rape immunity, but also for enacting a gender-neutral scheme of sexual assault laws that was intended to focus on the violence rather than the sexual nature of the assault.[74]

Rebuttals to the historical rationales for the marital rape immunity were also put forward. Those seeking to repeal the immunity argued that marital rape is actually more serious than rape outside of marriage given its context of trust, dependencies and coercive potential,[75] and that the sanctity and preservation of the marriage is a fruitless concern in light of the relationship breakdown inherent in marital rape cases.[76] The marital rape immunity was called a 'barbaric anachronism' that 'has no place in a society which recognizes women as equal human beings and wives as more than the property of their husbands'.[77] Women also cited the prevalence and severe consequences of spousal violence, including rape and other forms of sexual violence, as a justification for removing the immunity.[78]

Not all feminists supported the sexual assault reforms that were eventually passed in Bill C-127.[79] For example, Snider argued that the success of Bill

[68] National Association of Women and the Law, *A New Image for Sexual Offences in the Criminal Code: A Brief in Response to Bill C-53* (Ottawa, NAWL, 1981) 9.

[69] See NAC, *Status of Women News* (1977) (n 67) 15.

[70] Canadian Charter of Rights and Freedoms, Part 1 of the Constitution Act, 1982, being Schedule B of the Canada Act, 1982 (UK), 1982, c 11 (the Charter). Section 15, the equality rights provision, did not take force until 1985.

[71] See eg Boyle (n 49) 196–97; Backhouse and Schoenroth (n 49) 53–54; Fus (n 53) 497–98; McIntyre (n 51) 2.

[72] Fus (n 53) 498, citing J McFadyen, 'Inter-Spousal Rape: The Need for Law Reform' in JM Eekelaar and S Katz (eds), *Family Violence: An International and Interdisciplinary Study* (Toronto, Butterworths, 1978) 194.

[73] Fus, ibid, citing McFadyen, ibid.

[74] Fus, ibid, citing DC Cashman, 'Negotiating Gender: A Comparison of Rape Laws in Canada, Finland, and Pakistan' (2000) 9 *Dalhousie Journal of Legal Studies* 120, 128–29. The Law Reform Commission of Canada also supported this approach in its *Report on Sexual Offences* (Ottawa, Minister of Supply and Services, 1978) 14–15.

[75] Backhouse and Schoenroth (n 49) 54; Boyle (n 49) 193.

[76] Backhouse and Schoenroth, ibid, 52–3; Boyle, ibid, 200; NAWL, *A New Image for Sexual Offences* (n 68) 9.

[77] Backhouse and Schoenroth, ibid, 57, quoting D Drucker, 'The Common Law Does not Support a Marital Exception for Forcible Rape' (1979) 5 *Women's Rights Law Reporter* 181, 200.

[78] Backhouse and Schoenroth, ibid, 53, citing Lenore Walker, *The Battered Woman* (1979) 108.

[79] McIntyre (n 51) 75.

C-127 was due largely to support from law-enforcement agencies, and the fact that women's interests in sexual assault reform coincided with the interests of the state meant that 'this was not essentially a pluralist or feminist victory over patriarchy'.[80] Cohen and Backhouse noted the 'improbability of desexualizing rape', and argued that the repeal of a separate rape offence would make it difficult to gather statistics on the incidence of that form of violence. They also pointed out that the Bill did not sufficiently deal with the burden on complainants to prove lack of consent.[81] Predictably, however, there were no feminist critics of the abolition of the marital rape immunity.

Institutional commentators were more circumspect. In its Working Paper on Sexual Offences, the Law Reform Commission of Canada recommended the repeal of the immunity where the husband and wife had separated, but did not achieve consensus on the question of eliminating the immunity altogether.[82] After consultations, however, the Commission's final report advocated complete abolition of the marital rape immunity.[83] More generally, the Commission recommended that sexual offence reform be guided by the following principles: '(1) protecting the integrity of the person, (2) protecting children and special groups, [and] (3) safeguarding public decency'.[84] Women were not specifically defined as a 'special group'. While the Canadian Bar Association was 'basically supportive' of repealing the immunity, the Criminal Lawyers' Association was critical of the removal of defences for persons accused of sexual assault, including removal of the marital rape immunity.[85] NAWL's brief also referenced the 'misguided attempts of certain right-wing campaigns' against the repeal of the marital rape immunity, based on upholding the institution of marriage.[86]

Despite these objections, feminist law reform efforts prevailed, and Canada's marital rape immunity was repealed in 1983 amongst a package of reforms to sexual offence law, as the next section discusses.

IV. The New Legal Framework for Addressing Marital Rape in Canada

On 1 January 1983, Bill C-127 came into effect. Jean Chrétien, then Justice Minister and later Prime Minister of Canada, spoke of the 'inequity of the present law' and

[80] Snider (n 52) 350. Snider also notes that many of the liberalising reforms sought by gay rights groups were not won (ibid, 347).

[81] L Cohen and C Backhouse, 'Desexualizing Rape: A Dissenting View on the Proposed Rape Amendments' (1980) 2(4) *Canadian Woman Studies* 99, 101–03.

[82] Law Reform Commission of Canada, *Working Paper on Sexual Offences* (Ottawa, Minister of Supply and Services, 1978) 17.

[83] Law Reform Commission of Canada, *Report on Sexual Offences* (n 74) 16–17.

[84] ibid, 8.

[85] Snider (n 52) 344.

[86] NAWL, *A New Image for Sexual Offences* (n 68) 9. See also Snider, ibid, 347.

the 'unfair burden on female victims of sexual assault', and explicitly rejected arguments that the repeal of the marital rape immunity would undermine the institution of marriage.[87]

Bill C-127 replaced the offences of rape and indecent assault with a new, gender-neutral scheme of offences in the Criminal Code dealing with 'sexual assault'. The scheme grouped offences according to levels of seriousness. Sexual assault was punishable by a maximum of 10 years imprisonment, sexual assault with a weapon or causing bodily harm by 14 years, and aggravated sexual assault (ie causing wounding or disfigurement) by life imprisonment.[88]

Although not defined, 'sexual assault' was not limited to conduct occurring outside a marriage. A specific section was added to the Criminal Code to make it clear that sexual assaults were criminal within the context of marriage whether the parties were living together or not:

> **246.8** A husband or wife may be charged with an offence under section 246.1, 246.2 or 246.3 in respect of his or her spouse, whether or not the spouses were living together at the time the activity that forms the subject-matter of the charge occurred.[89]

The reforms to sexual assault laws in Canada generally had several positive effects. They served as an example of the influence of the women's movement over criminal law reform, and they recognised women as a 'strong political lobby'.[90] The reforms paved the way for further changes to the criminal law regarding consent, procedural and evidentiary protections, sentencing reforms, and policies on domestic violence.[91] More specifically with respect to marital rape, the reforms achieved formal equality between wives and non-wives, which, although not sufficient, was an important starting point for women's equality. As Boyle noted: '[S]ince it is accepted that non-consensual intercourse can legitimately be defined as criminal, the distinction between wives and other rape victims is invidious and a denial of the full humanity of a wife in a sexual context.'[92] Bill C-127 also served as an important symbolic change in terms of taking sexual assault and sexual violence in intimate relationships seriously.[93] Furthermore, compared to reforms achieved by judicial interpretation, the legislative approach to abolishing the marital rape immunity may have had more legitimacy in the eyes of the public, perhaps making it more difficult for police and prosecutors to resist than judicial change.[94]

[87] Snider, ibid.

[88] Bill C-127, SC 1980-81-82-83, c 125 enacted ss 246.1, 246.2 and 246.3 of the Criminal Code (now ss 271, 272 and 273 of the Criminal Code, RSC 1985, c C-46).

[89] Bill C-127, ibid, s 246.8 (now s 278 of the Criminal Code, 1985, ibid).

[90] K-L Tang, 'Rape Law Reform in Canada: The Success and Limits of Legislation' (1998) 42 *International Journal of Offender Therapy and Comparative Criminology* 258, 262.

[91] Fus (n 53) 501–02.

[92] Boyle (n 49) 197.

[93] B Schissel, 'Law Reform and Social Change: A Time-Series Analysis of Sexual Assault in Canada' (1996) 24 *Journal of Criminal Justice* 123, 134; Snider (n 52) 352.

[94] Fus (n 53) 503, 505, 507–08.

Not surprisingly, there were very few specific criticisms of the abolition of the marital rape immunity in Canada. However, several weaknesses have been noted with respect to the sexual assault reforms generally, and may serve as cautions for law reform efforts in other jurisdictions. For example, feminists have argued that the formal equality approach taken by the sexual assault reforms failed to account for the pervasiveness of myths about women and sexual violence and women's broader inequalities in Canadian society.[95] Moreover, feminists argued that criminal law may only achieve change at the level of individual cases and not on a systemic, political level.[96] While changes to criminal law may be important as symbolic recognition of women's equality and right to bodily integrity, such reforms may also 'symbolically [close] the issue and [make] it difficult for women to campaign against the conditions that generate rape'.[97] Women's law reform efforts around male violence may also be co-opted or resisted by the state[98] and may cause backlash or new strategies for undermining women's human rights.[99] Importantly, there is very little discussion in the literature and few studies at the time of Bill C-127 about the impacts the reforms might have on women and men who are marginalised by racialisation, culture, disability, poverty, sexual orientation or gender identity.[100] There also was no discussion of the implications of the reforms for Indigenous peoples in Canada and their sovereignty over resolving issues of interpersonal violence.[101]

On the eve of the reforms, Boyle wrote that: '[O]ne does not need to be a pessimist to predict that the law, as reformed, will not effect significant change in a practical sense.'[102] True to this prediction, and as outlined above in section II, reporting rates for sexual assault continue to be very low.[103] Studies show that reported sexual offences increased between 1983—the year that the reforms took effect—and 1993, after which the number of reported sexual offences declined somewhat but remained higher than the 1983 rates into the 2000s.[104] While this seems encouraging, studies suggest it is difficult to isolate the actual impact of the sexual assault law reforms from other factors that may have contributed to increased reporting.[105] Reporting rates also remain particularly low for some groups of

[95] McIntyre (n 51) 74–75; Sheehy (n 51).

[96] McIntyre, ibid, 78; Boyle (n 49) 194, 207.

[97] Tang (n 90) 267.

[98] D Currie, 'Battered Women and the State: From the Failure of Theory to a Theory of Failure' (1990) 1 *Journal of Human Justice* 77.

[99] McIntyre (n 51) 72; Tang (n 90) 267; A Girard, 'Backlash or Equality? The Influence of Men's and Women's Rights Discourses on Domestic Violence Legislation in Ontario' (2009) 15 *Violence Against Women* 23.

[100] For an exception, see Snider (n 52).

[101] For an account of the exclusion of Aboriginal women from feminist law reform efforts around intimate violence, see J Koshan, 'Sounds of Silence: The Public/Private Dichotomy, Violence, and Aboriginal Women' in S Boyd (ed), *Challenging the Public/Private Divide: Feminism, Law and Public Policy* (Toronto, University of Toronto Press, 1997) 97–101.

[102] Boyle (n 49) 199.

[103] See above section II.

[104] Brennan and Taylor-Butts (n 4) 8; Kong et al (n 18) 3.

[105] Brennan and Taylor-Butts, ibid, 10; Schissel (n 93).

women. The Native Women's Association of Canada has argued that criminal law reforms are unlikely to increase reporting rates for Aboriginal women, and that 'an active policy to encourage Aboriginal women to come forward' is required.[106] Even when Aboriginal women do come forward with reports of sexual violence—even those against the police—law enforcement and other authorities in Canada have often disregarded their claims.[107]

Furthermore, it continues to be rare for men to be charged with sexually assaulting their wives or partners.[108] The Canadian Panel on Violence Against Women's 1993 report attributed low reporting rates for sexual violence in spousal relationships to 'systemic barriers' such as 'moral obligations and dependency in marriages and families' and 'the implicit and explicit assumption that women have a "duty" to perform any sexual act their partners desire, whenever they so desire'.[109] Randall cites studies which show that 'the closer the relationship between the sexual aggressor and the victim, the less likely it is that a female victim will elect to report her experience of sexual violation or intrusion, and the less likely she will be to seek legal intervention'.[110]

There is a vast literature on 'victim reluctance' to report or testify in sexual assault and domestic violence matters, and the ways in which such reluctance may be affected by factors of racialisation, Aboriginality, immigration status, class, disability and sexual orientation.[111] Moreover, recent empirical research shows that the practices of defence lawyers and Crown prosecutors in marital rape cases continue to be influenced by myths and stereotypes about women as wives and sexual partners.[112] However, these are problems of enforcement that should not be permitted to justify maintaining an exemption for marital rape. As Boyle has argued, such justifications would logically demand the repeal of other criminal prohibitions of violence against women which receive discriminatory enforcement and prosecution.[113] There are other ways of dealing with these enforcement

[106] NWAC, *Perspective of Aboriginal Women* (n 9) 5.

[107] Committee on the Elimination of Discrimination against Women, *Report of the Inquiry Concerning Canada of the Committee of the Elimination of Discrimination against Women under Article 8 of the Optional Protocol to the Convention on the Elimination of All Forms of Discrimination against Women*, CEDAW/C/OP.8/CAN/1 (March 2015) para 3; Ingrid Peritz, 'Aboriginal Women "Feel Anger" No Charges Laid Against Val-d'Or Officers', *The Globe and Mail*, 18 November 2016.

[108] N Bala, *Protections for Victims of Spouse Abuse & Their Children: Responses in the Justice System & the Role of Health Care Professionals* (2004, unpublished, on file with author) 1.

[109] *Changing the Landscape* (n 14) 30.

[110] M Randall, 'Sexual Assault in Spousal Relationships, "Continuous Consent", and the Law: Honest But Mistaken Judicial Beliefs' (2008) 32 *Manitoba Law Journal* 144.

[111] See eg K Crenshaw, 'Mapping the Margins: Intersectionality, Identity Politics, and Violence against Women of Color' (1990) 43 *Stanford Law Review* 1241; E Faulkner, 'Lesbian Abuse: The Social and Legal Realities' (1991) 16 *Queen's Law Journal* 261; Koshan (n 101) 97–99; NWAC, *Perspective of Aboriginal Women* (n 9); D Martin and J Mosher, 'Unkept Promises: Experiences of Immigrant Women with the Neo-Criminalization of Wife Abuse' (1995) 8 *Canadian Journal of Women and the Law* 3.

[112] R Lazar, 'Negotiating Sex: The Legal Construct of Consent in Cases of Wife Rape in Ontario, Canada' (2010) 22 *Canadian Journal of Women and the Law* 329.

[113] Boyle (n 49) 200.

problems, including specialised training of justice system personnel, victims' services, and public education and awareness campaigns, which I will return to in section VI.[114]

V. Additional Laws, Policies and Reforms Affecting the Legal Treatment of Marital Rape in Canada

In order to place Canadian marital rape reforms into their broader contexts, it is important to review some of the other elements of and reforms to sexual assault laws that were enacted in the 1980s and 1990s. This overview shows that abolition of the marital rape immunity is only one step in the process of responding to sexual violence in spousal relationships.[115] Issues relating to consent, mistaken belief in consent, evidentiary and procedural issues, and sentencing are often relevant to the continuing difficulties in reporting, charging, prosecuting and obtaining convictions in marital rape cases.

A. Sexual Assault: Definition and Elements

As noted above, since 1983 Canada's substantive sexual offences have been sexual assault, sexual assault with a weapon or causing bodily harm, and aggravated sexual assault. Sexual assault is not defined in the Criminal Code, but has been judicially defined as

> an assault … committed in circumstances of a sexual nature, such that the sexual integrity of the victim is violated. The test to be applied in determining whether the impugned conduct has the requisite sexual nature is an objective one. … The part of the body touched, the nature of the contact, the situation in which it occurred, the words and gestures accompanying the act, and all other circumstances surrounding the conduct, including threats which may or may not be accompanied by force, will be relevant.[116]

The *actus reus* of sexual assault consists of two elements: touching of a sexual nature and lack of consent to that touching. The *mens rea* requirement is intent to touch in a sexual manner, and knowledge of or recklessness or wilful blindness as to the complainant's lack of consent.[117]

[114] See Tang (n 90) 264, 268.

[115] Other reforms relevant to women's ability to seek redress for spousal sexual violence, such as specialised domestic violence courts and civil domestic violence legislation, are beyond the scope of this chapter.

[116] *R v Chase* [1987] 2 SCR 293, para 11.

[117] *R v Park* [1995] 2 SCR 836, para 16.

B. Consent

Prior to 1983, lack of consent was an element of the offence of rape, unless the complainant's consent was a result of extortion by threats or fear of bodily harm, impersonation of her husband, or false and fraudulent representations as to the nature and quality of the act.[118] Between 1983 and 1992, consent was not defined in the Criminal Code in connection with the new sexual assault offences. In *R v Park*, Justice L'Heureux Dubé of the Supreme Court of Canada critiqued the common law approach to consent, stating that it 'may perpetuate social stereotypes that have historically victimized women and undermined their equal right to bodily integrity and human dignity'.[119]

This perspective underpinned the 1992 reforms to the Criminal Code in Bill C-49, which—like the criminalisation of marital rape—were achieved as the result of feminist law reform efforts.[120] Consent is now defined to mean 'the voluntary agreement of the complainant to engage in the sexual activity in question'.[121] The Criminal Code also stipulates that consent cannot be obtained in certain circumstances, including where the complainant is incapable of consenting, the accused induces the sexual activity by abusing a position of power, or the complainant expresses a lack of agreement to engage in or continue in the activity.[122] This reform can be read as a codification of women's right to withhold and revoke consent, and not to be presumed to have consented because of a spousal relationship.

In *R v Ewanchuk*, the Supreme Court confirmed that there is no doctrine of implied consent recognised in Canadian sexual assault law.[123] Furthermore, the Court elaborated that the consent element is an affirmative one which can be satisfied by evidence that the complainant did not say 'yes', as well as by evidence that she said 'no'.[124] As the Court earlier acknowledged in the *MLM* decision, it is erroneous to require the complainant to 'offer some minimal word or gesture of objection' and to '[equate] lack of resistance … with consent'.[125] Consent is to be assessed subjectively, from the perspective of the complainant.

C. Mistaken Belief in Consent

Related to consent is the defence of mistaken belief in consent. In 1980, the Supreme Court of Canada held in *R v Pappajohn* that a mistaken belief in consent

[118] Section 143 of the Criminal Code, 1970 (n 1).
[119] *Park* (n 117) paras 38, 47.
[120] See eg McIntyre (n 51).
[121] Criminal Code, 1985 (n 88) s 273.1.
[122] ibid.
[123] *R v Ewanchuk* [1999] 1 SCR 330, para 31.
[124] ibid, para 45, citing *Park* (n 117) para 39.
[125] *R v M(ML)* [1994] 2 SCR 3.

would negate the *mens rea* for the crime of rape.[126] The belief had to be honestly held but not necessarily reasonable; however, if the accused was reckless or wilfully blind to the existence of consent, the defence would not succeed. In a subsequent case, *R v Sansregret*, the Supreme Court considered the defence in the context of marital rape, and clarified that the *mens rea* for rape required knowledge (or recklessness) that the complainant was not consenting, or was consenting due to fear of violence.[127] In the circumstances of the case, the Court held that the defence of honest but mistaken belief in consent was not available, as the accused was wilfully blind to the fact that the complainant's 'consent' was induced by fear of violence.

The Bill C-49 amendments to the Criminal Code in 1992 enacted a provision that no defence exists for sexual assault where the accused believes that the complainant consented, if the accused's belief arose from self-induced intoxication, recklessness or wilful blindness, or if the accused did not take reasonable steps to determine consent.[128] There must be an air of reality to the defence of mistaken belief in consent, a requirement set out in the Criminal Code for all assault-related offences.[129] Recent cases make it clear that in order for the air of reality requirement to be met, there must be evidence that supports the accused's claim.[130] Where the accused 'has subjectively adverted to the absence of consent' a defence of mistaken belief in consent will not lie.[131] However, because the defence deals with a mistake of fact, Vandervort notes that appellate courts may be quite deferential to trial judges, which may in turn influence future decisions to lay charges and prosecute sexual offences.[132]

D. Evidentiary and Procedural Rules—Corroboration, Recent Complaint, Sexual History/Reputation and Production of Records

Before 1983, the Criminal Code and the common law contained several rules that adversely affected prosecutions of sexual offences. For instance, if a complainant's evidence was not corroborated, the trial judge was obliged to instruct the jury that it was unsafe to convict. Furthermore, the common law rule of recent complaint

[126] *R v Pappajohn* [1980] 2 SCR 120.

[127] *R v Sansregret* [1985] 1 SCR 570.

[128] Bill C-49, An Act to amend the Criminal Code (prohibiting the admission of sexual history evidence), SC 1992, c 38. This provision is currently found in Criminal Code, 1985 (n 88) s 273.2.

[129] Criminal Code, ibid, s 265(4). In *R v Osolin* [1993] 4 SCR 595, a sexual assault case, the Supreme Court upheld the air of reality requirement as constitutional.

[130] *R v Esau* [1997] 2 SCR 777, para 63; *Ewanchuk* (n 123) para 56; *R v Davis* [1999] 3 SCR 759, para 86.

[131] *Davis*, ibid, para 87.

[132] L Vandervort, 'Honest Beliefs, Credible Lies, and Culpable Awareness: Rhetoric, Inequality, and Mens Rea in Sexual Assault' (2004) 42 *Osgoode Hall Law Journal* 625, 638–39.

permitted a rape complaint made shortly following the assault to be entered into evidence to bolster the complainant's credibility on the logic that virtuous women would raise a prompt 'hue and cry' soon after the alleged event. In the absence of an immediate complaint, the jury was to be instructed that it could draw an adverse inference as to the complainant's credibility. Finally, evidence of the complainant's sexual history and sexual reputation was also admissible under common law rules that equated lack of chastity with a propensity to consent to any and all sex, and a propensity to lie about prior consent.[133]

In 1983, the rules concerning corroboration and recent complaint were abrogated and new provisions—the so-called 'rape shield' provisions—were enacted to limit the admissibility of sexual history evidence.[134] Evidence of the complainant's general and specific sexual reputation was now inadmissible in relation to her credibility, while evidence of her sexual activity with someone other than the accused was admissible only in limited circumstances: as rebuttal evidence, evidence going to identity, or evidence relating to consensual sexual activity on the same occasion as the alleged incident. The 1983 rape shield provisions did not limit evidence of past sexual contact between the complainant and the accused, a significant omission in the context of marital rape.

In *R v Seaboyer; R v Gayme*, the rape shield provisions were challenged as contrary to the fair trial rights of accused persons under the Charter.[135] The Supreme Court unanimously upheld the prohibition on sexual reputation evidence; however, a majority struck down the sexual history provision on the basis that it was too restrictive in setting out the circumstances in which such evidence might be relevant.[136] The majority's examples of where evidence of past sexual contact might also be relevant—to the defence of mistaken belief in consent, motive to fabricate or establishing a pattern of similar conduct—are all germane in the marital rape context. The Court established a new approach to the admission of sexual history evidence, whereby evidence of the complainant's past sexual conduct, including that with the accused, would not be admissible in relation to her credibility or consent, but would be admissible for other purposes where it possessed probative value that was not substantially outweighed by the danger of unfair prejudice flowing from the evidence.[137] Justice L'Heureux Dubé wrote a strong dissent in the case, tying arguments about the relevance of sexual history evidence to myths and stereotypes about women and sexual violence.[138]

The Bill C-49 reforms to the Criminal Code in 1992 were later said by the Supreme Court to have 'essentially codifie[d]' the rules in *Seaboyer*.[139] However,

[133] Stanley (n 64); Boyle (n 46) 14–16.
[134] Bill C-127 (n 88) s 19, enacting ss 246.4, 246.5, 246.7 and 246.8 of the Criminal Code.
[135] *R v Seaboyer; R v Gayme* (n 48).
[136] ibid, paras 50–53.
[137] ibid, para 101.
[138] ibid, paras 125–273.
[139] *R v Darrach* [2000] 2 SCR 443, para 1.

this view does not do justice to feminist law reform efforts.[140] In addition to strengthening the laws on consent and mistaken belief in consent, these efforts led to the establishment of procedural protections in sexual history applications, requiring the defence to file a written affidavit substantiating the relevance of the evidence sought to be admitted and a *voir dire* to determine its admissibility.[141] Several factors must be considered in assessing the admissibility of the evidence, including society's interest in encouraging sexual assault reporting, the need to remove discriminatory beliefs or biases from the trial process, the potential prejudice to the complainant's personal dignity and privacy, and her rights to personal security and the full protection and benefit of the law. These provisions were upheld as constitutional in *R v Darrach*.[142]

As a result of the restrictions on evidence created by the rape shield provisions, defence counsel adopted a new tactic: seeking production of complainants' personal records from third parties.[143] In *R v O'Connor*, a majority of the Supreme Court established a procedure for the production of such records that was seen as largely favouring the accused.[144] Law reform advocacy by women's groups, and government consultations with a wide range of stakeholders in the aftermath of *O'Connor*, led to the enactment of Bill C-46 in 1997.[145] Bill C-46 enacted a legislative scheme limiting the production of records in sexual assault cases.[146] This legislation was found to strike a constitutional balance between the rights of accused persons and the rights of sexual assault complainants in *R v Mills*.[147] While this was a positive outcome, *Mills* also reinforces the discretion of trial judges to order the production of complainants' private records, which has led commentators to question whether the spirit of the production provisions is being adequately implemented.[148]

[140] See eg Women's Legal Education and Action Fund, *Submission to the Legislative Committee of Parliament on Bill C-49, An Act Respecting Sexual Assault* (Toronto, LEAF, 1992); NWAC, *Perspective of Aboriginal Women* (n 9); McIntyre (n 51).

[141] Bill C-49 (n 128) enacted what are now ss 276.1, 276.2 and 276.3 of the Criminal Code, 1985 (n 68).

[142] *Darrach* (n 139).

[143] K Busby, 'Discriminatory Uses of Personal Records in Sexual Violence Cases' (1997) 9 *Canadian Journal of Women and the Law* 148. This is not to say that the restrictions on rape shield evidence are always properly applied. See E Craig, "Section 276 Misconstrued: The Failure to Properly Interpret and Apply Canada's Rape Shield Provisions" (2016) 94 *Canadian Bar Review* 1.

[144] *R v O'Connor* [1995] 4 SCR 411.

[145] See D Oleskiew and N Tellier, *Submissions to the Standing Committee on Bill C-46, An Act to Amend the Criminal Code in Respect of Production of Records in Sexual Offence Proceedings* (Ottawa, National Association of Women and the Law, 1997); J Scott and S McIntyre, *Submissions to the Standing Committee on Justice and Legal Affairs, Review of Bill C-46* (Toronto, LEAF, 1997).

[146] Bill C-46, An Act to amend the Criminal Code (production of records in sexual offence proceedings), SC 1997, c 30, enacting ss 278.1 to 278.91 of the Criminal Code, 1985 (n 88).

[147] *R v Mills* [1999] 3 SCR 668.

[148] See eg L Gotell, 'The Ideal Victim, the Hysterical Complainant, and the Disclosure of Confidential Records: The Implications of the Charter for Sexual Assault Law' (2002) 40 *Osgoode Hall Law Journal* 251; J Koshan, 'Disclosure and Production in Sexual Violence Cases: Situating *Stinchcombe*' (2002) 40 *Alberta Law Review* 655.

Both the rape shield provisions and the rules for production of personal records raise issues in the marital rape context. Accused persons will likely know the sexual history of their victims and of the existence and location of their personal records, and the potential admission of this kind of evidence may further deter women from reporting spousal sexual assaults.[149]

E. Sentencing

Prior to 1983, rape carried a maximum penalty of life imprisonment, although the average sentence was 5–7 years.[150] Since 1983, the sexual assault provisions in the Criminal Code carry progressively more serious maximum sentences where the assault causes bodily harm, is committed with a weapon, or results in wounding or maiming.

Some appellate courts have established sentencing ranges and guidelines for particular categories of offences, a practice that has received some support from the Supreme Court of Canada.[151] While no courts have established sentencing guidelines for marital rape convictions, section 718.2(a)(ii) of the Criminal Code requires 'a court that imposes a sentence [to consider] … evidence that the offender … abused [his] spouse or common-law partner' as an aggravating factor.[152] Referencing this section in *R v Stone*, a case dealing with spousal homicide, the Supreme Court stated that 'prevailing social values mandate that the moral responsibility of offenders be assessed in the context of equality between men and women in general, and spouses in particular'.[153] Even before this section of the Code was enacted, courts in some jurisdictions treated the context of intimate relationships as an aggravating factor at the stage of sentencing.[154]

At the same time, section 718.2(e) of the Criminal Code provides that 'all available sanctions other than imprisonment that are reasonable in the circumstances should be considered for all offenders, with particular attention to the circumstances of Aboriginal offenders'.[155] As noted by the Supreme Court in *R v Gladue*, this section is remedial in nature and is in part intended to respond to the overincarceration of Aboriginal peoples in Canada.[156]

Studies vary in their assessments of sentencing trends in cases of sexual and other forms of intimate violence, and there is little specific information on sentencing in marital rape cases. In a 2003 Statistics Canada report, sexual offences

[149] The application of these provisions in marital rape cases is addressed in chapter 9 of this volume.
[150] Stanley (n 64) 111–12.
[151] *R v Stone* [1999] 2 SCR 290.
[152] *Criminal Code*, 1985 (n 88) s 718.2(a)(ii).
[153] *Stone* (n 151) para 240.
[154] ibid, para 241.
[155] *Criminal Code*, 1985 (n 88) s 718.2(e).
[156] *R v Gladue* [1999] 1 SCR 688, para 64. See also *R v Wells* [2000] 1 SCR 207 and *R v Ipeelee*, 2012 SCC 13. The application of this section in marital rape cases is addressed in chapter 9 of this volume.

were found to be more likely to result in prison sentences than other violent offences.[157] In contrast, a 2005 study conducted by Justice Canada reviewed differences in sentencing outcomes for various forms of spousal and non-spousal violence between 1997 and 2002 in 18 urban areas. Generally, those convicted of spousal violence were found to be less likely to be sentenced to jail terms (19 per cent) than those convicted of non-spousal violence (29 per cent). For sexual assault offences, spouses were more likely (24 per cent) to receive a conditional sentence—one that is served in the community—than non-spouses (15 per cent),[158] calling into question the impact of section 718.2(a)(ii) of the Criminal Code. Recent reforms to the Criminal Code have eliminated the possibility of conditional sentences for indictable sexual offences,[159] but these statistics still suggest that sexual violence in intimate relationships may be treated less seriously by some sentencing courts.

The interpretation and application of the provisions relating to consent, mistaken belief in consent, evidentiary issues and sentencing in marital rape cases often belie the rights-promoting intentions behind these reforms, as chapter 9 demonstrates. The next section discusses ways of deploying rights-based arguments to deal with problematic state (in)action around marital rape.

VI. Rights-Based Arguments for Implementing Marital Rape Laws in Canada

As noted earlier, the focus of the sexual assault reforms on women's rights to equality, sexual autonomy, security of the person and privacy was unquestionably influenced by the advocacy of Canadian women before courts, legislatures and the general public.[160] These interventions have asserted that sexual violence is both a cause and effect of women's subordinate position in Canadian society, and that some women are more vulnerable to sexual violence and may experience it in unique ways because of circumstances of colonisation, poverty, racialisation, disability and heterosexism. The overarching theme of these arguments is that sexual assault laws must be enacted, interpreted and applied in ways that repudiate marital rape myths and that are cognisant of the multiple inequalities faced by marginalised women.

[157] Kong et al (n 18) 9.

[158] M Gannon and K Mihorean, 'Sentencing outcomes: A Comparison of Family Violence and Non-Family Violence Cases' (2005) 12 *JustResearch* 42, 44–45.

[159] *Criminal Code*, 1985 (n 88) s 742.1.

[160] See eg Oleskiew and Tellier (n 145); Scott and McIntyre (n 145). The Women's Legal Education and Action Fund (LEAF) has put forward equality-based arguments in numerous sexual assault cases, often in coalition with other women's groups; see www.leaf.ca/legal/search-cases/.

The Canadian Constitution, including the Charter of Rights and Freedoms, binds government rather than private actors,[161] so there are no Charter remedies available against men who rape their wives. However, if government actors fail to take proper steps to enforce marital rape laws, they may be liable for a breach of the Charter. Courts must also interpret sexual assault laws in accordance with Charter rights.[162]

A leading Canadian case in the area of police inaction and sexual assault is *Jane Doe v Metropolitan Toronto Police.* In *Jane Doe*, the Ontario Divisional Court held that the Toronto police force had breached the equality rights guarantee in section 15 of the Charter when it failed to warn women of the risk of attack by a serial rapist in their neighbourhood. The Court found that this failure was 'motivated and informed by the adherence to rape myths as well as sexist stereotypical reasoning about rape, about women, and about women who are raped'.[163] Furthermore, the police had violated Jane Doe's security of the person under section 7 of the Charter 'by subjecting her to the very real risk of attack by a serial rapist' when, although they were aware of the risk, they deliberately failed to inform her about it.[164] Jane Doe was granted a declaration that her rights under the Charter had been violated, and was awarded damages for breach of the Charter and negligence. The Supreme Court affirmed damages as a constitutional remedy in *Vancouver (City) v Ward*, a case involving excessive police action, which might also arise in the marital rape context (for example, if a woman was improperly charged for using force in defending herself against sexual violence).[165]

Not all cases seeking to hold the government accountable for failure to respond to spousal violence have been as successful, however. In *Mooney v British Columbia*, a woman's claim in negligence against the Royal Canadian Mounted Police (RCMP) for failing to investigate domestic violence was dismissed. Mooney had complained to the RCMP about threatening actions by her estranged abusive common law husband, and was told to contact a lawyer to get a restraining order. A few weeks later, he broke into her home, shot and killed her best friend,

[161] Section 32 of the Charter (n 70) provides that it applies to federal and provincial governments, and has been interpreted to preclude application to non-government actors unless they are implementing government policies. See *Eldridge v British Columbia (AG)* [1997] 3 SCR 624.

[162] See eg *R v Daviault* [1994] 3 SCR 63, where the Supreme Court modified the defence of intoxication in accordance with the Charter.

[163] *Jane Doe v Metropolitan Toronto (Municipality) Commissioners of Police* (1998) 39 OR (3d) 487 (Div Ct), para 162, leave to appeal dismissed, [1991] OJ No 3673 (CA). For comments on this case, see M Randall, 'Sex Discrimination, Accountability of Public Authorities and the Public/Private Divide in Tort Law: An Analysis of *Doe v Metropolitan Toronto (Municipality) Commissioners of Police*' (2000) 26 *Queen's Law Journal* 451; E Sheehy, 'Causation, Common Sense, and the Common Law: Replacing Unexamined Assumptions with What We Know about Male Violence against Women or from *Jane Doe* to *Bonnie Mooney*' (2006) 17 *Canadian Journal of Women and the Law* 97. See also Sheehy (n 43) for a series of essays evaluating the legacy of *Jane Doe.*

[164] *Jane Doe* (Div Ct) (n 163) para 163.

[165] *Vancouver (City) v Ward*, 2010 SCC 27.

wounded one of her daughters, and fatally shot himself. The BC Supreme Court, in a decision upheld by the Court of Appeal, dismissed Mooney's action, finding that although the RCMP had a duty of care, the actions of the officer in question did not cause or materially contribute to the shootings.[166] This was so even though the officer was aware of and failed to comply with investigative policies for relationship violence in BC, as the police were 'guardians, not guarantors, of public wellbeing'.[167] Unfortunately, *Mooney* was not mounted as a Charter claim in the alternative to negligence. Equality-based arguments were raised on appeal by an intervener, Vancouver Rape Relief and Women's Shelter, yet these arguments did not appear to influence the Court of Appeal's reasoning on causation. Sheehy argues that if raised at the outset, a claim under section 15 of the Charter may have made a difference by contextualising the causation analysis, and because discrimination is a stand-alone wrong.[168]

What are the implications of these cases for marital rape? *Jane Doe* is important for its recognition of the myths and stereotypes that may underlie police responses to sexual violence against women. If police failure to adequately respond to marital rape—for example, by failing to investigate or lay charges—could be attributed to discriminatory understandings of sexual relations within a spousal context, then a section 15 Charter claim may be viable. Arguments could include attention to gender inequality as well as other inequalities based on racialisation, Aboriginality, religion, disability and class where police (in)action was grounded in marital rape myths concerning marginalised women. Similarly, police failure to protect women from marital rape could be seen as a violation of their rights to security of the person and liberty (including sexual and reproductive autonomy) under section 7 of the Charter.

By extension, a prosecutor's failure to proceed to trial might similarly be found to violate sections 7 and 15 of the Charter if it could be tied to an increased risk of violence and was based on discriminatory understandings of marital rape. Although exercises of prosecutorial discretion are only reviewable for abuse of process in Canada, 'a judge may exceptionally override a Crown tactical decision in order to prevent a Charter violation'.[169]

The Supreme Court has emphasised that a fair trial implicates the rights of both accused persons and complainants, such that the right of an accused to make full answer and defence must be balanced with the rights of a complainant to equality, security of the person and privacy.[170] Judges are obliged to ensure that marital rape proceedings maintain a proper balancing of these rights, whether dealing

[166] *Mooney v British Columbia (AG)*, 2001 BCSC 419, para 61; appeal dismissed, *BM v British Columbia (AG)*, 2004 BCCA 402; leave to appeal dismissed, *Mooney v Canada (AG)* [2004] SCCA No 428.

[167] *Mooney* (BCSC) (n 166) para 64.

[168] Sheehy (n 163).

[169] *R v Anderson* [2014] 2 SCR 167, para 60.

[170] See eg *Osolin* (n 129) paras 165–66; *Mills* (n 147) para 90.

with sexual history and production applications (which actually mandate this balancing explicitly), or in rejecting arguments that seek to reintroduce marital rape myths in relation to matters such as credibility.

As seen in the review of cases in chapter 9, however, judges themselves sometimes reinforce marital rape myths. While the Charter cannot be used to directly challenge judicial decisions, Charter values must inform judicial decision-making. As Boyle puts it: '[A]n impartial judge cannot have a mind closed to the possibility of inequality in the law relating to … sexual assault trials.'[171] Judicial decisions where findings related to consent, mistaken belief in consent, evidentiary issues and sentencing are imbued with discriminatory rationales about sexual violence in spousal relationships should be appealed by the Crown. Moreover, efforts to provide judicial education on domestic violence and sexual violence should be mandatory and should be broadened to include material on marital rape and the issues it raises.[172]

A related strategy would be to train prosecutors to routinely rely on Charter-based arguments in marital rape cases. This might include, for example, the introduction of evidence of a history of domestic violence between the parties and any relevant cultural context as a lens through which to assess the credibility of the complainant's actions.[173] Professional Codes of Conduct for lawyers include duties of non-discrimination, and could be mobilised to prevent defence tactics that rely on or fail to dispel marital rape myths.[174] Judges are also professionally bound by duties of non-discrimination, and in cases where they show disdain or disregard for the law in sexual assault cases, they may be subject to inquiry and sanction by the Canadian Judicial Council or, in the most egregious cases, removed from the bench by Parliament.[175] In a recent example, a judge's use of rape myths to discredit and humiliate a young, poor Aboriginal woman in a sexual assault trial, and his antipathy for sexual assault law, led the Canadian Judicial Council to recommend his removal from the bench, and the judge resigned.[176]

[171] C Boyle, 'Reasonable Doubt in Credibility Contests: Sexual Assault and Sexual Equality' (2009) 13 *International Journal of Evidence and Proof* 269, 290.

[172] The National Judicial Institute (NJI) provides electronic bench books on domestic violence and sexual offenders, but these resources are available only with an NJI password, and it is unclear whether they include resources on marital rape. See NJI, 'Judicial Education in Canada', online: www.nji-inm.ca/index.cfm/judicial-education/judicial-education-in-canada/.

[173] Cases which have employed this strategy are discussed in chapter 9.

[174] Federation of Law Societies of Canada, *Model Code of Professional Conduct* (2014) s 6.3–5, online: flsc.ca/wp-content/uploads/2014/12/conduct1.pdf. See also E Craig, 'The Ethical Obligations of Defence Counsel in Sexual Assault Cases' (2014) 51 *Osgoode Hall Law Journal* 427.

[175] Canadian Judicial Council, *Ethical Principles for Judges* (Ottawa, CJC, 2004) ch 5, 'Equality', online: www.cjc-ccm.gc.ca/cmslib/general/news_pub_judicialconduct_Principles_en.pdf.

[176] Canadian Judicial Council, *In the Matter of Section 65 of the Judges Act, RSC 1985, c J-1, and of the Inquiry Committee convened by the Canadian Judicial Council to review the conduct of the Honourable Robin Camp of the Federal Court: Report of the Canadian Judicial Council to the Minister of Justice*, 8 March 2017. The case that led to the complaint was *R v Wagar*, Docket No 130288731P1 (ABPC, unreported); overturned 2015 ABCA 327.

However, Charter challenges may also be raised in sexual violence cases by the defence where they allege that particular legislative provisions violate the accused's Charter rights. As noted above, the fair trial rights of accused persons must be interpreted in light of women's rights to equality, security of the person, sexual autonomy and privacy. Women's rights may also be invoked in government arguments seeking to justify sexual assault laws as reasonable limits under section 1 of the Charter.[177] These arguments have had some success in defence challenges to the sexual assault law reforms of the 1990s in decisions such as *Ewanchuk*, *Mills* and *Darrach*, although some commentators have suggested that fair trial rights are still likely to trump women's Charter rights in the event of a conflict.[178] Rights-based arguments have also had success in a more proactive way in drafting sexual assault laws that respond to women's equality, security of the person and privacy rights, as seen with Bill C-49 and Bill C-46.[179] These Bills include both preambles and substantive provisions referencing women's rights to equality and security of the person.[180]

Another way that women's Charter rights could be protected would be to advocate for reforms to the Criminal Code that deal specifically with marital rape. For example, language could be added to provisions on consent, mistaken belief in consent and evidentiary rules to provide that if sexual violence occurs in a spousal context, the standards in relation to these rules should not be attenuated. This kind of reform would need to be grounded in arguments about the importance of dispelling marital rape myths and to encourage reporting of sexual violence in spousal relationships. Precedent exists for this sort of interpretive clause in the sections of the Criminal Code dealing with sexual history evidence and production of personal records, which stipulate factors which must be considered when judges are ruling on these applications in sexual assault cases.[181]

If these sorts of provisions were enacted, they would inevitably be challenged as contrary to the Charter rights of those accused of sexual assault, and arguments related to women's Charter rights would have to be mounted in support of the provisions. There is extensive literature in Canada framing sexual violence as a women's equality issue which could be drawn upon in such

[177] Section 1 of the Charter (n 70) allows governments to impose reasonable limits on Charter rights that are demonstrably justified in a free and democratic society.

[178] See eg L Gotell, 'When Privacy Is not Enough: Sexual Assault Complainants, Sexual History Evidence and the Disclosure of Personal Records' (2005–06) 43 *Alberta Law Review* 743; M Denike, 'Sexual Violence and "Fundamental Justice": On the Failure of Equality Reforms to Criminal Proceedings' (2000) 20(3) *Canadian Woman Studies* 151.

[179] S McIntyre, 'Redefining Reformism: The Consultations that Shaped Bill C-49', in J Roberts and R Mohr (eds), *Confronting Sexual Assault: A Decade of Legal and Social Change* (Toronto, University of Toronto Press, 2004) 293.

[180] Bill C-49 (n 128); Bill C-46 (n 146). Consistent with Canadian legislative practice, the preambles do not appear in the amended versions of the Criminal Code.

[181] *Criminal Code*, 1985 (n 88) ss 276(3), 278.3(4) and 278.5(2).

arguments,[182] some of which examines particular issues faced by marginalised women.[183] However, rather than introducing legislative reforms that would likely be challenged and take years to defend, strategies focused on judges and lawyers and their rights-based obligations in marital rape trials might be more fruitful.

International norms guaranteeing women's security of the person and equality generally and as spouses could support arguments challenging state (in)action on marital rape and advocating that sexual assault laws must be interpreted in light of women's human rights. As discussed in chapter 3, the Convention on the Elimination of All Forms of Discrimination against Women (CEDAW),[184] taken together with General Recommendation 19[185] requiring states to take action on violence against women, would provide support for such arguments, as would the explicit recognition of marital rape in the Declaration on the Elimination of Violence Against Women.[186] Other treaties and declarations, such as the Convention on the Rights of Persons with Disabilities[187] and the United Nations Declaration on the Rights of Indigenous Peoples[188] would be relevant in the case of women experiencing intersecting forms of inequality. Recent international case law is also

[182] In addition to the literature cited elsewhere in this chapter, see S Martin, 'Some Constitutional Considerations on Sexual Violence against Women' (1994) 32 *Alberta Law Review* 535; C Boyle, 'The Role of Equality in Criminal Law' (1994) 58 *Saskatchewan Law Review* 203; J McInnes and C Boyle, 'Judging Sexual Assault Law against a Standard of Equality' (1995) 29 *University of British Columbia Law Review* 341; I Grant, 'Second Chances: Bill C-72 and the Charter' (1995) 33 *Osgoode Hall Law Journal* 379; D Majury, 'The Charter, Equality Rights, and Women: Equivocation and Celebration' (2002) 40 *Osgoode Hall Law Journal* 297; R Cairns Way, 'Incorporating Equality into the Substantive Criminal Law: Inevitable or Impossible?" (2005) 4 *Journal of Law and Equality* 203; K Busby, 'Every Breath You Take: Erotic Asphyxiation, Vengeful Wives, and Other Enduring Myths in Spousal Sexual Assault Prosecutions' (2012) 24 *Canadian Journal of Women and the Law* 328; E Cunliffe, 'Sexual Assault Cases in the Supreme Court of Canada: Losing Sight of Substantive Equality?' (2012) 57 *Supreme Court Law Review* 295; L Gotell, 'Governing Heterosexuality through Specific Consent: Interrogating the Governmental Effects of *R v JA*' (2012) 24 *Canadian Journal of Women and the Law* 359; J Benedet, 'Marital Rape, Polygamy, and Prostitution: Trading Sex Equality for Agency and Choice' (2013) 18 *Review of Constitutional Studies* 161; E Craig, 'Capacity to Consent to Sexual Risk' (2014) 17 *New Criminal Law Review* 103.

[183] See eg ML Nightingale, 'Judicial Attitudes and Differential Treatment: Native Women in Sexual Assault Cases' (1991) 23 *Ottawa Law Review* 71; S Razack, 'What Is to Be Gained by Looking White People in the Eye? Race in Sexual Violence Cases' in *Looking White People in the Eye: Gender, Race, and Culture in Courtrooms and Classrooms* (Toronto, University of Toronto Press, 1998) 56; P Fournier, 'The Ghettoisation of Difference in Canada: "Rape by Culture" and the Danger of a "Cultural Defence" in Criminal Law Trials' (2002) 29 *Manitoba Law Journal* 81; Benedet and Grant (n 37).

[184] Convention on the Elimination of All Forms of Discrimination against Women, 18 December 1979, 1249 UNTS 13, Art 2(b) and (c), 15, 16 (CEDAW).

[185] Committee on the Elimination of Discrimination against Women, General Recommendation No 19, *Violence Against Women* (11th Sess 1992) comments 1, 4, 6, 7, 9, 23 and 24.

[186] Declaration on the Elimination of Violence Against Women, 20 December 1993, GA Res 48/104, Art 2(a).

[187] International Convention on the Protection and Promotion of the Rights and Dignity of Persons with Disabilities, UN Doc A/61/49 (2006), Arts 3, 6, 16.

[188] UN General Assembly, United Nations Declaration on the Rights of Indigenous Peoples, 2 October 2007, A/RES/61/295, Art 22(2).

relevant, and establishes a state duty not to create a climate of impunity around domestic and sexual violence.[189]

VII. Conclusion: Lessons from the Criminalisation of Marital Rape in Canada

The Canadian experience with the criminalisation of marital rape demonstrates the powerful role that feminist law reform advocates can play in convincing governments to take stronger action against sexual violence. Abolition of spousal immunity is a key first step, and ideally should be accomplished with legislative clarity similar to that in the Canadian provision, making it explicit that spouses can be charged with sexual assault. Abolition should also be accompanied by legislative definitions of consent and mistake of fact as well as evidentiary rules and sentencing norms that account for women's full rights to equality, sexual autonomy and security of the person.

However, even if such legislative provisions are in place, judicial interpretations of these provisions must be informed by principles that fully recognise women's rights under both domestic and international law and avoid marital rape myths, as chapter 9 further shows. Robust and ongoing judicial education programmes are essential in order to equip and support judges in the proper interpretation and application of the law in relation to spousal sexual assault.

If legislative reforms or more proactive state responses in furtherance of women's rights to be free from spousal sexual violence are not forthcoming, constitutional challenges may be an option. The Canadian experience with such challenges has been mixed, but could be supported by relevant norms of international law. All of these strategies can benefit from the support of feminist civil society organisations with expertise in sexual assault law.

Finally, fundamental structural responses dealing with the compound socio-economic, physical, psychological, dignitary and spiritual harms of poverty, social and political inequality, and colonisation must be implemented to combat the interlocking relations of oppression that enable marital rape and underpin legal rules and practices favouring immunity for its perpetrators.

[189] *Lenahan (Gonzales) et al v United States*, Case 12.626, Report No 80/11 (Inter-American Commission on Human Rights, 2011); *CK et al v The Commissioner of Police et al* [2013] eKLR (High Court of Kenya).

6

Legislating against the Odds: Lessons Learned from Efforts to Legislate against Marital Rape in Malawi

NGEYI RUTH KANYONGOLO AND SEODI WHITE

I. Introduction

Marital rape is a form of sexual assault and abuse of power that violates the human right to be free from violence. Marital rape is far more likely to be perpetrated against women by men, reflecting the broader social problem of unequal power relationships between men and women. Because marital rape is predominantly a gendered crime, failure to provide adequate protection from this type of sexual assault violates the equal right of women to the enjoyment of all civil and political rights, including sexual integrity and autonomy.[1] Marital rape is a problem the world over, including in Malawi.

Research demonstrates that marital rape and sexual violence against women in relationships is a pervasive problem in Malawi. Available evidence points to the prevalence of sexual (and physical) violence against Malawian women. According to the Malawi Demographic and Health Survey 2010, 52 per cent of Malawian women surveyed reported experiencing sexual or physical violence in the past 12 months; 24 per cent reported experiencing violence 'often'. One in four women in Malawi between the ages of 15 and 49 have experienced sexual violence, and a current husband or partner is the most commonly reported perpetrator of sexual violence (39 per cent), followed by a former husband or partner (14 per cent), and a current or former boyfriend (9 per cent).[2] Of the women experiencing violence, 43.8 per cent of women who have experienced only physical violence have never

[1] Human Rights and Equal Opportunity Commission, *Discussion Paper on the Law of Consent and Sexual Assault* (Sydney, Human Rights and Equal Opportunity Commission, 2007).

[2] National Statistical Office (NSO) and ICF Macro, *Malawi Demographic and Health Survey 2010* (Zomba, Malawi and Calverton, MD, NSO and ICF Macro, 2011) 243, 245.

sought help, compared to 69.9 per cent of women who have experienced only sexual violence.[3]

In an earlier study from 2004, the National Statistical Office of Malawi found that the most common forms of spousal violence include forced intercourse or marital rape (13 per cent) and being forced into sexual acts (4 per cent). Further, the survey found that only 17.9 per cent of women who had experienced physical or sexual violence in the last year reported that they could refuse sex to their husbands.[4] A 2013 survey conducted by the National Statistical Office, whose main objective was to provide baseline information regarding the prevalence of gender-based violence in selected districts of Malawi, found that 68.4 per cent of females had experienced multiple incidents (ie two or more incidents) of sexual abuse.[5]

These findings suggest that sexual violence, including marital rape, is a common occurrence in Malawi, and that women are the primary victims. It has also been found that 'due to cultural norms in Malawi, which discourage the discussion of sexual or conjugal issues, marital violence … may [be] underreported'.[6]

On 26 April 2006, the Malawi National Assembly passed the Prevention of Domestic Violence Act. The Act provides for the prevention of domestic violence and protects persons affected by domestic violence through protection orders, orders for the occupation of the household residence and other civil remedies, as well as penalties for breach of orders.[7] This law was passed primarily through the efforts of Women and Law in Southern Africa Research and Educational Trust (WLSA Malawi), a women's legal rights NGO based in Malawi. WLSA Malawi conceived the idea and facilitated the passing of the law, which included, among other things, encouraging political will from the executive and legislative arms of the government to support this legislation. What prompted WLSA Malawi to engage in the process of facilitating the enactment of this law was the clear fact that gender-related crimes were not ably handled by the state, in particular, gender-related crimes of domestic violence, including marital rape.

This chapter examines the legal treatment of marital rape in Malawi and related law reform efforts championed by WLSA Malawi. It explores the challenges of legislating against and criminalising marital rape, which is generally deemed to be a private matter outside the realm of the state. This discussion arises out of the work by one of the authors (S.W.), who was one of the activists engaged in efforts to legislate against marital rape from 1999 to 2006 on behalf of WLSA Malawi. It was the position of WLSA Malawi that marital rape should be one of the forms of domestic violence included within the proposed new law. To the surprise of

[3] ibid, 260.

[4] CD Chakwana, 'Domestic Violence' in National Statistical Office, *Malawi Demographic and Health Survey 2004* (Zomba, Malawi and Calverton, MD, NSO and ORC Macro, 2005) 273.

[5] Government of Malawi, *Violence against Children and Young Women in Malawi: Findings from a Survey 2013* (Ministry of Gender, Children, Disability and Social Welfare 2014) 23.

[6] ibid, 63.

[7] Prevention of Domestic Violence Act, 29 December 2006, Chapter 7:05 of the Laws of Malawi.

the activists involved, the effort to legislate against marital rape was the most contentious aspect of the law reform process. In the end, although the Prevention of Domestic Violence Act was passed, marital rape was not explicitly legislated against, let alone criminalised. The chapter also raises some issues regarding how the public and policy-makers may respond to a process aimed at enacting a law that will provide a human rights-based approach to the legal treatment of women with regard to domestic violence, including marital rape.

The chapter begins in section II by providing background to the rationale behind WLSA Malawi's efforts towards regulating and/or criminalising marital rape that arose in 1999. Then, in section III, we discuss Malawi's domestic laws and international legal obligations to protect women's human rights to be free from violence, in particular, sexual violence in marriage. This discussion includes cases that describe the legal treatment of marital rape in civil and criminal cases by the Malawian courts. In section IV, we describe some studies undertaken by WLSA Malawi, which highlight societal attitudes towards marital rape and sexual violence. Understanding these attitudes, as well as the challenges posed by legal pluralism, help to explain why there was resistance to legislating against marital rape. The chapter concludes in section V by outlining how the new law addressed sexual violence and why this was a missed opportunity to criminalise or legislate against marital rape in Malawi. We argue that explicit protection from marital rape must be included in the law of Malawi.

II. Context and Background: WLSA Malawi and the Problem of Gendered Violence

Although the actual consultative process on the Prevention of Domestic Violence Act took place in 2001, WLSA Malawi started its work on developing a law aimed at preventing domestic violence in 1999. These activities were prompted by a number of things.

First, WLSA Malawi's research findings on the justice system and its impact on women in Malawi revealed that the system, both 'formal' and 'informal', delivers justice from a male paradigm rather than from a paradigm that embraces gender equality.[8] Because traditional justice itself is patriarchal, it leaves out a great part of the population, namely women. WLSA Malawi therefore recommended that justice delivery structures, which include the police, courts, district assemblies, *ankhoswe*,[9] families and churches, should begin a deliberate process of making their systems gender responsive.

[8] WLSA Malawi, *In Search of Justice: Women and the Administration of Justice in Malawi* (Blantyre, Malawi, Dzuka Publishing House, 2000).

[9] In Malawi traditionally when a man and a woman want to get married, they are supposed to be represented by two individuals named *ankhoswe*: usually these are males coming from each side of the family who deal with all of the processes required in order for a marriage to be recognised.

Second, WLSA Malawi's Legal Aid and Services programme had been bombarded with an alarming number of cases relating to violence suffered by women at the hands of their intimate partners. Ninety per cent of all cases that WLSA handled in 2000, 2001 and 2002 dealt with domestic violence. At the time of writing, this trend continues. Most women sought legal aid and services and continue to do so from WLSA offices after suffering from a series of abusive incidents for a long time. Their heart-breaking stories involve every form of abuse.

For example, in the case of physical abuse, women reported being heavily battered even in front of domestic workers and children, and being stripped naked and thrown outside the house. Cases of emotional abuse included situations where the husband slept with girlfriends in the house and where the husband refused to eat food cooked by the wife but instead sent children of the marriage to collect cooked food from a girlfriend which he then ate in the marital home. In the case of economic abuse, this included situations where the husband locked all food cupboards when going to the office and left the wife and children to starve at home, and cases of unlawful dispossession of widows upon the death of their husbands. In terms of sexual abuse, WLSA Malawi heard of many cases of husbands forcing their wives to have sex with them against their will. In a focus group discussion conducted by WLSA Malawi in 1999 in Chiradzulu district, one woman explained as follows:

> In a marriage sometimes you reach a point where you can't stand the sight of your husband, for a number of reasons you stop loving him. You cannot bear him touching you. However, in the end you still find yourself pregnant with his child: how do you think that happened?[10]

Faced with these cases, women sought help from WLSA Malawi to invoke the justice system on their behalf. One of the critical issues that arose was the issue of the gender-blind nature of the criminal laws at that time and to a large extent even now. For example, battery against a woman falls under the offence of 'assault occasioning actual bodily harm' or 'common assault'.[11] Due to the patriarchal mind-sets of agents of the state in charge of implementing the laws, domestic violence matters were not being prosecuted by the police, as they were deemed not to fall under the definition of assault occasioning bodily harm or common assault. Accordingly, when WLSA Malawi referred a battered woman client to the police

Once the marriage is ongoing they are responsible for resolving marital disputes. See LJ Chimango, 'Woman without Ankhoswe in Malawi' (1977) 15 *African Legal Studies* 54 (analysing the case of *Christina Mhango v Amadu Ali*, Civil Appeal (TC) No 15 of 1970 (High Court of Malawi), in which the Court ruled that the absence of the *ankhoswe* rendered the union of the parties a nullity). Section 22(5) of the Constitution of Malawi (Republic of Malawi, Act No 20 of 1994) would now recognise the union as marriage though the requirement for *ankhoswe* persists today.

[10] As part of WLSA Malawi's outreach programmes, the organisation conducted various focus group discussions which were part of their legal rights education programme, and this statement was made by one of the women who attended.

[11] Penal Code, Chapter 7:01, Laws of Malawi, 1930, ss 253 and 254.

so that charges of assault could be laid against the abuser, more often than not, the police tended to ignore such problems simply because the offender was a husband. Already overloaded with criminal matters, the police preferred pursuing a case against a 'hard-core criminal' who had assaulted a stranger, rather than a husband. WLSA Malawi was concerned to hold violent husbands accountable through the justice system, and opted to facilitate the enactment of a law that would deal with this problem. Before we describe WLSA Malawi's efforts, we next discuss the state of the law in Malawi related to marital rape and domestic violence, beginning with the constitutional provisions that provide the framework for all Malawian laws.

III. Marital Rape in Malawi: The Law and the Reality

A. Malawi's Domestic Laws

(i) The Constitution

The Malawian Constitution has a number of provisions relevant to marital rape. These include provisions on the promotion of gender equality and women's rights,[12] the right to dignity,[13] the right to marry,[14] the right to development,[15] the right to life,[16] and the values and principles that underpin the interpretation of the law.[17] The Constitution prescribes under section 5 that: 'Any act of Government or any law that is inconsistent with any of the provisions of this Constitution shall, to the extent of such inconsistency, be invalid.'

(a) Promotion of Gender Equality and Promotion of Women's Rights

Equal treatment of men and women is at the core of the promotion of women's rights, including the right not to be discriminated against on the basis of gender. A number of provisions in the Malawi Constitution recognise gender equality and the rights of women that are critical in advancing their protection in the family. Under section 13, the Constitution requires that the 'State shall actively promote the welfare and development of the people of Malawi by progressively adopting and implementing policies and legislation aimed at achieving' gender equality, among other goals, including the implementation of policies to address social issues such as domestic violence.

[12] Malawi Constitution (n 9) ss 13, 20 and 24.
[13] ibid, s 19(1).
[14] ibid, s 22(3).
[15] ibid, s 30.
[16] ibid, s 16.
[17] ibid, ss 10 and 11.

Section 20 of the Constitution prohibits all forms of discrimination and guarantees all persons, under any law, 'equal and effective protection against discrimination on grounds of race, colour, sex, language, religion, political or other opinion, nationality, ethnic or social origin, disability, property, birth or other status'. The state is further obligated under this provision to pass legislation 'addressing inequalities in society and prohibiting discriminatory practices and the propagation of such practices and may render such practices criminally punishable by the courts'.

Under section 24 of the Constitution, 'women have the right to full and equal protection by the law, and have the right not to be discriminated against on the basis of their gender or marital status' including 'the right to be accorded the same rights as men in civil law'. Furthermore, laws that discriminate against women based on gender or marital status 'shall be invalid and legislation shall be passed to eliminate customs and practices that discriminate against women, particularly practices such as … sexual abuse, harassment and violence'. Therefore, the Constitution mandates the enactment of a legal framework that explicitly prohibits marital rape.

(b) The Right to Dignity

The national legal framework is further strengthened by provisions on dignity. Section 19(1) of the Malawi Constitution provides that 'the dignity of all persons shall be inviolable'. Subsection 2 provides that 'in any judicial proceedings or in any other proceedings before any organ of the State … respect for human dignity shall be guaranteed'. Further, under subsection 3, 'no person shall be subject to torture of any kind or to cruel, inhuman or degrading treatment or punishment'. This provision provides a basis for outlawing any acts of indignity including marital rape. More importantly, the provision obliges the state to enforce this right.

(c) The Right to Marry

The law in Malawi takes special recognition of the institution of marriage and people's protection within the family. Section 22(1) of the Constitution provides that 'the family is the natural and fundamental group unit of society and is entitled to protection by society and the State'. Subsection (2) provides that 'each member of the family shall enjoy full and equal respect and shall be protected by law against all forms of neglect, cruelty or exploitation'. Subsection (3) guarantees all men and women the right to marry and found a family. Again, this right is broad enough to require protection against marital rape.

(d) The Right to Development

Section 30 of the Constitution provides that everyone has the right to development. Marital rape is a form of social injustice affecting the victim, the family unit and the state. It inhibits social and economic development. The state has the obligation to take measures for the realisation of this right to development, and to 'introduce reforms aimed at eradicating social injustices and inequalities' such as marital rape.

(e) The Right to Life

The potential for HIV transmission increases greatly in situations of marital rape, especially given the likelihood that condom usage is very low. Since forced sex directly increases a woman's risk for HIV infection, it is a critical element in the violation of women's right to life, which is guaranteed to every person under section 16 of the Constitution.

(ii) The Offence of Rape and the Prevention of Domestic Violence Act

The offence of rape is covered under section 132 of Malawi's Penal Code, which states that:

> [A]ny person who has unlawful carnal knowledge of a woman or girl, without her consent, or with her consent if the consent is obtained by force or means of threats or intimidation of any kind, or by fear of bodily harm, or by means of false representations as to the nature of the act, or in the case of a married woman, by impersonating her husband shall be guilty of the felony termed rape.[18]

According to this section, there are three elements to be proved by the prosecution to obtain a conviction for the offence of rape: (1) sexual intercourse (penetration), (2) lack of consent and (3) the identity of the accused person.[19] Consent is not defined, but the section highlights circumstances under which consent will not be an acceptable defence—where such consent is obtained through force, intimidation, threats or fear of bodily harm, or there was misrepresentation as to the nature of the act.

Consent has also been elaborated upon in Malawi case law. In *Mariette v Republic*, the High Court stated that lack of positive consent to sexual intercourse by a woman, though no force is used at all, amounts to rape.[20] This approach was applied in the case of *Republic v Nzina* in which the accused was convicted of rape after having had sexual intercourse with a woman while she was asleep and therefore incapable of consenting to the sexual act, although no force was used at all.[21]

Some judicial officers have taken a lenient view on issues of rape between intimate partners, as manifested in the case of *Rashid Hussein James v The Republic*, decided in January 2000.[22] The accused appealed against his sentence of 12 years'

[18] Penal Code (n 11) s 132.

[19] *Republic v Kaluwa* [1964–66] 3 ALR (Mal) 356 (High Court of Malawi, 12 August 1965) 360.

[20] *Mariette v Republic* [1966–68] 4 ALR (Mal) 119.

[21] *Republic v Nzina* [1966–68] 4 ALR (Mal) 263.

[22] *Rashid Hussein James v The Republic*, Criminal Appeal No 12 of 1999 (High Court of Malawi, January 2000).

imprisonment by the Chief Resident Magistrate on a charge of rape. In exercising its power of review, the High Court stated that the facts of the case revealed that the accused and the victim had been at one point intimate. The facts also revealed that the victim had resisted the advances of the accused, but the accused had forced himself on her. In his ruling, the Honourable Justice Kumange stated:

> I do not wish to be duped by the talk of forcing her down. Who doesn't know that women are naturally difficult and pretentious when sex demands are in the fore? After all these people were negotiating for sex at a strange place. May be the woman wanted it at the house of the appellant or her own house. In meeting resistance to his demands, no doubt that man had to use any form of violence to force her down. That he did and she succumbed to sex in normal circumstances. I therefore, observe that the facts do not satisfy the elements of the rape.[23]

Rape is a brutal and violent crime. Usually, it is also an act of hate and spite. With such perceptions, the judge might have it felt improper to associate such a heinous crime with someone who was once intimate with the complainant. However, the judge's statement displayed high levels of misogyny and a deep collusion with patriarchy that 'sometimes men just have to do what it takes', thereby legitimating a man's use of violence against a former intimate partner.

The common understanding of marital or spousal rape in Malawi is that it does not exist as an offence under the Penal Code. However, section 132 of the Penal Code does not make any reference to the position of husband and wife (except as regards impersonation). There has never been an explicit exemption for marital rape; it is the interpretation of consent and the word 'unlawful' that results in the legal impunity for marital rape in Malawi.[24]

It should be noted that Malawian law originated from the English legal system and thus British common law has had much influence on the law in Malawi. In early English decisions the understanding was that one of the terms of the marriage contract was that the wife consented to sexual intercourse throughout the marriage. Thus there was no need for the husband to seek consent any time he wanted sex with his wife. As noted in the nineteenth-century English case *R v Clarence*:

> The wife submits to her husband's embraces because at the time of the marriage she gave him an irrevocable right to her person. The intercourse, which takes place between a husband and wife after marriage is not by virtue of any special consent on her part, but is mere submission to an obligation imposed on her by law. Consent is immaterial.[25]

Malawi law has embraced this interpretation of rape law; there have been cases which have interpreted section 132 of the Penal Code to mean that non-consensual

[23] ibid (no pagination).

[24] F Sampson, *The Legal Treatment of Marital Rape in Canada, Ghana, Kenya and Malawi: A Barometer of Women's Human Rights* (Toronto, Equality Effect, 2010), online: www.theequalityeffect.com/pdfs/maritalrapebarometer.pdf at 23.

[25] *R v Clarence* [1886–90] All ER 133, 150.

sexual intercourse in marriage is not 'unlawful' and therefore cannot be criminal. For example, in the *Mwasumola* decision of 6 June 1968, Bolt J of the High Court stated:

> The question has been raised whether a wife can lawfully refuse intercourse at any time, that is to say, irrespective of custom and place, etc. In this connection, it would seem reasonable for a respectable wife to refuse her husband, eg, in a public place in front of other people. But in a normal way, I doubt whether she can do so. … It has been observed that a man can never be guilty of raping his wife and conversely that she can never refuse her consent. Whether this is a sound argument or not, I am inclined to the view … that a wife cannot lawfully refuse her husband intercourse.[26]

In marriage, therefore, there is a presumption that consent to sexual intercourse is by mutual, ongoing matrimonial consent; thus it has been argued that penal laws in Malawi do not criminalise marital rape. In 1996 there was a proposal to include marital rape as an offence under Malawi law, but this was rejected in the National Assembly on the basis of presumed and perpetual consent to sex in marriage.[27]

Efforts to capture the offence of marital rape as an issue of domestic violence in the proposed Prevention of Domestic Violence Act—which provides civil remedies for domestic violence—were met with very strong resistance in the various consultative forums where the proposed law was being discussed. WLSA Malawi's view was that the need for such a law was great if one considers the fact that, wrongful as it is, it is difficult to charge a husband with rape under the Penal Code because rape can only be committed by a person who has *unlawful* carnal knowledge with the victim. Culturally and to a certain extent legally as discussed above, it is 'lawful' for a husband to have carnal knowledge with his wife (impliedly no matter by what means), so long as it is in line with the 'order of nature'. The common law position has been that 'the husband cannot be guilty of rape committed by himself upon his lawful wife, for by their mutual matrimonial consent and contract, the wife hath given herself in kind unto the husband which she cannot retract'.[28] As Finkelhor and Yllo have argued, this provides husbands with an exemption from prosecution for raping their wives—in short, 'a license to rape'.[29] As noted in section I, however, despite of the efforts of WLSA Malawi and other stakeholders, the Prevention of Domestic Violence Act, as currently enacted, does not explicitly include marital rape.

The Malawian law reflects an era in Britain when women were not regarded as persons once they married; by marriage spouses became one legal personality, and

[26] *R v Mwasumola* [1966–68] 4 ALR (Mal) 569 (High Court of Malawi, 6 June 1968) 572.

[27] N Kanyongolo et al, *Customary Law and Women's Rights: The Case of Malawi* (Zomba, University of Malawi, 2010) (no pagination).

[28] Lord Matthew Hale, quoted in DE Russell, *Rape in Marriage* (Bloomington, Indiana University Press, 1990) 17.

[29] D Finkelhor and K Yllo, *License to Rape: Sexual Abuse of Wives* (New York, Holt, Rinehart & Winston, 1985), cited in M Motalingoane-Khau, 'But He is My Husband! How Can That Be Rape? Exploring Silences Around Date and Marital Rape in Lesotho' (2007) 74 *Agenda: Empowering Women for Gender Equity* 58, 63.

the 'one person' created was the husband. According to Sir William Blackstone, the marital status of men and women under the common law was as follows:

> By marriage, the husband and wife are one person in law; that is, the very being or legal existence of the woman is suspended during the marriage, or at least is incorporated and consolidated into that of the husband: under whose wing, protection, and cover, she performs everything.[30]

It was therefore impossible to imagine the husband raping his wife, as she was a part of him. Although these ideas long ago lost validity in Britain so that marital rape was no longer countenanced in that society,[31] Malawi maintains these relics in its laws. Identification of such colonial baggage and its deconstruction offers an opportunity to develop laws that originate from Malawians, and which, through the Constitution, can promote the equal rights of Malawian women.[32]

The framework of decolonisation calls for confronting the issue of marital rape from the perspective that Malawi carries a colonial legacy which continues to oppress Malawian women even in this post-independence era.[33] Colonisation generally involves dislocation and devaluation of the way of life of the original peoples inhabiting a land by outside peoples.[34] The colonial laws Malawi inherited from the British are laws influenced by British values and culture imposed on the Malawian people.[35] Since customary law in Malawi is area specific,[36] and in the absence of anthropological studies of precolonial Malawi in relation to marital rape, it is difficult and rather unsafe to make conclusions as to whether the British treatment of marital rape prior to its criminalisation in *R v R*[37] was similar to how customary law of the time treated marital rape in Malawi.

As it stands, the de facto exemption of marital rape completely fails to provide equal protection from sexual violence to all women. This is inconsistent with the constitutional provision that guarantees equal protection regardless of marital status and sex.[38] It is also inconsistent with the constitutional protection against inhuman and degrading treatment.[39] Marital rape is a highly degrading experience,

[30] Sir William Blackstone, *Commentaries on the Laws of England*, vol 1 (Oxford, Clarendon Press, 1765–69) 430.

[31] See NK Stafford, 'Permission for Domestic Violence: Marital Rape in Ghanaian Marriages' (2008) 29 *Women's Rights Law Reporter* 63, 63–64 (providing a history of the background to marital rape from British common law); and see *R v R* [1992] 1 AC 599 (HL) 623 (declaring that 'in modern times the supposed marital exception in rape forms no part of the law of England').

[32] See generally K Cochrane, 'Resolving Violence Against Women in Intimate Relationships through International Guidance and Self-Determination' (University of British Columbia, unpublished, 2010).

[33] Malawi was under British rule officially from 1891 to 1964 when it gained independence.

[34] HN Weaver, 'The Colonial Context: Reflections' (2009) 24 *Journal of Interpersonal Violence* 1552, 1553.

[35] See generally S Wiessner, 'Rights and Status of Indigenous Peoples: A Global Comparative and International Legal Analysis' (1999) 12 *Harvard Human Rights Journal* 57.

[36] *Kamphoni v Kamphoni*, Matrimonial Cause No 7 of 2012 (High Court of Malawi, 26 August, 2012) (no pagination).

[37] *R v R* (n 31).

[38] Malawi Constitution (n 9) s 20.

[39] ibid, s 19(3).

and the failure to protect women from marital rape violates this section of the Malawian Constitution. Continued exemption of husbands from criminal liability for marital rape has been criticised as conveying the message that such acts of aggression are somehow less reprehensible than other types of rape. Importantly, it indicates an acceptance of the archaic understanding that wives are the property of their husbands and the marriage contract provides an entitlement to sex.[40]

Malawian women, therefore, still suffer as a result of colonial legal relics and of more contemporary resistance to criminalising marital rape. An explicit prohibition of marital rape must form a part of Malawian law for women to be protected.

(iii) The Civil Law

Although it is widely accepted that marital rape is not an offence in Malawi at present, there is evidence that women complain of actions amounting to marital rape in civil cases. This mostly occurs in the context of divorce proceedings on grounds of sexual abuse or cruelty. As the cases discussed in this section illustrate, the subordinate courts in Malawi who hear divorce cases are generally not willing to recognise marital rape as such.

In the 2007 case of *Roger Moffat v Grace Moffat*,[41] the petitioner husband and respondent wife had been married since 1997 and had two children. The petitioner contended that the wife had deserted him in 2006 and had chased him away from their matrimonial home for no proper reason. In her evidence, however, the respondent wife told the Court that the husband had been adulterous and cruel to her. She testified that the husband had appeared to have lost sexual desire for her but forced her to sleep with him when she was having her periods, and that the husband forced her to sleep with his friends in turn and that she was humiliated by all of these experiences. She also alleged that the husband used to have sexual intercourse with her when she was unconscious, and she suspected that he had a sexually transmitted disease. The wife told the Court that she had deserted her husband partly due to his sexual abuse. The Court held that the husband was the one in the wrong and was responsible for cruelty and sexual abuse towards the wife. The Court was satisfied that the man had been adulterous and abusive and that these reasons justified ending the marriage. However, the Court did not go further to pronounce the husband's actions as marital rape, even though the husband was having sex with the wife when she was unwilling and thus without her consent.

A similar case from 2009 is *Susan Zambezi v Francis Zambezi*.[42] The petitioner wife and the respondent husband were in a marriage from 1994 and had four

[40] Blackstone (n 30) 430.

[41] *In the Matter of Roger Moffat v Grace Chinga Moffat*, Civil Cause No 10 of 2007 (Chief Resident Magistrate Court, Blantyre 2010).

[42] *Susan Zambezi v Francis Zambezi*, Civil Cause No 49 of 2009 (Blantyre Magistrate Court), His Worship Mzondi Mvula presiding.

children. She wanted to divorce him on grounds of cruelty. She told the Court that the husband developed a habit of beating her. She also said that the respondent used to force her to have sex despite her not being willing, would beat her if she refused, and that he had even destroyed her underwear in a struggle to force her to have sexual intercourse with him. The husband also called her a prostitute in public. The Court held that cruelty had been established, as there was evidence that the petitioner had undergone humiliation, torture and trauma at the hands of the respondent. The Court ordered the respondent to compensate the petitioner for the pain she suffered, and also ordered him to build a house for her. The Court did not, however, go into detail on the issue of forcing the petitioner to have sexual intercourse, but rather generalised the experience she had undergone with the respondent as establishing cruelty which justified ending the marriage.

In *Brandina Chipofya v John Chipofya*,[43] the parties got married in 2005 but later started experiencing problems. The husband had other sexual relations outside marriage and had a child with another woman. At some point he was diagnosed with cancer. Later he and his wife both tested HIV positive and were counselled to use condoms as protection when having sexual intercourse. However, the husband forced the wife to have sexual intercourse without protection and threatened to divorce her if she insisted on the use of condoms. When the wife decided to sleep in a different room, he got angry and told her that she was not respecting his leadership in the family, and because she was refusing him in bed she had better divorce him. The Court found as a fact that the husband was cruel and unfaithful to the wife. Furthermore, 'he was not deterred in his promiscuous behaviour even after being tested HIV positive. He even wanted to be having sexual intercourse with her without any protection.'[44] The Court ordered dissolution of the marriage, but as in previous cases, did not identify the husband's behaviour as marital rape.

Lastly, in *Christina Mpanga v Lazaki Phiri*,[45] the parties were in a marriage and at some point the husband was incarcerated for two and half years. Upon his return from prison, relatives recommended that the two have tests for sexually transmitted diseases before having sexual intercourse. However, the husband forced the wife into having sexual intercourse before the test. The husband also asked the wife if a snake could suck her private parts. When she refused, the husband hit her. The wife told the Court that the husband would also force her to have sexual intercourse when she was having her periods. He had been threatening to kill her if she did not listen to him. The Court held that the husband had subjected the wife to sufficient cruelty to justify divorce. However, the Court did not dwell so much on the forced sexual intercourse but rather on the other violent acts of the husband towards the wife to establish the irretrievable breakdown of the marriage.

[43] *Brandina Chipofya v John Chipofya*, Civil Cause No 342 of 2009 (Zomba Magistrate Court), His Worship Likwanya presiding.

[44] ibid (no pagination).

[45] *In the matter of Christina Mpanga v Lazaki Phiri*, Civil Cause No 35 of 2010 (Mulunguzi Magistrate Court), Senior Resident Magistrate Kacheche presiding.

It is safe to conclude from these cases that the pattern by the subordinate courts—which are very important in Malawi as they comprise the most accessible form of formal justice—is to shy away from acknowledging marital rape. In fact, even when it seems obvious in these cases that the husbands raped their wives, the judges fail to name this fact. Thus, it is apposite for Parliament to enact a law that explicitly prohibits marital rape rather than expecting the courts to interpret the current laws to recognise marital rape, as they have so far failed to do so.

B. The International Legal Framework

The Republic of Malawi has several international obligations and commitments to protect women from domestic violence and in particular from marital rape, in recognition of the fact that, globally, marital rape has come to be seen as a violation of human rights. At the national level, the country's obligations exist under its Constitution, as discussed above. At the international level, its commitments and obligations arise under the Convention on the Elimination of All Forms of Discrimination against Women (CEDAW), which Malawi ratified in 1987.[46]

CEDAW guarantees women equal rights with men in all spheres of life, including education, employment, healthcare, nationality and marriage. This is in recognition by state parties of the fact that a change in the traditional roles of men and women in society and in the family is needed to achieve full equality between men and women. CEDAW therefore affirms the need for the elimination of discrimination against women.

Pursuant to this goal, General Recommendation 19 of the CEDAW Committee states that:

> Gender based violence, which impairs and nullifies the enjoyment by women of human rights and fundamental human freedoms under general international law or under human rights conventions, is discrimination. Under general international law and specific human rights covenants, States may also be responsible for private acts if they fail to act with due diligence to prevent violation of rights or to investigate and punish acts of violence, and for providing compensation.[47]

This is a key recommendation related to domestic violence and marital rape. It imposes upon state parties an obligation to, among other things, prevent violations of rights in the private sphere, and punish acts of violence in that sphere. Under CEDAW itself, all state parties are under an obligation to adopt appropriate legislative and other measures prohibiting discrimination against women.[48] This specifically creates a commitment upon Member States to eliminate all forms

[46] Convention on the Elimination of All Forms of Discrimination Against Women, General Assembly Resolution 34/180 of 18 December 1979, entry into force 3 September 1981 (CEDAW).

[47] UN Committee on the Elimination of Discrimination Against Women, General Recommendation 19: Violence Against Women, 11th Session, 1992, UN Doc A/47/38, para 7.

[48] CEDAW (n 46) Arts 2, 3.

of discrimination against women, including domestic violence and marital rape, through legislation.[49]

By virtue of section 211(2) of the Malawi Constitution, CEDAW is part of the laws of Malawi and therefore needs to be given full and immediate effect.[50] Malawi's Supreme Court of Appeal has addressed the issue of whether international conventions ratified before the enactment of the Constitution form part of the laws of Malawi in accordance with section 211.[51] The Court was of the view that:

> The correct reading of that section is to follow the clear language that has been employed. If one does that; one will find that the clear thread that runs through the fabric of all the subsections of section 211 of our Constitution is that all international agreements entered into prior to the Constitution or after the Constitution are only binding if they are not in conflict with the clear provisions of our statutes. Put differently, whether an international agreement forms part of our law, regardless of when it was entered into, will depend on whether there is no Act of Parliament that provides to the contrary. And the question whether customary international law forms part of our law will depend on whether it is consistent with our Constitution or our statutes.[52]

Our position is that CEDAW—which was ratified by Malawi in 1987, before the Constitution was adopted in 1994—does not conflict with the Constitution. In fact, it is in tandem with Malawi's constitutional protections of women's equality, dignity and marriage rights, and therefore forms part and parcel of the laws of Malawi. Another relevant source of Malawi's obligations to end marital rape is the Beijing Platform for Action, which states that one of the fundamental sexual and reproductive health rights of women is the right to have control over, and decide freely on matters related to their own sexual and reproductive health free from coercion, discrimination or violence.[53]

It must be understood, however, that the implementation of CEDAW and the Beijing Platform for Action requires an examination of relationships between men and women, between family members, and between family and state, that affect every citizen personally as well as theoretically.[54] Another challenge is

[49] For further discussion of international obligations, see Vasanthi Venkatesh and Melanie Randall, 'Normative and International Human Rights Law Imperatives for Criminalising Intimate Partner Sexual Violence: The Marital Rape Impunity in Comparative and Historical Perspective', chapter 3 in this volume.

[50] Malawi Constitution (n 9) s 211(2).

[51] See *In the Matter of the Adoption of Children Act* (Chapter 26:01) and *In the Matter of CJ (A Female Infant)*, MSCA Adoption Appeal No 28 of 2009, [2009] MWSC 1 (Malawi Supreme Court of Appeal).

[52] ibid (no pagination).

[53] United Nations, Beijing Declaration and Platform for Action, *Fourth World Conference on Women* (September, 1995) para 97.

[54] MA Freeman, 'Measuring Equality: A Comparative Perspective on Women's Legal Capacity and Constitutional Rights in Five Commonwealth Countries' (1990) 5 *Berkeley Women's Law Journal* 110, 130–31 (analysing domestic courts' decisions resolving issues concerning customary law, patriarchy, women's rights and international law); M Freeman, 'Women, Development and Justice: Using the International Convention on women's rights' in J Kerr (ed), *Ours By Right* (London, Zed Books, 1993) 100.

the trickledown effect of international legal instruments; that is, how are these obligations going to be 'felt', understood and granted legitimacy at the grassroots level in order to be implemented? We address this issue in the next section of this chapter.

C. Customary Law and Community Perceptions of Marital Rape

Studies undertaken by WLSA Malawi suggest that the Malawian population is divided on the issue of marital rape.[55] For these studies, WLSA organised discussion groups with people in the southern region of Malawi from 2005 to 2006 to discuss the issue of marital rape in the context of trying to understand factors that created women's vulnerability to HIV transmission. In the course of the meetings organised by WLSA, many people expressed the opinion that marital rape is not consistent with the institution of marriage, by virtue of which a husband inherits a right to access his wife even without the necessary consent. This section examines community viewpoints, which are informed by customary law, practice and perceptions in Malawi.

(i) Customary Law

In Malawi there are two major systems of contracting marriages under custom: the dominant matrilineal system, which prevails in most parts of the central region and in most parts of the southern region, and the patrilineal system, which prevails in the whole of the northern region, in certain parts of the central region, and in certain parts of the southern region.[56] Under the matrilineal system of marriage, there is no payment of dowry but various gifts may be exchanged between the contracting parties.[57] Under the patrilineal system of marriage, dowry is paid by the man's family to the woman's family in the form of livestock or money.[58] Most marriages in Malawi are characterised by unequal power relations, which sometimes manifests in injustices such as spousal violence, including marital rape. This is caused and rooted in gender inequalities that underlie the presumed superior status of the husband.

Customary law in both systems of marriage does not recognise the concept of marital rape. In both systems a husband is entitled to exclusive sexual intercourse with his wife. Denial of sexual intercourse by the wife is a common

[55] WLSA Malawi, *Sexual Violence and Women's Vulnerability to HIV: A Rights Issue* (Research Report submitted at a Regional Research Conference for all WLSA Countries held in Harare, September 2006).

[56] M. Chigaŵa, *Customary Law Marriages and Social Development: De Jure Marriages at Customary Law in Malawi* (Zomba, unpublished, 1987).

[57] JO Ibik, *The Law of Marriage and Divorce* (London, Sweet & Maxwell, 1970) 183.

[58] ibid, 43.

ground for divorce. However, customary law in both systems recognises certain circumstances in which a spouse can justifiably withhold consent to sexual intercourse, which include during advanced pregnancy, immediately after childbirth, during menstruation and during mourning for a deceased close relative of either spouse.[59]

It is therefore arguable that it is not the payment of dowry as such which leads to the custom of presuming a wife's ongoing consent to sex in marriage. Even in those marriages that do not recognise the practice of dowry, consent to sex throughout the marriage is assumed to be given at the time of marriage.

(ii) Community Perceptions of Marital Rape

WLSA Malawi wanted to understand more fully people's perceptions on forced sex within a marriage, particularly given the strong opinions of some that the concept of marital rape violated the sanctity of marriage, and the idea that rape in marriage was impossible. To this end, WLSA Malawi held discussions on domestic violence with grassroots communities in several villages.[60]

Although many women generally viewed forced sex within marriage as violence, in most cases they provided justifications as to why men engage in such violent acts. A group of women in the Traditional Authority (TA) of Mabuka in Mulanje district viewed forced sex in marriage as violence only in special circumstances. For example, they highlighted that in situations where a woman is ill, tired or menstruating, forced sex would be viewed as violence. Conversely, they argued that if a woman refuses to have sex with her husband without valid reasons, she is the one who is violating her husband's rights.

Similarly, a group of women in Nkando in Mulanje felt that in Malawian culture, a woman cannot claim to have been raped by her husband because by virtue of getting married, a woman has consented to everything, including sex as and when the husband chooses. For some women, the experience of forced sex has to be endured because marriage possibilities are scarce and, due to the social pressures that single women endure, one cannot afford to lose a husband. All of these factors highlight the interconnected social, cultural and psychological factors that negatively affect the realisation of women's sexual autonomy and that promote marital rape.

In Namani village, TA Njema in the same district of Mulanje, a focus group discussion of women was divided in their views on whether or not forced sex within marriage qualifies as violence. One perspective was that this is not violence, because by forcing a wife to have sex, the man symbolises that he is committed to them only, and does not want other women. Such an attitude may reflect a

[59] ibid, 59.

[60] WLSA Malawi (n 55).

position of internalised oppression, whereby notions of what constitutes a valid relationship are determined by experiences of domination. However, another perspective was that forced sex in a marriage is outright violence, although the fact that the perpetrator is one's husband legitimises the violence. One woman living with AIDS in Mulanje, who was aged 40 years and had four children at the time of the interview, attested to this view by sharing her story:

> She divorced with her first husband in 1996 and got married to another man whom she believes infected her with HIV. Her cousin knew about the sero status of the second man but never disclosed to her because he was his friend. The man too never disclosed his status and now when she recalls the events, she believes he just came to destroy her. He used to come home at night while drunk and rape her. She claims that she withstood such abuses because marriages are scarce and therefore [she] did not want to lose him but also she did not have the strength to resist it. Although she knew that what she was experiencing was sexual abuse, at that time she did not really mind because it was her husband doing it, unlike if it was a boyfriend.[61]

Many focus group discussions of men generally viewed forced sex as unacceptable only when it is perpetrated unreasonably, like in cases of illness or menstruation, but not otherwise. An exception was found in Nkando village, where some men pointed out that:

> The fact is she does not want [sex]. Having sex should be viewed as a right for both men and women. Both are supposed to have independent thoughts and decisions over sexual matters. Besides, damage to the woman's body may be occasioned as you force her, which just underscores the fact that forced sex is violence. Sometimes, your wife may tell you she cannot have sex because she is menstruating. However, you may insist on physically examining her, which is violence as well as degrading.[62]

The above descriptions of WLSA Malawi's focus group discussions highlight the different perspectives which exist on whether forced sex can be considered violence, and whether it is acceptable within the confines of marriage or long-term unions. By unpacking the interpretation of forced sex, it is easy to see the ways that marital rape occurs, partly as a result of pre-existing gender power dynamics, partly as a result of women's subordinate status within the family, and also due to the construction of sex and sexuality within society. Sex is often constructed in such a way that male partners dictate the terms of sex, including the right to use force if sex is unwanted or being refused by a female partner. The community perceptions of marital rape discussed in this section provide a key backdrop for thinking about the role of the state and civil society organisations such as WLSA Malawi in responding to this form of violence against women.

[61] ibid, 68.
[62] ibid, 63.

IV. A Critical Overview of the Legal Reform Process: Challenges and Opportunities

A. Perceptions on the Role of the State

For many women, the state has been a focus of feminist efforts to redress injustices arising from gender differences on the ground. The state is assumed to have a degree of autonomy from patriarchy; hence to the degree that the state assumes responsibility for women's interests, it can provide a resort of appeal against the power of men in more intimate institutions such as the family.[63] However, as will be discussed below, states are definitely not autonomous from patriarchy; in fact they are patriarchal. Goetz, in her theory of the gendered nature of states, cites Connell to suggest that they are largely oriented to male interests for historical reasons; state institutions have been constructed and staffed by men and tend therefore to be oriented to advancing their class and gender interests.[64] Therefore, gender equity concerns must be institutionalised so that women's as well as men's concerns and experiences are integral to the design, implementation, monitoring and evaluation of all legislation, policies and programmes to ensure that women benefit equally and inequality is not perpetuated.[65]

It is this conceptual framework that led WLSA Malawi to call for a Malawian justice system committed to gender equality. In 2001, WLSA Malawi decided that in order to understand how various Malawian sectors understood the issue of domestic violence, it should hold several consultative forums with the organs of the state. WLSA's goal was the introduction of a law that would contribute to the protection of women from violence in their homes, including marital rape.

The tool used by WLSA Malawi to facilitate these consultative meetings was an issues paper designed to elicit reaction from the various consultative forums. The gist of the argument posed in the paper was that domestic violence, including marital rape, is prevalent in Malawi and that this was a violation of women's rights under Malawi's international and domestic legal obligations.[66] This paper was made available at consultative workshops that WLSA organised to raise awareness about and mobilise support for laws to end domestic violence.

Even before the consultations based on the issues paper, a number of advocacy events had taken place in Malawi. Beginning in November 2000, WLSA organised a Round Table discussion on domestic violence as a prelude to an event

[63] AM Goetz, 'Institutionalizing Women's Interests and Accountability to Women in Development' (1995) 26(3) *IDS Bulletin* 1, 3.

[64] RW Connell, *Gender and Power* (Cambridge, Polity Press, 1987), cited in Goetz, ibid, 3.

[65] H Derbyshire, *A Practical Guide for Development Policy Makers and Practitioners* (London, DFID Social Development Division, 2000) 9.

[66] WLSA Malawi, *Issue Paper on the Enactment of Domestic Violence Legislation in Malawi* (Blantyre, unpublished, 2001).

'16 Days of Activism against Gender-Based Violence'.[67] To facilitate this event, WLSA produced a video documentary, *Unveiling the Unspeakable*, in which women who had experienced domestic violence told their stories. This video was first shown at the Round Table and aroused many discussions at that event and in the media afterwards. On 25 November 2000, WLSA organised a March Against Violence Against Women, launching the White Scarf Campaign in which marchers wore white scarves as a symbol of resistance to violence against women. It was the first march of its kind and the First Lady of the Republic of Malawi, Madame Shanil Muluzi, participated. It was after these events that the discussion around domestic violence gained momentum and gripped the country. Questions were being raised by Malawians in both electronic and print media such as: Does domestic violence exist? Do we have to talk about marital rape? Does Malawi have to legislate against domestic violence?

In was during this momentum that WLSA Malawi developed the issues paper on domestic violence legislation. From April to November 2001 WLSA Malawi held a range of activities, including Expert and Community Discussions as well as video-recorded discussions on domestic violence with grassroots communities in Mdala Village in Mulanje district, Chiwamba Village in Lilongwe district, and Chilembwe Village in Mangochi district. Furthermore, WLSA organised five Stakeholder Consultative Workshops to include discussions with technical experts, traditional leaders, judges and government officials, religious leaders and civil society organisations. These consultative workshops were held in Mangochi district at Sunbird Nkopola Lodge.

On the face of it, this process should have been a relatively simple matter. The bottom line was that crimes were being committed (and continue to be so) in homes, and women formed a majority of the victims of such crimes. Furthermore, it is the duty of the state to protect those who are victims from further violence, and to ensure that acts of similar violence in other homes must not happen. However, once WLSA started working on this project we realised that we had entered into difficult terrain.

Many of the state actors that WLSA Malawi engaged with did not consider violence against women to be an issue. In particular, some state actors thought of marital rape as a very 'private' issue of sex that forms the central core of marriage.[68] Some people believed that rape could not be viewed in the same vicinity as marriage. That rape was a despicable and shameful word, and that marriage is a

[67] The 16 Days of Activism Against Gender-Based Violence is an international campaign first organised by the Center for Women's Global Leadership in 1991. See UN Women, online: www.unwomen.org/en/what-we-do/ending-violence-against-women/take-action/16-days-of-activism.

[68] See also WLSA Malawi, *Living Dangerously: The Intersection between Women's Right to Life and the Feminisation of the HIV and AIDS Epidemic* (research conducted by WLSA Malawi between 2004 and 2009, highlighting the centrality of sex to the institution of marriage in Malawi. One woman in a focus group in Nkhotakota said: 'The reason why you marry is to have real and good sex. My father can give me everything that matters—food, clothes etc. But I want a man to give me sex, and that is why I left my father to come and stay with him').

sacred space in which rape cannot happen, led to the position that one should not even talk about marital rape, let alone legislating against it. What was therefore at stake was to convince those in power that this issue was important and that the state was under an obligation to pass a law against marital rape.

On the ground, WLSA Malawi found a lack of public consensus about accepting and adopting laws preventing domestic violence, and in particular a resistance to seeing marital rape as an issue. As consultations proceeded, it became apparent that many of the people WLSA consulted somewhat agreed that domestic violence should be subject to sanctions by the state (with some variations to this position), but they totally disagreed that marital rape should be included as a form of domestic violence. The main reason given for this position was that rape and marriage are mutually exclusive and therefore marital rape cannot be included in a law that was aimed at preserving marriage. In fact, WLSA Malawi's core argument was that the law was being proposed to save the institution of marriage rather than undermine it. This position was taken in order to convince various parties that a domestic violence law that included marital rape would protect spouses within marriage and preserve the institution of marriage.

This lack of public consensus on the problem of marital rape can be understood at many levels and is multifaceted in nature, relating to male bias in the justice system in responding to gender-related crimes (particularly sexual assault between intimate partners), the failure of the justice system to operate effectively due to a lack of resources, and the challenges posed by legal pluralism. Each of these issues will be examined in turn.

B. Male Bias in the Justice System in Response to Gender-Related Crimes

A lack of public consensus is evidenced by the negative and biased attitudes of personnel in the justice system in dealing with cases relating to gender-based violence. This deters women from accessing formal and informal justice structures with regard to crimes committed against them in the private sphere. A study undertaken by WLSA Malawi in 2000 into the justice system and its impact on women found that in one rape case, the police refused to take down a complainant's statement unless she took off her clothes to show them where she was raped.[69] This victimised the woman twice and humiliated her as she suffered repeated violence. The study revealed that the police looked at gender-based violence cases as domestic matters only and typically only encouraged parties to reconcile.[70]

In another survey, WLSA Malawi assessed 12 police stations in 12 districts in Malawi on their views of what should be in the proposed domestic violence

[69] WLSA Malawi (n 8) 88.
[70] ibid, 87.

legislation.[71] Some of the respondents—all of whom were members of the police force—were sceptical about the legislation and stated that they would not support the enactment of such a law, as it would be tantamount to breaking up marriages. According to one respondent, 'How can I arrest someone in this case when I know I also beat up my wife as well?'[72] In addition, some of the police officers thought that if the law was enacted, it might oppress men. The major reason for this attitude amongst the police personnel related to the fact that all of them came from the Malawian cultural context, in which there is a clear separation of private and public and a belief that men have a right to use violence against the women who are their wives. This separation even extends to issues which can properly be described as criminal. Our argument was that the state itself has enforced such mind-sets by not providing for a precise law to address such 'domestic' wrongs. The laws and procedures that existed at the time, and in some respects continue to exist now, have proven to be ineffective to address these wrongs.

In Malawi some police stations have Victim Support Units that were established long before the domestic violence law. The purpose of the Victim Support Units is to provide a safe space for survivors of domestic violence to report their cases in a private environment to an officer who is trained in gender analysis and domestic violence. There is mounting evidence, however, that the challenge being faced with regard to these units is that they are not safe. Police personnel who are placed there are not trained in gender analysis and use traditional values to help women. Some women have reported to WLSA Malawi offices that police shout at them and accuse them of causing the violence perpetrated against them.

There is also evidence that some Malawi courts hold traditional values that perpetuate myths and stereotypes of women who suffer sexual abuse. There are some myths among Malawian society that entrench the view that women's consent in sexual matters is not necessary. One of these myths is that women and girls are very 'coy' in sexual matters, and that in most cases when they say 'no' to sexual advances they actually mean 'yes'. These myths are not part of Malawian customary law but they do carry much weight, so much so that they have actually found their way into the Malawian courts. There have been court decisions supporting the stereotypes, such as the *James* case discussed above in section III.[73]

It is this kind of attitude by the personnel in the justice system that makes it hard for women to gain equality through strategic interventions such as laws preventing domestic violence. These attitudes suggest that there are many deep layers of sexist beliefs about women, making it difficult to pass laws supporting women's equality and autonomy in sexual matters and to apply criminal penalties

[71] WLSA Malawi, *Report on the Crisis Management Survey of Selected Police Stations in Malawi* (Blantyre, unpublished, 2001).

[72] ibid.

[73] *James v The Republic* (n 22).

to violations of women's rights to sexual autonomy. Alda Facio outlines this point quite effectively when she says:

> [T]here cannot be sustainability in development if male biased administration of [the] justice system continues in developing as well as the so-called developed nations. This is because if the administration of justice is male biased, women's human rights violations remain unpunished. If women are understood as persons 'entitled' to benefits of development, one of which is a right to a non-sexist administration of justice, this necessarily implies that violations of women's rights will not go systematically unpunished.[74]

C. Lack of Resources within Justice Administration Structures

The second point relevant to a lack of public consensus is that over and above male bias within the system, the nature and operation of the justice delivery structures themselves show a severe lack of necessary and adequate resources to effectively perform their duties. A study conducted by seven southern African countries in 1999 shows that most of the justice delivery structures are inundated with problems relating to lack of resources.[75] This pertains to simple things such as stationery and infrastructure, and to more strategically complicated things such as lack of proper training among personnel, intimidating court procedures (including the use of English by court personnel), and large distances from many villages.

Whilst this lack of resources was found to have negative implications on the general populace, it had even greater implications on women as it meant long-distance travel to these places, which consumed a lot of valuable time interfering with their productive and reproductive roles. It also meant spending money on transport, which women usually did not have. In addition, since there was a lack of stationery, court users were expected to provide their own, which most of the women could not afford. Most women therefore gave up on the formal justice system.

Another study of access to justice in Malawi conducted on behalf of the Kenyan Section of the International Commission of Jurists in 2009 included discussions with court personnel and revealed a number of dynamics showing the challenges that the judiciary faces.[76] Discussions were undertaken with the Justice of the

[74] A Facio, 'Women in Development: The Rights of Women and Children' in C Sweetman (ed), *Women and Rights*, vol 3 (London, Oxfam, 1995) 1, 16.

[75] Women and Law in Southern Africa (WLSA Zimbabwe), *In the Shadow of the Law. Women and Justice Delivery in Zimbabwe* (Harare, WLSA Trust, 1999); WLSA Malawi (n 8); Women and Law in Southern Africa (WLSA Botswana), *Chasing the Mirage: Women and the Administration of Justice* (Gaborone, WLSA Trust, 1999); Women and Law in Southern Africa (WLSA Zambia), *Women and Justice. Myth or Reality in Zambia* (Lusaka, WLSA Trust, 1999); Women and the Administration of Justice (WLSA Lesotho), *Women and the Administration of Justice. Where Do women in Lesotho Go?* (Maseru, WLSA Trust, 2000).

[76] 'Seodi V-R White, *Baseline Survey on Access to Justice. Access to Justice for the Poor and Marginalised in Malawi. The Malawi Country Report*, a study commissioned by the Kenyan section of the International Commission of Jurists, African Human Rights and Access to Justice Programme (AHRAJ) (2009).

Supreme Court, the Registrar of the High Court, and two Assistant Registrars of the High Court. The study found that challenges with access to justice are not deliberate on the part of the judiciary, but stem from systemic governance issues both in historic terms as well as in economic terms.

The annual budget allocation for the judiciary is the most constricting factor for improving access to justice for marginalised people. A report by Edge Kanyongolo shows that, in general, Malawi officials say funding for the justice sector is inadequate.[77] The funding inadequacies probably reflect the fact that the justice sector does not appear to be a high priority for the government despite its inclusion in the Poverty Reduction Strategy Paper.[78] Approved budgets are much lower than estimated expenditures for the year would suggest. In addition, there is no guarantee that funds will be released from the Treasury according to the approved budget. Funds are released on an irregular basis and in greatly varying amounts.

In the 2005–06 national budget for example, the government allocated almost the same funding to state residences as it did to the Anti-Corruption Bureau, the Human Rights Commission and the Ministry of Justice and Constitutional Affairs headquarters combined.[79] Inadequacy in the funding of the justice sector must be understood in the context of the general problem of inadequacies in the funding of all public-sector institutions in Malawi.

In light of the fact that women are overrepresented among the poor,[80] the inadequacies of the justice system have a profound negative impact on women. This state of affairs means that a majority of women fail to access the justice system and thus fail to resolve their problems and defend their rights. In the case of the domestic violence law when it was being proposed, there were concerns that the majority of the women would fail to use it and thus would not be protected by it.

D. Legal Pluralism

The third area related to the lack of public consensus on Malawi's proposed domestic violence law and the opposition to criminalising marital rape is that of legal pluralism.[81] Over and above male bias and an inadequate legal system, legal pluralism also contributed to the resistance to this law because the multiple legal orders in Malawi—including customary law and state laws—create conflicting messages about the social acceptability of marital rape. For instance, in the event

[77] FE Kanyongolo, *Malawi: Justice Sector and Rule of Law* (London, Open Society Initiative for Southern Africa, 2006) 65–66.

[78] Malawi Government, *Malawi Poverty Reduction Strategy Paper* (Lilongwe, Malawi Government, 2002) 74.

[79] Kanyongolo (n 77) 66.

[80] P Newell and JG Frynas, 'Beyond CSR? Business, Poverty and Social Justice: An Introduction' (2007) 28 *Third World Quarterly* 669, 675.

[81] See Vasanthi Venkatesh, 'Pluralistic Legal Systems and Marital Rape: Cross-National Considerations', chapter 4 in this volume for an analysis of legal pluralism, customary law and marital rape.

that state laws were to make provision for marital rape, enforcement would be hampered by customary laws in which marital rape is not recognised; customary law is enforced by chiefs who are predominantly males with entrenched patriarchal interests.

Traditional legal anthropology views legal pluralism as a system of different orders, conceived of as separate entities coexisting in the same political space.[82] It consists of different bodies of law that form part of the state legal system.[83] As Dow and Kidd argue: '[S]tate law is not the only body of rules governing social behaviour, and … there exists in a society elaborate and complex and sometimes competing rules that govern people's action and behaviour.'[84]

The interplay between state laws, customary laws, religious laws and other laws is a critical issue in the determination of women's rights. This is because there are tensions and competition among the various laws that operate within one country setting. In the context of Malawi, von Benda Beckmann puts this as follows:

> The law that is applied in Malawi has different foundations of validity. Although it is now common to speak of a legal dualism, this … is a clumsy characterisation of the co-existence of different laws, that is 'English' law is composed of different kinds of law, it is more appropriate to speak of legal pluralism. On the whole, four complexes can be distinguished: local statutory law, English law, the customary law of the Malawian tribes and the religious law.[85]

The theory of legal pluralism explains the fact that within any given field, laws of various provenances may be operative, or more than one source of law may be observable. It describes a situation in which 'law and legal institutions are not all subsumable within one "system" but have their sources in the self-regulatory activities of all … social fields present … which may support, complement, ignore or frustrate one another'.[86]

This situation mainly arises from the historical tenets of these kinds of societies. Most sub-Saharan African states are ones 'where the colonial masters left legal regulation in certain areas to the indigenous population, [and] they gave rise to the co-existence of a plurality of normative systems'.[87]

In discussing the gendered dynamics of domestic violence as a subject of legal surveillance, Sally Engle Merry argues that the hegemonic view of gender

[82] B de Sousa Santos, 'Law: A Map of Misreading. Toward a Postmodern Conception of Law' (1987) 14 *Journal of Law and Society* 279, 293.

[83] ibid.

[84] U Dow and P Kidd, *Women, Marriage and Inheritance Research Report* (Gaborone, WLSA Botswana, 1994) 4.

[85] F von Benda Beckmann, *Legal Pluralism in Malawi: Historical Development 1858–1970 and Emerging Issues* (Blantyre, Kachere Monographs, 2007) 55.

[86] J Griffiths, 'What Is Legal Pluralism?' (1986) 24 *Journal of Legal Pluralism and Unofficial Law* 1, 39.

[87] R Odgaard and AW Bentzon, 'The Interplay Between Collective Rights and Obligations and Individual Rights' (1998) 10(2) *European Journal of Development Research* 105, 108.

and gendered relationships is what promotes domestic violence in the subjective context.[88] Citing Comaroff and Comaroff, she makes the point that:

> Conceptions of gender which are culturally defined as natural constitute that sphere of culture which [they] define as hegemony. … Their distinction between ideology and hegemony is valuable in understanding the redefinitions of gender. It points to the shifting and ambiguous line between those beliefs, understandings, and knowledges which exist at the level of such general acceptance that they are not only unquestioned but perhaps even unthought, and those which are the subject of more articulate discussion and recognition. They refer to the former as hegemony, the latter ideology. Hegemony is that part of the dominant world view which has been naturalized and comes to exist without question, as habitual, while ideology is the more explicitly recognized worldview of a particular group.[89]

Merry's experience in Hawaii shows that: 'Recent efforts to control domestic violence have undermined the hegemonic understanding of violence as a natural part of gender relationships.'[90] Moreover:

> As judges, attorneys, and advocates talk about domestic violence, it slips from the unseen to the seen, from the natural to the cultural, from the hegemonic to the ideological. Actions that were the normal order of the family relationships acquire new names such as abuse. And abuse, unlike the violence embedded in patriarchal authority, is reconstituted as crime, subject to carceral response. The law is unsettling hegemonic categories of gender inequality through mobilisation of feminist discourse of relationships.[91]

How this hegemonic view plays out in the context of legal pluralism is that ordinarily, despite the existence of multiple laws and systems, there is usually a dominant system which competes with all the other systems. In sub-Saharan Africa and in Malawi, customary laws and practices form the dominant legal system. This is so despite that fact that enforceability of rights is officially through the state formal legal system. Therefore, in Malawi customary law and practices form a dominant legal system creating subjective hegemonic views about various facets of life. This includes the view in customary law that forced sex in marriage is legitimate (with few exceptional cases such as during menstruation or mourning), so there can be no such thing as marital rape.

It is this hegemonic understanding of domestic violence within the context of legal pluralism and gender relations that creates a lack of public consensus about what domestic violence is, as evidenced in section IV.E below. In the process of developing the domestic violence law in Malawi, this hegemonic attitude was displayed in the resistance the general populace showed to some aspects of regulating

[88] SE Merry, 'Gender Violence and Legally Engendered Selves' (1995) 2(1–2) *Identities* 49.

[89] ibid, 52, citing J Comaroff and JL Comaroff, *Of Revelation and Revolution: Christianity, Colonialism and Consciousness in South Africa* (Chicago, University of Chicago Press, 1991) 24–25.

[90] Merry, ibid, 52.

[91] ibid, 52–53.

domestic violence, notably refusing to recognise marital rape as a type of domestic violence. During the campaign to pass the Prevention of Domestic Violence Act, the majority of the public's response to this issue was negative, given the predominance of customary law in Malawi's context of legal pluralism.

E. Submissions Concerning Marital Rape

As we highlighted in section IV.A above, in order to facilitate workshops aimed at eliciting views on the content of the proposed domestic violence law, WLSA Malawi produced an issues paper. This paper led to a discussion paper which contained the specific views of some the participants in the consultative workshops.[92]

The views are classified under two central categories: submissions (views) that support the inclusion of marital rape, and submissions (views) against the inclusion of marital rape as a form of sexual abuse. Various submissions were also made supporting the inclusion of marital rape as a form of sexual abuse under the proposed legislation, but suggesting a change in terminology. All submissions (views) are quoted verbatim.

The following are some of the submissions that WLSA Malawi received *in favour of including* marital rape in the domestic violence law:

> Our definition of sexual abuse should adopt the South African legislation. It should also explicitly include marital rape. (First Technical Experts Workshop)

> Rape results when an individual has not consented to sex. If you force your wife, it is rape. The problem is that men think women can be used anytime. If somebody forces himself on his partner then, there is no love—it is pure abuse. That is why the law is necessary to protect the weaker partner in terms of power in the relationship. (Faith Leaders)

> Marital rape should be included as a form of sexual abuse, as it is a big problem, both in the urban and rural areas. In the words of one participant: 'A man goes drinking off all his money, has sex with other women, and then comes home and also demands sex. He is selfish, treats his wife with no respect, like a dog. Now, this is worrisome in light of the HIV/Aids epidemic. (Parliamentarians)

> Marital sex is a gift from God, which must be consented to, so that both parties can enjoy and derive satisfaction from it. Though it was submitted that in Islam, a husband can *approach* his wife at any time (and therefore marital rape should not be recognized as a wrong), I would like to submit that 'approach' should be the catchword, and not force. The husband should approach, so that it is up to the wife to say yes or no. (Her Honour Rachel Zibelu Banda, Assistant Deputy Registrar, High Court of Malawi (as she then was))

> The definition should include marital rape, as it is evil. The definitions from South Africa and Namibia should also be adopted. (Faith Leaders)

[92] WLSA Malawi, *Discussing the Prevention of Domestic Violence Legislation in Malawi: Recommendations and Submissions 2000–2002* (Blantyre, unpublished, 1st edn, 2003, 2nd edn, 2009).

> The concept that a woman is 'obliged to sexually submit to her husband' has no place in a democratic society based on the principles of human rights. The provision recognizing that violence includes 'compelling a spouse by force or threat to engage in any conduct or act, sexual or otherwise' include compulsion as a result of *economic threat* or *threat to another* (ie threat to harm a child of the marriage) as well as lack of consent. (Malawi Human Rights Resource Centre)

> Justice Tambala's position is untenable. The damage is therefore immeasurable. Further still, the existing law makes the woman's consent to have sex in marriage irrelevant and subjugates her wishes to those of her husband. This clearly goes to the root of a woman's dignity and reduces her to a tool to be used by her husband. Her right to control her body is denied. The abuser has the legitimacy of marriage to carry out his assaults. The proposed law needs to reflect the seriousness of marital rape. (Chikosa Banda, Law Lecturer, Chancellor College)

The following are some of the submissions that WLSA Malawi received *against inclusion of marital rape* in the domestic violence law:

> The offence of marital rape would be inconsistent with the continued existence of marriage. The essential element constituting the offence of rape is lack of consent. By entering into marriage, each spouse is taken to have consented to sexual intercourse during the existence of his or her marriage. It can safely be argued that such consent is irrevocable during the time that the marriage exists. (Justice Duncain Tambala, WLSA: 2002, now Justice of the Supreme Court)

> If the marital rape proposal were to become law, it would have scandalous repercussions that would subsequently make women victims of their own invention. (*The Nation*, 4 February 2002).[93]

> Why should a husband rape his wife after all, they are married for that? In Islam the husband can approach his wife anytime. (Faith Leaders)[94]

> Gender activists are going too far with their freedoms and human rights. I am not against all the rights these women are fighting for. The subject of marital rape is a non-starter. Surely, you do not expect our male members of Parliament to support this kind of amendment to the law when the consequences are clearly spelt out that 75% of innocent men will end up in prison for no 'proper' offence and cause a lot of suffering to their families. (Saizi Aipira, in an article in *The Nation*, 12 December 2002, entitled 'Marital Rape in Malawi')

> While accepting that sexual abuse of the nature reported might well be common place, I fail to see the link as to how merely criminalizing the conduct can save the victim from her ordeal. (Worship Chifundo Kachale, Senior Resident Magistrate, Blantyre)

[93] Editorial, 'Comment Marital Rape', *The Nation*, 4 February 2002, 2. This was a comment by the editors of *The Nation* newspaper expressing their views on the efforts undertaken by WLSA and other stakeholders aimed at recognising marital rape.

[94] These are the sentiments of the only representative amongst the faith leaders who opposed the inclusion of marital rape as an act of domestic violence.

> The law would then encourage promiscuity, and that marital rape has no place in our culture, whereby the wife is under an obligation to sexually submit to her husband if he needs her, and vice versa. (Traditional Leaders)

The following are some of the submissions that WLSA Malawi received *supporting the inclusion of marital rape but suggesting a change in terminology*:

> There is need to find a more positive word for marital rape. In as much as we acknowledged marital rape occurs, there may be resistance to incorporate it in the legislation due to the very use of the word 'rape'. Rape as we know it is a very evil crime, and should not be associated with marriages. (Workshop For Parliamentarians)

> The few who did not object [to] the inclusion of marital rape were however uncomfortable with the use of the term 'marital rape' (*kugwilirana*) itself. They suggested that a more politically correct word should be used, ie, '*unwanted sexual intercourse*.' (Workshop for Traditional Leaders)

> I would agree with various submissions that we should be thinking of an alternative terminology. In this regard, I would propose two terms: *unconsented sexual intercourse, or conjugal rights abuse*. If the Mauritian definition is to be adopted, we should also add the words compelling a spouse by undue influence, ie blackmail or intimidation. (Her Honour Rachel Zibelu Banda, Assistant Deputy Registrar of the High Court (now Chairperson of the Industrial Relations Court))

> There is need for change of terminology; we should not be using the word 'marital rape'. Let us find a more polite word to reflect that this is a marriage situation. (Ms Queen Gondwe, AFEWO)

On the other hand, there were also submissions that advocated *maintaining the terminology of marital rape*:

> It is not a question of the term but the attitudes that we have. Marital rape happens. In the course of my Ministry, a lady approached me from DRC who fled to Malawi; she was married to a soldier who was raping her about 8 times a day. She had to flee from the man. She could not walk properly as a result of the rape. (Pastor Nyirenda, Workshop for Faith Leaders)

> There is no need for the use of a 'positive' term to describe marital rape. Rape is a very evil crime, just as the other forms of domestic violence. The fact that marital rape is regarded as too heavy or evil a term to be associated with marriages does not make it cease to exist in marriages. Whether or not a positive term is used, it does not lessen the trauma and the effects it has on the victim. If it is bad, then it need not have any positive aspect related with it. Persistency in ignoring it or describing it positively defeats part of the principle of this legislation ie criminal activities should not go unpunished and disregarded because the victim is related by consanguinity or affinity with the perpetrator. (Wezi Mesikano, fourth-year law student, Chancellor College, now Controller of Legal Services, Office of the Ombudsman)

> Any form of forced sexual contact is violence against a woman. The fact that it happens in her home and by her husband/partner only makes the violence worse, as she has no safe refuge or ability to protest against the perpetrator's conduct. The use of the word *rape* carries with it a meaning which is lost if the more generic descriptor of sexual assault is used. The

violation of a woman should not be lessened by using a less offensive term to describe the violation of a woman by marital rape. (Malawi Human Rights Resource Centre)

V. Conclusion: Reflections on Marital Rape and the Prevention of Domestic Violence Act

How did these differing views on the issue of marital rape and its recognition in the domestic violence legislation play out? The law went through various stages before it was passed. First, in order to assist the government with writing its draft Bill, WLSA Malawi engaged experts to draft what was termed the 'Principles of the Proposed Bill'. This document was a prototype of what the proposed legislation should look like. It was submitted to the Ministry of Gender, which is the ministry responsible for coordinating gender equality policies and programmes. In turn, the Ministry of Gender submitted this prototype to the Ministry of Justice, which then developed the first draft of the proposed Bill.

The government's proposed Prevention of Domestic Violence Bill, which was introduced in 2004, included the following definition of 'sexual abuse' as part of the definition of 'domestic violence':

> **Sexual abuse**, ***whether parties are married or not, includes any sexual conduct*** that abuses, humiliates, degrades or otherwise violates the dignity of the complainant and includes sexual intercourse against the will or without the consent of the complainant, and refusal to cooperate in contraception when the complainant reasonably requires it.

The draft Bill collected dust on the shelves of the Ministry of Justice, which is responsible for pushing the conveyor belt of laws on to the Cabinet and finally to the Parliament. State actors in this ministry showed very little interest in putting this law on the conveyor belt, as the majority of these actors had never dealt with such a gendered piece of legislation and lacked the technical expertise to deal with such a statute.

In January and February 2006, tragic events relating to domestic violence were reported in print and electronic media in Malawi. One story was of a woman in the district of Dowa whose hands had been chopped off with a *panga* knife by a jealous estranged husband.[95] The second story was that of a women who was doused in petrol and set alight by yet another estranged husband in Blantyre City.[96]

[95] Interview, 'He Sliced my Arms and Both had to be Amputated', *IRIN News*, www.irinnews.org/report/81942/malawi-he-sliced-my-arms-and-both-had-be-amputated.

[96] Women's UN Report Network, 'When Police Announced Recently that They had Detained a Man in the Northern Town of Karonga for Allegedly Killing his Wife after She Refused Him Sex', *WUNRN*, www.wunrn.com/2006/02/malawi-blantyre-feb-9-ips-when-police-announced-recently-that-they-had-detained-a-man-in-the-northern-town-of-karonga-for-allegedly-killing-his-wife-after-she-refused-him-sex/.

Finally came the story of a woman who was killed by her husband in Karonga district for refusing sex; she was also HIV positive.[97] These three stories enraged Malawians and caused the Head of State to address the nation, condemning these acts of domestic violence. WLSA seized this opportunity to pressure the government to speed the passing of the domestic violence law. The law did indeed pass on 26 April 2006 after six years of engagement with the state, but with changes to the sexual abuse provision.[98]

The law as finally enacted did not explicitly include marital rape as the draft Bill had done. The Prevention of Domestic Violence Law defines sexual abuse as follows:

> **Sexual abuse** includes sexual contact of any kind that is made by force or threat and the commission of, or an attempt to commit any of the offences under chapter XV of the Penal Code.[99]

One can argue that marital rape is included in this definition. However, the problem we outlined above—that the definition of rape under the Penal Code excludes marital rape through the term 'unlawful'—still applies, given the reference to the Penal Code in the Prevention of Domestic Violence Act. We are not convinced that on the basis of the 2006 law a woman can go to the police and report that her husband raped her, and we are not aware of any cases where charges have been laid in this context. Furthermore, the Prevention of Domestic Violence Act does not give women power to obtain protection orders and other civil remedies in cases of marital rape since marital rape is not recognised under Malawi's penal law.

We believe that a law explicitly criminalising or legislating against marital rape would be more effective than the current law in Malawi and thus is necessary. Our societies are increasingly demanding that the state enact laws that better protect them, and are increasingly questioning cultural practices that are oppressive in nature. It has been years since the Prevention of Domestic Violence Act was passed. The world has become more connected, and oppression is more abhorred. The conversation around criminalising or legislating against something so private as forced sex in a marital bed was shocking in 2000 and even in 2006, but we are of the view that that position no longer prevails. Women may wish to bring a complaint of marital rape against their husbands should they deem it necessary to do so. However, the very existence of efforts to explicitly legislate against marital rape, and the publicity around those efforts, show that marital rape is not yet an offence properly understood in Malawi. Legally, it would be more likely than not for judges and magistrates to acquit any man who was charged with such an offence.[100]

[97] ibid.

[98] See Prevention of Domestic Violence Law (n 7).

[99] ibid, s 2.

[100] It is a trite rule of construction that where a statute imposes criminal liability and the statute is ambiguous or uncertain, it should be construed in favour of the accused individual. See *A Ltd v Commissioner of Taxes* [1968–70] 4 ALR (Mal) 630 (Court of Special Arbitrator for Income Tax 18 October 1968) 636.

Although there may be an ongoing lack of public consensus on the illegality of marital rape, women's rights activists should not give up on legislating against it. What is important is to find strategies that work in keeping with the plurality of the societies where the laws are being introduced. WLSA, in a 2002 Working Paper, provides some guidance on how this might be achieved:

> The first point of departure is a recognition that custom and customary law will shape and mould the lives of the people in these societies either through the medium of the formal legal system or as a dynamic force within the community. If we accept that custom is embedded within the society, it is necessary to assist governments to identify the positive and negative aspects of custom as they apply to women.[101]

In this regard, Nyamu-Musembi argues for an engagement with local norms and practices to pursue change.[102] In her view, human rights activists should not set aside local norms and practices which appear to contradict aspects of gender equality, as this legitimises their status and makes it harder for change to happen. Nyamu-Musembi argues for the vernacularisation of human rights as articulated by Merry.[103] According to Nyamu-Musembi, paying attention to the local norms and practices is part of the process of internal discourse and cross-cultural dialogue and is necessary for the legitimisation of human rights principles in all cultures.[104]

With the above analysis in mind, we believe it is dangerous to depict the picture as totally immovable. It must be pointed out that there were pockets of acceptance in Malawi for legislating against marital rape; for example the fact that there was space created for the process of enactment of the domestic violence law was in itself a great step forward. Following Nyamu-Musembi's arguments, one can exploit that space by using an actor-oriented perspective on human rights—'an understanding of human rights needs and priorities that is informed by the concrete experiences of the particular actors involved in and who stand to gain directly from the struggles in question'.[105] Law should not be seen as a set of principles and norms that is independent from the social context, but instead needs to focus on the different relationships between rights and obligations in both formal and living law.[106] In feminist analysis, this perspective facilitates an engagement that starts with women's experiences in the process of life management and examines the normative structures and groups that affect their lives.

[101] WLSA, 'Uncovering Reality, Excavating Women's Rights in an African Family Law', WLSA Working Paper No 7 (Harare, WLSA Regional Office, 2002) 11–12.

[102] C Nyamu-Musembi, *Towards an Actor-Oriented Perspective on Human Rights* (Brighton, Institute of Development Studies, 2002).

[103] ibid, 6, citing SE Merry, 'Legal Pluralism and Transnational Culture: The *Ka Ho'okolokolonui Kanaka Maoli* Tribunal, Hawai'i, 1993' in R Wilson (ed), *Human Rights, Culture and Context: Anthropological Perspectives* (London, Pluto Press, 1997) 29.

[104] C Nyamu-Musembi, 'Are Local Norms and Practices Fences or Pathways? The Example of Women's Property Rights' in A An-Naim (ed), *Cultural Transformation and Human Rights in Africa* (New York, Zed Books, 2002) 126, 143ff.

[105] ibid.

[106] Odgaard and Bentzon (n 87) 111.

In Malawi, the pain and suffering that has been caused by HIV/AIDS is a good entry point to reignite a conversation on the importance of consent, and the responsibility of the state to ensure that all forms of sex are consensual, including sex in marriage. This is particularly so in the light of the fact that it is couples in long-term relationships who are most vulnerable to HIV transmission. We remain hopeful that despite the setback of the exclusion of explicit protection against marital rape in the Prevention of Domestic Violence Act, Malawians will in the near future actually demand that social problems such as marital rape be legislated against or even criminalised.

7

Dismantling Barriers to Women's Equality: Making the Case for the Criminalisation of Marital Rape in Kenya

WINIFRED KAMAU, PATRICIA NYAUNDI AND JANE SERWANGA

The African woman never says YES
Her NO or SILENCE are YES
If she says YES or comes to you
RUN
Unless you want a prostitute
Anonymous

I. Introduction[1]

The status of women in any society is crucial to their participation in its development. Despite the steps taken toward gender equality, and although women form just over half of the population,[2] Kenyan women remain disadvantaged socially, politically and economically. There is a high prevalence of gender-based violence in Kenya, which mostly occurs in domestic settings.[3] Domestic violence includes sexual violence, which is often perpetrated by intimate partners and disproportionately affects women.

[1] Earlier excerpts of this chapter were published in Winifred Kamau, Patricia Nyaundi and Jane Serwanga, *The Legal Impunity for Marital Rape in Kenya: A Women's Equality Issue* (Equality Effect, 2010), online: theequalityeffect.org/wp-content/uploads/2013/04/Marital-Rape-Paper-Winnie-Kamau-Final-edited-July-18.pdf.

[2] See Kenya National Bureau of Statistics, *The 2009 Kenya Population and Housing Census*, vol 1C (Nairobi, Kenya National Bureau of Statistics, 2009) 23.

[3] See Kenya National Bureau of Statistics, *Kenya Demographic and Health Survey, 2014: Key Findings* (Nairobi, Kenya National Bureau of Statistics, 2015) 38 (indicating that 41% of women had experienced physical or sexual violence from their spouse or partner).

The concept of patriarchy provides an illuminating lens through which to understand sexual violence by men against women. According to Sultana, patriarchy refers to 'male domination, to the power relationships by which men dominate women', and can be characterized as 'a system whereby women are kept subordinate in a number of ways'.[4] The subordination that women face takes various forms, including 'discrimination, disregard, insult, control, exploitation, oppression, [and] violence'.[5] Sexual violence is an expression of women's oppression by men. It is deployed to control and subjugate women, thus maintaining patriarchal power.

One form of sexual violence is marital rape (also known as spousal rape and rape within marriage), that is, non-consensual sex in which the perpetrator is the victim's spouse. Marital rape is often an aspect of domestic abuse, affects women physically, emotionally and mentally, and has a significant negative impact on individuals, families and society in general.[6]

Feminists have identified the gendered nature of the public/private divide on which human rights law has traditionally rested as the main obstacle to the protection of women's rights, as it 'obscures the experiences of women and fails to challenge women's disadvantage'.[7] Arising from the second-wave feminist position that emphasised women's autonomy over their bodies, marital rape has received wide attention since the 1970s and a number of countries in the world have moved to criminalise it.[8]

In Kenya, however, although rape is a serious criminal offence punishable with severe penalties under the Sexual Offences Act 2006 (SOA), an exemption for marital rape exists in section 43(5) of the Act.[9] Kenya therefore does not currently criminalise marital rape. While the Act has been lauded as a progressive piece of legislation that addresses a variety of important issues for women, it fails to address the issue of marital rape. The effect of the exemption is to establish the basis for legal impunity for marital rape, leaving no protection against spousal sexual violence for married women. This constitutes discrimination against women based on marital status and sex, and is a violation of their fundamental human rights, particularly the rights to equality, dignity and bodily integrity.

This chapter examines the legal treatment of marital rape in Kenya, tracing the roots of the marital rape exemption from Kenya's British colonial heritage, and

4 A Sultana, 'Patriarchy and Women's Subordination: A Theoretical Analysis' [July 2010–June 2011] *The Arts Faculty Journal* 2, quoting K Bhasin, *What Is Patriarchy?* (Women Unlimited, New Delhi, 2006) 3.

5 Sultana, ibid, 7.

6 African Population and Health Research Centre, 'Marital Rape and its Impacts: A Policy Briefing for Kenyan Members of Parliament', Policy Brief No 3 (2010) 1.

7 I Radacic, 'Human Rights of Women and the Public/Private Divide in International Human Rights Law' (2007) 3 *Croatian Yearbook of European Law and Policy* 443, 443.

8 See Vasanthi Venkatesh and Melanie Randall, Normative and International Human Rights Law Imperatives for Criminalising Intimate Partner Sexual Violence: The Marital Rape Impunity in Comparative and Historical Perspective', chapter 3 in this volume for a discussion of criminalisation efforts globally.

9 Sexual Offences Act, Act No 3 of 2006 (Kenya) (SOA).

exploring how this intersects with the customary law/traditional framework for sexual violence. Drawing from international, regional and constitutional standards as yardsticks for evaluating Kenyan domestic law and practice, the chapter challenges the failure to recognise marital rape in Kenya's sexual offences legislation and argues for its criminalisation. Further, the chapter considers the possibilities offered by the Constitution of Kenya, 2010,[10] and the recently enacted Protection Against Domestic Violence Act,[11] which for the first time recognises sexual violence within marriage, a step towards protection for victims of marital rape. Using a contextual approach that considers the concrete and complex socio-cultural and economic realities of married women in Kenya, we explore the most viable legal and non-legal options for dealing with marital rape.

II. Definition and Context of Marital Rape

Marital rape, non-consensual sex in which the perpetrator is the victim's spouse, is a form of intimate partner violence. Ahmed and Shaba define marital rape as 'any unwanted intercourse or penetration (vaginal, anal, or oral) obtained by force, threat of force, or when [the] wife is unable to consent'.[12] We would add that marital rape also includes situations where the wife does not consent for whatever reason. Marital rape can include couples who are legally married, separated, divorced or cohabiting without formal marriage.[13] Marital rape is usually perpetrated by men against women, although on rare occasions men are also victims. The available literature suggests that marital rape has historically fallen through the cracks of the focus on domestic violence on the one hand, and on sexual violence on the other hand, not fully encompassed by either form of violence but traversing both.[14]

As marital rape mostly occurs in the context of abusive relationships, it has usually been conceptualised in the context of domestic violence. However, some scholars have argued against subsuming marital rape under the heading of domestic violence, as this has 'led to rape in marriage being overlooked as a

[10] Constitution of Kenya, 2010, promulgated on 27 August 2010.

[11] Protection Against Domestic Violence Act, Act No 2 of 2015 (Kenya).

[12] R Ahmed and NJ Shaba, 'Critical Analysis on Marital Rape and its Legal Consequences: Bangladesh Perspective' (2016) 21 *IOSR Journal of Humanities and Social Science* 7.

[13] The Marriage Act, 2014, Act No 4 of 2014 (Kenya), recognises that persons in Kenya may get married under any of five systems of marriage: Christian, Civil, Customary, Islamic and Hindu. The Act defines 'cohabitation' as 'an arrangement in which an unmarried couple lives together in a long-term relationship that resembles a marriage'. Kenyan courts have developed the common law presumption of marriage to confer marital rights and duties on cohabiting couples.

[14] For further discussion of this point, see Melanie Randall, 'Marital Rape and Violence against Women in Intimate Relationships: The Hidden Form of Domestic Violence', chapter 2 in this volume.

distinctive problem'.[15] As argued by Bergen and Barnhill, 'it is necessary to recognise marital rape as a distinctive form of violence' due to the devastating trauma suffered by women who are battered and raped, which often needs to be specifically addressed by service providers.[16] In addition, it cannot be assumed that marital rape survivors are all battered by their partners; some women experience marital rape but not other forms of violence. To see marital rape merely as a form of domestic violence may serve to exclude such women and their experiences.[17]

For a clear understanding of marital rape, it is important to see it in all of its forms and complexities. Marital rape may be categorised into three forms, namely violent rape, 'force only' rape and sadistic rape.[18] Violent rape occurs, as the name suggests, when the abuser uses enough physical violence to cause injury to the victim, apart from any injuries due to the rape itself. Examples would include the husband punching his wife or injuring her with a knife—the rape being part of a violent assault, or the violence being a part of the rape. 'Force only' rape occurs where a man uses only that degree of force needed to coerce his wife into sexual activity. Sadistic rape indicates that in addition to the rape itself, the victim is forced to comply with or undergo deeds designed to further humiliate her. Examples of this would be the rapist urinating on the victim, acting out a fantasy of torturer, or using an object during a rape.[19] Women also submit to unwanted sexual activity due to fear of violence or due to their economic dependence on their husbands, as well as societal pressure to conform to culturally accepted notions of 'wifely duty'.[20]

III. Situational Analysis of Marital Rape in Kenya

A. Prevalence of Marital Rape

The prevalence of marital rape in Kenya is difficult to determine. This is due to several factors that make the collection of data on the subject difficult. The key factor appears to be the dominant culture of silence that surrounds rape. Further, since Kenya does not categorise marital rape as a crime, there are no official

[15] Raquel Kennedy Bergen, with contributions from Elizabeth Barnhill, *Marital Rape: New Research and Directions* (February 2006) *VAWnet: The National Online Resource Center on Violence Against Women*, www.vawnet.org, 4.

[16] ibid, 4, citing D Finkelhor and K Yllo, *License to Rape: Sexual Abuse of Wives* (New York, Holt, Rinehart & Winston, 1985). See also African Population and Health Research Centre (n 6) 2.

[17] Bergen et al (n 15) 4. See also K Painter, 'Wife Rape in the United Kingdom', paper presented at the American Society of Criminology 50th Anniversary Meeting (1991) 5.

[18] Bergen et al (n 15) 3–4, citing Finkelhor and Yllo (n 16).

[19] 'Hidden Hurt, Domestic Abuse Information: Marital Rape', www.hiddenhurt.co.uk/marital_rape.html#types.

[20] See Bergen et al (n 15) 3, 4.

government statistics on incidents of marital rape. Any available information is fragmented because it is non-state actors who often document marital rape. The dearth of information has compromised advocacy efforts targeting legal protection against marital rape. There is, however, limited data from which one can make reliable deductions regarding the incidence and magnitude of marital rape in Kenya.

In 2006, UN AIDS reported that two-thirds of women in Kenya who were physically and sexually abused identified the abusers to be their husbands. Furthermore, approximately 16 per cent of married, divorced or separated women experienced sexual assault by their spouses.[21] A 2008 study undertaken by the Federation of Women Lawyers (FIDA) Kenya found that 74.5 per cent of respondents reported being physically abused within the home. Respondents experienced various forms of violence, including physical, economic, sexual, psychological and emotional violence. This report indicated that the most common form of sexual violence reported by women participants was marital rape. The women lamented that their abusive husbands treated them as property and disregarded any notions of consent to sexual activity.[22] According to the Kenya Demographic and Health Survey of 2014, 14 per cent of women aged 15–49 and 14 per cent of ever-married women have experienced sexual violence at least once in their lifetime. Ten per cent of women had experienced spousal sexual violence in the past 12 months, with the most common form cited as being physically forced to have sex against their will.[23] These findings point to the relatively large scale on which women in Kenya experience sexual violence in their intimate relationships with men.

B. Impact of Marital Rape

Research undertaken in Kenya debunks the myth that rape by one's partner is a relatively minor occurrence with insignificant effects. On the contrary, as in other jurisdictions, research shows that marital rape often has serious and far-reaching consequences for women.[24]

According to one study conducted among battered women in a shelter run by the Women Rights and Awareness Programme (WRAP) in Kenya,[25] intimate partner violence (including marital rape) has negative mental and physical ramifications for victims. The study reviewed 1253 client records over a span of seven years. Nine per cent of the clients explicitly mentioned victimisation by

[21] UN AIDS, *Violence Against Women and Girls in the Era of HIV and AIDS: A Situation and Response Analysis in Kenya* (UN AIDS, June 2006) 14.

[22] Federation of Women Lawyers (FIDA) Kenya, *Gender Based Domestic Violence in Kenya* (Nairobi, FIDA Kenya, 2008) 26–27.

[23] *Kenya Demographic and Health Survey, 2014* (n 3) 306, 335.

[24] Bergen et al (n 15) 5.

[25] J Crichton et al, 'Painful Tradeoffs: Intimate-Partner Violence and Sexual and Reproductive Health Rights in Kenya', IDS Working Paper, University of Sussex, (2008).

sexual violence, including rape and other forced sexual acts and harassment.[26] The study observed that this may be an underestimation of those affected owing to underreporting, based on the stigma associated with sexual violence. Impacts indicated in the study included both physical and emotional harms. On account of the forceful nature of the sexual acts, clients suffered trauma to their reproductive tracts and also reported cases of sexually transmitted infections, including HIV. Pregnancies in these relationships were often unplanned and the clients reported being under pressure to terminate these pregnancies, often through backstreet abortions, thereby exposing them to health risks. These abusive relationships exposed the clients to discomfort, pain, humiliation and anxiety.[27]

The consequences for the women in the WRAP study were aggravated by the social contexts of the victims. The vulnerability of the women to abuse and their 'tolerance' was increased by the fact that they were economically dependent on their abusive spouses. Health risks were aggravated by the fact that a number of the clients did not seek health services as they did not fully appreciate the impact of the violence on their health. Others were hampered from accessing health services on account of the high cost.[28] Thus, for many women, sexual and reproductive well-being was subordinated to basic material needs, as the women were often forced to 'make a trade-off between economic survival and their right to be free from violence', with detrimental effects for themselves and their children.[29]

A particular concern for women who experience spousal rape is the high risk of contracting HIV/AIDS. According to a 2006 UN AIDS study, Kenyan women and girls are particularly vulnerable to HIV/AIDS infection due to their subordinate societal position, which makes it difficult for them to negotiate safe sexual practices such as use of condoms.[30]

Women who have been sexually abused by their partners experience pain, humiliation and distress, constituting emotional and psychological harm in addition to the physical harms we have already noted. Sexual assaults are likely to be repeated several times over the course of the marital relationship, resulting in both short-term and long-term emotional and psychological consequences. These effects include anxiety, shock, fear, depression, suicidal ideation, disordered sleeping and eating, distorted body image and negative self-regard.[31] The psychological harm also extends to children who witness sexual violence at home. To make things worse, mothers of such children may find it difficult to care for them as a result of the violence.[32]

[26] ibid, 21.

[27] ibid, 21–22.

[28] ibid, 54.

[29] ibid, 54.

[30] UN AIDS (n 21) 7. HIV prevalence among women aged 15–49 is 8% as compared to 4.3% among men; See also National AIDS Control Council of Kenya, *Kenya AIDS Response Progress Report, 2014: Progress Towards Zero* (March 2014) 4, indicating the 2012 prevalence among women at 6.9% compared to 4.2% among men.

[31] Bergen et al (n 15) 5.

[32] African Population and Health Research Centre (n 6) 1.

Despite the adverse physical and psychological consequences of marital rape, little attention is given to it. To begin with, many abused women are afraid to report the violence since they rely financially on their husbands for their upkeep and that of their children. There is also fear of retaliation, humiliation and shame, as well as cultural inhibitions against public discussion of issues of sex, thereby promoting a culture of silence. Further, since rape is generally perceived as an act involving a stranger, the victim of spousal rape may not view demands of sex from her partner as a crime. In addition, intimate partner violence is often perpetrated over a long period and it may be difficult for the victim to keep track of the specific events and dates when the acts were committed.[33] Even when such incidents are reported, the police often treat them as 'domestic matters' which do not warrant intervention by the criminal justice system. This is compounded by a slow and inefficient criminal justice system and scarcity of doctors who can provide the evidence necessary to convict offenders.[34]

Notwithstanding the demonstrated debilitating consequences of spousal sexual violence for its victims, Kenyan law does not clearly prohibit marital rape. This legal immunity against marital rape is partly explained by the societal response to marital rape discussed in the next section.

C. Societal Response to Marital Rape

As we will elaborate on in section IV, the response to marital rape by the Kenyan criminal justice system is dismal. This is also true of the response by society at large, which is a reflection of the prevailing attitudes towards violence against women. Factors contributing to violence against women include gender stereotypes as well as negative cultural norms and practices that condone or tolerate violence against women, thus perpetuating the subordinate position of women in Kenyan society. Some forms of domestic violence, such as wife beating, are still considered normal or as routine chastisement[35] and marriage is deemed to provide blanket consent to marital sex.[36] This violence against women is not viewed as a crime warranting harsh punishment but rather a mere infraction for which the offender can be mildly reprimanded. This attitude has meant that marital rape as a wrong is inconceivable, particularly in a society where most issues between husband and wife are viewed as 'bedroom matters' and there is general acceptance of a man's entitlement to sex and a woman's acquiescence to sex as part of her wifely duties.[37] Violence is used as an instrument to ensure conformity to

[33] CW Kung'u, *Criminalisation of Marital Rape in Kenya* (LLM thesis, University of Toronto, 2011) 2–3.

[34] UN AIDS (n 21) 22. As we will discuss in the section IV, corroboration—such as medical evidence—is required in sexual offence cases in Kenya.

[35] Amnesty International, *Kenya: Rape—The Invisible Crime* (2002) AFR 32/001/2002, 43.

[36] ibid, 12.

[37] FIDA Kenya (n 22) 12–13.

traditional roles for women and dominance of husbands.[38] Women's vulnerability to domestic violence and marital rape is compounded by the cultural ideologies that link women's identity and self-esteem to their relationships to males, be they fathers, husbands or sons.[39] Because of this reality, women in abusive relationships might stay on in their marriages so as not to lose their social standing.

IV. Legal Framework Relating to Marital Rape in Kenya

A. Customary/Traditional Framework

Customary law plays a crucial role in the maintenance of cultural norms about the place of women in the family and society. Customary law is a source of law in Kenya along with statutes and English common law and is particularly relevant in the realm of family law. It is applicable in civil matters 'in which one or more of the parties is subject to it or affected by it, so far as it is applicable and is not repugnant to justice and morality or inconsistent with any written law'.[40] For Kenyan women, custom is particularly important as it defines their identity within society, and mediates their family relationships, entitlements and access to resources. Traditional African societies were governed on the basis of patriarchal structures where women's individual interests were subsumed under the interests of the group, dominated by males.[41]

Rape is generally recognised as an offence under the customary laws of Kenyan communities. In the marital context, the expectation is that the woman will avail herself to her husband for sexual relations and failure to do so may constitute grounds for divorce. However, there are specific instances where a woman is permitted to withhold sex from her husband, namely during menstruation, during pregnancy, shortly after childbirth or during a period of mourning. It is difficult to say with certainty whether marital rape was permitted in traditional African societies. However, there were, and continue to be, several cultural norms and practices sanctioned by customary law that contribute to women's subordination to men, and to the condoning of violence against women.[42]

[38] CG Bowman, 'Theories of Domestic Violence in the African Context' (2003) 11 *American University Journal of Gender Social Policy and Law* 847, 855.

[39] P Kameri-Mbote, 'Violence Against Women in Kenya. Analysis of Law, Policy and Institutions', International Environmental Law Research Centre, IELRC Working Paper 2000–1, 2.

[40] Section 3(2) of the Judicature Act, Chapter 8, Laws of Kenya.

[41] P Kameri-Mbote, 'The Land Has its Owners! Gender Issues in Land Tenure under Customary Law', International Environmental Law Research Centre, IELRC Working Paper 2005–9, 5.

[42] R. Aura, 'Situational Analysis and the Legal Framework on Sexual and Gender-Based Violence in Kenya: Challenges and Opportunities', Kenya Law, www.kenyalaw.org/kl/index.php?id=4512, 21–22.

One of these practices is the payment of bride-wealth or dowry. Bride-wealth is paid by the husband to the wife's family and is intended to seal the marriage contract and to be a symbol of unity between the two families. While such payment is not intended as purchase of the woman, it is sometimes seen as a way of validating a man's right to 'own' his wife such that wives may be viewed as the property of their husbands. This can be used as a justification for perpetrating violence against a wife, framed in terms of 'disciplining' her.[43]

Another cultural practice is wife inheritance, where a woman whose husband has died is obligated to marry her husband's brother in order to ensure that she and her children are taken care of by her husband's family. Young widows are inherited by a brother-in-law or any other suitor chosen by the village elders. The practice was originally intended to ensure that a young widow's sexual needs were provided for and her children were taken care of. Although in theory the wife is free to refuse to be inherited, the reality is that such a woman faces the prospect of social exclusion and disenfranchisement.[44] Related to wife inheritance is the practice of 'widow cleansing', where a widow is obligated to undergo ritual cleansing in order to be integrated into the community. Cleansing involves having sexual intercourse with a man appointed by the husband's clan, who may be suffering from mental illness. The widow usually has no choice over whether to accept being cleansed or as to the man involved in the activity. Wife inheritance and widow cleansing have contributed significantly to the spread of HIV/AIDS in the communities where they are practised.[45] These cultural practices reinforce the notion that a woman must have an attachment to a male for status within the society, which increases the vulnerability of women to abuse and violence.

Early marriages performed under customary law also contribute to violence against women. Under customary law, there is no set minimum age for marriage and a person is deemed ready for matrimony upon reaching puberty and after the accompanying initiation rites. In some communities, young girls are married off to men much older than themselves. Due to the unequal balance of power inherent in such marriages, young wives are often subjected to violence by their husbands and have little ability to withhold consent to sex during the marriage. However, no protection is afforded to such girls due to the marital rape exemption.[46] As we elaborate in section V, this practice is contrary to the Constitution as well as to the Children Act.[47]

[43] Kung'u (n 33) 21.

[44] ibid, 19–20.

[45] B Perry et al, 'Widow Cleansing and Inheritance among the Luo in Kenya: The Need for Additional Women-Centred HIV Prevention Options' (2014) 17 *Journal of the International AIDS Society* 19010.

[46] C-C Undie, 'Addressing Sexual Violence and HIV Risk among Married Adolescent Girls in Rural Nyanza', Kenya Population Council, Brief No 19 (2011) 1.

[47] Children Act, Chapter 141, Laws of Kenya.

Another harmful practice is female genital mutilation (FGM, also known as female circumcision), which sometimes results in reproductive health problems as well as reduction in women's sexual response. Although FGM is prohibited under the Children Act[48] and the Prohibition of Female Genital Mutilation Act,[49] the practice continues to thrive in some communities and prosecutions are rare. FGM is a reflection of gender norms in society where women's autonomy over their bodies is curtailed and is part of the wider context of violence against women which condones sexual violence within marriage.[50]

Culture is often invoked in society to block attempts at legal reform. In Kenya, the predominantly male legislators in Parliament have been generally reluctant to pass legislation that challenges cultural norms, for fear of upsetting the status quo and/or of recrimination or loss of voter support. Such legislation is usually depicted as foreign and contrary to African culture. For example, during debate on the Marriage Bill in 1968, the proposal by the Commission on the Law of Marriage and Divorce to outlaw wife beating was strongly opposed and the draft section was deleted. One MP felt particularly strongly against the provision and expressed the opinion that corporal punishment was necessary for disciplining wives in order to teach them 'manners' as this was the normal African way. Another MP stated that a wife should be beaten as it was a pleasure to her, and was a way of expressing love under the customs of his community.[51]

Similarly, in the debate on the Sexual Offences Act in 2006, one MP used the practice of dowry payment to oppose arguments for the criminalisation of marital rape:

> I have paid dowry for my wife and we are formally married. I cannot rape her by any chance. You can see the damage that western indoctrination has done to us. I cannot rape my wife! I don't think there is one man who can rape his wife … you can rape someone else.[52]

However, customary law in Kenya is only applicable in civil cases and cannot therefore be directly appealed to as the basis for a marital rape exemption in a criminal case.[53] Further, customary law has been subordinated to the Constitution, as we will discuss in section V.[54] Nevertheless, custom continues to be raised in opposition to the criminalisation of marital rape, intersecting with the historical legal framework discussed in the next section.

[48] ibid, s 14.

[49] Prohibition of Female Genital Mutilation, Act No 32 of 2011 (Kenya), Part IV.

[50] Kung'u (n 33) 21–22.

[51] PM Asiyo, 'Gender Issues and the Legislative Process in Kenya' in M Adhiambo Mbeo and O Ooko-Ombaka (eds), *Women and Law in Kenya, Perspectives and Emerging Issues* (Nairobi, Public Law Institute, 1989) 42.

[52] Kenya National Assembly Official Record (Hansard), Second Reading of the Sexual Offences Bill, 27 April 2006, 780, cited in Kung'u (n 33) 21.

[53] Judicature Act (n 40) s 3.

[54] Constitution of Kenya 2010 (n 10) Art 2(4).

B. Historical Legal Background

The establishment of British colonial rule in Kenya in the late nineteenth century was accompanied by the superimposition of English law over the Indigenous peoples. This resulted in legal plurality, with customary law coexisting with state law. The law as received was infused with British values and culture. At the time, the British concept of the family was that of a nuclear husband/wife arrangement in which the husband was the breadwinner and head of household, while the wife was the 'domesticated', economically dependent consumer.[55] Thus Kenyan law reflected an era in Britain when married women were not regarded as persons; upon marriage, spouses became one legal personality and the 'one person' created was the husband. This principle of coverture was described by Blackstone in the eighteenth century as follows:

> By marriage, the husband and wife are one person in law: that is, the very being or legal existence of the woman is suspended during the marriage, or at least is incorporated and consolidated into that of the husband.[56]

It was therefore inconceivable that a husband could rape his wife, as she was part of his person. This position was exemplified by Lord Matthew Hale's proposition (known as the Hale doctrine) that:

> The husband cannot be guilty of a rape committed by himself upon his lawful wife, for by their mutual matrimonial consent and contract the wife hath given up herself in this kind unto her husband, which she cannot retract.[57]

This idea laid the basis for the common law exemption which provided that a husband could not be accused of raping his wife.[58] Within marriage, a wife's consent was implied, so under the law, all sex-related activity, including rape, was legitimate. This common law position was reinforced by customary law norms in Kenya that lent credence to the idea that upon marriage a woman became part of her husband's property for him to do with as he pleased. The interplay of common law principles with customary norms and practices generally worked to the disadvantage of women and served to entrench the patriarchy inherent in both systems.[59]

[55] Barbara Rogers, *The Domestication of Women: Discrimination in Developing Countries* (London, Kogan Page, 1980) 62.

[56] Sir William Blackstone, *Commentaries on the Laws of England*, vol 1 (Oxford, Clarendon Press, 1765–69) 430.

[57] Sir Matthew Hale, *History of the Pleas of the Crown*, vol 1, ch 58, cited in W Larcombe and M Heath, 'Developing the Common Law and Rewriting the History of Rape in Australia: PGA v The Queen' (2012) 34 *Sydney Law Review* 785, 785.

[58] JA Bennice and PA Resick, 'Marital Rape: History, Research and Practice' (2003) 4 *Trauma, Violence and Abuse*, 228, 229.

[59] W Kamau, 'Customary Law and Women's Rights in Kenya' (Equality Effect, 2010), online: theequalityeffect.org/wp-content/uploads/2014/12/CustomaryLawAndWomensRightsInKenya.pdf, 6.

The current law in Kenya reflects the widespread cultural stereotype that marriage confers upon men presumed rights of sexual access to their wives.[60] This stereotype 'negates a woman's right to give or refuse consent in marriage … [a]ssuming that for a woman marriage implies her ongoing consent with her spouse'.[61]

Until 2006, sexual offences in Kenya were prosecuted under the Penal Code, where they were categorised as offences against morality.[62] While there was no explicit legislative marital rape exemption, the principles of the received English common law were applied in the application of the Penal Code. This encompassed the common law marital exemption under the Hale doctrine.[63] Under section 139 (now repealed) of the Penal Code, rape was defined as 'unlawful carnal knowledge of a woman or girl without her consent or with her consent if the consent is obtained through force, coercion or false representations as or *in the case of a married woman, by personating her husband*.'[64] The implicit assumption was that sex would not be rape if the impersonator were actually the husband, based on the premise that a married woman has given perpetual consent to sex with her husband.

The stance of the common law is reflected in the attitudes of the Kenyan judiciary in sexual offence cases. Judges are often inclined to assume that women have a tendency to lie in sexual matters or are ambivalent about saying yes or no to sexual advances. For instance, in *Maina v R*, the court stated that in sexual offence cases, 'girls and women are wont to tell an entirely false story which is very easy to fabricate, but extremely difficult to prove'.[65] This assumption is reflected in the common law requirement that applies in Kenya and some other Commonwealth countries for corroboration of the complainant's evidence in trials involving rape and other sexual offences,[66] on the rationale that in such cases there is always a possibility of 'trumped-up charges'. Other evidentiary rules which operate to disadvantage women victims of sexual offences include consideration of the complainant's sexual history and the existence of a prior sexual relationship between the complainant and the accused.[67] While it is laudable that the SOA has

[60] Kameri-Mbote (n 39) 14.

[61] M Randall and V Venkatesh, 'The Right to No: The Crime of Marital Rape, Women's Human Rights, and International Law' (2015) 41 *Brooklyn Journal of International Law* 153, 192.

[62] Penal Code, Chapter 63, Laws of Kenya.

[63] Section 3 (now repealed) of the Penal Code, ibid, required that the Code be interpreted in accordance with the principles of legal interpretation obtaining in England.

[64] Penal Code (n 62) s 139 (emphasis added).

[65] *Maina v R* [1970] EA 370, 371.

[66] *Chila v Republic* [1967] EA722, 723 para C: 'The Judge should warn … himself of the danger of acting on uncorroborated testimony of the complainant, but having done so he may convict in the absence of corroboration if he is satisfied that her evidence is truthful. If no such warning is given, then the conviction will normally be set aside unless court is satisfiofed that there has been no failure of justice.'

[67] Section 34 of the SOA (n 9) prohibits the production of evidence of the complainant's previous sexual experience or conduct except with the leave of the court and only in specified circumstances.

substantially done away with these rules, vestiges still remain. A notable example is section 38 (now repealed) of the SOA, which made it an offence for a complainant to make false charges against a person, the offence attracting the same penalty as that complained of. This clause had the effect of deterring victims of sexual violence from reporting their offenders for fear of being criminalised.[68]

In 1991, the English House of Lords, in *Regina v R*, recognised that the common law had evolved in light of changing social and cultural developments, and finally conceded to a wife's right to withdraw her consent to sex. As stated by Lord Keith of Kinkel:

> Hale's proposition ... reflected the state of affairs in those respects as at the time it was enunciated. Since then, the status of women and particularly married women has changed out of all recognition. ... [One] of the most important changes was that marriage in modern times was regarded as a partnership of equals and no longer one in which the wife was to be the subservient chattel of the husband ... on the grounds of principle there was no good reason why the whole proposition of marital exemption to rape should not be held inapplicable in modern time.[69]

Lord Keith went further to state that the doctrine of implied consent served no useful purpose today, and that the marital rape exemption was a 'common law fiction which had never been a true rule of English law'.[70]

Earlier, in the 1984 US case of *People v Liberta*, the constitutionality of section 130.35 of the Penal Law of New York—which provided a marital rape exemption for the offences of forcible rape and forcible sodomy—was considered. Judge Wachtler found 'no rational basis for distinguishing between marital rape and non-marital rape'.[71] He stated that 'the various rationales which have been asserted in defense of the exemption are either based upon archaic notions about the consent and property rights incident to marriage or are simply unable to withstand even the slightest scrutiny', and therefore declared the marital rape exemption in New York to be unconstitutional.[72] Referring to Lord Hale's notion of an irrevocable implied consent by a married woman to sexual intercourse, Judge Wachtler stated as follows:

> Rape is not simply a sexual act to which one party does not consent. Rather, it is a degrading, violent act which violates the bodily integrity of the victim and frequently causes severe, long-lasting physical and psychic harm. ... To ever imply consent to such an act is irrational and absurd. ... Certainly, then, a marriage license should not be viewed as a

However, under s 163(1)(d) of the Evidence Act, Chapter 80 of the Laws of Kenya, the credibility of a woman complainant in a rape case may be impeached by showing that she was of generally immoral character.

[68] W Onyango-Ouma et al, *The Making of the Sexual Offences Act, 2006: Behind the Scenes* (Nairobi, Kwani Trust, 2009) 25.

[69] *Regina v R* [1992] 1 AC 599, 616.

[70] ibid, 623.

[71] *People v Liberta*, 64 NY 2d 152, 164 (1984).

[72] ibid, 163.

> license for a husband to forcibly rape his wife with impunity. A married woman has the same right to control her own body as does an unmarried woman.[73]

We acknowledge that culture and the common law are not static. The above two cases are illustrative of the willingness of courts to interpret the law in line with prevailing social realities to safeguard women's rights to equality, dignity and sexual liberty. As we discuss in section V, under the Constitution of 2010, Kenyan courts have a similar obligation, which they ought to exercise to negate the marital rape exemption inherited from the English common law and codified in the SOA.

C. The Marital Rape Exemption under the Sexual Offences Act 2006

The SOA represents a major step forward in efforts to protect victims of sexual violence, who are predominantly women.[74] The SOA has been lauded as a progressive piece of legislation, as it was the first statute to comprehensively address sexual offences in Kenya and reflects a significant change of orientation in the handling of sexual offences. Prior to 2006, sexual offences were dealt with under the Penal Code and were categorised as offences against morality. Under the SOA, these offences are now treated as crimes of sexual violence. The SOA was a culmination of debate and negotiation in the context of high incidences of rape, defilement and incest in Kenya, as well as the scourge of HIV/AIDS, new social realities such as child sex tourism and developments in the field of forensics such as DNA profiling. The SOA repealed most of the sexual offences under the Penal Code and substituted its own provisions, introduced new offences,[75] imposed minimum mandatory sentences,[76] and provided for the setting up of a DNA data bank and a sex offenders' registry, among other measures.[77]

The new definition of rape introduced by the SOA contemplates that the perpetrator or the victim may be either male or female, unlike the Penal Code which provided only for the rape of women or girls. Section 3(1) of the SOA provides that:

> A person commits the offence termed rape if he or she intentionally and unlawfully commits an act which causes penetration with his or her genital organs; the other person does not consent to the penetration; or the consent is obtained by force or by means of threats or intimidation of any kind.[78]

[73] ibid, 164.
[74] SOA (n 9).
[75] The new offences include gang rape, sexual assault, sexual harassment, deliberate infection with HIV/AIDS and child trafficking for sexual exploitation and child pornography. See SOA, ibid, ss 10, 14–16, 23, 24, 26–29.
[76] See eg SOA, ibid, s 11, which imposes minimum sentences for defilement.
[77] ibid, s 39.
[78] ibid, s 3(1).

Other sexual offences include sexual assault and indecent acts, which may also be committed by men or women. Sexual assault covers unlawful penetration of the genital organs with objects other than for 'proper and professional hygienic or medical purposes', as well as digital penetration.[79] Indecent acts are defined as intentional acts causing contact between the genital or sexual organs of a person and another person, or exposure or display of pornographic material to any person against their will.[80]

Unlike the Penal Code, the SOA contains comprehensive provisions on consent. Section 42 provides that 'a person consents if he or she agrees by choice, and has the freedom and capacity to make that choice'.[81] Although the section does not elaborate on the meaning of choice or freedom, this definition appears to emphasise the importance of free will and the ability to make a decision about whether or not to take part in the sexual activity at the time in question, in the absence of coercion or deceit.

The SOA also provides for rebuttable and irrebuttable presumptions of lack of consent, which are intended to make it easier for the prosecution to prove this element. Under section 44, lack of consent will be presumed where it is proved that the following circumstances existed with the knowledge of the accused: (a) any person used or threatened violence against the complainant at the time of the act or immediately before the first sexual activity began; or (b) any person caused the complainant to fear at the time of the act or immediately before the first sexual act that violence was being used or would be used immediately against another person.[82]

This is an evidential presumption, which may be rebutted where sufficient evidence is adduced to raise an issue as to whether the complainant consented. Conclusive (irrebuttable) presumptions as to consent are provided in section 45 of the SOA, and cover impersonation of persons known to the complainant, which would include the husband; implicitly this assumes that it would not be 'rape' if the assailant were actually the husband or intimate partner of the victim.[83]

As noted above, rape consists of 'an intentional and unlawful' act causing penetration.[84] Under section 43 of the SOA, intentional and unlawful acts are those committed in coercive circumstances, which includes the use of force against the complainant or her property and the threat of harm to the complainant or her property. A reading of these provisions indicates that they cover situations of marital rape, where one spouse engages in sexual activities without the other's consent, or where consent is obtained through coercive means, that is by use of violence, threats or intimidation.

[79] ibid, s 5.
[80] ibid, s 2.
[81] ibid, s 42.
[82] ibid, s 44(2). This is not an exhaustive list of the presumptions.
[83] ibid, s 45.
[84] ibid, s 3.

However, during the debate on the Sexual Offences Bill, a majority of the Members of Parliament voted to exempt legally married persons from the rape provisions in order to provide immunity for spouses.[85] They did this by adding sub-section (5) to section 43, which expressly declares that the section's definition of 'intentional and unlawful acts' '*shall not apply in respect of persons who are lawfully married to each other*'.[86] The effect of section 43(5) is to exclude spouses from the application of the sexual violence provisions, as the offences of rape, sexual assault and indecent assault all require intentional and/or unlawful acts. This failure to criminalise marital rape denies spouses the protection of the SOA. The wording of section 43(5) suggests that the exemption applies equally to both married men and women. However, the gender-neutral language obscures the inherently unequal position of married men and women and the fact that victims of marital rape are predominantly women. Therefore, it is married women who suffer most from lack of legal protection against marital rape. This burdens married women with exposure to sexual violence, and denies them the right to equal protection of the law.[87]

A review of the drafting process of the SOA is instructive in unearthing the reasons behind the marital rape exemption. From the outset, the Sexual Offences Bill, which culminated in the Act, was the product of much negotiation and compromise and fuelled much controversy among the Kenyan public.[88] In Parliament, battlelines were drawn between the traditionalists, who saw the provisions of the Bill as running counter to African culture, and the liberals, who were in favour of equal rights for women. According to Onyango-Ouma et al,[89] the original version of the Bill—which did not include section 43(5)—had the effect of criminalising rape in marriage, among other contentious issues.[90] However, this version of the Bill was strongly objected to by some Members of Parliament, who argued that it would be difficult to prove rape in marriage. They also argued that conjugal rights were conferred by the marriage covenant entered into between the parties, and that there could therefore be no rape in marriage. This argument was extended to infer that there was no notion of marital rape in the African context. According to one MP:

> An activity between a man and his wife in his bedroom cannot within reason be constituted to be rape. Many people believe this is not an African issue. Marriage creates sexual licence to each party … that is the licence they get by saying 'I do'.[91]

[85] Kung'u (n 33) 14.

[86] SOA (n 9) s 43(5) (emphasis added). As indicated in n 13 above, there are five recognised systems of marriage in Kenya: Customary, Statutory, Christian, Muslim and Hindu systems. Cohabitation is not recognised as 'marriage'; however, Kenyan courts may apply the common law presumption of marriage to cohabiting couples if they meet the criteria for this presumption.

[87] Kung'u (n 33) 14–15.

[88] The Sexual Offences Bill, 2006 was also referred to as the Njoki Ndungu Bill, after the MP who sponsored the Bill. She is currently serving as a Judge in the Kenyan Supreme Court.

[89] Onyango-Ouma et al (n 68) 22.

[90] Other contentious issues in the Bill related to chemical castration, female genital mutilation, rape shield provisions, burden of proof, definition of a child and the age of consent for sex.

[91] Onyango-Ouma et al (n 68) 22.

During the debate, one MP declared that 'women usually say "No" to sex, even if they mean "Yes", unless they were prostitutes', prompting 12 of Kenya's 18 female MPs to walk out in protest. Others felt that the law would prevent men from courting women and this would be a 'serious impediment to the young who would want to marry'.[92] Several male MPs feared that the original Bill went too far and could lead to a spate of false accusations by women. Another concern was the possibility of marital rape being abused as a way of settling scores in marriage, and the corresponding need to protect families from such abuses.

On the other hand, supporters of the inclusion of marital rape as an offence were emphatic in their contention that rape in marriage was very common in Kenya and constituted a violation of women's rights. They argued that marriage did not automatically confer conjugal rights if there was no consent.[93]

Eventually, legislators included section 43(5) in subsequent versions of the Bill, including the final version. This was done as part of a strategy by the mover of the Bill as a trade-off to ensure other contentious clauses, including a clause prohibiting sexual harassment, were accepted by opponents. However, the majority legislators insisted on the insertion of section 38, which made it an offence for a person to make false allegations of a sexual offence against another person, with a penalty equivalent to that of the offence complained of. This clause was harmful to women, as it discouraged them from reporting sexual crimes for fear of being prosecuted themselves. It also insinuated that women are liars and are therefore likely to bring up false cases of sexual violence. Happily, that section has now been repealed.[94]

The SOA was a lost opportunity to criminalise marital rape in Kenya. As we discuss in the next sections, there are alternatives available under Kenyan law to deal with spousal sexual violence, but none of these alternatives treat marital rape as a criminal offence.

D. Assault Provisions in the Penal Code

Due to the ongoing marital rape exemption in the SOA, married women (and men) who are victims of sexual violence are left only with the option of using the assault provisions provided under the Kenyan Penal Code. Relevant offences include common assault (assault that does not amount to bodily harm) as well as assault occasioning actual bodily harm and grievous bodily harm.[95] However, these provisions are grossly inadequate for several reasons.

Firstly, the provisions do not deal explicitly with gender-based violence but with violence generally. Assault-related offences under the Code are not gender-specific

[92] *BBC News*, 'Anger at Kenya's Diluted Rape Law', 1 June 2006.
[93] Onyango-Ouma et al (n 68) 22.
[94] See Statute Law (Miscellaneous Amendments) Act, 2012 (Kenya).
[95] Penal Code (n 62) ss 250, 251 and 234, respectively.

and do not take into account the different experiences of men and women as perpetrators and as victims of assault. Unlike the SOA, the Code does not provide for specific measures to allow for the protections of victims of gender-based violence, such as protections against sexual history and character evidence.[96]

Secondly, assault under the Penal Code is very narrowly conceived as it covers only physical injury or threat of physical injury. 'Harm' is defined as any bodily hurt, disease or disorder, whether permanent or temporary. 'Grievous harm' is defined to include maiming and dangerous harm that does or is likely to seriously or permanently injure health, or which causes permanent disfigurement, as well as permanent or serious injury to any external or internal organ, membrane or sense.[97] Other types of harm, such as emotional and psychological harm, or economic harm and threats to livelihood, are not covered.

Thirdly, the assault provisions require physical proof of injury in order to distinguish between actual harm and grievous harm and to determine punishment. However, it is often difficult to prove injury in marital rape cases, where the sexual coercion does not involve any other form of physical harm. Further, charges relating to assault usually require witnesses or evidence of a physical struggle. As marital rape takes place in the privacy of the home, there will almost never be witnesses. Evidence of a physical struggle is not usually available, as many women do not resist when their partners try to force them to have sex, to avoid further violence or to protect their children from seeing the abuse.[98]

Finally, the penalties for assault-related offences are very lenient, especially in comparison to those under the Sexual Offences Act.[99] Moreover, attempts by women to prosecute cases of physical violence in marriage have not been effective. For instance, in the widely publicised case of *Wilmina Achieng*,[100] a man had pushed the broken legs of a stool into his wife's genitals. During his court appearance, he justified his cruelty on the grounds that 'his community allowed such punishments' and he was merely punishing his wife for having left home 'with no valid reason'. He was convicted of assault causing actual bodily harm to his wife and fined 10,000 Kenyan shillings (approximately US$100). After paying the fine, he went home and beat his wife again, threatening to kill her, and was once again charged with assault and sentenced to 6 months imprisonment. Shortly afterwards he was pardoned under a presidential amnesty.[101]

[96] See SOA (n 9) s 34.

[97] Penal Code (n 62) s 4.

[98] African Population and Health Research Centre (n 6) 2.

[99] For instance, the penalty for assault occasioning actual bodily harm is a maximum of 5 years' imprisonment (s 210 Penal Code) compared to the penalty for rape which is a minimum of 10 years' imprisonment, which may be increased to life imprisonment (s 3 SOA).

[100] Criminal Case No 177736 of 1998 (unreported).

[101] See Kameri-Mbote (n 39) 17.

E. Marital Rape and HIV/AIDS

Kenyan law contains provisions intended for the protection of partners of persons with HIV/AIDS. Under section 26(1) of the SOA, it is an offence for a person to deliberately transmit HIV or any other life-threatening sexually transmitted disease to another person; the penalty for such an offence is a minimum term of 15 years imprisonment and a maximum of life imprisonment. It is noteworthy that this provision explicitly operates whether or not the parties are married to each other.[102] Thus, it seems possible for one party in a marriage to have the other prosecuted for this sexual offence, and it is immaterial whether or not the other party consented to the act. Given the explicit language of section 26(1), we presume that spouses would not enjoy the immunity under section 43(5) of the SOA, but the interactions between the two sections have yet to be tested in court.

A similar provision is found in the HIV and AIDS Prevention and Control Act 2006 (HIV/AIDS Act).[103] Under section 24, an infected person who 'knowingly and recklessly places another person at risk of becoming infected with HIV' is guilty of an offence, '*unless that other person knew that fact and voluntarily accepted the risk of being infected*'.[104] The penalty for this offence is a fine not exceeding 500,000 Kenyan shillings, 7 years imprisonment, or both. This section contemplates the possibility of a sexual partner (including a spouse) refusing consent to a sexual act with the infected person. Like section 26 of the SOA, section 24 of the HIV/AIDS Act does not provide an exemption based on marital status. However, the defence of 'voluntary acceptance of risk of infection' may operate to the detriment of women, as they are often unable to bargain on equal terms with men in sexual matters due to their subordinate socioeconomic status and the presence of, or threats of, violence from their partners. It is therefore very difficult for such women to refuse to have sex with their partners even where there is a risk of infection.

In 2010, the HIV/AIDS Act was challenged in the case of *AIDS Law Project v Attorney General & Director of Public Prosecutions.*[105] The petitioner contested the constitutionality of section 24 of the Act on the ground that the section contained language that was vague and overbroad, and argued that it should be declared invalid because it failed to precisely communicate its purpose in law.[106] Further, the petitioner claimed that this provision was unconstitutional as it infringed on the right to privacy of persons living with HIV.[107] The Center for Reproductive Rights, which appeared as *amicus curiae*, argued that the section could be

[102] SOA (n 9) s 26(1).
[103] HIV and AIDS Prevention and Control Act, Act No 14 of 2006 (Kenya).
[104] ibid, s 24(2) (emphasis added).
[105] [2010] eKLR, Petition No 97 of 2010.
[106] ibid, para 4.
[107] ibid, para 6.

interpreted to criminalise women living with HIV who expose or transmit the virus to a child during pregnancy, delivery or breastfeeding.[108] The Center argued that criminalising HIV exposure and transmission does not protect women, but instead exacerbates existing stigma and discrimination against women, exposing them to risk of prosecution.[109] In its decision, the three-judge bench applied the principle of legality to section 24, especially the failure to define precisely the meaning of 'sexual contact'. The Court agreed with the petitioner that the provision was vague and overbroad and violated their rights to privacy and confidentiality, and was therefore unconstitutional.[110]

Although the similar provision in section 26 of the SOA has not been challenged in court, it is likely that the outcome of any such challenge would be the same, based on the doctrine of *stare decisis*. As argued by the Center for Reproductive Rights, the criminalisation of transmission of HIV/AIDS serves to increase the vulnerabilities of women. They are blamed for spreading HIV because they are the first to know their status if they are married and child-bearing, as it is usually a requirement that they be tested during obstetric care. Fear and stigma, on the other hand, keeps the man away from testing, and when the woman discloses first, the consequences may include spousal violence.

The realities of HIV/AIDS testing suggest that recourse for women seeking protection from spousal sexual violence does not lie in criminalising the transmission of HIV/AIDS. The HIV/AIDS Act and section 26 of SOA are not adequate substitutes for the criminalisation of marital rape itself.

F. Marital Rape and Divorce Law

Although marital rape is not currently treated as a criminal offence in Kenya, lack of consent in marital sexual relations can be considered as a form of cruelty constituting a ground for divorce and dissolution of marriage in civil cases, even though it is not explicitly recognised under Kenyan family law. For example, in *Esther Nangwana Nandi v John Chewe Bobo*, the wife sought dissolution of her marriage on the grounds of cruelty and adultery because her husband had assaulted her, locked her out of their matrimonial home, and forced her to have sex with him while he was drunk.[111] The High Court found that the husband's behaviour constituted cruelty of a serious nature that endangered her life and health. Such cruelty could not be accepted as the usual 'wear and tear of married life' and of living together amidst marital problems.[112] Significantly, the court held that

[108] ibid, para 47.

[109] ibid, para 50.

[110] *Aids Law Project v Attorney General & 3 others* [2015] eKLR, paras 88–89.

[111] *Esther Nangwana Nandi v John Chewe Bobo* [2006] eKLR, 1.

[112] ibid, 2.

non-consensual sex, even within a marriage, was an act of cruelty by the respondent and hence a ground for dissolution of the marriage.[113]

Under the recently enacted Marriage Act of 2014,[114] cruelty and exceptional depravity are grounds for divorce in four of the systems of marriage recognised in Kenya: Christian,[115] Customary,[116] Civil[117] and Hindu.[118] Further, irretrievable breakdown of marriage, which is a ground of divorce under all these systems of marriage, includes cruelty.[119] It is arguable that exceptional depravity can be interpreted to include forced sexual activity within marriage, but this is an issue that still needs to be tested in the Kenyan courts.

G. Recent Legislative Developments: The Protection Against Domestic Violence Act, 2015

In 2015, the Kenyan Parliament passed the Protection Against Domestic Violence Act (PDVA).[120] This was the first statute in Kenya specifically to address the issue of domestic violence. The new law was the product of a 'long and protracted journey' of negotiation and cooperation among the civil society and Members of Parliament.[121] Some male MPs opposed the law, as they felt it constituted a challenge against the existing patriarchal structures.[122] By passing the Act, Kenya was fulfilling its international obligations regarding protecting individuals from violence as well as giving effect to several articles in the Bill of Rights of the Constitution of Kenya, 2010.[123]

The preamble of the Act provides that it is intended 'to provide for the protection and relief of victims of domestic violence; to provide for the protection of a spouse and any children or other dependent persons, and to provide for matters connected therewith or incidental thereto'.[124] Section 3 of the PDVA defines 'domestic violence' to mean violence against or threat of violence or imminent danger to a person perpetrated by another person in a domestic relationship with the victim. Under section 4, a 'domestic relationship' covers persons in a subsisting

113 ibid, 3.
114 The Marriage Act, Act No 4 of 2014 (Kenya).
115 ibid, s 65(b) and (d).
116 ibid, s 69(b) and (d).
117 ibid, s 66(b) and (c).
118 ibid, s 70(d), (e) and (f).
119 ibid, ss 65, 66, 69 and 70. The dissolution of Islamic marriages, the fifth system of marriage in Kenya, is governed by Islamic law. See ibid, s 70.
120 Protection Against Domestic Violence Act (n 11).
121 Heinrich Boll Stiftung, 'The Protection Against Domestic Violence Act (PADV) 2015' (8 August 2015), online: ke.boell.org/2015/08/27/protection-against-domestic-violence-act-padv-2015.
122 ibid.
123 Constitution of Kenya 2010 (n 10) Arts 29(c), 45 and 50(9).
124 PDVA (n 11) preamble.

or previous marriage or a marriage that has been dissolved or declared null, or persons who are or have been engaged to be married. It also covers persons living in the same household.[125] While the definition of domestic relationship does not expressly cover persons in a cohabiting relationship, the expression 'persons living in the same household' may be interpreted to cover cohabiting couples. Similarly, it is not clear whether the PDVA covers situations where a woman is separated or divorced from her husband, but in our view, such situations are likely covered in light of the wide definition of 'domestic relationship'.

The PDVA adopts a wide definition of 'violence' which encompasses physical, sexual, emotional, psychological and economic abuse. Under section 3(a), violence also includes 'child marriage, female genital mutilation, forced marriage, forced wife inheritance, *sexual violence within marriage*, virgin testing and widow cleansing'.[126] This definition recognises that violence may be derived from cultural, customary and religious practices. By specifically including sexual violence within marriage in the definition of violence, the Act takes a bold step towards recognising the reality of marital rape. This is laudable as it offers hope for women to obtain remedies which had previously been unavailable.

However, the PDVA is not a penal statute and does not create any offences relating to domestic violence or marital rape. The only time there are penal sanctions under the Act is when a person contravenes a court order.[127] The PDVA is more in the nature of a civil statute—the main remedy it provides for victims of domestic violence is in the form of protection orders, including urgent interim orders that cover threats of violence. Jurisdiction is vested in the Resident Magistrates' Courts, which are more accessible and affordable than the High Court. Section 8(1) provides that a person who is in a domestic relationship with another person may apply to the court for a protection order in respect of that other person.[128] This means that a woman who has suffered marital rape or other forms of sexual violence within marriage can apply for a protection order in respect of her husband. This is the first time that any law in Kenya has provided for such orders.

Under section 13 of the PDVA, the court may make a protection order if it is satisfied that the respondent is using or has used domestic violence against the applicant and/or a child of the applicant's family, and that the making of an order is necessary for their protection. A protection order may direct that a respondent desist from any action that amounts to 'abuse' of the protected person. The abuse that can be covered by protection orders is widely defined to include physical or sexual abuse, damage to property, intimidation, harassment, stalking amounting to emotional, verbal or psychological abuse, economic abuse, and engagement in cultural or customary rites or practices that abuse the protected person. Threats

[125] ibid, s 4 (excluding landlord–tenant and employment relationships).

[126] ibid, s 3(a) (emphasis added).

[127] ibid, ss 22 and 31.

[128] ibid, s 8(1).

of abuse are also covered.[129] Under section 22, the contravention of a protection order which has been duly served upon a respondent is an offence, attracting a fine not exceeding 100,000 Kenyan shillings, 12 months imprisonment, or both.

A unique aspect of the PDVA is that it empowers the courts to direct parties to participate in counselling and conciliation programmes or any other programme acceptable to the court.[130] The counselling is aimed at ensuring respect for the law prohibiting domestic violence, the promotion of a protective environment for all within the family and the promotion of harmonious domestic relations between and among the parties. This approach is in line with Article 159 of the Constitution, which encourages settlement of disputes through alternative dispute resolution mechanisms.[131] This kind of approach is likely to be more acceptable to Kenyan women who have suffered spousal violence but do not necessarily wish to see their husbands in jail, as it promotes the continuation of marriage, which is so important in the Kenyan sociocultural context.

The PDVA places a duty on police officers to whom a complaint of domestic violence has been made to advise the complainant of all relief measures available to her, including access to shelters and medical assistance. It also imposes a duty to advise the complainant of her right to apply for relief under the Act and how she may lodge a criminal complaint.[132] Further, the Inspector-General of Police is required to ensure the development of procedures, including training police officers, to deal with family-related matters and domestic violence.[133] The Inspector-General also has an obligation to develop procedures that facilitate more friendly, expeditious and efficient reporting processes.[134] Thus the Act seeks to provide an environment that is friendly to complainants and makes it easier for them to report incidents of domestic violence (including marital rape) and obtain protection.

The Act also provides for orders excluding or restricting the respondent's access to the applicant's home (except where the two have consented to live in the same house), and for orders requiring the respondent to meet the applicant's living expenses. The court is also empowered to order compensation for victims of domestic violence payable by the perpetrators of the violence.[135]

One major weakness of the PDVA is that, unlike the 2012 Bill that preceded it, it makes no provision for a fund for financial and other welfare assistance to victims of domestic violence or for any support programmes for victims. Further, the Act is silent on the establishment of shelters or safe houses and other relevant services for the protection of victims of domestic violence. This is unfortunate as there

[129] ibid, s 19.
[130] ibid, s 14.
[131] Constitution of Kenya 2010 (n 10) Art 159.
[132] PDVA (n 11) s 6.
[133] ibid, s 6.
[134] ibid, s 6(4).
[135] ibid, s 32.

is dire need for shelters and safe houses in Kenya. Moreover, the Act is still in its infancy and the mechanisms for its implementation are not yet in place.

Notwithstanding its shortcomings, the Act is important because of the clear message it sends that domestic violence in all its forms—including marital rape—is unacceptable. The non-penal approach enables courts to deal with violence without necessarily resorting to criminal proceedings, even though a protection order is not a bar to criminal prosecution. However, the question remains of whether criminalisation of marital rape is required under international and constitutional norms, and is addressed in the next section.

V. International, Regional and Local Standards for Protection against Marital Rape

Kenya is a party to several international and regional human rights instruments that relate to the issue of gender-based violence, including sexual violence. Kenya also promulgated a new Constitution in 2010 which contains important principles and protections relevant to gender-based violence. These documents constitute standards against which the current legislative framework in Kenya relating to marital rape must be measured. It is notable that under Article 2 of the Constitution of 2010, the general rules of international law, as well as any treaty or convention ratified by Kenya, form part of the law of Kenya.[136] This is a significant shift from the previous approach, where Kenya could not apply international conventions that it had ratified until Parliament had enacted domesticating legislation. The new approach has positive implications for the promotion of gender equality and the protection of women's rights by the courts, as it means that international instruments ratified by Kenya, such as the Convention on the Elimination of All Forms of Discrimination against Women, are now deemed to form part of its law.[137] Kenya now has a constitutional obligation to enact and implement legislation to fulfil its international obligations in respect of human rights and fundamental freedoms, including those that protect the right to be free from marital rape.[138]

[136] Constitution of 2010 (n 10) Art 2.

[137] There has been controversy on the precise meaning of Art 2, with some commentators arguing that 'ratification' would entail domestication of treaties through legislation by Parliament. For further discussion, see EO Asher, 'Incorporating Transnational Norms in the Constitution of Kenya: The Place of International Law in the Legal System of Kenya' (2013) 11 *International Journal of Humanities and Social Science* 266; EBN Abenga, 'The Place of International Law in the Hierarchy of Valid Norms under the 2010 Kenyan Constitution' (17 October 2011), ssrn.com/abstract=2101565.

[138] Constitution of 2010 (n 10) Art 21(4).

A. International standards

The Universal Declaration on Human Rights, 1948[139] and the International Covenant on Civil and Political Rights,[140] to which Kenya is a signatory, provide foundational principles for equality and non-discrimination, and fundamental rights such as the right to dignity, security of the person and freedom from torture and inhuman treatment.[141] These are important and relevant rights for women who are victims of marital rape.

Further, Kenya ratified the Convention on the Elimination of All Forms of Discrimination against Women (CEDAW) in 1984.[142] While there is no explicit reference in CEDAW to violence against women,[143] the CEDAW Committee has interpreted the definition of discrimination to include gender-based violence, including sexual violence. In General Recommendation 19 of 1992, the Committee recognised gender-based violence as a form of discrimination that seriously inhibits women's ability to enjoy rights and freedoms on a basis of equality with men and urged state parties to adopt penal sanctions in order to protect women from such violence. This recommendation also urges states to include in their periodic reports to the Committee information about the legislation in force to protect women against violence (including sexual violence) and to provide statistical data on the incidence of violence against women.[144]

In 1993, the United Nations General Assembly adopted the Declaration on the Elimination of Violence against Women (DEVAW).[145] This landmark document was the result of global efforts to address violence against women. Although DEVAW does not have the binding legal authority of a convention or treaty, it is universal in coverage and a strong statement to the international community on the issue of violence against women. Article 1 defines 'violence against women' to mean any act of gender-based violence that results in, or is likely to result in, physical, sexual or psychological harm or suffering to women, including threats of such acts, coercion or arbitrary deprivation of liberty, whether occurring in public or in private life.[146] Under Article 2, violence against women is further defined to

[139] UN General Assembly, Universal Declaration of Human Rights, 10 December 1948, GA Res 217 A (III) (UDHR).

[140] UN General Assembly, International Covenant on Civil and Political Rights, 16 December 1966, 999 UNTS 171, acceded to by Kenya March, 1976 (ICCPR).

[141] Arts 1, 3 and 5 UDHR (n 139) and Arts 7, 9 ICCPR (n 140).

[142] Convention on the Elimination of All Forms of Discrimination against Women (New York, 18 December 1979), 1249 UNTS 13, 19 ILM 33 (1980), entered into force 3 September 1981, acceded to by Kenya March 1984.

[143] Art 6 CEDAW, ibid, calls for the suppression of all forms of traffic in women and exploitation of prostitution of women.

[144] UN Committee on the Elimination of Discrimination against Women, General Recommendation 19: Violence Against Women, adopted in the 11th Session of the CEDAW Committee, UN Doc A/47/38 1992, paras 7, 9 and 24.

[145] UN Declaration on the Elimination of Violence against Women (DEVAW), GA Res 48/104, 1993.

[146] ibid, Art 1.

include physical, sexual and psychological violence occurring in the family, including battering, sexual abuse of female children in the household, dowry-related violence, *marital rape*, FGM and other traditional practices harmful to women, non-spousal violence and violence related to exploitation.[147] This was the first time that an international instrument explicitly recognised marital rape as constituting gender-based violence.

In 2008, the CEDAW Committee called for the criminalisation of marital rape by Kenya. It also called for the repeal of section 38 of the SOA—which, as noted above, criminalised the making of false charges—and the enactment of domestic violence legislation, which eventually led to the PDVA.[148] The Committee noted that the continuing prevalence and belief in negative gender stereotypes contribute to and reinforce the existence of violence against women and harmful practices against them and urged Kenya to take systematic action to modify or eliminate such stereotypes and negative cultural values and harmful practices.[149]

In its General Recommendation 28 of 2010 regarding the core obligations of state parties to respect, protect and fulfil women's rights, the Committee again stressed the duties of state parties to impose penal sanctions on perpetrators of domestic and other forms of violence against women:

> States parties have a due diligence obligation to prevent, investigate, *prosecute and punish such acts* of gender-based violence. … Where discrimination against women also constitutes an abuse of other human rights, such as the right to life and physical integrity in, for example, *cases of domestic and other forms of violence, States parties are obliged to initiate criminal proceedings, bring the perpetrator(s) to trial and impose appropriate penal sanctions.*[150]

Kenya's failure to criminalise marital rape is a breach of its international obligations as set out in these human rights documents.

B. Regional Standards

The principle regional human rights instrument relevant to Africa is the African Charter on Human and Peoples' Rights (the so-called Banjul Charter), which Kenya ratified in 1992.[151] The Charter does not contain overt provisions on gender-based violence or sexual violence. However, it does provide general protections which are relevant to marital rape. The Charter provides for the right to

[147] ibid, Art 2 (emphasis added).

[148] Concluding Observations and Recommendations of the 48th Session of the CEDAW Committee on 2 February 2011, CEDAW/C/KEN/CO/7, paras 21–22.

[149] ibid, paras 17–18.

[150] CEDAW, General Recommendation No 28: The Core Obligations of States Parties under Article 2 of the Convention on the Elimination of All Forms of Discrimination against Women, 47th session, 2010, paras 19 and 34 (emphasis in original text).

[151] Organization of African Unity (OAU), African Charter on Human and Peoples' Rights, 27 June 1981, CAB/LEG/67/3 rev 5, 21 ILM 58 (1982), entered into force 21 October 1986.

equality and equal protection of the law,[152] the right to respect for life and integrity of the person,[153] and the right to inherent dignity.[154] It also prohibits all forms of exploitation and degradation including torture, cruel and inhuman punishment and treatment.[155] Further, it places on states the duty to eliminate all forms of discrimination against women.[156]

The subsequent Protocol to the Banjul Charter on the Rights of Women in Africa, ratified by Kenya, contains more detailed provisions for the protection of women from all forms of violence.[157] The Protocol defines 'violence against women' widely to include all acts perpetrated against women which cause or could cause them physical, sexual, psychological and economic harm, including threats to take such acts, whether in private or public life in peacetime and during situations of armed conflict or of war.[158] State parties are required to take appropriate and effective measures to enact and enforce laws to prohibit all forms of violence against women, including unwanted or forced sex, whether the violence takes place in private or public.[159] This provision encompasses a duty to take measures to prohibit marital rape. States must also take measures to actively promote education through curricula and social communication in order to eradicate elements in traditional and cultural beliefs, practices and stereotypes which legitimise and exacerbate the persistence and tolerance of violence against women.[160]

C. The Constitution of Kenya, 2010

The Constitution of 2010 represents a major victory for women's human rights. The national values and principles of governance on which Kenya is founded are stated to include human dignity, equity, social justice, inclusiveness, equality, human rights, non-discrimination and protection of the marginalised.[161] Chapter 4 contains an extensive Bill of Rights, which has elaborate provisions relating to fundamental rights and freedoms and thus provides increased space for addressing human rights. Notably, the Constitution explicitly provides for gender equality and non-discrimination. Article 27(1) provides that every person is equal before the law and has the right to equal protection and equal benefit of the law.

[152] ibid, Art 3.
[153] ibid, Art 4.
[154] ibid, Art 5.
[155] ibid.
[156] ibid, Art 2.
[157] Protocol to the African Charter on Human and Peoples' Rights on the Rights of Women in Africa, adopted by the Meeting of Ministers, Addis Ababa, Ethiopia on 28 March 2003, and the Assembly of the African Union at the second summit of the African Union in Maputo, Mozambique, 21 July 2003. Kenya ratified the protocol on 6 October, 2010.
[158] ibid, Art 1.
[159] ibid, Art 4(2)(a).
[160] ibid, Art 4(2)(d).
[161] Constitution of 2010 (n 10) Art 10.

Equality includes the full and equal enjoyment of all rights and fundamental freedoms.[162] Under Article 27(3), women and men have the right to equal treatment, including the right to equal opportunities in political, economic, cultural and social spheres. Article 27 prohibits discrimination by the state or any other person, whether directly or indirectly against any person on any ground, including *sex*, pregnancy and *marital status*.[163] For the first time, anti-discrimination provisions target not just the state but also non-state actors. This protection enables women to obtain redress from individuals, groups and corporate bodies in relation to discriminatory action, repudiating the public/private dichotomy and providing an obligation on the state to address the violation of rights by third parties. Further, women have been recognised as a category of vulnerable or marginalised groups and an obligation is imposed on all state organs and public officers to address the needs of such groups, including through affirmative action measures.[164] Relatedly, Article 50(9) directs Parliament to enact legislation providing for the protection, rights and welfare of victims of offences.[165]

Apart from recognising general principles related to respect for human rights, gender equality and non-discrimination, the Constitution provides more specific rights relevant to the issue of gender-based violence. Article 29 provides for the right to freedom and security of the person, which includes the right not to be subjected to any form of violence from *either public or private sources*, to torture in any manner, whether physical or psychological, to corporal punishment, or to be treated or punished in a cruel, inhuman or degrading manner. This right is not subject to any limitation, which means that no law or policy can operate to derogate from it.[166] Article 28 recognises the inherent dignity of every person and the right to have that dignity respected and protected.[167]

Another important provision is that all laws in force before the passing of the Constitution 'shall be construed with the alterations, adaptations, qualifications and exceptions necessary to bring it into conformity with this constitution'.[168] The implication of this provision is that existing legislation must be interpreted in a manner that is consistent with the Constitution, thus providing a basis for the invalidation of a law that is overtly discriminatory and contrary to other rights, such as the marital rape exemption in section 43(5) of the SOA.

Further, customary law is clearly subordinated to the Constitution in Article 2(4), and any conflicts are to be resolved in favour of the Constitution,

[162] ibid, Art 27(2).

[163] ibid, Art 27(4) and (5) (emphasis added). The other grounds are race, health status, ethnic or social origin, colour, age, disability, religion, conscience, belief, culture, language and birth.

[164] The obligation is imposed by Art 21(3) read together with Art 260, which defines 'marginalised group' to mean a group of people who are disadvantaged by discrimination on one or more of the grounds in Art 27(4). Some of the grounds of discrimination in that clause relevant to women include sex, pregnancy, marital status and dress. See also Art 27(5) and (6) on affirmative action measures.

[165] ibid, Art 50(9).

[166] ibid, Arts 29, 25(a).

[167] ibid, Art 28.

[168] ibid, Art 7(1) of Schedule 6.

which includes the Bill of Rights and the principles of non-discrimination and equality.[169] This provision removes the ambivalence in the repealed Constitution with regard to the application of customary and religious laws in the realm of personal law and is a welcome development.[170] It is therefore not permissible to defend gender-based violence or other discriminatory practices on the basis that they are allowed under customary law. Practices that are legitimated by customary law, such as spousal beating, child marriages, FGM, widow inheritance and widow cleansing, may be challenged on constitutional grounds. Such a challenge would reinforce the message of non-acceptability of all forms of gender-based violence, including marital rape.

The Constitution also recognises the right of every adult to marry a person of the opposite sex, based on the free consent of the parties. Parties to a marriage are entitled to equal rights at the time of the marriage, during the marriage and at the dissolution of the marriage.[171] Article 45 reinforces the position that a marriage is a union of equal partners and so women can negotiate their rights (including sexual rights) within the marriage. While the Constitution grants recognition to multiple marriage and family law systems, including customary law, such marriages are subject to the Constitution, which includes the Bill of Rights and the equality and non-discrimination provisions.[172] Thus forced marriages or marriages of under-age girls are not permissible under the Constitution. To the extent these practices are tied to marital rape, the Constitution's marriage rights also provide a basis for challenging the marital rape exemption.

D. Application of International, Regional and Constitutional Provisions to Support the Criminalisation of Marital Rape

The above international, regional and constitutional provisions clearly provide a firm basis for protection of married women against gender-based violence, and can be used as a springboard for reform of the law relating to marital rape. In particular, Article 29(c) of the Constitution provides 'that no one shall be subjected to any form of violence from either public or private sources'.[173] The Constitution therefore does not countenance legal immunity for marital rape. Furthermore, Article 19 provides an important framework for law reform on marital rape by stating that:

> (1) The Bill of Rights is an integral part of Kenya's democratic state and is the framework for social, economic and cultural policies. (2) The purpose of recognising and

[169] ibid, Art 2(4).

[170] Despite a prohibition against sex discrimination in s 82 of the repealed Constitution (Constitution of Kenya, Revised Edition 2009), the 'claw-back' provisions in sub-s 4 effectively allowed discrimination in the area of personal law, including marriage, divorce and succession.

[171] Constitution of 2010 (n 10) Art 45(1).

[172] ibid, Art 45(3). This clause is echoed in s 3(2) of the Marriage Act, Act 4 of 2014.

[173] Constitution of 2010 (n 10) Art 29(c).

> protecting human rights and fundamental freedoms is to preserve the dignity of individuals and communities and to promote social justice and the realisation of the potential of all human beings.[174]

As we have demonstrated, marital rape dehumanises and has numerous negative physical and psychological implications for the victim. As the supreme law of Kenya, the Constitution requires the government to revise both customary law and statutory law to bring them into alignment with the Constitution. This duty is supported by the international and regional human rights instruments discussed earlier. The existing statutory framework which exempts marital rape from criminal consequences is not tenable under the government's current constitutional and human rights obligations. Kenya must follow the path of other countries that have moved to criminalise marital rape.

Criminalisation of marital rape is essential, as it represents the requisite opprobrium towards this form of spousal violence. Stiff penalties will go a long way in communicating legal intolerance of the offence and may have a deterrent effect on would-be perpetrators. However, as we discuss in the final section, criminalisation of marital rape may take different forms, and must be accompanied by other legal and social measures to be truly effective.

VI. Recommendations for Dealing with Marital Rape

As we have argued, the current state of the law in Kenya is such that marital rape is not criminalised, and the failure to prohibit this form of gender-based violence violates international and regional norms as well as the Constitution of 2010. The following strategies are proposed towards ensuring protection of women from marital rape.

A. Criminalisation of Marital Rape

Criminal law serves an important function in not only protecting individuals against harms but also in addressing threats to the well-being of society as a whole. Where conduct is prohibited by the criminal law, this sends a strong message to society that such conduct is unacceptable and will be punished. In addition, criminal law offers a remedy in the form of sanctions such as imprisonment, which also serve as a deterrent to continuation of further criminal conduct. Criminalisation therefore has significant normative value.

Criminalisation of marital rape is an important step in the protection of married women who are victims of sexual violence perpetrated by their spouses.

[174] ibid, Art 19.

There are three options open to the Kenyan legislature to criminalise marital rape. One is to remove the exemption contained in section 43(5) of the SOA without additional language. The effect of this amendment would be that marital rape and rape by any other person would be treated the same way. The second option would be to enact provisions specifically proscribing marital rape, either by specifying that a husband can be held liable for the rape of his wife,[175] or by adding that the fact that the perpetrator is married to the complainant is no defence to a charge of rape.[176] Thirdly, the legislature could enact additional legislation protecting women from spousal sexual violence.

The third option, which entails introducing new legislation, is the most unlikely to succeed. Lessons from the debates related to the passage of the SOA make it clear that legislation seeking to improve the legal status of women by challenging assumptions about patriarchy will face a huge backlash and opposition from some members of civil society and government. The same challenges would hold for the second option, namely explicit criminal prohibition of marital rape. In the circumstances, the first option—repeal of the spousal exemption in section 43(5) of the SOA—is the most promising, as there is sufficient support to demonstrate that 'the criminality of sex without consent cannot depend on the relational context'.[177] In addition, the successful campaign for the repeal of section 38 of the SOA can serve as a precedent for the repeal of section 43(5).

However, while criminalisation is a necessary step in the protection of women from marital rape, it is not adequate as the only remedy. This is because of the inherent limitations of criminal law. First, the criminalisation of conduct does not necessarily result in change of people's attitudes towards the conduct. Further, where penal provisions go against the established status quo, there is a high possibility of backlash, as happened with the imposition of section 38 in the SOA criminalising the making of false charges. In addition, due to the complexity of marital relationships, women may be reluctant to report their husbands where there is the prospect of a jail term upon conviction, particularly where the woman is economically dependent on the man as is often the case. It is therefore important that alternative measures be taken to deal with marital rape in addition to criminalisation, including legislation that provides civil remedies and mandates use of alternative dispute resolution mechanisms such as mediation where appropriate. A good example is the PDVA discussed in section IV above.

B. Judicial Intervention, Education and Training

Courts have a primary role in the enforcement and protection of human rights, and an active and creative judiciary can be critical in the protection of married

[175] See eg the South African Prevention of Family Violence Act, Act No 133 of 1993, s 5. See also the Canadian Criminal Code, discussed in chapter 3 of this volume.

[176] See eg the Zimbabwean Criminal Law (Codification and Reform) Act, Act No 23 of 2004, s 68(5).

[177] Randall and Venkatesh (n 61) 156.

women from spousal sexual violence. An important tool at the disposal of the Kenyan judiciary is their power of judicial review, which includes nullifying and striking down unconstitutional legislation.[178] A constitutional challenge should therefore be brought against the marital rape exemption in section 43(5) of the SOA under the relevant clauses of the Constitution, particularly Article 27(4), which clearly outlaws discrimination on the grounds of sex and marital status. From a strategic point of view, bringing a constitutional challenge may be easier than legislative change, as litigation would avoid the publicity and likely polarisation of legislative reform. Legislative change can then follow as happened in the case of section 38 of the SOA, the repeal of which was spurred by a constitutional challenge.[179]

In conjunction with the power of judicial review, judicial training and education is crucial in order to raise awareness of gender issues among judges. This should include instruction on the incorporation of international law norms and use of equality analyses in judicial decision-making. Judges also need to be aware of gender biases and stereotypes, including their own, that contribute to women's subordination. It is notable that the Constitution provides a requirement for continuing judicial training.[180] Such training should be included as part of the curriculum for the mandatory induction course for newly appointed judges as well as for refresher courses at the Judiciary Training Institute. A good example of such training is the Jurisprudence of Equality Programme that was carried out in the 2000s.[181]

C. Police Training

Proper treatment of marital rape by the police is key to providing protection to victims of this type of violence. Previous studies suggest that there is trivialisation of violence against women by the police.[182] Police require specialised training on gender-based violence that will enhance their capacity to manage these cases properly. In addition, with the passage of the PDVA, it is necessary to train the police on the law and how they can contribute to its effective implementation, including in cases of marital rape.

178 This power is found in Art 2 of the Constitution of 2010 (n 10), which declares the supremacy of the Constitution, rendering void any law (written or unwritten) which is inconsistent with the Constitution.

179 *FIDA Kenya and Anor v The Hon Attorney General*, Nairobi High Court Petition No 751 of 2006. The matter did not proceed to trial as the Attorney General repealed s 38 of the SOA.

180 Constitution of 2010 (n 10) Art 172(1)(d).

181 The successes of the programme are detailed in A Pacht and S Glazebrook (eds) *The IAWJ: Twenty-Five Years of Judging for Equality* (International Association of Women Judges, 2016) 163–68.

182 Crichton (n 25) 45.

Emanating from a court decision in a constitutional petition challenging police inaction in cases of defilement in Meru Kenya,[183] the National Police Service has partnered with the Equality Effect[184] and the Kenya National Commission on Human Rights to train police officers on the investigation and management of defilement cases. To date, close to 2000 officers have been trained, and indications are that the training has contributed towards a change in attitude towards defilement by the officers so that they no longer trivialise the offence. As a result of this intervention, cases that had previously stagnated have been prosecuted and convictions have been secured.[185]

For sustainable results, it is essential that training on sexual and gender violence be incorporated into the police curriculum. Institutions such as FIDA Kenya have developed training materials that can be used for this purpose.[186] The National Police Service also ought to include training on gender and human rights as essential training for promotion. Such training would ensure that the senior officers in the Service are apprised on emerging and current trends in domestic violence, including marital rape, hopefully providing institutional transformation in the handling of these issues.

D. Public Education and Awareness-raising

There is also need for sustained public education and awareness-raising on the issue of gender-based violence with a view to dismantling gender stereotypes and negative cultural attitudes against women. Both women and men need to be aware of the physical, psychological and economic harms caused by spousal sexual violence at an individual and societal level. They also need to be aware of the equality and non-discrimination principles in the Constitution, as well as the other provisions of the Constitution that require the prohibition of marital rape. Further, it is important to challenge prevailing notions of masculinity and gender relations, particularly in marriage. In fostering public awareness, it would be useful to engage traditional and community justice structures in such a campaign with a view to making them more democratic and gender sensitive. Notwithstanding that they do not have criminal jurisdiction, these structures are critical in mobilising for transformation at the community level as the elders who preside over them are acknowledged as opinion-shapers. In 2005, the Kenya National Commission on Human Rights implemented a project in which it worked with the Luo Council of

[183] Petition No 8 of 2012, High Court of Meru, *CK (A Child) & 11 others v Commissioner of Police/Inspector General of the National Police Service & 2 Others* [2012] eKLR.

[184] The Equality Effect is an international NGO with its head office in Toronto, Canada. See equalityeffect.org/.

[185] See Equality Effect, 'International Day of the Girl Child 2016 Update', theequalityeffect.org/international-day-of-the-girl-child-2016-update/.

[186] FIDA-Kenya, *Police Training Manual on Gender and Human Rights* (FIDA-Kenya, 2008).

Elders to promote women's rights to property.[187] The project successfully secured property rights for women whose rights had previously been hampered by the application of cultural practices that did not recognise their rights to inherit land. These justice structures are culturally recognised and accepted and are therefore influential within communities.

VII. Conclusion

Kenyan law is currently inadequate to protect married women from sexual violence perpetrated by their spouses. The Kenyan state is under an obligation at the international and regional levels to enact or amend its legislation and take other measures to ensure protection against marital rape, including criminalisation of this practice and measures to deal with underlying gender stereotypes and negative cultural attitudes and practices. The Constitution also provides a solid basis for reform of the law. The enactment of the PDVA is an important first step, as it provides the much-needed legal recognition of the existence of marital rape and offers remedies to victims through protection orders. The PDVA provides additional protection to victims as it attaches penal sanctions to the breach of protection orders, which may have a deterrent effect on perpetrators of this violence. It is important to note, however, that criminalisation—though necessary—is not adequate and must be supplemented by additional measures including judicial training and police training as well as public education and awareness-raising.

[187] D Nyong'o and O Ongalo (eds), *From Despair to Hope: Women's Right to Own and Inherit Property* (KNCHR and Policy Project, 2005).

8

Marital Rape under Ghanaian Law

RENEE AKU SITSOFE MORHE

I. Introduction

Countries whose laws do not criminalise marital rape or effectively deal with it are permitting violence against women. Research suggests that rape occurring within marital relationships has the same, and sometimes even more, adverse physical and psychological impacts as rape by strangers.[1] Legal impunity for marital rape undermines women's equality in marriage and in society. Currently, there is no statute criminalising marital rape in Ghana and no single reported case on marital rape.[2] One reason for the lack of marital rape cases is Ghana's legal history, which has allowed husbands to use force against their wives. Another reason is the continuous presence of sociocultural and religious beliefs and norms associated with marriage that support patriarchy and reinforce women's inequality.

Until 2007, under Ghanaian law, a husband could legally rape his wife because she could not revoke consent which was considered given for the purposes of marriage.[3] Under this law a husband's right to demand sex from his wife included a right to use physical force against her. But women should be able to refuse sexual intercourse and other kinds of sex within marriage, and violence should not be the solution for this refusal. In 2007, an amendment to the Criminal Offences Act, 1960 (Act 29) abolished the provision granting spousal consent to use of force in

[1] M Adinkrah, 'Criminalising Rape within Marriage: Perspectives of Ghanaian University Students' (2011) 55 *International Journal of Offender Therapy and Comparative Criminology* 982, 983, citing P Mahoney, 'High Rape Chronicity and Low Rates of Help-Seeking among Wife Rape Survivors in a Nonclinical Sample: Implications for Research and Practice' (1999) 5 *Violence Against Women* 993.

[2] See RAS Morhe, A Assan Jr and EKS Morhe, 'Criminalising Marital Rape under Ghanaian Law' in *Proceedings of Second International Conference on Advances in Women's Studies* (Toronto, Unique Conferences Canada Publication, 2015) 100. Morhe et al, however, noted that there are murder cases in which husbands have assaulted and killed their wives for refusal of marital intercourse. See also Adinkrah (n 1) 986, where the author referred to reports in which husbands who claimed that they had been denied sex by their wives brutally murdered them.

[3] Criminal Code, 1960 (Act 29) s 42(g).

marriage.[4] Again, in 2007, the Domestic Violence Act, 2007 (Act 732) prohibited use of force in the domestic setting.[5] Yet these legal reforms were not sufficient.

Under these two statutes, marital rape is no longer explicitly exempted from Ghanaian law. However, the laws in Ghana do not fully criminalise marital rape because not all cases of rape involve use of force. Additionally, despite these statutes, a wife is still deemed in Ghanaian law to give her implied consent to sex in marriage and if she reports sexual assault she bears the burden of proving that she has revoked her consent. This makes the issue of consent highly significant in marital rape cases in Ghana.

Proving lack of consent has been very problematic in many cases of rape, with courts insisting on corroboration of the rape victim's evidence. Although corroboration is not necessary to establish the offence of rape, Ghanaian courts, in practice, still rely not only on circumstantial evidence but also on corroborative evidence, such as medical reports on the victim and evidence from witnesses, to establish the crime of rape. There is need for more reform to Ghanaian law, practice and procedure, on the matter of rape generally and marital rape in particular. Also, more specific legislation is needed which explicitly criminalises rape in marriage. Public education on marital rape also needs to be undertaken to promote women's equality and freedom from sexual abuse in marriage and other intimate relationships, and to give criminalisation of marital rape real effect.

This chapter is divided into three sections. In the first section, I outline the historical endorsement of marital rape under Ghanaian law. First, I point out that Ghana's legal history is based on English common law, which prevented married couples from bringing actions in court for marital rape. Second, I examine how Ghana's sociocultural background, beliefs, practices and norms affect marital rape discourse in the country. I argue that these sociocultural beliefs, practices and norms prevent marital rape reporting.

In the second section, I discuss the legal developments and reforms to Ghanaian law under the Criminal Offences Act, 1960 (Act 29) and the Domestic Violence Act, 2007 (Act 732). I argue that despite lack of explicit marital rape legislation in the country, the Criminal Offences Act, 1960 (Act 29) and the Domestic Violence Act, 2007 (Act 732) are statutes that could, in theory, be used to prosecute cases of marital rape.

Finally, in the third section, I make the case that there is need for further law reform to address marital rape. Law reform should involve passage of a marital rape law that abolishes the requirement of establishing the elements of force and corroboration to establish rape. I propose that in the interest of the clarity of the law, to promote the reporting of marital rape and to protect women from suffering rape at the hands of husbands, former husbands or estranged husbands and

[4] Criminal Offences Act, 1960 (Act 29) s 42(g). Section 42(g) of the Criminal Offfences Act repeats that consent to use of force can be revoked but it omits the old exception to this rule regarding consent of husband and wife.

[5] Domestic Violence Act, 2007 (Act 732) ss 1(b)(i), 2 and 3.

boyfriends, Ghana needs a direct criminal law prohibiting marital rape and rape in other intimate relationships. I also argue that a direct criminal law prohibiting marital rape is required in order for Ghana to fulfil its constitutional guarantees of gender equality and its international obligations under human rights instruments such as the Convention on the Elimination of All Forms of Discrimination against Women (CEDAW).[6]

I argue, however, that even a reformed law on marital rape will not be effective and women will still be unwilling to report marital rape cases unless certain strategies are adopted to counter the effects of sociocultural beliefs and norms that prevent marital rape reporting and keep this crime private. These necessary strategies include providing legal support, undertaking public education on the law and also providing for the use of alternative methods of redress (such as court-supervised mediation, offered under the Domestic Violence Act, 2007 (Act 732))[7] in cases where the relief sought by the victim is not incarceration of her husband.

II. Historical Endorsement of Marital Rape under Ghanaian Law

Under the 1992 Constitution of Ghana, the laws of Ghana include received English common law and Ghanaian customary law practised amongst various communities in Ghana.[8] Historically, both systems of law, English common law and Ghanaian customary law, permitted marital rape. Prior to 2007, married couples could not bring criminal actions against each other for any offence involving the use of force. Under section 42(g) of the Criminal Code, 1960 (Act 29), which was based on English common law, the provision on consent read as follows:

> A person may revoke any consent which he has given to the use of force against him, and his consent when so revoked shall have no effect for justifying force; save that the consent given by a husband or wife at marriage, for the purposes of marriage, cannot be revoked until the parties are divorced or separated by a judgment or decree of a competent Court.[9]

This provision meant that married couples were allowed to use force or violence against each other and such violence was not viewed as criminal. In terms of marital rape, acceptable use of force in marriage included use of force for marital intercourse. Apart from being incongruous, this provision invariably affected

[6] Convention on the Elimination of All Forms of Discrimination against Women (New York, 18 December 1979) 1249 UNTS 13, 19 ILM 33 (1980), entered into force 3 September 1981, Art 1.

[7] Section 24 of the Domestic Violence Act, 2007 (Act 732) (n 5) allows courts to promote reconciliation especially when violence is not severe and the demand for mediation is made by the victim.

[8] Constitution of the Republic of Ghana 1992, s 11(1).

[9] Criminal Code (n 3) s 42(g).

women negatively because it is undeniable that men are to a large extent physically stronger than women.[10] It is my position that this biological factor of male strength accounts for the almost universal phenomenon where women are, in most cases, the victims of sexual violence including rape. I concede, however, that not all cases of rape fit the forceful model.[11] Research on the reality of women's experiences show that rape can be achieved through coercion and manipulation.[12]

Many theories have been propounded to explain why forced sexual intercourse in marriage has been considered permissible. The unity of property theory, for example, assumes that a wife is part of her husband's property. Indeed, on this view, the husband can do with his wife what he wills and the wife must obey and fulfil her husband's demands. Much of this argument is based on the old English common law notion that as she was his property, the husband could use force to chastise his wife.[13] According to Blackstone, 'the husband also (by the old law) might give his wife moderate correction. For, as he is to answer for her misbehaviour, the law thought it reasonable to entrust him with the power of restraining her, by domestic chastisement.'[14]

Another theory explaining the common law acceptance of marital rape is the theory of implied consent to sexual intercourse in marriage, such that upon marriage a woman consents irrevocably to sexual intercourse with her husband every time and at all times. On this view, the consent is implied in the marriage contract between the parties. Yet another theory, the unity of person theory, justifies the marital rape exclusion because historically, upon marriage, a woman is deemed to become one with her husband, and has no separate legal identity. Being one with her husband, a woman could not possibly report her husband for marital rape because such an action would amount to him bringing an action against himself, a legal impossibility.[15]

The fact that consent by husband and wife to use of force cannot be withdrawn during marriage except when the parties are separated or divorced was confirmed in *R v O'Brien*.[16] In that case, after a divorce, the accused forcibly had intercourse with his former wife and upon being charged, defended himself on the basis that

[10] E Bortei-Doku Aryeetey and A Kuenyehia, 'Violence against Women in Ghana' in WalWa, *Women and Law in West Africa, Situational Analysis of Some Key Issues Affecting Women* (Accra, Women and Law in West Africa, 1998) 272, 274. The authors mention that men are traditionally associated with physical strength which placed them in positions of authority over women and children and which also invariably results in unequal gender relations.

[11] K Baker, 'Once a Rapist? Motivational Evidence and Relevancy of Rape Law' (1997) 110 *Harvard Law Review* 563, 570.

[12] ibid, 576.

[13] W Blackstone, *Commentaries on the Laws of England* (1765–69) vol 1, ch 15, 444,445.

[14] ibid.

[15] See H Barnett, *Sourcebook on Feminist Jurisprudence* (London, Cavendish, 1997) 378–79. See also KT Bartlett and DL Rhode, *Gender and Law: Theory, Doctrine,Commentary*, 4th edn (New York, Aspen, 2006) 811, where it is noted that 'at common law, the concept of marital unity viewed husband and wife as one, and a married man, therefore, could not be liable for raping himself'.

[16] *R v O'Brien* [1974] 3 All ER 663.

she was still his wife. The court held for the wife only because divorce effectively terminated their marriage and the consent given at the time of marriage could not be pleaded as a defence. The conclusion to be drawn from the case is that had the parties still been married, the court would have ruled in the husband's favour. The law anticipated that husband and wife consent to use of force in marriage to achieve the purpose of marriage, which includes sexual intercourse. Consequently, refusal of sexual intercourse is sufficient grounds for divorce. According to Sarkodee J. in *Addo v Addo*:

> It is now settled that a wife has a right to the consortium of her husband and these rights are reciprocal. … An incident to consortium is the mutual right to sexual intercourse. But a wilful refusal to have intercourse at all will entitle the party suffering as a result of it to leave the other.[17]

The cumulative effect of the common law in Ghana is that in marriage there is implied consent to sexual intercourse, making an action for sexual assault in marriage legally impossible. Historically and contemporarily, the notion that in Ghana a woman cannot report her husband for marital rape is also reflected in sociocultural beliefs, practices and norms associated with marriage, as discussed below.

A. Marriage: Polygamy and Child Brides

Ghanaian law recognises three types of legally valid marriages:[18] customary marriage,[19] Christian marriage[20] and marriage of Muslims.[21] Generally, marriage in Ghana is contracted by families on behalf of their sons and daughters. Payment of a bride-price or dowry to the wife's family is a common practice in Ghanaian communities. Most ethnic groups in Ghana accept polygamy—marriage of one man to two or more women—as part of their culture. Customary marriage and Muslim marriage favour polygamy. Such marriages are said to be potentially polygamous because after marriage the husband has the capacity to choose either to stay married to one wife or to marry more wives. Hence, under customary law, a man in Ghana can marry as many wives as he chooses. The marriage of Muslims limits a man to four wives.[22] Wives can sue their husbands for bigamy when married under Christian marriage but cannot do so when married under either customary law or Muslim marriage.

[17] *Addo v Addo* [1973] 2 GLR103.

[18] Marriages Act, 1884–1985 (CAP 127) parts one–three.

[19] ibid, part one.

[20] ibid, part three.

[21] ibid, part two. See also E Kom, *Kofi Mensah and the Law: Inheritance, Marriage and Divorce* (Accra, Asempa, 1993) 59.

[22] Al Islam, Ahmadiyya Muslim Community, the Holy Quran, English translation, ch 4:4, which states that: 'And if you fear that you will not be fair in dealing with orphans, then marry women as may be agreeable to you, two or three or four; and if you fear you will not deal justly, then marry only one or what your right hands possess' (www.alislam.org/quran/tafseer/?page=82&region=E2).

A recent survey in Ghana shows that 16 per cent of married women and 7 per cent of married men age 15–49 are in polygamous unions.[23] The greater the number of wives a man has, the more successful he is seen to be, as it is generally believed that only a wealthy man is capable of taking care of several wives and children.[24] Another explanation for polygamy is that a man needs many wives and children to help him on his farm. Invariably, these wives and children contribute to the accumulation of wealth, although wives are hardly credited for their husband's wealth. Barrenness may be a cause for polygamy, but polygamy is also practised in order to 'teach [outspoken] women a lesson'[25] in submission and obedience to their husbands, who are assumed to be in charge of the family.

Modernity and increased female education has done little to change perceptions about polygamy or the notions of male dominance.[26] Polygamy puts women at a disadvantage socially because it teaches that the man is the head of the household, the provider and the ultimate decision-maker. The husband's wishes, including sexual advances, must be fulfilled and society does not countenance any deviation from such teaching. In Ghanaian customary marriages women must defer to their husband's authority. As Adinkrah observed: 'There is a general cultural expectation that women demonstrate respect, obedience, submissiveness, and acquiescence toward men, particularly with respect to husbands' wishes and demands.'[27] Customary law and practices accept husbands' rights to 'discipline' their wives for failing to follow their directives.

Ofei-Aboagye has noted that in Ghanaian traditional societies, wife beating is not an unusual occurrence; traditional folk tales include stories such as a man beating his wife to maintain law and order, and Ghanaian folk songs often have themes that encourage husbands' mastery of their wives.[28] Sarpong analyses the ways that patriarchy, gender stereotypes and roles that support the impunity of marital rape function in Ghanaian traditional societies, and has observed that in Ghanaian traditional societies, wives are expected to obey their husbands and cook, clean, bear children and satisfy their husbands sexually. The families of both a husband and wife would deem the wife to have failed in her duties, and to deserve reprimand, including being divorced by her husband, should she fail

[23] Ghana Demographic and Health Survey (2014) 49, www.dhsprogram.com/pubs/pdf/FR307/FR307.pdf.

[24] A Nwoye, 'The Practice of Interventive Polygamy in Two Regions of Africa: Background, Theory and Techniques' (2007) 31 *Dialectical Anthropology* 383.

[25] A Kuenyehia and E Ofei Aboagye, 'Parenting, Fostering, Adoption and Domestic Employment' in WalWa, *Women and Law in West Africa, Gender Relations in the Family—A West African Perspective* (Accra, Women and Law in West Africa, 2003) 38, 67.

[26] ibid, 70.

[27] See Adinkrah (n 1) 987. See also NC Cantalupo, LV Martin, K Pak and S Shin, 'Domestic Violence in Ghana: The Open Secret' (2006) 7 *Georgetown Journal of Gender & the Law* 531, 539–51 for discussion of the traditional beliefs, economic dependence and customary practices that perpetuate domestic violence in Ghanaian communities.

[28] R Ofei-Aboagye, 'Domestic Violence in Ghana: An Initial Step' (1994) 4 *Columbia Journal of Gender Law* 1.

in carrying out any of these duties.[29] A woman marrying under customary law is advised to obey her husband's directives, and in sexual matters she is advised to be ready to have sex whenever her husband wants to have sex.[30]

Customary law appears to support marital rape, and complaints from a wife to her family that she has been raped by her husband tend to attract questions about why she refused her husband sex in the first place. It is typically assumed that her husband has the right to use force to have sex with her since, as a married woman, she cannot refuse sex. Some husbands rape and beat their wives for refusing to have sex with them and this violence is also considered legitimate. In addition, in Ghana, as in most African countries, a man pays dowry to marry his wife. The practice of dowry creates the impression that husbands have bought and therefore own their wives.[31] Thus, married women often have no say in how they are treated, and when their husbands want sex, they have no right to say no.

One practice associated with polygamy is marriage of underage girls. In Ghana, the minimum age of marriage of any kind is 18 years[32] and the age of sexual responsibility is 16 years.[33] Therefore, a person can only be prosecuted for defilement or sexual intercourse with a minor, if the minor (girl) is below 16 years of age.[34] According to Mensah Bonsu,[35] the previous age of sexual consent was 14 years and was raised to 16 years with the intention of 'arresting the growing incidence of child marriages, teenage motherhood and child prostitution'.[36] Sometimes, particularly in Islamic unions, girls 16 years of age and younger are married to much older adult males. According to the 2014 Ghana Demographic and Health Survey, 8 per cent of Ghanaian women marry before age 15 and 29 per cent by age 18.[37] This survey shows that increasing the age of sexual consent has not done much to prevent underage marriage.

Under Ghanaian law, these marriages of girls below 18 years of age are illegal, and the 2014 survey shows many people's utter disregard for the law. The practice of marriage of girls 15 years of age and younger promotes and perpetuates the phenomenon of child brides in Ghana. Further, when female children marry in their adolescence, they have very little bargaining power in marriage. These girls become women who are socialised to accept every sexual advance from their

[29] PK Sarpong, *Ghana in Retrospect, Some Aspects of Ghanaian Culture* (Accra, Ghana Publishing Corporation, 1974) 70.

[30] See B Duncan, 'Marital Rape as a Form of Domestic Violence and the Need for Law Reform in Ghana' in J Bond (ed), *Voices of African Women: Women's Rights in Ghana, Uganda and Tanzania* (Durham, NC, Carolina Academic Press, 2005) 148.

[31] See S Appiah, 'Dowry Should not Enslave Women—FIDA—Ghana', *Daily Graphic*, October 2014, www.graphic.com.gh/news/general-news/31598-dowry-should-not-enslave-women-fida-ghana.html.

[32] Children's Act, 1998 (Act 560), s 14(2).

[33] Criminal Offences Act, 1960 (Act 29) (n 3) s 101. 'Sexual responsibility' means capacity to consent to sex.

[34] ibid.

[35] HJAN Mensah Bonsu, *The General Part of Criminal Law: A Ghanaian Case Book*, vol 2 (Accra, Black Mask, 2001) 275–76.

[36] ibid.

[37] Ghana Demographic and Health Survey (2014) (n 23).

husbands and to accept the inevitable consequences of any refusal on their part. It is culturally unacceptable and unthinkable that these child brides would report their husbands for forced spousal sexual relations or marital rape. The occurrence of marital rape could be reduced if child marriage was not only prohibited but the laws were enforced and public education was undertaken.

B. Domestic Violence in Marriage

The ill-treatment of women in Ghana and the idea that a woman is her husband's property is also observable in the high incidence of domestic violence in the country. In Ghana, in addition to rape, defilement, widowhood rites, forced marriages and female circumcision perpetrated on women by members of their families, wife battery is a common occurrence.[38] In a two-day study of 214 pregnant women who attended the Komfo Anokye Teaching Hospital, in Kumasi, Ghana, the prevalence of physical violence was found to be 16.8 per cent.[39] The study revealed that out of 36 perpetrators of the physical violence, 41.7 per cent were husbands, 13.9 per cent were boyfriends and 19.4 per cent were strangers.[40] Furthermore, 72 per cent of the battered women did not want to talk about their experiences. A significant point noted by the authors of the survey was that the women who were assaulted had not complained about their experiences of domestic violence and they would not have been identified had they not been asked specifically about their experiences of violence and abuse.

Violence against women is a significant challenge in Ghana. According to a 1998 national survey on violence against women, 'violence is a reality for a substantial number of women'.[41] The survey found that 8 per cent of female respondents said men had forced sex with them and 5 per cent of the male respondents indicated that they had forced sex on their wives and girlfriends. However, 59 per cent of the female respondents said they never reported these experiences of forced sex to anybody.[42]

This data is similar to those from other African countries. Even in South Africa, for example, where marital rape is a criminal offence, research revealed that many

[38] MI Amoakohene, 'Violence against Women in Ghana: A Look at the Women's Perceptions and Review of Policy and Social Responses' (2004) 59 *ScienceDirect, Science & Medicine* 2373.

[39] KA Danso and H Lamptey, 'Physical and Sexual Violence against Pregnant Women Attending Komfo Anokye Teaching Hospital, Kumasi, Ghana' (1999) 3 *Ghana Medical Journal* 33.

[40] ibid.

[41] M Pappoe and E Ardayfio-Schandorf, *The Dimensions and Consequences of Violence against Women in Ghana* (Accra, National Council for Women and Development, 1998).

[42] ibid. See also DC Appiah and K Cusack (eds), *Breaking the Silence and Challenging the Myths of Violence against Women and Children in Ghana* (Accra, Gender Studies and Human Rights Documentation Centre, 1999) 65, where the authors in a 1999 national study on domestic violence found that one-third of Ghanaian women were experiencing physical violence at the hands of current or previous partners.

battered women suffer marital rape but few report their husbands for the offence.[43] Further, Ghana's 2003 Demographic and Health Survey indicated that there is a widespread belief that a husband is entitled to sexual intercourse from his wife at his behest and may act upon this entitlement by force. According to this 2003 Survey, 10.1 per cent of men and 19.9 per cent of women considered it justified if a husband beat his wife for refusing to have sex with him.[44] In order 'to protect their family' women are not expected to report these abuses.[45]

Women are often expected to endure abuse silently, and reporting husbands or other family members to the police may mean being ostracised from family and community.[46] The culture of silence surrounding domestic violence in general and marital rape in particular accounts for the lack of legal cases on the matter. The culture of silence surrounding domestic violence is reinforced by religious beliefs. Ghana is a religious country and the Bible and Koran are interpreted or used as tools of oppression of women. The Bible reinforces the position of the man as the head of the house and the woman as the helper. Women are to be submissive to their husbands and the correlation is for men to love their wives. The position of women is also affected by Islamic doctrines. Some Islamic practices, such as seclusion and veiling of women, repress and undermine the ability of women to claim equality with men.[47] These religious beliefs and doctrines have contributed to Ghanaian married women choosing not to report sexual violence.

C. Poverty and General Low Social Status of Ghanaian Women

In Ghana, poverty is an especially significant reason for women's unwillingness to report husbands for marital rape. Decades of patriarchy in customary law rules of inheritance and succession rights have contributed to female impoverishment and the low social status of Ghanaian women.

Ghanaian customary law rules of inheritance are structured in favour of men. For example, for the purpose of intestate succession to property among the traditional Akan ethnic community in Ghana, wives do not form part of their

[43] IH Frieze, 'Investigating the Causes and Consequences of Marital Rape' (1983) 8 *Signs* 532. See also R Gelles, 'Power, Sex and Violence: The Case of Marital Rape' (1977) 26 *Family Coordinator* 339, 343, where he notes that there is a correlation between battery and rape but battered women who are invariably raped by husbands, after the act of battery, never complain about rape.

[44] See Ghana Demographic and Health Survey (2003) 50–52, http://dhsprogram.com/pubs/pdf/FR152/FR152.pdf.

[45] See F Kaganas and C Murray, 'Law Reform and the Family: South African Rape-in-Marriage Legislation' (1991) 18 *Journal of Law and Society* 287, 291. See also R Copelon, 'Intimate Terror: Understanding Domestic Violence as Torture' in RJ Cook (ed), *Human Rights of Women: National and International Perspectives* (Philadelphia, University of Pennsylvania Press, 1994) 116, 116, where Copelon mentioned that intimate partner violence is often viewed as a private or family matter.

[46] See Copelon (n 45).

[47] ASMD Halim, 'Challenges to the Application of International Women's Human Rights in the Sudan' in Cook (n 45) 397, 407.

husband's family and do not inherit his property. Prior to the Intestate Succession Law, 1985 (PNDC Law 111) it was the nephew of the husband who inherited his property upon his death. Children are allowed to reside in their father's house only upon showing good behaviour.[48] Among the Ewe ethnic community in Ghana, sons inherit from their father but wives and daughters only have life interests in their father's estate.[49] The Ghanaian Constitution and Intestate Succession law have made inroads into correcting these customary law rules of inheritance by allowing women and children to inherit portions of their father's property, but decades of oppression have affected the status of women and many still live in poverty. As a consequence, in marriage, the husband is usually the breadwinner. Many wives would be reluctant to report their husbands for marital rape, especially if the penalty for marital rape is incarceration that would lead to loss of family income.

Women's increased access to education has not bridged the gap between men and women in Ghanaian society. The general society—including Ghanaian media, television drama and films—tends to portray women in gender-specific roles and emphasises men's social dominance and women's subordination.[50] Indeed, many Ghanaian idiomatic expressions also allude to the smallness, inferiority or weakness of a woman's mind. Women themselves often quote these expressions to excuse any folly on their part. Consequently, few women aspire to leadership positions.

Women are underrepresented in governance structures in Ghana. As of 2013, women made up 29 per cent of government ministers, 23 per cent of deputy ministers, 16 per cent of chief directors and 8 per cent of district/municipal/metropolitan chief executives.[51] In the judiciary, women made up 5 out of the 13 Supreme Court judges, 9 out of 26 of the Court of Appeal judges, 25 out of the 103 judges at the High Court and 30 out of the 275 parliamentarians.[52] A similar situation prevails in traditional governance structures. Ghana's Minister of Gender, Children and Social Protection, in her report to the CEDAW Committee, observed that efforts were being made to 'ensure active participation of queen-mothers in the Traditional Councils and Houses of Chiefs',[53] structures that are predominantly male dominated.

[48] See the following: A Kuenyehia, 'Women and Family Law in Ghana' (1986–90) XVII *University of Ghana Law Journal* 83 and C Dowuona-Hammond, 'Women and Inheritance in Ghana' in WalWa (n 10) 132, 139.

[49] NA Ollenu, *The Law of Testate and Intestate Succession in Ghana* (London, Sweet & Maxwell, 1966) 231.

[50] See generally K Dako, 'The Culture of Sexist Language among Male University Students in Ghana' (2013) 3 *World Journal of English Language* 19.

[51] See Ghanaweb.com, 'CEDAW Commends Ghana' (25 October 2014), www.ghanaweb.com/GhanaHomePage/regional/artikel.php?ID=332045.

[52] ibid.

[53] ibid.

Although women constitute 53.4 per cent of Ghana's economically active (employed and unemployed) population[54] they do not enjoy a high economic status. The dominant occupation for both men and women in Ghana is skilled agricultural, forestry and fishery work (44.9 per cent of economically active men and 37.7 per cent of economically active women).[55] The second highest occupation is service and sales work, where women dominate in informal sector activities such as wholesale and retail trade (31.7 per cent of economically active women compared to 10.2 per cent of economically active men are engaged in service and sales work).[56] Women's involvement in both the agricultural and informal sector activities tends to be at a low level, such as small-scale farming and petty trading in the private informal sector.

The private sector is Ghana's largest employer; 93.1 per cent of economically active persons are in that sector, with the private informal sector comprising 86.1 per cent of employers and private formal sector making up the remaining 7.0 per cent.[57] Thus, the private informal sector is the largest employer of Ghana's working population for both women and men. Women in the private informal sector are slightly more likely to be self-employed than men and are more likely to be engaged as contributing family workers.[58] Few women have jobs in the sectors that tend to pay higher wages.[59]

Ghanaian women are concentrated at the lower levels of economic activity and so do not significantly influence policy decisions. Amu has attributed women's low economic status to their poor access to education and other economic resources and their generally low self-esteem, all of which are attributable to the way females are socialised into subordination in Ghanaian society.[60] A 2009 study found that 'a woman's contribution to household expenditures, in some instances, increases her participation in conjugal decision-making in Ghana'.[61]

[54] See Ghana Statistical Service, *2010 Population and Housing Census Summary Report of Final Results* (Accra, Sakoa Press, 2012) 21.

[55] ibid, 9, 74.

[56] ibid.

[57] ibid, 11. The second largest employer is the public sector which employs only 6.3% of economically active Ghanaians.

[58] ibid, 10, where it is stated that females are slightly more likely to be self-employed (69.4%) than males (60.0%). In addition, more females (14.2%) than males (8.7%) are engaged as contributing family workers.

[59] ibid, 77. Ghana's economically active women constitute the following percentages in the indicated industries: information and communication, 0.2%; financial and insurance activities, 0.5%; real estate activities, 0%; professional scientific and technical activities, 0.7%; administrative and support services activities, 0.3%.

[60] NJ Amu, *The Role of Women in Ghana's Economy* (Ghana, Friedrich Ebert Stiftung, 2005). The report quoted the Ghana Statistical Service, 2000 Population and Housing Census, Summary Report of Final Results. The 2010 Ghana Population Census does not reflect any significant change in this area.

[61] H Warren, 'The Relationship between Women's Contribution to Household Expenditures and their Participation in Conjugal Decision-Making in Ghana' (2009) 98 *Radical Statistics* 50, 55, 60. Warren analysed respondents to the Ghana 2003 Demographic and Health Survey (DHS), looking at the dataset of women categorised as married or living with their partner; this comprised 3,694 respondents in total. She focused on questions in the Ghana 2003 DHS covering these women's

It appears that if Ghanaian women who are highly educated and make financial contributions to their households comparable to that of their spouses share in household decision-making, they are also better able to negotiate sex and seek redress where their sexual rights are abused. This suggests that advancing women's economic empowerment and equality in the domestic sphere are important ways to end marital rape.

D. Cumbersome and Costly Court Processes, Consent and Corroboration as Barriers to Justice

Apart from poverty or financial dependence on husbands, other factors preventing women from reporting sexual assault in marriage include fear of police and the cumbersone and lengthy court processes in Ghana (as in other African countries).[62] In Ghana, the criminal process is initiated by the police or by the Attorney-General's Department. But these processes are very slow moving, and often costly, making it difficult for women to bring charges against their husbands.

Furthermore, the difficulty in establishing marital rape in court presents a major barrier to reporting rape in marriage. Ghana's Criminal Offences Act, 1960 (Act 29) is the main statute governing criminal law.[63] Chapter 6 of the Criminal Offences Act deals with sexual offences. The first provision of the chapter, section 97, provides that rape is a first-degree felony and an accused person is liable on conviction to a term of imprisonment of 'not less than five years and not more than twenty-five years'. Thus, the penalty for rape under Ghanaian law is severe. The next section, section 98, defines rape as 'the carnal knowledge of a female of not less than sixteen years without her consent'. Carnal knowledge refers to sexual intercourse.[64] For a rape conviction, prosecutors must establish lack of consent, which is usually exhibited through evidence of use of force.

It appears there is low reporting of rape cases and even lower prosecution rates of rape cases, hence there are limited cases on rape in the law reports. A search for cases on sexual offences in two major Ghanaian law reports, the Ghana Law Reports (GLR) and the Supreme Court of Ghana Law Reports (SCGLR),[65] yielded only seven cases in the GLR series and one case in the SCGLR series.

participation in household decisions on (1) making large household purchases; (2) making household purchases for daily needs; and (3) visits to family or relatives. Warren's conclusion cautioned that 'to provide a comprehensive picture of factors affecting women's conjugal decision-making a number of other aspects would need to be taken into account, including other resource contributions and "cultural" factors such as different gender ideologies' (60).

[62] G Hancox, 'Marital Rape in South Africa: Enough Is Enough' (2012) *BUWA! A Journal on African Women's Experiences* 70, 73, www.osisa.org/sites/default/files/70-74.pdf. See also Kaganas and Murray (n 45).

[63] See Preamble to the Criminal Offences Act, 1960 (Act 29) (n 4), which refers to the Act as 'an Act to consolidate and amend the law relating to criminal offences'.

[64] P K Twumasi, *Criminal Law in Ghana* (Accra, Ghana Publishing Corporation, 1985) 281.

[65] The GLR has been published from 1959 to 1996 while the SCGLR began in 2000 with the most recent volume being the 2013–14 report.

Of the cases located, four were rape cases involving females over 16 years of age, the rest were cases of defilement (meaning the victim was an adolescent or child). Defilement is defined as 'the natural or unnatural carnal knowledge of a child under sixteen years of age'.[66] There is great public abhorrence of rape of children and such cases receive significant media and public attention compared to rape cases involving women. As for marital rape, it remains below the radar; there are no reported cases of marital rape in Ghana.

In the earliest of the four reported cases of rape of adult women, *State v Gyimah*,[67] the evidence adduced at the trial proved that there was full penetration and the only issue for consideration of the court was whether or not there was consent. The accused person's defence was that the sexual intercourse took place with the full and free consent of the complainant, and that the complainant had been his girlfriend with whom he had had sex several times before.

The court found that the accused and the complainant had been caught in the act by the complainant's mother, and it was only upon her mother's arrival on the scene that the complainant started shouting and crying. When asked what she was doing in the accused person's room the complainant did not answer her mother; meanwhile two men who had been outside the room as well as the landlord had heard no shouts until the complainant's mother appeared on the scene. The accused claimed that the story of rape was concocted by the complainant and her parents after he declined to comply with their demand for money as compensation and in order to prevent the matter being reported to the police. Justice Lassey acquitted and discharged the accused, holding that there was no evidence of the complainant fighting back and the doctor had found her hymen broken but no recent injury. The court's reliance on the lack of evidence of the complainant fighting back as indicative of consent can be problematic in cases where a complainant does not fight back out of fear of the accused or only starts to fight when others arrive on the scene.

In *Republic v Dapaah*[68] the sole issue was whether or not the complainant had consented. The facts were that on the pretext of giving the complainant money to buy something for him, the accused pulled the complainant into his room and while threatening her with a knife, forcibly had sexual intercourse with her twice. Three witnesses testified that they heard the complainant pleading with the accused to let her go as 'he was killing her' and they intervened. The accused maintained that the complainant was a girlfriend with whom he had had sexual intercourse several times previously. The court found as a fact that the complainant was not a girlfriend and on the issue of consent held that the evidence

[66] Section 101(1) of the Criminal Offences Act, 1960 (Act 29) (n 4). Hence defilement is a term that covers any sexual act committed against a child below the age of 16 years.

[67] *State v Gyimah* [1963] 2 GLR 446.

[68] *Republic v Dapaah* [1968] GLR 513.

of the witnesses corroborated the complainant's version. In the words of Justice Campbell:

> [T]he evidence that she was heard crying and shouting in the room, corroborated as it is by the evidence of the third, fourth and fifth prosecution witnesses is evidence that she could not have been consenting to what was being done to her in the room.[69]

Just as in *Gyimah*, the court relied on the extent of resistance put up by a complainant to determine whether or not there was consent in this rape case. Also significant for the courts in the two cases above was the corroboration of the complainant's version of events by witnesses. Twumasi has observed that although there is no legal provision requiring corroboration in Ghanaian law, the practice is that the courts look for corroboration in sexual offence cases. In this regard the Ghanaian courts draw on the common law's use of corroboration in rape cases.[70]

The third case identified, *Hanson v the Republic*,[71] focused on the issues of corroboration and misdirection on identity. In that case, the complainant, the wife of a private in the army, alleged that on the pretext of giving her a lift, the accused drove her out of the barracks and had sex with her against her will, and then drove her back to the barracks. The accused's appeal against his conviction (for conduct prejudicial to good order and discipline by a court martial) was allowed, on the basis that the prosecution had not proved beyond a reasonable doubt that the complainant had sexual intercourse with him specifically. The court allowed the appeal because there was no proof of penetration and no corroboration. The legal reasoning in this case was defective because the court took into account the fact that there were no witnesses to support the complainant's version of events, again showing the corroboration requirement.

Corroborative evidence is usually sought in rape cases to prevent false incrimination or to prevent fabrication, lying or exaggeration by the victim.[72] But corroboration is not an element of the crime of rape and neither is it demanded in many other criminal offences. Armstrong argues that demanding that evidence of a rape victim be corroborated puts the victim in the situation where she is put on trial for her veracity.[73] Corroboration can be obtained through medical reports that establish violence or force. The problem is that rape is not always obtained through force. It can also be obtained through manipulation and threats of force and some victims do not put up a fight for fear of death or physical harm. Hence, a court's reliance on a doctor's report to show force, as is usually the case in order to corroborate a report of rape, could prove fatal to the case. At best therefore, corroboration may be helpful but it must not be the deciding factor in rape cases, yet it appears that it often—and incorrectly—is determinative.

69 ibid.

70 Twumasi (n 64) 285.

71 *Hanson v the Republic* [1978] GLR 477.

72 A Armstrong, 'Evidence in Rape Cases in Four Southern African Courts' (1989) 33 *Journal of African Law* 172.

73 ibid.

The fourth case, *G/CPL Valentino Gligah & Anor v The Republic*,[74] involved the appeal of two policemen against their rape convictions. The appellants had invited a woman who sold used clothes into the police station, pushed her into a store room and took turns forcing her to have sex with them without her consent. They appealed their rape convictions on the grounds that the trial court failed to consider their defence that the alleged act was not rape and that a material witness was absent. The Supreme Court dismissed their appeal, finding that the prosecution had established its case against them based on the evidence of the complainant, a medical officer and the circumstantial evidence of two other witnesses. The Supreme Court also found that failure of the prosecution to call the police officer who was in charge of the store room where the rape had occurred had not been fatal to the prosecution's case.

The court observed that the whereabouts of this officer and where he kept the key to the store room were irrelevant since the prosecution had established that the appellants had access to the store room. In this case, the complainant gave a vivid description of the store room and referred to the loss of her earring stopper which the investigators later found stuck in foam in the store room. However, it appears that it took more than her evidence for the court to reject the appellants' defence. The Supreme Court affirmed and quoted the trial judge's direction to the jury by stating that:

> It is PW1's word that it was the accused persons who had sex with her without her consent against that of the accused person. Nobody else was present but them so that evidence becomes crucial. I warn myself and also warn you to be cautious when evaluating the evidence of PW1. Since there was nobody else present to confirm what she says in other words there has been no direct corroboration of PW1's allegation that she has been raped. You can however use the surrounding circumstances to determine the truth or otherwise of PW1's claims. If these circumstances implicate, connect or link the accused with the offence then they amount to corroboration.[75]

Thus, the complainant's evidence appears to have been insufficient to establish that non-consensual sex had occurred. The court also relied on the strength of the circumstantial and corroborating evidence.

The question remains as to whether the evidence of a complainant alone will be enough to convict in rape cases in Ghana's courts. The cases discussed reflect the traditional problem with prosecuting sexual offences when the cases are reduced to his word against her word. It is likely that this traditional problem of insistence on corroboration will be imported into marital rape situations. Hence, for marital rape, the onus and burden will be upon the wife (1) to show she was actually raped by her husband and that the act took place without her consent; and then (2) to provide corroboration for her claim of rape. The practice of courts asking for support for a rape victim's story through the provision of corroborating evidence holds victims to a higher burden of proof vis-a-vis rapists, and must be abolished.

[74] *G/CPL Valentino Gligah & Anor v The Republic* [2010] SCGLR 870.
[75] ibid, 876.

On the issue of revocation of consent, the problem is that lack of consent cannot be easily established in marital rape situations because of the bonds of affinity which are usually present between the parties. In other jurisdictions, some cases hold that the wife's revocation of consent to sexual relations must be exhibited by a manifest intent to terminate the marital relationship.[76] Such intent could be exhibited through total separation but if the wife's revocation is equivocal, ambivalent or ambiguous, then a charge of marital rape would not lie.[77]

Mensah Bonsu argues that using separation or intent to divorce as a yardstick of a wife's lack of consent is not a viable option in Ghana because 'customary marriages are hardly ever, even though it is possible to do so, dissolved in court'.[78] In reality, she asserts, many customary marriages 'merely fizzle out, and are never formally dissolved'.[79] This is one important reason why a specific Ghanaian criminal law on marital rape is needed, one that does not require separation or a show of intent to separate as the hallmark of lack of consent.

III. Law Reform: Domestic Violence Act and the Criminal Offences Act

Ghanaian law did not sanction marital rape as an offence until 2007, because irrevocable consent to sexual relations between spouses was implied in marriage. The general unwillingness of Ghanaians to recognise a wife's right to bring an action of marital rape against her husband was evident in positions taken by parliamentarians and other politicians during the debate that led to passage of the Domestic Violence Act, 2007 (Act 732).[80]

Much of the debate revolved around whether or not marital rape should be included as a type of domestic violence. According to one lawmaker:

> You cannot restrict the benefit of conjugal rights when it is acquired within the process of marriage ... if this country was to go through the process of making marital rape an offence, the purpose of maintaining matrimonial harmony and ensuring cohesion within families would not be attained.[81]

Another argued that marital rape legislation would enable women to use

> sexual starvation as punishment for their husbands ... these are acts that provoke the men beyond limit, and all those men who cannot contain the situation have only one

[76] *Weishaupt v Commonwealth of Virginia*, 315 SE 2d 847, 855 [Va 1984].
[77] *Kizer v Commonwealth of Virginia*, 321 SE 2nd 291 [Va 1984].
[78] See Mensah Bonsu (n 35) 360–61.
[79] ibid.
[80] Domestic Violence Act, 2007 (Act 732) (n 5).
[81] See Official Report on Parliamentary Debates (Department of Official Report, Parliament House) Fourth Series (2006) vol 54, no 19, 1495.

way out; that is to reduce their wives to punching bags and lowering them into involuntary submission.[82]

This statement seems to justify and excuse force to obtain sexual relations in marriage. Some refuse to accept criminalisation of marital rape because it would restrict the husband's enjoyment or benefit of conjugal rights which he acquires through marriage. These positions, together with the sociocultural factors discussed above, have contributed to the powerlessness and helplessness of women to seek legal protection when their husbands sexually assault them.

Other politicians who were also opposed to adding marital rape as a form of domestic violence under Ghanaian laws argued that it would contradict Ghanaian culture. These opponents of criminalising marital rape also accused criminalisation advocates of seeking to import foreign ideas into Ghanaian culture. For instance, Dr Edward Mahama, a medical practitioner and then presidential candidate of the People's National Convention party said that: '[I]f we talk about marital rape, it means we are going into the bedroom, and we have no right to go there.'[83] He added his opinion that: '[Y]ou cannot legislate on such issues.'[84] Professor Evans Atta Mills, who was later elected President of Ghana, called for protection of the 'sanctity' of marriage.[85] Chiefs in the Upper East Region concluded at a meeting that the Domestic Violence Bill was 'meant only for urban dwellers' and that 'the proposed law on marital rape [was] anti-Ghanaian'.[86]

On one hand, the views and concerns expressed about the impact that criminalising marital rape would have on Ghanaian marriages and society are archaic and need revision, given that what happens in Ghanaian homes has for a long time remained a private matter. It is hard for traditionalists, and mostly men, to envisage husbands being held accountable for sexual violence committed against their wives.[87] These views reveal the reluctance of many Ghanaians to expose intimate details of their private lives and the reluctance of many women to report marital rape to the police. On the other hand, failing to tackle the issue of marital rape ignores the fact that sexual violence occurs in Ghanaian marriages. One parliamentarian who did support inclusion of marital rape in the domestic violence law noted that women often became slaves in marriage:

> We all know what happens; we should not be ostriches and bury our heads in the sand. We know what happens to several wives, particularly wives in our homes. It … occasionally … happens to men. We know how some men treat their wives as if they were their slaves. Once they paid the dowry, she became a chattel in the house.[88]

[82] ibid, 1514.

[83] NK Stafford, 'Permission for Domestic Violence: Marital Rape in Ghanaian Marriages' (2008) 29 *Women's Rights Law Report* 63, 63.

[84] ibid.

[85] ibid.

[86] ibid.

[87] See Adinkrah (n 1) 996, where he mentioned that one respondent believed that rape between couples in Ghana is a normal thing.

[88] See Official Report on Parliamentary Debates (n 81) 1493.

Marital rape adversely affects women's lives. Ignoring marital rape reinforces married women's inequality, attacks the security of their person and denies their right to equal self-determination. The need for change and law reform was championed by the National Coalition on Domestic Violence Legislation (DV Coalition) in 2003.[89] The DV Coalition, which was made up of women's groups and various NGOs,[90] advocated for passage of the Domestic Violence Act, 2007 (Act 732). The work of the DV Coalition also led to the repeal of the clause in the criminal law that allowed use of force in marriage.[91]

A. Ghana's Domestic Violence Act, 2007 (Act 732)

The law against domestic violence in Ghana is the Domestic Violence Act, 2007 (Act 732), which according to the preamble is: 'An Act to provide protection from domestic violence particularly for women and children and for connected purposes.'[92] Although the Act applies to all in Ghana, it was developed out of a particular concern to protect women and children from domestic violence.

Prior to the establishment of the Domestic Violence Victims Support Unit (DOVVSU) in the Ghana Police Service and the passage of the Domestic Violence Act, 2007 (Act 732), the police mostly asked those with complaints arising from domestic settings to go and settle the matter at home. This situation meant complainants had recourse only to family elders who very often failed to effectively protect women and children from violence and abuse.

Throughout 2006, the DV Coalition lobbied Members of Parliament and the Ministry for Women and Children's Affairs. Members of Parliament received information and data on violence against women.[93] The then Minister for Women and Children's Affairs, Hajia Alimah Mahama, who had a civil society and development work background, supported the DV Coalition. At the 36th Session of the CEDAW Committee that discussed Ghana's periodic reports, the DV Coalition put pressure on the government by presenting a shadow report which stressed the need for legislation on domestic violence and urged the repeal of the criminal law provision on implied consent to use of force in marriage.[94]

[89] Ghanaian Chronicle, 'The Law and Gender-Based Violence', www.modernghana.com/news/317627/1/the-law-and-gender-based-violence.html.

[90] Some of the groups belonging to the DV Coalition are the Ghana Centre for Democracy and Development (CDD-Ghana), The Ark Foundation, Commonwealth Human Right Initiative (CHRI), Concerned Citizens of Ghana, Domestic Violence Bill Coalition, and Women in Law and Development in Africa (WiLDAF) Ghana.

[91] See B Sam, 'Advocacy for a Domestic Violence Act using CEDAW', WiLDAF, Ghana, unpublished report (2009). Though unpublished, this report is relied on here because it is a first-hand account of Sam and her organisation, WiLDAF's, direct involvement, as part of the DV Coalition, in the advocacy that led to the passage of the Domestic Violence Act, 2007 (Act 732) in Ghana.

[92] The opening statement or Preamble to the Domestic Violence Act, 2007 (Act 732) (n 5).

[93] See Sam (n 91).

[94] See NGO Shadow Report to 3rd, 4th and 5th Periodic Report of Ghana on CEDAW (2006).

The DV Coalition argued that the legal doctrine of implied consent to use of force in marriage contravened Articles 1 and 2 of CEDAW[95] and also Article 17 of Ghana's 1992 Constitution,[96] both of which prohibit gender discrimination. The CEDAW Committee's concluding comments included language that called on Ghana to legislate on domestic violence.[97] Specifically, at paragraph 24 of its concluding comments on Ghana, the CEDAW Committee raised the issue of marital rape as one of its principal areas of concern and recommended that the country ensure the speedy adoption of the Domestic Violence Bill and repeal section 42(g) of the Criminal Code, 1960 (Act 29), which exempted husbands from prosecution for marital rape.

Parliament passed the Domestic Violence Act, 2007 (Act 732) on 21 February 2007. One newspaper captured the moment in these words:

> It was a sight to behold as female members across the political divide, who are united by their gender sensitivity, flew their handkerchiefs and embraced each other when the speaker of the House … pronounced the Bill passed at exactly 11.45 a.m. The reaction in Parliament was reflective of national relief from years of an emotionally charged debate during which various organizations, such as the National Coalition on Domestic Violence assumed frontline roles.[98]

The Domestic Violence Act, 2007 (Act 732) creates a summary conviction offence for domestic violence in section 3, provides police with powers of arrest under section 9, and allows victims to obtain protection orders under sections 11–22. It covers persons in marriage relationships as well as intimate relationships more broadly in section 2.

The definition of domestic violence under the Domestic Violence Act, 2007 (Act 732) covers physical, sexual, economic and psychological violence and also sexual harassment.[99] However, the Act does not mention marital rape. Members of Parliament argued that it was not necessary to include the words 'marital rape' in the domestic violence law, because the offence was implied under section 4 of the Act, which prohibited use of force in the domestic setting. Section 4 provides that 'use of force in domestic setting is not justified on the basis of consent'.[100] Since marriage is a relationship in the domestic setting, then henceforth, any form of sexual relations obtained through violence within marriage without consent, in theory, qualifies as domestic violence.

[95] CEDAW (n 6). Ghana ratified CEDAW on 2 January 1986.

[96] Ghana's 1992 Constitution (n 8) Art 17 prohibits discrimination on the basis of gender.

[97] See Committee on the Elimination of Discrimination Against Women, Thirty-Sixth session, 7–25 August 2006, Concluding Comments of the Committee on the Elimination of Discrimination against Women: Ghana, CEDAW/C/GHA/CO/5.

[98] E Adu-Gyamerah, 'House Clears Hurdle, Domestic Violence Bill Passed at Last', *Daily Graphic*, 22 February 2007, 3. Presidential assent to the Act was granted in May 2007.

[99] Domestic Violence Act, 2007 (Act 732) (n 5) s 1.

[100] ibid, s 4.

B. Amendment to the Criminal Offences Act

Two months after the passage of the Domestic Violence Act, 2007 (Act 732) the marital rape exemption under Ghanaian criminal law was also amended through a rather less direct legislative process. The government of Ghana, acting under the authority of the Laws of Ghana (Revised Edition) (Amendment) Act, 2006 (Act 711), appointed a Statute Law Revision Commissioner to prepare a revised edition of all Ghanaian Acts and subsidiary legislation in force as at 1 January 2005. After completion of the task, the Commissioner submitted the set of revised laws in bound volumes to the Minister of Justice, and these laws were laid before, and approved by, Parliament. After parliamentary approval, the President by Executive Instrument 2007 (EI 3) established the volumes as effective from 16 April 2007, making the laws currently in force the Laws of Ghana (Revised Edition).

As part of the statute revision, the name 'Criminal Code' gave way to the 'Criminal Offences Act'. Couples could not report each other for marital rape under the now-repealed section 42(g) of the Criminal Code, 1960 (Act 29), but the current revised criminal law, the Criminal Offences Act, 1960 (Act 29), under the new section 42(g) omitted the old exception to revocation of consent to use of force in marriage. The persuasive argument for the revision was that the old provision was unconstitutional on the basis that it allowed men to use force against their wives, thereby contravening chapter 5 of the Ghanaian Constitution, which protects the human rights of all and prohibits torture and inhumane and degrading treatment as well as prohibiting discrimination based on gender.[101]

The current version of section 42(g) of the Criminal Offences Act, 1960 (Act 29) states that: 'A person may revoke any consent which he has given to the use of force against him, and his consent when so revoked shall have no effect for justifying force.'[102] The effect of this amendment is that married women can now withdraw consent to sexual relations with their husbands, and can report their husbands to the police if force is used to obtain sex.

Ghanaian law seems to have taken a cue from current English law, which removed the marital rape exemption to criminal prosecution in the 1990s. According to the dictum of Lord Keith of Kinkel in the 1991 English case of *R v R*:

> The rule that a husband cannot be criminally liable for raping his wife if he has sexual intercourse with her without her consent no longer forms part of the law of England since a husband and wife are now to be regarded as equal partners in the marriage and it is unacceptable that by marriage the wife submits herself irrevocably to sexual intercourse in all circumstances or that it is an incident of modern marriage that the wife consents to intercourse in all circumstances, including sexual intercourse obtained by force.[103]

[101] Constitution of Republic of Ghana 1992 (n 8) ss 12(1), 15(2)(a) and 17(2).
[102] Criminal Offences Act (n 4).
[103] *R v R* [1991] 4 All E R 481, 484.

The legal effect of the two Ghanaian statutes discussed above, the Domestic Violence Act, 2007 (Act 732) and the Criminal Offences Act, 1960 (Act 29), is that marriage is no longer a bar to revocation of consent to use of force, including use of force to obtain sexual relations. The problem remains, however, that force is not always present in rape offences and both statutes are therefore insufficient in establishing the offence of marital rape. In addition, neither law specifically mentions or uses the words 'marital rape'. Reform is still needed to ensure certainty in the laws and to remove all doubts about marital rape being a criminal offence. Specifically, the Criminal Offences Act needs a provision stating that a husband or a wife can be charged with a sexual offence against the other.

IV. Strategies for Law Reform and Ending Marital Rape

Currently, Ghana's Domestic Violence Act, 2007 (Act 732) and the Criminal Offences Act, 1960 (Act 29) can be used to prosecute husbands for marital rape.[104] The sum effect of these two Acts suggests that a spouse could be charged for marital rape when he or she uses force to obtain sexual intercourse without the consent of the other. However, the legal possibility that husbands can now be prosecuted for marital rape under Ghanaian law is yet to be tested in the courts. Nine years have passed since these legal reforms and Ghana still has no case on marital rape.

The removal of the marital rape exemption from Ghanaian law and the lack of case law precedents provides an opportunity for pursuing test case litigation. Women's rights organisations in Ghana could identify a client to support, and working with legal practitioners and academics, mount test case litigation to pave the way for cases of marital rape to reach the courts.

However, the law also ought to be more explicit. The term 'marital rape' ought now to be introduced into the Ghanaian legal lexicon and not shied away from as if it were an affront to the institution of marriage. I argue that the criminal law needs further reform and that Ghana needs specific marital rape legislation to protect women from physical abuse—particularly physical abuse in sexual relations. The current lack of a specific law on marital rape is a limiting factor to marital rape reporting.

First, a reformed law must clearly criminalise marital rape, sending out a clear message that marital rape is illegal and that spouses are not exempted from prosecution.

Second, the legislative reforms must ensure that the issue of lack of consent in the definition of rape does not only rest on proof of use of force. In this regard, analysis of statutory provisions on rape and cases from different countries would

[104] See Morhe et al (n 2), where the authors came to similar conclusions.

be beneficial. For example, in its definition of rape, the Kenyan Sexual Offences Act adds the concept of consent obtained by intimidation or threats. The statute states that a person commits rape

> if (a) he or she intentionally and unlawfully commits an act which causes penetration with his or her genital organs (b) the other person does not consent to the penetration or the consent is obtained by force or by means of threats or by means of intimidation of any kind.[105]

Third, the procedural and evidentiary aspects of marital rape prosecutions need to be carefully examined to ensure that the trial process does not frustrate the successful prosecution of perpetrators of marital rape. In this regard, Canada's experiences with marital rape law offer helpful insights for Ghana. Our countries' shared history of colonialism and a common law legal system offers common grounds from which to develop strategies for tackling marital rape. Canadian law on marital rape applies to all spouses and the criminal law abolished spousal exemption in 1983.[106]

Ghanaian law does not prescribe separation before a charge of marital rape can be brought. Hence, where parties are still married and the victim does not want criminal prosecution, the remedy for marital rape may lie in looking for a prompt, cost-effective and less traumatic means of redress, such as using alternative dispute settlement mechanisms, which could, for example, include properly supervised mediation efforts, preferably under the auspices of a court, in order to prevent impunity of offenders. Stiffer measures such as detention and imprisonment could be used only as a last resort for an incorrigible spouse or cases where parties are separated and the 'home' is already broken. Protection orders could be used in some cases, with the aim of preventing recurrence of the offence and for the protection of women.

In addition to criminal law, therefore, alternative means of redress such as mediation could also be employed in order to promote marital rape reporting. As noted above, the Domestic Violence Act, 2007 (Act 732) provides both civil and criminal remedies. Moreover, mediation has always been part of the Indigenous African judicial process.[107] In preliterate communities of Africa, there were two

[105] See Kenyan Sexual Offences Act, 2006 (Act No 3) which entered into force on 21 July, 2006, s 3(10)(a)–(c). See also Winifred Kamau, Patricia Nyaundi and Jane Serwanga, 'Dismantling Barriers to Women's Equality: Making the Case for the Criminalisation of Marital Rape in Kenya', chapter 7 in this volume, for a discussion of the Kenyan law on marital rape.

[106] J Koshan, 'The Criminalisation of Marital Rape and Law Reform in Canada', chapter 5 in this volume. See also F Sampson, *The Legal Treatment of Marital Rape in Canada, Ghana, Kenya and Malawi—A Barometer of Women's Human Rights* (Equality Effect, 2010) http://theequalityeffect.org/pdfs/maritalrapebarometer.pdf, 1, 26.

[107] AS Rattray, 'Ashanti Law and Constitution' in Eugene Cotran and Neville Rubin (eds), *Readings in African Law* (Oxford, Oxford University Press 1938) 53, where it is mentioned that cases can be settled privately or unofficially before a person acting as a mediator and conciliator rather than prosecutor or judge.

types of cases: those that were sent to the palace of the chief or headsman, mostly adjudicated by men (although a few tribunals were headed by queen mothers),[108] and those that were adjudicated by the immediate family heads or other persons with a reputation for wisdom and common sense.[109] Modern-day African courts have embraced mediation as an acceptable alternative method to settle certain disputes, including domestic violence. Ghanaian courts, for example, have always allowed parties to withdraw their cases for settlement. Sometimes courts, on their own motion, advise parties to settle the case between themselves out of court. This is usually done when parties are related. Mediation is also often proposed as a means to decongest the courts. Section 24(1)(a) of the Domestic Violence Act (Act 732) allows the courts to promote reconciliation and provides that when the complainant expresses the desire to have the matter settled out of court, the court shall refer the case for settlement by an alternative dispute resolution method.

Despite the need for specific legislation and prosecution or mediation of marital rape argued above, legislation and litigation alone is not enough to protect women from this form of gendered violence. Other hurdles to reporting marital rape, such as patriarchal sociocultural practices and beliefs, still exist and need to be overcome in order for women to take advantage of the laws. These hurdles could be overcome through well-targeted educational programmes on intimate partner violence and marital rape; such programmes should be undertaken to raise awareness and break the culture of silence and myth surrounding marital rape.

Public education is crucial for advancing the argument that to effectively tackle marital rape requires ensuring women's equality in Ghanaian society. Public education tends to be effective when it involves dialogue, rather than the mere imposition of ideas on a people. Education on marital rape as an equality issue is needed at every level of society to ensure that the message of achieving full realisation of women's rights gets to all. There is also the need for education of the public to support rather than stigmatise women who experience marital rape and to shame the perpetrators of this crime, not the victims. Those in the criminal justice system, especially those involved in prosecuting and adjudicating cases of sexual violence, need to be educated on the adverse effects of marital rape on women's lives and rights. Sensitisation in this area would help promote successful prosecution of marital rape cases.

Public education can take various forms, such as presentations to groups and organisations, radio dramas, television programmes, posters, texting to mobile phones, and community outreach programmes. A range of organisations can also offer good opportunities to present the message on marital rape, including church

[108] SA Brobbey, *The Law of Chieftaincy in Ghana* (Accra, Advanced Legal Publications, 2008) 75. Queen mothers are female chiefs and, according to Brobbey, they usually deal with disputes relating to women and some females also sit as members of chiefs' councils.

[109] See Rattray (n 107).

groups, educational institutions, traditional authorities, shelters, mobile legal aid providers, district and municipal authorities, and corporate organisations. Ghana's women's rights advocacy groups can draw on fruitful initiatives from similar organisations in Africa and beyond.

Chapter 5 of the 1992 Constitution of Ghana is also important because it protects the fundamental human rights and freedoms of every person in Ghana, and thereby affirms gender equality. All government organs, agencies, and natural and legal persons are required to respect and uphold, and the courts to enforce, these rights without discrimination.[110] Chapter 5 also provides for the protection of the right to life[111] and the personal liberty of every person.[112] Article 15 of the 1992 Constitution provides that 'the dignity of all persons shall be inviolable', and it denounces 'torture or other cruel, inhuman and degrading treatment'.

There are other important Ghanaian constitutional protections relevant to marital rape. Article 16 of the 1992 Constitution provides protection against slavery or servitude and forced labour. Further, Article 17 of the 1992 Constitution states categorically that 'all persons shall be equal before the law', and that there shall not be discrimination on any grounds including gender, ethnic origin, religion, and social or economic status. The same article enjoins Parliament to enact laws that further protect peoples' rights. On cultural rights and practices, the 1992 Constitution provides at Article 26 that:

> (1) Every person is entitled to enjoy, practice, profess, maintain and promote any culture, language, tradition or religion subject to the provisions of this Constitution.
> (2) All customary practices which dehumanize or are injurious to the physical and mental well-being of a person are prohibited.

Furthermore, Article 39 of the Constitution on cultural objectives encourages 'the integration of appropriate customary values' into national life while abolishing 'traditional practices which are injurious to the health and well-being of the person'. Thus, while the Constitution promotes customary law and practices, it also makes it clear that such practices are subject to the Constitution as the supreme law of the land. The above-noted provisions of Ghana's current Constitution have enough substance to tackle the discriminatory nature of marital rape because of their clear stance on equality, human dignity, and the denouncement of discrimination and injurious cultural practices.

Commenting on the progressive nature of the 1992 Constitution, one scholar noted that the Constitution was drawn up by a consultative committee which consulted contemporary constitutions the world over, and came up with provisions that 'renounce all forms of violence against women and children, including violent

[110] Constitution of the Republic of Ghana 1992 (n 8) Ch 5, Art 12.
[111] ibid, Art 13.
[112] ibid, Art 14.

traditional practices and rituals'.[113] Further, the directive principles of state policy at Chapter 6 of the 1992 Constitution provide objectives which specifically relate to women. The state's political objectives include state prohibition of discrimination and prejudice on grounds such as gender.[114]

Furthermore, as party to CEDAW and also the Protocol to the African Charter on Human and Peoples' Rights on the Rights of Women in Africa (the Maputo Protocol),[115] Ghana has an obligation to proscribe and abolish discriminatory laws and practices that are inimical to the rights of women. Article 2 of both documents enjoin Ghana as a state party to combat all forms of discrimination against women through appropriate legislative, institutional and other measures. The Maputo Protocol goes a step further to instruct that all state parties commit themselves to modify the sociocultural patterns of conduct of women and men through public education, information, education and communication strategies, with a view to achieving the elimination of harmful cultural and traditional practices and all other practices which are based on the idea of the inferiority or the superiority of either of the sexes, or on stereotyped roles for women and men.

It is pursuant to these obligations that Ghana's Parliament has enacted the laws that advance women's rights, such as the Domestic Violence Act, 2007 (Act 732) and new Criminal Offences Act, 1960 (Act 29). These legal protections also offer an opportunity to lobby the Ghanaian state to effectively tackle marital rape as a way of preventing discrimination and practices that are injurious to women. These strategies for tackling marital rape, including law reform, test case litigation, mediation and public education, are all important in encouraging more women to report marital rape and to advance women's right to equality.

V. Conclusion

Ghanaian law on marital rape is not very direct or clear. However, with the passage of the domestic violence legislation and the amendments to the criminal law in 2007, a spouse can now be charged and prosecuted for marital rape when he or she uses force to obtain sexual intercourse without the consent of the other. There is need, however, for more specific legislation on marital rape because marital rape can occur without the use of force, especially through threats or

[113] R King, 'Is it Time for a Progress Report on Violence against Women in Ghana?' (2006) 7(2) *Human Rights Review* 75.

[114] Constitution of the Republic of Ghana 1992 (n 8) Art 35.

[115] African Union, Protocol to the African Charter on Human and People's Rights on the Rights of Women in Africa (11 July 2003), www.refworld.org/docid/3f4b139d4.html. Ghana signed the Protocol on 31 October, 2003 and ratified it on 13 June 2007.

intimidation, trickery or coercion. In addition, there is the need to dispense with the strict requirement for corroboration in rape cases (including marital rape), in particular because this puts a disproportionately heavy burden of proof on rape victims. These reforms are required by Ghana's constitutional commitments to gender equality and the protection of human rights, and are also required by Ghana's international obligations under CEDAW and other human rights instruments. These reforms are necessary to ensure that a wife can refuse sex and have her decision respected.

9

The Judicial Treatment of Marital Rape in Canada: A Post-Criminalisation Case Study

JENNIFER KOSHAN*

I. Introduction

This chapter analyses the judicial treatment of marital rape in Canada from 1983 until 2013. This review of 30 years of case law—the first comprehensive review of marital rape decisions in Canada since criminalisation—allows an assessment of whether the sexual assault laws that women advocated are being applied as intended.[1] Section II discusses the reported cases of marital rape in Canada over this period, focusing on issues related to consent, mistaken belief in consent, evidence and sentencing. This analysis reveals that, although there are some positive developments, there are significant ongoing challenges with fulfilling the goal of protecting women's rights in the application of sexual assault laws in the spousal context. Section III concludes by highlighting the overall trends in the case law and identifying potential responses to the continuing challenges.

As noted in chapter 5, reforms to the Criminal Code in 1983 abolished the marital rape immunity in Canada and, along with other reforms to the sexual assault provisions in the Criminal Code, sought to recognise women's rights to equality and security from sexual violence. However, the interpretation of these provisions

* This chapter is an updated and revised version of Jennifer Koshan, *The Legal Treatment of Marital Rape in Canada and Women's Equality: An Analysis of the Canadian Experience* (Equality Effect, 2010), http://theequalityeffect.org/pdfs/maritalrapecanadexperience.pdf. The author wishes to thank Sheila McIntyre, Melanie Randall and Elizabeth Sheehy for their feedback on the original report.

[1] For other literature on the judicial treatment of marital rape, see eg C Boyle, 'Sexual Assault as Foreplay: Does *Ewanchuk* Apply to Spouses?' (2004) 20 *Criminal Reports* 359; M Randall, 'Sexual Assault in Spousal Relationships, 'Continuous Consent', and the Law: Honest but Mistaken Judicial Beliefs' (2008) 32 *Manitoba Law Journal* 144; E Craig, 'Ten Years after *Ewanchuk* the Art of Seduction Is Alive and Well: An Examination of the Mistaken Belief in Consent Defence' (2009) 13 *Canadian Criminal Law Review* 247; J Benedet, 'Marital Rape, Polygamy, and Prostitution: Trading Sex Equality for Agency and Choice?' (2013) 18 *Review of Constitutional Studies* 161.

by the courts has sometimes made it difficult to obtain appropriate legal redress for marital rape, as can be seen in the review of the case law which follows.

II. The Judicial Treatment of Marital Rape in Canada from 1983 to 2013

A. Introduction

For this study, I analysed just over 400 marital rape cases decided between the time of criminalisation in 1983 and the end of 2013. The case law search was designed to capture all reported decisions involving sexual violence in spousal relationships where the parties had cohabited and/or had children in an intimate relationship whether they were legally married or not.[2] A sample of over 6,000 decisions was produced and reviewed to determine which cases met these criteria, resulting in a total sample of approximately 400 relevant cases.[3]

A few preliminary observations are in order. First, every case except one involved a male accused person and female complainant(s),[4] and no reported cases of same-sex spousal violence or cases involving transgender persons were identified.[5] This result alone speaks to the ongoing nature of marital rape as a gendered and patriarchal practice.

Second, several cases involve statements or conduct by the accused that indicate the ongoing power of the myths underpinning the marital rape exemption.

[2] Searches for decisions reported in English in each Canadian province and territory were conducted on the Canadian database Quicklaw using the terms 'sexual assault' or 'rape' in the same paragraph as one of the following words: 'partner' OR 'girlfriend' OR 'boyfriend' OR 'spous!' OR 'wife' OR 'relation!' or 'consent'. The search was designed by Vasanthi Venkatesh. All cases were noted up, sometimes leading to more decisions in the same case not initially produced by the search. One limitation of this study is that Quebec, a French-language province, is not fully covered. I have also included any Supreme Court of Canada cases on marital rape through to the end of March 2017.

[3] This review and other research support was provided by volunteer and paid research assistants. Many thanks to Samantha Albright, Steve Carey, Kelsey D'arcy, Antonio Giambardino, Miriam Gibbs, Brynne Harding, Michelle Johnston, Lisa Kuti, Joshua Lam, Stephen Lajeunesse, Monica Lee, Marco Maduri, Nicole Ludwig, Tara MacDougall, Elaine Ng, Charles McRoberts, Lindsay Merrifield, Gabrielle Motuz, Orlagh O'Kelly, Vignesh Pillai, Ramsha Shafaq, Carolyn Stroz, Meghan Tonner, Elizabeth Whitsitt, Lindsay Wright and Miriam Yosowich. Given the large sample size and the sharing of subsamples amongst different volunteers, the list of relevant cases produced for this study, listed in the Appendix, should be seen as reasonably comprehensive.

[4] *R v DC*, 2012 SCC 48 (female accused ultimately acquitted of sexual assault where she did not disclose HIV status to male partner).

[5] While there is research which documents these forms of violence, it also identifies challenges in reporting it. See eg C West, 'Lesbian Intimate Partner Violence: Prevalence and Dynamics' in SM Rose (ed), *Lesbian Love and Relationships* (Binghamton, NY, Harrington Park Press, 2002) 121, 123; N Murphy, 'Queer Justice: Equal Protection for Victims of Same-Sex Domestic Violence' (1995–96) 30 *Valparaiso University Law Review* 335. See also chapter 5 in this volume, n 25.

For example, in *R v RG*, the accused told his wife that 'he had the right, as her husband, to have sexual intercourse with her'.[6] In *R v Lefebvre*, the accused was quoted as 'deny[ing] society's right to intervene in [his] private life'.[7] In *R v BSS*, a man responded to his wife's refusal to engage in sexual relations by stating that 'she was his wife'; his 'patriarchal and proprietary attitudes' were noted in a psychological evaluation.[8] In other cases, men have forced their partners to work as prostitutes,[9] have burned, cut and disfigured them 'to stop other men from getting the impression that she was "available"',[10] and have sexually assaulted and killed them.[11]

As my analysis will show, the practices of some legal actors continue to reflect and reinforce marital rape myths as well. For example, some judges have characterised spousal sexual offences as involving 'lovers'[12] or 'love making',[13] romanticising particular encounters in spite of allegations of unwanted sex. Myths relating to implied consent, marital harmony and wives' propensity to fabricate also persist. Lawyers' practices may be problematic as well, including defence lawyer tactics seeking to reintroduce marital rape myths, and failures on the part of the Crown to properly prosecute marital rape cases.[14]

The Supreme Court of Canada has decided several cases involving spousal sexual violence,[15] but has not yet taken the opportunity to denounce marital rape myths. Some of these decisions involved issues that were peripheral to the sexual assault, such as jurisdiction in sentencing matters.[16] However, other Supreme Court cases have squarely raised the issues typically engaged in marital rape matters, namely those concerning consent,[17] mistaken belief in consent,[18] credibility[19] and evidence.[20] In these cases, a majority of the Court has never discussed the

[6] *R v RG* [2003] NJ No 82; aff'd 2003 NLCA 73, para 2.

[7] *R v Lefebvre* [1991] BCJ No 2054 (SC) 3.

[8] *R v BSS*, 2006 BCPC 135, paras 6, 18.

[9] See eg *R v DF* [2002] OJ No 5004 (SCJ); [2005] OJ No 2148; leave to appeal refused [2005] SCCA No 477.

[10] *R v JJC* [1997] BCJ No 1817 (CA), para 2. See also *R v RKJ* [1998] NBJ No 483 (CA).

[11] See eg *R v MacFie*, 2001 ABCA 34; *Grey v R*, 2010 QCCA 1776; *R v Volker*, 2013 ABCA 319. The killing was not always contemporaneous with the sexual assault in these cases.

[12] See eg *R v AR* [1996] OJ No 367, para 42.

[13] See eg *R v AB*, 2003 ABPC 180, para 13. For a critique of this language, see *R v LEG* [1999] SJ No 318 (PC) para 10.

[14] For cases where the Crown failed to lay sexual assault charges where the circumstances appeared to warrant it, see eg *R v AB* (n 13); *R v Nitsiza*, 2010 NWTSC 22; *R v Truong*, 2012 ABQB 661; 2013 ABCA 373. See also R Lazar, 'Negotiating Sex: The Legal Construct of Consent in Cases of Wife Rape in Ontario, Canada' (2010) 22 *Canadian Journal of Women and the Law* 329; E Craig, 'The Ethical Obligations of Defence Counsel in Sexual Assault Cases' (2015) 51 *Osgoode Hall Law Journal* 427.

[15] *R v Sansregret* [1985] 1 SCR 570; *R v W(G)* [1999] 3 SCR 597; *R v DGS*, 2005 SCC 36; *FJ c R*, 2007 QBCA 541, aff'd 2008 SCC 21 (*R v Mathieu et al*); *R v JAA*, 2011 SCC 17; *R v JA*, 2011 SCC 28; *R v DC* (n 4); *R v Hutchinson*, 2014 SCC 19; *R v Sipos* [2014] 2 SCR 423; *R v SB*, 2017 SCC 16. These cases will be discussed in more detail at relevant points of this chapter.

[16] *R v W(G), R v Mathieu, R v Sipos*, ibid.

[17] *R v DGS; R v JAA; R v JA; R v DC; R v Hutchinson*; all (n 15).

[18] *R v Sansregret* (n 15).

[19] *R v JAA; R v DC; R v SB* (n 15).

[20] *R v JAA; R v SB*, ibid.

broader context surrounding spousal sexual violence, ignoring its prevalence, the issues these cases raise for women's human rights and the importance of avoiding reasoning based on marital rape myths. Some cases cried out for such a response—in particular *R v JAA*, where the risk of post-separation violence was overlooked by a majority of the Court in reviewing the trial judge's credibility assessments;[21] *R v JA*, where the Court failed to contextualise issues related to advance consent;[22] *R v DC*, where the Court did not comment on the trial judge's attribution to the female accused of a motive to fabricate;[23] and *R v SB*, where the Court allowed an appeal based on erroneous admission of sexual history evidence without providing its own reasons.[24] Although minority judges in some of these cases did discuss myths pertaining to sexual assault[25] and the rights of complainants to autonomy, dignity and integrity,[26] these were more generalised statements about sexual assault rather than spousal sexual violence specifically.

This reticence can be contrasted with other cases outside the area of marital rape where the Supreme Court has elaborated on the contexts surrounding domestic violence[27] and sexual assault[28] more generally. It also stands in contrast to some lower court decisions that have explicitly rejected marital rape myths. For example, in *Lefebvre*, in response to the accused's assertion that the state was interfering with his privacy, the court commented that: 'A man and woman's private life is their own, but when it involves violence from one spouse to another, make no mistake, that is society's business and the law will intervene as it has done now.'[29] In *R v GOG*, the court rejected the defence of mistaken belief in consent as 'rape fantasy' on the part of the accused,[30] and in *R v HV* the Ontario Court of Justice impugned rape myths in the sentencing context.[31] As this section will show, however, there are also several cases where marital rape myths appear to be at work, demonstrating that the Supreme Court still needs to expressly denounce such myths.

A third initial observation is that in many cases, the sexual violence occurs in the context of an ongoing abusive relationship. Some cases also involve sexual

[21] ibid, para 14 (Charron J for the majority). But see the reasons of Rothstein J, dissenting, paras 18–20.

[22] *R v JA* (n 15).

[23] *R v DC* (n 14) para 26.

[24] *R v SB* (n 15). The Supreme Court allowed the appeal for the reasons of Green CJ, writing in dissent at the appellate level (2016 NLCA 20, finding the erroneous admission of sexual history evidence and failure to allow the Crown to rebut evidence of recent fabrication required a new trial).

[25] *R v W(G)* (n 15) para 29 (L'Heureux Dubé J).

[26] *R v Hutchinson* (n 15) paras 88, 98 (Abella and Moldaver JJ).

[27] See eg *R v Lavallee* [1990] 1 SCR 852; *R v Stone* [1999] 2 SCR 290; but see *R v Ryan*, 2013 SCC 3.

[28] See eg *R v Ewanchuk* [1999] 1 SCR 330; *R v Mills* [1999] 3 SCR 668; *R v Quesnelle*, 2014 SCC 46; but see *R v Shearing*, 2002 SCC 58.

[29] *R v Lefebvre* [1991] BCJ No 2054 (SC), para 3. See also *R v VM* [1999] OJ No 3905 (SCJ) and *R v JA*, 2013 NUCJ 7 (denouncing the view of wife as property).

[30] *R v GOG*, 2000 BCPC 10.

[31] *R v HV* [1998] OJ No 4694 (OCJ).

violence against children[32] and violence using animals.[33] Cases where there is violence and physical injury in addition to forced sex are typically easier for the courts, at least at the stage of determining guilt, because defences related to consent and mistaken belief in consent are more difficult to mount in these cases. The harder cases seem to be those where the courts are faced with isolated incidents of unwanted sex without evidence of physical injury, or where issues of consent and mistaken belief in consent arise in circumstances where there was intoxication or previous 'rough sex'. Even in cases where the accused pleaded or was found guilty, sentencing judgments indicate wide variance in the degree of seriousness with which marital rape is taken by the courts.

My analysis in this section is organised around the most frequent legal issues which arise in marital rape cases, issues that are closely linked to women's rights to equality, security of the person and autonomy: consent, mistaken belief in consent, evidentiary rules and sentencing.[34] Although it is relatively uncommon for judges to provide details about the social location of the accused and victim, I will also note cases where those matters appear to have influenced arguments or judicial reasoning in marital rape cases.

B. Consent

Enacted in 1992, section 273.1 of the Criminal Code defines consent as 'the voluntary agreement of the complainant to engage in the sexual activity in question'. It also stipulates that consent cannot be obtained in certain circumstances, including where the complainant is incapable of consenting, the accused induces the sexual activity by abusing a position of power, or the complainant expresses a lack of agreement to engage in or continue in the activity.[35] In *Ewanchuk*, the Supreme

[32] See eg *R v WRB* [1999] OJ No 1394; [1999] OJ No 1470 (OCJ); *R v MBM*, 2002 MBCA 154; *R v BT*, 2007 BCPC 268; *R v EKM*, 2012 NBCA 64.

[33] See eg *R v MHC*, [1988] BCJ No 2620 (CA); *R v Parsons*, 2010 BCCA 377.

[34] Other issues which arise in criminal cases include bail issues (see eg *R v HSH*, [1995] BCJ No 2855 (PC); *R v GD*, 2005 ABQB 163; *R v CH*, 2010 ONSC 1850); the elements of sexual offences (see eg *R v Rowsell* [1990] NJ No 364 (CA); *R v C (BJ)* [1991] NBJ No 436 (CA); *R v CK*, 2001 BCCA 379; 2002 BCCA 233; *R v DARC*, 2002 PESCAD 22; *R v TME* [2004] BCJ 844; 2005 BCCA 388); dangerous offender applications (see eg *R c J-MD* [2004] QJ No 13183; [2005] QJ No 6843; *R v SGB*, 2005 SKQB 510, 2009 SKQB 360; *R v RG*, 2009 ONCA 796; *R v OEC*, 2013 MBCA 60; *R v Sipos* (n15) affirming 2012 ONCA 751; [1998] OJ No 985); Charter applications (see eg *R v Hetsler*, 2000 SKQB 126; *R v CRG* [2005] OJ No 3764 (CA); *R v RPS*, 2010 ABQB 418; *R v Ian*, 2011 NUCJ 09; *R v CMW*, 2013 ONSC 4713); and applications for exemptions from the sexual offence registry (see eg *R v CC*, 2007 ABPC 337; *R v Butz*, 2009 SKCA 142). The sample also includes civil claims (*BW v PMM* [1994] OJ No 2241 (OCJ); *NC v WRB* [1999] OJ No 3633 (SC); *Kolofsky v Freedman* [2001] QJ No 3100 (SC); *Pilon v Nahri* [2006] OJ No 2640 (SC); *DG v RM*, 2012 SKQB 296); child protection cases (*X (Dans la situation de)* [2001] QJ No 8159 (QCYD); *Director of CFCS v DAJ*, 2010 BCPC 311); other family law proceedings (*LH v DH*, 2009 NLTD 153; *SM v RM*, 2010 ONSC 7069; *LCM v BAC*, 2010 NBQB 127; 2011 NBQB 283; *EA v LM*, 2010 QCCS 4390; *MDB v HLB*, 2012 ONSC 4822); and discipline matters (*Belong v Her Majesty the Queen in Right of the Attorney General of Canada et al*, 2013 NBCA 68; leave to appeal refused [2013] SCCA No 367).

[35] Bill C-49, SC 1992, c 38, s 273.1.

Court interpreted this provision to mean that implied consent is not recognised under Canadian sexual assault law—the consent requirement is a subjective, affirmative one which can be satisfied by evidence that the complainant did not say 'yes', as well as by evidence that she said 'no'.[36] As the Court earlier acknowledged in *MLM*, it is erroneous to require the complainant to 'offer some minimal word or gesture of objection' and to '[equate] lack of resistance … with consent'.[37]

Not surprisingly, consent is a live issue in many marital rape cases. At one end of the spectrum lie cases where there is clearly no consent as defined in the Criminal Code. For example, in *R v DS*, voluntary consent was found to be absent where the accused extorted sex from his former partner by threatening to disseminate nude photographs of her.[38] A husband who administered a stupefying drug to his wife and videotaped his act of forced intercourse with her was convicted in *R v SBG*.[39] Violence and fear of violence may vitiate consent as well,[40] although fear of being thrown out of the home without one's children apparently does not.[41]

While violence will normally vitiate consent, there are some marital rape decisions where courts acquitted the accused based on their perceptions of complainants' consent to participate in 'rough sex' or sex involving bondage, domination or sadomasochism.[42] One such case, *R v JA*, went to the Supreme Court of Canada, a majority of which held that complainants cannot consent in advance to sexual activity that is expected to occur while they are unconscious.[43] The ruling has generated critiques from feminists and law and sexuality scholars.[44] Chief Justice

[36] *Ewanchuk* (n 28) paras 31, 45, citing *R v Park*, [1995] 2 SCR 836, para 39.

[37] *R v M(ML)* [1994] 2 SCR 3.

[38] See *R v DGS*, 2005 SCC 36; affirming [2004] OJ No 3440 (CA). See also *R v CBR* [1991] NSJ No 663 (Co Ct), (extortion was a relevant factor in sentencing).

[39] *R v SBG* [2001] OJ No 3785 (SCJ).

[40] See eg *R v Payne* [1996] NWTJ No 112 (SC); *R v JA*, 2009 NUCJ 3.

[41] See *R v Mitchell* [2007] OJ No 163 (SCJ).

[42] See eg *R v Brunen*, 2007 MBQB 320; *R v CA*, 2011 ONSC 291; *R v AP*, 2011 ONSC 2716; 2013 ONCA 344 (overturning the accused's conviction and ordering a new trial). But see *R v GAL* [1992] BCJ No 2529 (CA); *R v RKJ* (n 10); *R v GOG* (n 30); *R v Bone*, 2007 MBCA 95. In some cases, evidence of the past sexual history of the parties was considered as relevant to issues of consent or mistaken belief in consent. See *R v RKJ*, ibid; *R v Went*, 2004 BCSC 1205; *R v Wilson*, 2008 ONCJ 418; *R v Ian*, 2011 NUCJ 09; *R v CA*, ibid. But see *R v Bone*, ibid; *R v GPS*, 2001 YKCA 10.

[43] *JA* (n 15).

[44] Benedet (n 1); K Busby, 'Every Breath You Take: Erotic Asphyxiation, Vengeful Wives, and Other Enduring Myths in Spousal Sexual Assault Prosecutions' (2012) 24 *Canadian Journal of Women and the Law* 328; B Cossman, 'Sex and the Unconscious (No, We Aren't Speaking of Freud)', Mark S Bonham Centre for Sexual Diversity Studies, www.uc.utoronto.ca/content/view/1114/2666/; E Craig, 'Capacity to Consent to Sexual Risk' (2014) 17 *New Criminal Law Review* 103; E Cunliffe, 'Sexual Assault Cases in the Supreme Court of Canada: Losing Sight of Substantive Equality?' (2012) 57 *Supreme Court Law Review* (2d) 295; L Gotell, 'Governing Heterosexuality through Specific Consent: Interrogating the Governmental Effects of *R v JA*' (2012) 24 *Canadian Journal of Women and the Law* 359; R Jochelson and K Kramar, 'Essentialism Makes for Strange Bedmates: The Supreme Court Case of JA and the Intervention of LEAF' (2012) 30 *Windsor Yearbook of Access to Justice* 77; J Koshan, 'Marriage and Advance Consent to Sex: A Feminist Judgment in *R v JA*' (2016) 6(6) *Onati Socio-Legal Series*, available at ssrn.com/abstract=2891024; U Khan, 'Take My Breath Away: Competing Contexts Between Domestic Violence, Kink and the Criminal Justice System in *R v JA*' (2016) 6(6) *Onati Socio-Legal Series*,

McLachlin's majority decision is almost entirely lacking in context, and fails to note the abusive nature of the relationship between the accused and complainant, for which the accused had been previously jailed.[45] Her language seems deliberately gender neutral, including her discussions of sexual exploitation and the historical stereotypes surrounding sexual assault.[46] The majority thus missed an important opportunity to situate the issue of advance consent within the broader context of domestic violence and marital rape. Nevertheless, the majority's holding that advance consent is not recognised under Canadian law may have a positive impact in cases where the complainant was intoxicated or otherwise incapacitated at the time of the sexual assault, as it clearly ruled that consent must be continuous during sexual activity.[47]

Also troubling is the dissent in *JA*. According to Justice Fish, failing to recognise advance consent 'would deprive women of their freedom to engage by choice in sexual adventures that involve no proven harm to them or to others'.[48] He noted that the complainant had consensual intercourse with the accused immediately after regaining consciousness, suggesting that this supported the view that she had consented to being anally penetrated while unconscious.[49] Furthermore, the majority's approach 'would also require us to find that cohabiting partners across Canada, including spouses, commit a sexual assault when either one of them, *even with express prior consent*, kisses or caresses the other while the latter is asleep'.[50] One point on which the dissent agreed with the majority was that the de minimus doctrine—the idea that some sexual touching during sleep would be too trifling to result in a conviction—was not a satisfactory response to concerns about the criminalisation of minor non-consensual touching in the sleeping spouse scenario.[51] Indeed, the majority closed by stating that '[i]n some situations, the concept of consent Parliament has adopted may seem unrealistic' and by

available at ssrn.com/abstract=2891048; I Olson, 'Asking for It: Erotic Asphyxiation and the Limitations of Sexual Consent' (2012) 4 *Jindal Global Law Review* 171; J Sealy-Harrington, 'Tied Hands?: A Doctrinal and Policy Argument for the Validity of Advance Consent' (2014) 18 *Canadian Criminal Law Review* 119. See also the factum of the Women's Legal Education and Action Fund (LEAF) in *JA*, www.leaf.ca/wp-content/uploads/2011/05/Factum_Finale_JA_Filed_SCC.pdf.

45 See *R v JA*, 2008 ONCJ 624, para 2. But see Khan (n 44) for a critique of the focus of some feminists on the domestic violence context.

46 *R v JA* (n 15) paras 3, 24, 60, 65.

47 ibid, paras 36–43. For cases prior to *JA* involving unconscious spouses, see eg *R v BT* (n 32) (accused pleaded guilty to sexually assaulting wife several times while she was unconscious from diabetic seizures); *DIDuB c R*, 2006 QCCA 460 (accused's appeal allowed based on reasonable doubt that complainant may have consented before becoming unconscious). See also J Benedet, 'The Sexual Assault of Intoxicated Women' (2010) 22 *Canadian Journal of Women and the Law* 435.

48 *R v JA*, ibid, para 73; see also paras 72, 110–11, 115–16, and 138 for references to sexual autonomy and freedom.

49 ibid, para 69.

50 ibid, para 74 (emphasis in original).

51 ibid, paras 121 and 63.

opening the door for a constitutional challenge in these circumstances.[52] The issue of whether advance consent is legally permitted is therefore still open.[53]

There are several marital rape cases involving sleeping spouses, many of which seem to come to attention only where the accused documented the sexual assault by photograph or videotape.[54] These cases demonstrate the risk of allowing advance consent in the sleeping spouse scenario, as this would permit the defence to argue consent in such cases.

Another developing area is that pertaining to consent and the risk of HIV transmission or pregnancy. The leading case in this area is *R v Cuerrier*, where the Supreme Court of Canada held that failure to disclose HIV status to a sexual partner may constitute fraud vitiating consent where there is significant risk of serious bodily harm.[55] This ruling was later clarified in *R v Mabior*, where the Court held that 'significant risk of serious bodily harm' requires disclosure if there is a realistic possibility of transmission of HIV, and can be negated if the accused had a low viral load at the time of sexual relations and used condom protection.[56]

There have been few marital rape cases to date involving consent and disclosure of HIV status.[57] In a companion case to *Mabior*, *R v DC*, the Supreme Court was faced with a female accused who allegedly failed to disclose her HIV status to a male partner with whom she later developed a common law relationship.[58] The case turned on whether DC and her partner had used a condom, with the Court holding that the trial judge, in convicting DC, had resorted to speculation in answering this question in the negative. Although the Court ultimately acquitted DC, it failed to critique the trial judge's finding that she had a motive to fabricate condom use so as to mask 'carelessness she had shown in having unprotected sexual relations with a new partner'.[59] Interestingly, this attribution of a motive to fabricate is similar to that which is typically directed at sexual assault complainants, and can be seen as similarly gendered and problematic.

Another marital rape case, *R v Hutchinson*, involved the comparable issue of how condom tampering by the accused affected what would otherwise have been consensual sex with his partner.[60] A majority of the Supreme Court, following *Cuerrier*, held that this sort of fraud would vitiate consent since the risk of pregnancy could be seen as a significant risk equivalent to serious bodily harm.[61]

[52] ibid, para 65.

[53] The other question that remains open following *JA* is whether individuals may consent to bodily harm during sexual activity and whether choking constitutes bodily harm. See ibid, para 21.

[54] *R v Berry*, 2013 BCSC 1878; 2014 BCSC 284; 2015 BCCA 210; *R. v. Truong*, 2012 ABQB 661; 2013 ABCA 373; *R v NW*, 2013 ABCA 393; *R v Cassels*, 2013 MBPC 47; *R v BJW*, 2011 ONSC 5584; *R v JH*, 2013 ONCA 693; *R v DR*, 2013 ONSC 161.

[55] *R v Cuerrier* [1998] 2 SCR 371.

[56] *R v Mabior*, 2012 SCC 47.

[57] See eg *R v McGregor*, 2008 ONCA 831 (a pre-*Mabior* case resulting in a conviction).

[58] *R v DC* (n 15).

[59] ibid, para 26.

[60] *R v Hutchinson* (n 15).

[61] ibid, para 70.

The concurring opinion took a different approach, relying on *R v JA* to find that consent requires the complainant's voluntary agreement to the manner in which sexual activity is carried out, including use of contraception. Their reasons were grounded in the rights of complainants to sexual autonomy, dignity and personal integrity, but did not deal specifically with the spousal sexual violence context.[62]

There are a number of marital rape cases where the courts have found consent to be implied in spite of the Supreme Court decision in *Ewanchuk*. For example, in *R v RV*, the trial judge stated that:

> [W]hen parties get married, they, by the very nature of the relationship, are consenting to engaging in sexual intercourse and consummating the marriage. Even after consummation, a marriage continues to imply that parties have joined together for various purposes including that of retaining or continuing their sexual relationship.[63]

At the Ontario Court of Appeal, the Court critiqued the equation of marriage and implied consent, but failed to overturn the acquittal.[64] In a subsequent case, *R v Wigle*, the Ontario Court of Appeal overturned a conviction for marital rape and allowed a new trial because, amongst other errors, 'regarding the issue of consent to the … sexual conduct, the trial judge did not address the incident in the context of the spousal relationship'.[65]

In many marital rape cases, consent is a matter of 'he said/she said' and the key issue is credibility. There are several marital rape cases where courts assessed credibility in favour of the complainant, and were not otherwise left with a reasonable doubt as to the guilt of the accused.[66] However, there are also cases where courts displayed problematic attitudes in their credibility assessments. In *R v JAA*, the Supreme Court ordered a new trial to allow the introduction of fresh evidence relating to an alleged bite mark on the finger of the accused, which was seen as relevant to the complainant's credibility.[67] A majority of the Court remarked that it seemed 'implausible that the appellant, who had never been depressed, violent, or aggressive in the 19 years the parties spent together, suddenly turned into the suicidal, violent rapist described by the complainant', thus ignoring the prevalence of first-time post-separation violence.[68] In contrast, the dissenting justices pointed out that the separation was against the wishes of the accused, the parties had not engaged in sexual activity for more than 18 months prior to the incident, and the complainant was 'observed to be in an hysterical and terrified state' shortly afterwards.[69]

[62] ibid, paras 88, 98. The majority also refers to equality and autonomy (at para 72).

[63] *R v RV* [2001] OJ No 5143, para 10. See also *R v Bodnar* [1990] MJ No 418 (PC) (although this case pre-dated *Ewanchuk* (n 28)).

[64] [2004] OJ No 5136, para 1.

[65] *R v Wigle*, 2009 ONCA 604, para 45.

[66] See eg *R v JA* [2001] OJ 5956 (OCJ); *R v DSC*, 2004 NSCA 135; *R v RH*, 2012 ONCJ 673; 2013 ONCA 676. For cases where such findings were overturned on appeal, see eg *R v Dutchek* [1995] AJ No 233 (CA); *R v Jackson* [2007] OJ No 3269 (ONSC); *R v TT*, 2009 ONCA 613; *R v HA*, 2009 ONCA 438.

[67] *R v JAA* (n 15).

[68] ibid, para 14. For a critique see Cunliffe (n 44) 304.

[69] *JAA*, ibid, paras 18–20.

Problematic credibility assessments are also apparent at the lower court level. In *R v SC*, the court's analysis of the complainant's credibility includes comments that she 'had a history of hospitalization for nervous breakdowns' and on the date of the alleged incident 'she was depressed and her nerves were bad'.[70] In *R v AR*, the court was 'suspicious' that the complainant, who married the accused 'by proxy' from Iran, 'was perhaps more interested in securing a permanent home in Canada than anything else', relying on a racialised marital rape myth about immigrant wives.[71] As for her husband: 'A selfish lover he may have been, but a person committing sexual assault has not been proven.'[72] In a number of other cases, credibility assessments have involved consideration, and sometimes acceptance, of defence arguments that the complainant had a motive to fabricate to gain an upper hand in custody disputes, effectively supporting the marital rape myth that women may fabricate claims to gain an advantage in family law proceedings.[73]

In other cases, courts have found complainants' credibility problematic because they had consensual intercourse with the accused following the alleged incident of sexual assault or because they did not leave the accused, perpetuating myths about how domestic violence victims should react.[74] The Ontario Court of Appeal recently chastised a lower court for relying on a similar myth that the victim was too 'feisty' as a witness to be credible as a victim of spousal sexual violence. The trial judge had also looked at a dating website to obtain information about the complainant out of court, leading to a finding of a reasonable apprehension of bias.[75]

With some exceptions, these cases demonstrate that a relaxed standard continues to be applied to the issue of consent in many marital rape cases—consent may be implied, credibility determinations may turn on marital rape myths, and courts may seek proof of resistance or lack of capacity to consent rather than the absence of affirmative agreement.[76] These issues also find their way into cases involving mistaken belief in consent, as the next section will show.

C. Mistaken Belief in Consent

The 1992 amendments to the Criminal Code enacted section 273.2, which provides that a mistaken belief in consent is no defence where the accused's belief arose from self-induced intoxication, recklessness or wilful blindness, or if the accused

[70] *R v SC* [1992] YJ No 93 (TC).

[71] *R v AR* (n 12) paras 1, 41.

[72] ibid, para 42.

[73] *R v Aysto*, 2010 ONCJ 353; *R v RT*, 2011 ONSC 1042; *R v AP*, 2011 ONSC 2716; 2013 ONCA 344; *R v MKK*, 2012 SKQB 531; 2014 SKCA 15; *R v RL*, 2013 ONSC 1247. See also *R v KFL* [1999] OJ No 2623 (SCJ) (complainant's allegations of marital rape allegedly made to bolster daughter's claim of abuse against accused).

[74] See eg *R v Tait*, 2008 ONCJ 629; *R v CA* (n 42).

[75] *R v CDH*, 2013 ONSC 7789; 2015 ONCA 102, para 17.

[76] Boyle (n 1); Randall (n 1).

did not take reasonable steps to determine consent.[77] These amendments thus introduce an element of objectivity into the mistake defence, which was traditionally entirely subjective.[78] The Canadian approach is that:

> [T]he *mens rea* of sexual assault is not only satisfied when it is shown that the accused knew that the complainant was essentially saying 'no', but is also satisfied when it is shown that the accused knew that the complainant was essentially not saying 'yes'.[79]

There are numerous marital rape cases where mistaken belief in consent was in issue, with several exemplifying problematic decisions by trial courts.[80] In *R v TV*, the trial judge did not take into account the history of violence between the parties as relevant to recklessness or wilful blindness as to consent, and seemed to impose an exit requirement on the complainant, remarking that 'there was nothing that prevented this complainant, who was economically independent, from simply leaving the home' before the incident.[81] In *R v SAW*, the trial judge found an air of reality to the defence of mistaken belief in consent, characterising the accused's testimony that he thought his wife was consenting to oral sex as 'rational' while the complainant was characterised as 'shrewd' and 'fanciful'.[82]

In other cases, the defence was accepted at trial but overturned on appeal, suggesting greater sensitivity amongst appellate judges to the requirements of this defence. For example, in *R v MacFie*, the trial judge held that the accused, who had a long history of physical and emotional abuse against his estranged wife and had violently abducted and raped her, was not guilty of sexual assault because he honestly believed that she was consenting.[83] The Alberta Court of Appeal overturned the acquittal and found that the accused was wilfully blind to the existence of consent.[84] Similarly, in *AWS*, the Manitoba Court of Appeal rejected an argument of mistaken belief in consent where the accused was rebuffed by his spouse following her abdominal surgery, but nevertheless removed her clothing and had sexual intercourse with her.[85] However, the Court stated that:

> [T]he law cannot ignore the reality of normal human behavior … [and] it would be wrong to conclude that a person involved in an ongoing intimate relationship must secure the express consent of his or her partner prior to initiating any sexual act.[86]

[77] Bill C-49 (n 35).

[78] See eg *Sansregret* (n 15).

[79] *Park* (n 36) para 39.

[80] For cases where the defence was rejected, see eg *R v RG* [1994] BCJ No 3094 (CA) and *R v Payne* [1996] NWTJ No 112 (previous violence by the accused); *R v GOG* (n 30) (rejecting the defence as 'rape fantasy'); *R v PS*, 2007 ONCA 299 (no air of reality).

[81] *R v TV*, 2006 ONCJ 338, paras 166, 170. The Crown's application for an extension of time to appeal the acquittal for sexual assault was denied; see [2007] OJ No 1300 (ONSC). See also *R v LB*, 2005 ONCJ 143 (accused acquitted of forced anal intercourse because of mistaken belief he was not hurting complainant).

[82] *R v SAW*, 2002 NSPC 40, paras 29, 32.

[83] *MacFie* (n 11) para 6.

[84] ibid, para 27. See also *R v JSY*, 2011 BCSC 1280; 2013 BCCA 451 (no air of reality to mistaken belief in consent because of accused's violence).

[85] *R v AWS* [1998] MJ No 26 (CA).

[86] ibid, para 12.

It also suggested that 'evidence as to the past sexual relationship of the parties' would be relevant to whether there was an air of reality to the claim of mistaken belief.[87]

There are also cases where appellate courts overturned convictions for marital rape on the basis that the trial judge did not give adequate consideration to mistaken belief in consent or misapplied the defence to the detriment of the accused. For example, in *R v Went*, the trial judge found that the accused was reckless in failing to inquire about the complainant's consent and was wilfully blind to her protests and body language. The appeal court found that the trial judge had been unable to decide who to believe in respect of essential evidence as to whether Went's belief in consent was reckless or wilful, and that in these circumstances, he should have had a reasonable doubt as to mens rea. It distinguished *Ewanchuk* on the basis that it was a case between strangers.[88]

In contrast, there are some positive decisions where courts explicitly and properly applied the 1992 amendments to the Criminal Code in the marital rape context. For example, in *R v Lemaigre*, the court rejected the accused's defence of mistaken belief in consent where he had sexual intercourse with his spouse while he was drunk, 'and was oblivious to whether she was consenting or not'.[89] In *R v WAT*, the court noted that: 'The existence of the marital relationship ... does not entitle a spouse to assume consent unless otherwise advised.'[90] However, there remain few marital rape cases where courts deal explicitly with the reasonable steps provision of section 273.2.[91] As Randall observes, the reasonable steps element of mistaken belief in consent often seems to disappear in the spousal context.[92]

D. Evidentiary Rules[93]

As noted in chapter 5, reforms to the Criminal Code in 1983, 1992 and 1997 included new evidentiary provisions related to sexual assault. The rules concerning corroboration and recent complaint were abrogated, signifying that adverse inferences should no longer be drawn where corroborating evidence is absent or the complainant failed to complain right away.[94] Evidence of the complainant's

[87] ibid, para 13. But see *R v DWH* [2006] OJ No 1009 (CA) (rejecting mistaken belief in consent and the relevance of sexual history evidence in similar circumstances).

[88] *R v Went* (n 42). See also *R v DWK* [1996] BCJ No 1148 (CA); *R v NPR* [1998] BCJ No 2908 (CA).

[89] *R v Lemaigre*, 2003 SKPC 144, para 35. See also *R v JLA* [1995] BCJ No 2978 (PC).

[90] *R v WAT*, 2011 ABQB 328, para 102.

[91] For a rare example, see *R v DWH* (n 87). See also *R v NPR* (n 88) (implicitly addressing the provision).

[92] Randall (n 1) 145, 161, 179.

[93] This section will focus on cases where evidentiary issues related to the interests of complainants are raised; for cases dealing with issues related to the admissibility of statements made by the accused, see eg *R v LSU* [1999] BCJ No 2618; 2001 BCCA 529; *R v Nelson* [2001] OJ Nos 2353, 2354, 2355 (SCJ); *R v McIsaac*, 2005 BCSC 385; *R v TCJ*, [2005] OJ Nos 4134, 5876 (OCJ); *R v Dahlman*, 2007 BCSC 1913.

[94] See Criminal Code, RSC 1985, c C-46, ss 274, 275.

general and specific sexual reputation is now inadmissible as to her credibility; evidence of her previous sexual activity is inadmissible in relation to credibility and consent, but is potentially admissible for other purposes.[95] Restrictions were also placed on the admission of personal records about the complainant.[96] Many of these provisions continue to be at issue in marital rape cases. In addition, courts have developed and applied other evidentiary rules to assist them in making determinations as to matters such as credibility, including the admission of similar fact evidence and evidence related to a history of domestic violence between the parties.

(i) Corroboration and Recent Complaint

Even though it is not required, corroboration is still raised as a defence argument in some marital rape cases. For example, in *R v GDM*, the accused unsuccessfully argued on appeal that the trial judge should not have convicted him 'unless the complainant's testimony was confirmed by independent evidence'.[97] It may be that continued references by the courts to corroborating evidence give the defence some ammunition in this respect. In *R v JAA*, the dissenting justices at the Supreme Court noted that while corroborative evidence is not required, it can still serve to bolster the complainant's version of events.[98]

In the realm of recent complaint, courts have rejected defence suggestions that the complainant's failure to raise an immediate hue and cry should impugn her credibility,[99] although there are also cases to the contrary.[100] For example, in *R v TV*, discussed above, the appellate court denied the Crown leave to appeal, stating that:

> While there can be misconceptions surrounding reasons why victims do and do not report or complain of being assaulted … it is nonetheless appropriate for a trial judge to consider a failure to report or complain as a factor in assessing the credibility and reliability of a complainant in a trial.[101]

In *R v GB*, the court found that the complainant's failure to mention previous incidents of sexual assault when prompted by the police undermined her credibility, notwithstanding the fact that she was Fijian, did not speak English, lacked an education and was said to be 'somewhat sheltered … from Canadian life'.[102]

[95] ibid, ss 276, 277.

[96] ibid, ss 278.2.

[97] *R v GDM*, 2000 ABCA 319, para 7. See also *R v DEB* [1993] NSJ No 46 (CA); *R v ASB*, 2006 BCPC 598 (PC).

[98] *R v JAA* (n 15) para 41. For other marital rape cases referring to the usefulness of corroborative evidence, see *R v JT* [1994] OJ No 3937 (OCJ); *R v GWM* [1998] OJ No 3122.

[99] See eg *R v AFL*, 2005 ABPC 367.

[100] See eg *R v DWC* [1995] OJ No 4360 (OCJ); *R v QMJ* [2003] OJ No 6012 (OCJ); *R v Singh* [2009] OJ No 840 (OCJ); *R v MJ*, 2011 ONCJ 412; *R v LW1*, 2012 ONCJ 270.

[101] *R v TV* (n 81) (SCJ) para 12.

[102] *R v GB* [2000] OJ No 5513 (SC) paras 4, 5. The accused was convicted of other sexual assaults against the complainant where there was corroborating evidence, and was eventually sentenced as a long-term offender.

(ii) Sexual History Evidence

Since the 1992 reforms, section 276 of the Canadian Criminal Code provides that evidence of sexual history with the accused or another person is inadmissible to support an inference that the complainant is more likely to have consented or is less worthy of belief simply because the other sexual activity occurred. Beyond those impermissible contexts, the accused must apply to introduce sexual history evidence and give detailed particulars showing that the evidence relates to specific instances of sexual activity, is relevant to an issue at trial, and 'has significant probative value that is not substantially outweighed by the danger of prejudice to the proper administration of justice'. The judge hearing the application must have regard to several factors in deciding on admissibility, including the right of the accused to make full answer and defence, society's interest in encouraging the reporting of sexual assault offences, the need to reject discriminatory beliefs or biases, and the rights of the complainant to personal dignity, privacy, security of the person, and to the full protection and benefit of the law.[103]

It appears that these applications are not always a precursor to the consideration of sexual history evidence by the courts in marital rape cases.[104] As Randall suggests, judges may be subverting the rape shield provisions by allowing sexual history evidence to 'creep in' without making a formal application.[105] This approach is problematic, as it allows judges to avoid consideration of the test for sexual history applications as well as the factors relevant to admission. Also problematic is the fact that judges sometimes allow sexual history evidence to be introduced by the Crown without an application. For example, in *R v NPR*, the Crown led evidence of the sexual relationship between the complainant and her husband 'to provide context for the manner in which the assault took place, and to rebut a defence of honest but mistaken belief'.[106] Similarly, in *R v JAA*, the dissenting justices at the Supreme Court considered sexual history evidence apparently introduced by the Crown as relevant to 'the logic and consistency of the complainant's version of events'.[107] Although section 276(2) of the Criminal Code only refers to applications to introduce sexual history evidence at the behest of the defence, section 276(1) refers to the admissibility of this evidence more broadly, and should be seen as applicable to Crown-led evidence as well as defence-led evidence.

[103] Criminal Code (n 94), s 276(2) and (3). For a key case interpreting these sections, see *R v Darrach* [2000] 2 SCR 443. See also L Gotell, 'When Privacy Is not Enough: Sexual Assault Complainants, Sexual History Evidence and the Disclosure of Personal Records' (2005) 43 *Alberta Law Review* 743; E Craig, "Section 276 Misconstrued: The Failure to Properly Interpret and Apply Canada's Rape Shield Provisions" (2016) 94 *Canadian Bar Review* 1.

[104] See eg *R v RG* [1994] NWTJ No 20 (SC); *R v RG* [1994] BCJ No 3094 (CA); *R v JLA* [1995] BCJ No 2978 (PC); *R v BA* [1996] BCJ No 268 (CA); *R v DT* [1997] OJ No 688 (OCJ); *R v RKJ* (n 10); *R v DIA* [1999] NBJ No 303 (CA); *R v LEG* (n 13); *R v RAG*, 2008 ONCA 829; *R v Aysto*, 2010 ONCJ 353; *R v CA* (n 42).

[105] Randall (n 1) 158.

[106] *R v NPR* [1998] BCJ No 2908 (CA) para 3.

[107] *R v JAA* (n 15) para 51.

There are some marital rape cases where sexual history applications were rejected by the courts. For example, in *R v TEP*,[108] the Ontario Court of Appeal confirmed that an application was required in circumstances where the accused wished to cross-examine the complainant as to whether they had slept in the same bed on a particular occasion, agreeing with the trial judge that this 'raised an inference of sexual activity'.[109] The Court also confirmed the trial judge's holding that this line of questioning should not be permitted—it had little probative value and to the extent that it may have suggested that sexual activity took place it had significant potential for prejudicial effect.[110]

However, in the vast majority of marital rape cases, applications to adduce evidence of sexual activity were allowed, at least in part. Most cases involved evidence of past sexual activity with the accused, although evidence of sexual activity with others has also been admitted.[111]

In marital rape cases where sexual history evidence was considered, it was typically found to be relevant to issues regarding consent, mistaken belief in consent, and fabrication.[112] For example, in *R v BJS*,[113] the court admitted evidence of a previous instance of sexual activity between the accused and complainant as relevant to the issue of mistaken belief in consent, as 'the applicant testified he believed that the complainant had given him permission to touch her for the purpose of inspecting her fidelity', which had allegedly happened previously.[114] Evidence of a previous alleged incident of fabrication by the complainant following consensual intercourse was seen as relevant to credibility, as this 'would tend to prove that the complainant is motivated to lie because she wanted him out of her life and wanted sole possession of their joint residence'.[115] This case and others suggest that the courts are failing to apply the rape shield provisions with rigour where spouses are involved. The judge in *BJS* arguably relied on two marital rape myths—that wives are the property of their husbands and are prone to fabricate rape complaints for advantage in family law proceedings.

[108] *R v TEP* [2004] OJ No 1904 (CA). For other cases where sexual history applications were rejected, see eg *R v RDD* [2001] SJ No 354 (PC); *R v AAM* [2004] OJ No 5306; *R v PS*, 2007 ONCA 299; *R v Allan*, 2009 MBQB 323.

[109] *TEP*, ibid, para 3.

[110] ibid, paras 4–5. See also *R v JW*, 2009 ABQB 332 (sexual history irrelevant to accused's denial of alleged sexual assault, following *Darrach* (n 103)); *R v SB* (n 15) (Supreme Court accepting appellate court's dissenting reasons that trial court improperly admitted sex tape with accused and sexually explicit texts with another man, requiring new trial).

[111] See eg *R v Munn* [1993] NBJ No 418 (QB); *R v TS*, 2012 ONSC 6244. But see *R v BB* [2009] OJ No 862 (disallowing evidence of the wife's sexual history with others but allowing evidence of sexual history with the accused).

[112] See eg *R v Maher* [1992] NWTJ No 148 (SC) (fabrication); *R v TJ* [1994] OJ No 4167 (OCJ) (consent); *R v AWS* [1998] MJ No 26 (CA) (mistaken belief in consent); *R v DIA* [1999] NBJ No 303 (CA) (mistaken belief in consent); *R v ARC* [2002] OJ No 5364 (SCJ) (fabrication); *R v Went* (n 42) (mistaken belief in consent); *R v Latreille* [2005] OJ No 4845 (OCJ) (consent); *R v KO* [2008] OJ No 4193 (SCJ) (consent); *R v Wilson*, 2008 ONCJ 418 (consent); *R v MJT*, 2008 BCPC 131 (consent); *R v BB* (n 111) (consent); *R v DGS*, 2013 SKCA 6 (credibility, mistaken belief in consent).

[113] *R v BJS*, 2005 ABPC 158, para 41.

[114] ibid, para 55.

[115] ibid, para 57.

(iii) Production of Records

Similar to the situation for sexual history evidence, an application is now required before an accused can seek access to a complainant's personal records under Canada's Criminal Code. The application must provide particulars of the record, the name of the record holder, and the grounds relied upon to establish the record's relevance to an issue at trial or the competence of a witness to testify. The factors that a judge must consider in an application for personal records are largely the same as those that apply in applications to introduce sexual history evidence, including whether production of the record is based on a discriminatory belief or bias.[116]

Relatively speaking, there are few reported marital rape cases involving applications for production of personal records, suggesting that these records are 'creeping in' just as evidence of sexual history does. This is perhaps not surprising, given that the accused will often have knowledge of the existence of such records and the means to acquire them. In *Shearing*, a majority of the Supreme Court found that a production application is not required where the accused was already in possession of the records through his own devices. However, the Court also held that the probative value of the record must be weighed against its prejudicial effects to determine whether the record is admissible.[117]

Shearing was not referenced in any marital rape decisions involving personal records in the hands of the accused, suggesting that the judges in these cases did not even turn their minds to whether it was appropriate to receive and consider the records in question.[118] For example, in *R v RAG*, the Ontario Court of Appeal remarked upon the evidentiary weight, but not the admissibility, of a letter to a former lover taken from the complainant's purse by the accused. The Court found the letter to be 'a critical piece of evidence' as the complainant had alleged the sexual assault by the accused caused her pregnancy, while the letter called this into question.[119] There was no evaluation of the prejudicial effects this evidence might have on the complainant's interests.

In the marital rape cases where production applications were considered, the results are more encouraging.[120] In *R v RC*, the Ontario Court of Appeal found that the Criminal Code production provisions applied to joint records involving the accused and complainant—in this case, records relating to

[116] Criminal Code (n 94) s 278.1–278.5. For the leading case on production of person records, see *R v Mills* (n 28). See also K Busby, 'Discriminatory Uses of Personal Records in Sexual Violence Cases' (1997) 9 *Canadian Journal of Women & the Law* 148; J Koshan, 'Disclosure and Production in Sexual Violence Cases: Situating *Stinchcombe*' (2002) 40 *Alberta Law Review* 655; Gotell (n 103).

[117] *Shearing* (n 28) (complainant's diary in hands of accused, alleged cult leader).

[118] See eg *R v QMJ* (n 100) (allowing complainant's diary into evidence as relevant to credibility); *R v TV* (n 81) (allowing into evidence complainant's journal and two 'love letters' from man with whom she was having an affair; letters and journal had been stolen by accused).

[119] *R v RAG* (n 104) para 18.

[120] But see *R v WCD*, 2012 MBQB 128 (production of counselling records ordered as relevant to credibility, recent complaint).

counselling sessions.[121] Although there might be a 'somewhat reduced expectation of privacy' for such records, a production application was still required. Further, because the accused would know the content of the records in such a case, 'he should be in a position to provide specific details of the information sought'. The Court upheld the trial judge's decision not to order production of the records in this case, as the application consisted of 'largely nothing more than vague assertions' related to the complainant's credibility.[122] Similarly, in *R v AAM*, the trial judge declined to order production of the complainant's medical and counselling records to the accused.[123] According to the court, the records were of limited to no probative value, were not necessary to the accused to make full answer and defence, and had a high expectation of privacy associated with them, particularly the medical records which related to 'matters of a sexual or reproductive nature'.[124] The court also referenced other factors stipulated in the Criminal Code, including the likelihood of prejudice to the personal dignity and right to privacy of the complainant, society's interest in encouraging the reporting of sexual offences, and society's interest in encouraging the obtaining of treatment by complainants of sexual offences. These reasons exemplify the importance of rigorous application of the production provisions in spousal sexual assault cases, in order to protect the privacy, dignity and equality rights of women sexually assaulted in marriage.

(iv) Similar Fact Evidence, Evidence of Domestic Violence, Recanting Witnesses

Similar fact evidence—typically led by the Crown as to the accused's prior bad acts—is presumptively inadmissible unless, based on the similarity of the alleged acts, 'the probative value of the evidence in relation to a particular issue outweighs its potential prejudice'.[125] The rules on similar fact evidence in Canada are judge made rather than codified in the Criminal Code.

A leading case on the admissibility of similar fact evidence in the marital rape context is *R v CPK*.[126] The trial judge had admitted evidence of the accused's conduct towards his previous spouse, both general and related to six incidents of domestic violence, as relevant to the credibility of the complainant, who alleged several instances of assault and sexual violence over a four-day period. The Ontario Court of Appeal held that this evidence was too broad to frame the relevant issue for admissibility of similar fact evidence as the credibility of the complainant; the

[121] *R v RC* [2002] OJ No 865 (CA). For a case where counselling records of the accused seized via a search warrant were found to be admissible, see *R v TCJ* [2005] OJ No 5876 (SCJ).

[122] *R v RC*, ibid, para 68. However, the court ordered a new trial based on misapprehensions of other evidence at trial.

[123] *R v AAM* [2004] OJ No 5306 (SCJ).

[124] ibid, paras 14–15. The court also denied the accused's application to cross-examine the complainant on her sexual history with him.

[125] *R v Handy*, 2002 SCC 56, para 55; *R v Grant*, 2015 SCC 9, para 31. See also *Shearing* (n 28).

[126] *R v CPK* [2002] OJ No 4929 (CA).

focus should have been on whether the alleged acts occurred.[127] Even with this focus, the court found that evidence of the conduct against the previous spouse was not sufficiently similar to the alleged incidents against the complainant, primarily because there were no reported incidents of sexual violence against the former spouse, nor was there anything particularly distinctive about the conduct of the accused.[128]

The reasoning of the Court of Appeal on the lack of sufficiency of similarity is arguably problematic. As the Crown argued in *CPK*, assault and sexual assault could be seen as 'just different forms of violence', similar in the sense that 'in the context of abusive domestic relationships in which the appellant used fear as a means of control, the sexual assaults described by the complainant were simply another method of asserting control'.[129]

Nevertheless, there are marital rape cases subsequent to *CPK* where similar fact evidence involving conduct towards other women was admitted. For example, in *R v TJD* the Ontario Court of Appeal admitted similar fact evidence of a sexual assault against the accused's former spouse as relevant to the issue of consent.[130] In that case and others, past violent conduct of the accused towards the complainant, sexual and otherwise, has also been admitted as relevant to 'the narrative or context of events' and 'to show animus or motive' on the part of the accused,[131] as well as to explain the complainant's actions in not reporting the violence and in continuing to reside with the accused.[132]

Expert evidence may also be admissible for similar purposes. For example, in *R v DSF*, expert evidence on the 'tendency of persons who have been abused to remain in the relationship for some time and to not immediately disclose the abuse' was admitted at trial, and this ruling was upheld on appeal.[133] There are a number of marital rape cases where judges made negative credibility rulings regarding complainants that would have benefited from the admission of this sort of evidence, as they exhibit a lack of understanding and indeed a perpetuation of myths about the dynamics of abusive relationships.[134]

[127] ibid, paras 34–39 (following *Handy* (n 125)).

[128] ibid, paras 46, 51.

[129] ibid, para 20.

[130] *R v TJD* [2002] OJ No 2992, aff'd [2004] OJ No 1444 (CA).

[131] *TJD* (CA), ibid, para 4. See also *R v BR* [2004] OJ No 5969, aff'd [2006] OJ No 3404, para 38 (CA) (evidence of previous violence admitted as relevant to rebut defence of fabrication, to explain nature of relationship, and to show animus of accused towards wife); *R v DARC* (n 34) (evidence of past assaultive behaviour of accused admitted as relevant to animus towards complainant).

[132] See eg *R v SB* [1996] OJ No 1187 (OCJ); *R v WI* [1998] QJ 3563 (SC); *R v Chapman* [2006] OJ No 185 (CA); *R v NT*, 2011 ONCA 114. But see *R v McDowell* [1995] BCJ No 929 (PC).

[133] See *R v DSF* [1997] OJ No 5628; [1999] OJ No 688 (CA). See also *R v WI* [1998] QJ 3560 (SC). But see *R v Nelson* [2001] OJ No 2354 (expert evidence of domestic violence context was inadmissible where complainant herself had given such evidence).

[134] See eg *R v GEM*, 2004 BCSC 668; *R v JM* [2004] OJ No 5976 (SCJ); *R v Tait* (n 74); *R v BJW*, 2011 ONSC 5584; *R v CA* (n 42). The admissibility of expert evidence requires consideration of relevance, necessity in assisting the trier of fact, the absence of an exclusionary rule, and a properly qualified expert. See *R v Mohan* [1994] 2 SCR 9.

A related issue is that of recanting witnesses. Where victims of marital rape recant or refuse to testify at trial, courts may allow their previous statements into evidence if they meet the criteria of necessity and reliability.[135] Crown applications to admit fresh evidence that complainants have recanted due to threats from the accused have also been permitted.[136] Admission of this kind of evidence does not necessarily save the case, however; there are some examples of acquittals for marital rape in spite of such evidence.[137]

Defence applications to introduce fresh evidence on appeal that victims have recanted allegations of marital rape have sometimes been allowed as well.[138] For example, in *R v TS*, the Ontario Court of Appeal considered a defence motion to introduce fresh evidence—an allegation of sexual abuse against the daughter—that allegedly supported his argument that the complainant had fabricated her claim of sexual assault to succeed in a custody dispute. The Court stated that only in 'exceptional cases' will an accused be able to cross-examine the complainant in a new trial based on fresh evidence, so as not to 'repeat the stress and trauma of the legal process'; nor should the defence be permitted to 'rehash ground covered at trial' or undertake a 'fishing expedition' to uncover new evidence.[139] However, the Court decided that it was in the interests of justice to allow the defence to cross-examine the complainant on the allegations, once again supporting a discredited marital rape myth.

E. Sentencing

Since 1983, the Canadian Criminal Code carries progressively more stringent maximum sentences for sexual assault, sexual assault causing bodily harm or with a weapon, and aggravated sexual assault.[140] Subsequent amendments have increased the penalties where a firearm was used in the commission of the offence,[141] and have removed the possibility of conditional sentences (those served in the community) for indictable sexual offences.[142]

Sentences do tend to be higher in marital rape cases involving convictions for sexual assault with a weapon, sexual assault causing bodily harm or aggravated sexual assault. For example, in *R v DK*, the Ontario Court of Appeal upheld a

135 Generally see *R v KGB*, [1993] 1 SCR 740. In the marital rape context, see eg *R v CCB* [1999] SJ No 672; aff'd 2000 SKCA 72; *R v MAL*, 2000 NWTSC 61; *R v DJS*, 2002 BCSC 612; *R v KM*, 2013 ONSC 1271; 2015 ONCA 582.

136 See eg *R v DF* (n 9).

137 See eg *R v Samuel* [2001] OJ No 895 (OCJ); *R v MS*, 2004 ONCJ 397.

138 See eg *R v LGP*, 2009 ABCA 1 (ordering new trial where wife had recanted allegations of sexual assault in statutory declarations). But see *R v RSDL*, 2009 NSCA 74 (not admitting fresh evidence of recantation led by an unrepresented accused).

139 *R v TS*, 2009 ONCA 770, para 14. A new trial was ultimately ordered based on the fresh evidence; see *R v TS*, 2012 ONCA 289.

140 Criminal Code (n 94) ss 271–73.

141 SC 1995, c 39, s 145.

142 Criminal Code (n 94) s 742.1.

sentence of 10 years' imprisonment for five counts of sexual assault with a weapon, committed over a period of 12 years by the offender against his former wife. The Court emphasised both the brutality of the crimes and the relationship between the parties as aggravating factors.[143] In *R v JA*, involving sexual assault causing bodily harm amongst other offences, the Nunavut Court of Justice invoked a Criminal Code provision that allows judges to require that an offender serve half his sentence without eligibility for parole, noting 'the brutal nature of the offences, the overall degradation of women in general and his lack of remorse'.[144]

'Simple' sexual assault is the most frequent category into which marital rape cases fall, including cases of forced vaginal, anal or oral sex. In these cases, there is authority that the absence of 'gratuitous', 'extraneous' or 'additional' violence should not be seen as a mitigating factor for sentencing purposes.[145] In 2011 the Ontario Court of Appeal found that the typical range of sentences for sexual assault involving forced intercourse with a spouse was 21 months to 4 years incarceration.[146] Other appellate courts have established starting points for sentencing in this type of sexual assault case of 3 years imprisonment,[147] or ranges of 3–5 years,[148] and courts have applied these guidelines in marital rape cases.[149]

Also relevant is section 718.2(a)(ii) of the Criminal Code. Enacted in 1995, this section requires 'a court that imposes a sentence [to consider] … evidence that the offender … abused [his] spouse or common-law partner' as an aggravating factor.[150] Referencing this section in *Stone*, a case dealing with spousal homicide, the Supreme Court noted that 'prevailing social values mandate that the moral responsibility of offenders be assessed in the context of equality between men and women in general, and spouses in particular'.[151] Even before this legislative reform, courts in some jurisdictions established guidelines whereby violence in the context of intimate relationships was to be treated as an aggravating factor at the stage of sentencing.[152]

One would therefore expect sentences to be relatively higher in marital rape cases than in cases involving non-spouses. However, before the 1990s there was

[143] *R v DK* [2003] OJ No 562 (CA) para 7. See also *R v DF* (n 9) (16 years incarceration for offences including sexual assault with a weapon; upheld on appeal with the exception of the period of parole ineligibility); *R v DS*, 2013 ONCA 244 (12 years incarceration for forced sex involving weapons and friends of accused).

[144] *R v JA*, 2013 NUCJ 7, para 76 (relying on s 743.6(1) of the Criminal Code).

[145] *R v BM* [2008] OJ No 3653 (ONCA) para 7.

[146] *R v Smith*, 2011 ONCA 564, para 87. For a case following *Smith*, see eg *R v RH*, 2012 ONCJ 674.

[147] See eg *R v Sandercock* [1985] AJ No 817 (CA); *R v Arcand*, 2010 ABCA 363; *R v Adams* [1988] NWTJ No 141 (CA); *R c Bonnier* [1992] JQ 2061 (CAQ); *R v Cappo* [1993] SJ 571 (CA); *R v Savoie* [1993] NBJ No 319 (QB).

[148] See eg *R v Freake*, 2012 NLCA 10.

[149] See eg *R v RWF* [1992] AJ No 915 (PC); *R v ELD* [1992] MJ 445 (CA); *R v SJM* [1995] MJ 514 (CA); *R v DWG*, 1999 ABCA 270; *R v DS*, 2012 SKQB 118.

[150] SC 1995, c 22, s 6, enacting s 718.2(a)(ii).

[151] *Stone* (n 27) para 240.

[152] ibid, para 241.

little such recognition. For example, in *R v HLC*, the BC County Court considered an appropriate sentence in a case of forced sexual intercourse by a man on his wife of 19 years. According to the Court: 'With respect to the fact that this occurred during marriage in my view it is most difficult to assess this with respect to mitigation and aggravation. In my view I think it is a balance of both.'[153]

In later cases, courts in marital rape cases more commonly reference the aggravating nature of the spousal context in their sentencing reasons.[154] For example, in *R v LSU*, the accused, who had been in an arranged marriage with his wife, was convicted of a number of violent offences against her, including two sexual assaults. The BC Supreme Court noted the particular vulnerability of the victim, whom the accused had attempted to isolate from contact with her family, and described his treatment of her as 'an extreme abuse of his position of trust'.[155] Denunciation of the violence was seen to override the rehabilitation of the accused, and he was sentenced to 4 years imprisonment for the sexual assaults. In *R v BM*, the Ontario Court of Appeal overturned a sentence of 9 months and substituted a term of 2 years incarceration for an accused who had forced anal intercourse on his wife, who was described as developmentally delayed. In the words of the court: 'Individuals such as the respondent, who victimize their partners within the context of the marital relationship, in this case a spouse with particular vulnerabilities, must know that serious consequences will follow.'[156] The court also held that it was appropriate to consider previous violence by the accused against his wife, even if no charges were laid for those instances: '[P]rior abusive conduct may nonetheless be relevant at the sentencing stage to show the character and background of the offender as it relates to the principles of sentencing.'[157] In *R v OAP*, the Nova Scotia Supreme Court confirmed that consideration of abuse of trust continues to apply when the parties' relationship is breaking down, perhaps even more so given the prevalence of violence in this context.[158]

While many of these cases are framed in terms of the victim's vulnerability and dependency on the accused, some decisions use the language of equality and autonomy. For example, in *R v OFB*, the Alberta Court of Appeal stated that:

> Sexual assault committed by a domestic partner or former domestic partner violates the victim's emotional, psychological and physical autonomy in a way that may permanently

[153] *R v HLC* [1988] BCJ No 1299 (Co Ct). See also *R v Boliantz* [1987] SJ No 189 (CA); *R v Eisan* [1988] NJ No 241 (SC) (involving very low sentences, suggesting spousal sexual assault is less serious than sexual assault of stranger).

[154] See also *R v WR*, 2012 ONSC 3935, para 19 (court applied s 718.2(a)(ii) to offender in long-term relationship even though not spousal). But see *R v Squires*, 2012 NLCA 20 (appellate judges disagreeing whether presence of spousal relationship should be considered aggravating or mitigating factor).

[155] *R v LSU* [1999] BCJ No 2618, para 36.

[156] *R v BM* (n 145). See also *R v DGK* [1999] OJ No 5239 (SC) (vulnerability of deaf victim discussed).

[157] *BM*, ibid, para 11. See also *R v HV* (n 31) para 29 (history of abuse relevant to risk of recurrence).

[158] *R v OAP*, 2008 NSSC 365, para 38. See also *R v LAM*, 2010 ONCJ 742; 2011 ONCJ 387; 2013 ONCA 113.

> harm her intimate and trust relationships; relationships that most view as integral to a fulfilled life.[159]

Courts have also referenced the prevalence of marital rape myths. In *R v HV*, the Ontario Provincial Court recognised as follows:

> One of the myths associated with sexual offences has been that rape by an acquaintance—a husband, for example—is less serious than rape by a stranger. Part of that myth, of course, was until recently no myth at all, in that until 1983 husbands enjoyed immunity from prosecution for raping their wives. While it is now clear, surely, that the fact that the rapist is the husband of the complainant is not a mitigating circumstance, our long history of characterizing spousal rape as a non-criminal act gives rise to a legitimate concern that its gravity may not be properly appreciated.[160]

However, while the Court rejected a conditional sentence based on these considerations, it imposed a jail term of only 6 months for HV's forced sexual intercourse on his wife of 26 years.[161]

There are other marital rape cases where attention to equality and sexual autonomy are altogether absent. For example, some judges have taken into account the occurrence of consensual sex with the accused following the sexual assault[162] and 'poor choices' made by the victim, such as use of drugs and alcohol,[163] in mitigation of sentence. On the other hand, in *R v RH*, the offender's reaction to his spouse's infidelity was seen as aggravating:

> [He] physically and emotionally harmed [her] over a lengthy period of time because he felt he had the right to do so because she was unfaithful to him. He humiliated and degraded [her] by exerting his power over her … while their children slept in the same room.[164]

A related issue is whether courts should consider an ongoing relationship or the possibility of reconciliation between the parties as a mitigating factor. This is an area that raises complicated issues in terms of women's autonomy and equality. In some cases, courts have taken into account the fact that the parties remained together following the sexual assault as mitigating,[165] sometimes referencing women's (and children's) financial dependency on their partners.[166] Although this

[159] *R v OFB*, 2006 ABCA 207, para 12. See also *R v Schmidt* [1991] YJ No 84 (SC); *R v Pastiwet* [1993] NJ No 130 (SCTD); *R v GWP*, 2006 NLTD 136; *R v Woods* [2008] SJ No 200, reversed 2008 SKCA 40; *R v JA*, 2009 NUCJ 3; *R v Berry* (n 54) (referencing victims' physical and sexual integrity, dignity and self-respect).

[160] *R v HV* (n 31) para 38.

[161] See also *R v BRE*, 2012 NSSC 253 (recognising the spousal context as aggravating, but granting an absolute discharge).

[162] See eg *R v Woods* (n 159).

[163] See eg *R v CS*, 2005 ONCJ 391, para 18.

[164] *RH* (n 146) para 28. See also *R v DJ*, 2010 ONSC 3910; *R v AB*, 2013 NUCJ 15 (presence of children aggravating).

[165] See eg *R v KN* [1988] NBJ No 137 (QB); [1988] NBJ No 516 (CA) (reducing sentence of 10 months imprisonment to time served plus 2 years probation).

[166] See eg *R v BJS*, 2000 BCCA 117 (upholding a conditional sentence to allow BJS to support family).

may be a factual reality in many cases, this kind of thinking perpetuates the myth of marital harmony, reinforces women's dependency and ignores the role of the state in addressing women's financial inequality. In other cases, courts have found general deterrence to be an overarching consideration, and have not allowed the victim's wishes for a lenient sentence to prevail.[167] The prevalence of domestic violence in the community has also been a consideration in some cases.[168] One might see these cases as ignoring women's agency; however, courts have also expressed concern about putting too much weight on the victim's wishes given the potential for fear and dependency to influence requests for leniency.[169]

In addition to financial considerations, some courts have given priority to factors such as the lack of need for specific deterrence. Although Parliament has now eliminated conditional sentences for indictable sexual offences, there are several cases where such sentences were granted in the marital rape context prior to this time. In an egregious example, the Ontario Court of Appeal in *R v Nolan* allowed a Crown appeal of a 100-day sentence, but substituted a conditional sentence of 21 months plus 1 year probation in circumstances where the offender tied down his wife, duct taped her mouth, punched her in the face, cut off her underwear with a knife, threatened to cut her vagina, and eventually cut her loose and raped her.[170] In support of a conditional sentence, the Court relied upon his respect for court orders, the fact he had already served 100 days in jail and was 'doing well in the community', and his employment and financial support of his adult children.[171] The Court's statement that '[i]ndividuals, even first offenders such as the respondent, who victimize their partners within the context of the marital relationship, must know that serious consequences will follow' rings hollow in this case.[172]

Similarly, in *R v BJS*, the trial judge imposed a conditional sentence of 20 months, including a no-contact order in respect of the victim, for charges of sexual assault, forcible confinement, uttering threats and careless use of a firearm. Three months later, BJS breached the no-contact order by going to his wife's home and 'verbally assault[ing] and frighten[ing] her in an ill-considered attempt to persuade her to become reconciled with him'.[173] The Crown sought to have the offender serve the balance of his sentence in jail, but a majority of the BC Court of Appeal refused to make this order, relying on the fact that the breach did not involve physical violence, the original offences were committed during the deterioration of the relationship, BJS was employed and supporting his ex-wife and children, and he had

[167] See eg *R v RH* [1994] AJ No 124 (CA); *R v LRF* [1997] NWTJ No 103 (SC); *R v DWG* (n 149).

[168] See eg *R v Betsidea*, 2007 NWTSC 85 (SC).

[169] See eg *R v GSG* [1993] OJ No 466 (CA), 2 (but imposing only 18 months jail for vaginal and anal rape with a broomstick, even considering previous abusive conduct by GSG).

[170] *R v Nolan*, 2009 ONCA 727, para 2.

[171] ibid, paras 11, 12.

[172] ibid, para 6. For other marital rape cases where conditional sentences were given in spite of serious violence against the victim, see *R v JCT* [1998] OJ No 1688 (CA); *R v LER* [2000] NBJ No 407 (QB); *R v GAM*, 2001 ABPC 252. But see *R v RNA*, 2012 BCSC 1527 (facts too serious for conditional sentence).

[173] *R v BJS* (n 166) para 3.

the support of his extended family. According to the majority, 'this accused had made some very foolish errors of judgment, but was not a criminal in the usual sense'.[174] This decision was made in spite of a previous Supreme Court ruling that breach of a conditional sentence will presumptively require offenders to serve the remainder of their time in jail.[175]

Other factors seen as mitigating include the accused's youth and prospects for rehabilitation.[176] The potential for deportation may have some weight, although 'it cannot be a controlling factor when the objective and subjective gravity of the offence and the other factors that are applicable are also taken into account'.[177] Mental health issues on the part of the accused may also be seen as a relevant sentencing consideration.[178] Even stress experienced by the accused as a result of marriage breakdown has been treated as mitigating where the court viewed it as an explanation for the marital rape.[179] The accused's own victimisation by sexual abuse has been considered as well, but will not necessarily be seen as mitigating.[180]

Another factor for sentencing courts faced with Aboriginal offenders is section 718.2(e) of the Canadian Criminal Code, which provides that: '[A]ll available sanctions other than imprisonment that are reasonable in the circumstances should be considered.'[181] The Supreme Court noted in *R v Gladue* that this section is remedial in nature and responsive to the over-incarceration of Aboriginal peoples in Canada.[182] *Gladue* also stated that: '[G]enerally, the more serious and violent the crime, the more likely it will be as a practical matter that the terms of imprisonment will be the same for similar offences and offenders, whether the offender is aboriginal or non-aboriginal.'[183] This passage has often been relied upon by sentencing judges in sexual assault cases to justify custodial sentences for Aboriginal offenders.

174 ibid, para 14.

175 See *R v Proulx* [2000] 1 SCR 61, 2000 SCC 5, para 39.

176 See eg *R v ELD* (n 149) (2 years less a day plus probation for serious sexual assault based on young age and prospects for rehabilitation); *R v JJW*, 2012 NSCA 96 (upholding sentence of 5 months for forced anal sex even though demonstrably unfit, based on offender's efforts at rehabilitation).

177 *FJ c R*, 2007 QCCA 541, para 45, aff'd on other grounds, 2008 SCC 21. This approach was affirmed by the Supreme Court in *R v Pham*, 2013 SCC 15. See also *R v BSS* (n 8) para 50 (imposing sentence that would not 'trigger immigration scrutiny'; offender and victim were immigrants from India).

178 See eg *R v Enever*, 2009 ONCJ 49 (intermittent sentence so offender could obtain treatment for mental health issues). See also *R v RWV*, 2003 BCSC 1806 (offender with post-traumatic stress disorder (PTSD) given conditional sentence of 2 years less a day for breaking, entering and committing sexual assault against estranged wife). But see *R v Ward* [2007] OJ No 444 (SC) (finding no evidence of PTSD); *R v DC*, 2005 YKSC 30 (offender's diagnosis with fetal alcohol syndrome disorder seen as neutral factor).

179 See eg *R v Eisan* (n 153); *R v Gulliver* [1991] NJ No 145 (CA).

180 See *R v RKJ* (n 10) paras 14, 18 (offender's history as victim of sexual abuse not seen as mitigating, but potential for rehabilitation and willingness to seek treatment for substance abuse mitigating). But see *R v DJ*, 2010 ONSC 3910 (offender's history as victim of sexual abuse mitigating).

181 Criminal Code (n 94) s 718.2(e).

182 *R v Gladue* [1999] 1 SCR 688, para 64.

183 ibid, para 93. See also *R v Wells* [2000] 1 SCR 207.

However, a majority of the Supreme Court in a subsequent case, *R v Ipeelee*, clarified that sentencing courts have a duty in all cases, regardless of the level of seriousness, to

> take judicial notice of such matters as the history of colonialism, displacement, and residential schools and how that history continues to translate into lower educational attainment, lower incomes, higher unemployment, higher rates of substance abuse and suicide, and of course higher levels of incarceration for Aboriginal peoples.[184]

Marital rape cases involving the sentencing of Aboriginal offenders before *Ipeelee* was decided in 2012 must therefore be read with some caution. It is interesting to note that cases involving the sentencing of Aboriginal offenders for spousal sexual violence subsequent to *Ipeelee* have all involved custodial sentences.[185]

In *R v Betsidea*, the accused, a member of the Deliné First Nation, was convicted of sexual assault with a weapon against his wife to be. He had a previous conviction for assaulting her with a weapon. Community elders testified at the sentencing hearing about resources in the community to support Betsidea if he were granted a conditional sentence, and the Northwest Territories Supreme Court found that there were systemic background factors that contributed to Betsidea's criminal behaviour.[186] The offender was also noted to suffer from a degree of cognitive disabilities and to be a talented artist. However, ultimately rejecting a conditional sentence, the court remarked that:

> The aboriginal women in the north, indeed all women, have the right to live in safety in their community. Violence of this nature is not only a violation of the relationship between the offender and the victim. Especially in a smaller community such as Deliné, violence of this nature is a violation of the relationship between the offender and the entire community.[187]

Similarly, in another case from the NWT, *R v DB*, the competing nature of Criminal Code sections 718.2(a)(ii) and 718.2(e) was highlighted.[188]

In contrast, in *R v TC*, the Saskatchewan Court of Appeal upheld a short custodial sentence followed by a long period of probation for an Aboriginal man who was convicted of sexually assaulting his former common law wife. TC was a member of the Muskoday First Nation, and was said to be a role model in his community and an exceptional father.[189] He had no criminal record, and the sexual assault was an isolated incident for which he expressed deep remorse. The court noted that TC had a troubled upbringing and was a victim of abuse, members of the Muskoday Restorative Justice programme were willing to work with him, and his

[184] *R v Ipeelee*, 2012 SCC 13, para 60.

[185] See *R v McPherson*, 2013 BCPC 250; *R v JA*, 2013 NUCJ 7; *R v AB*, 2013 NUCJ 15; *R v OEC*, 2013 MBCA 60. See also *R v LW1* (n 100) (resulting in an acquittal).

[186] *R v Betsidea* (n 168) para 34.

[187] ibid, para 17.

[188] 2005 NWTSC 89 (2 years incarceration for forced intercourse with common law spouse).

[189] *R v TC*, 2009 SKCA 124, para 10.

wife had 'cautiously' forgiven him, leading to their reconciliation. Calling the case 'highly unusual', the Court of Appeal dismissed the Crown's sentence appeal.[190]

Although these cases may appear positive for considering the impact of colonisation at least to a degree, they are still a long way from recognising the sovereignty of Indigenous peoples in Canada to deal with interpersonal violence according to their own laws.[191] Moreover, in a number of cases the interests of Aboriginal women have been ignored when sentencing circles—a community-based sentencing process focused on restorative justice objectives—were held contrary to their wishes, denying these women autonomy.[192]

Overall, and as one might expect given the discretionary nature of sentencing and the competing factors that courts must balance, sentencing decisions in marital rape cases show great diversity. What is not a matter of discretion, however, and what continues to be downplayed by some courts, is the aggravating nature of the spousal context and its underlying connection to women's equality, security and autonomy interests.

F. Identity Issues

In the majority of marital rape cases in Canada, the courts did not make reference to the Aboriginality, ethnicity, religion, dis(abilities), socioeconomic position or other identity features of the accused and victim.[193] In other cases, these features were mentioned in passing, and were apparently seen as being irrelevant to the issues in the case.[194]

It is important not to essentialise women who are sexually violated by their partners, nor to paint all non-Western cultural norms as harmful to women.[195] At the same time, claims of culture asserted as defences or in mitigation of sentence for violence against women are widely rejected by scholars[196] and are contrary

[190] ibid, para 18.

[191] See eg Mary Eberts and Patricia Monture, 'Is "Customary Law" a Solution or a Continuing Problem of Colonial Oppression: The Case of Aboriginal Women in Canada' (unpublished, on file with author), see also chapter 4 in this volume.

[192] See eg *R v HKC* [1997] SJ No 577 (CA); *R v WBT* [1997] SJ No 826 (CA).

[193] In some cases, the parties' names or geographical location suggest they may belong to cultural minority groups, but there is no such reference by the courts. See eg *R v Singh* [2006] OJ No 4415; *R v Singh* [2009] OJ No 840 (OCJ); *R v JA*, 2008 NUCJ 8; 2009 NUCJ 3; *R v Sihota* [2009] OJ No 4590 (CA).

[194] See eg *R v GD*, 2005 ABQB 163 (parties 'immigrants'); *R v SGB*, 2005 SKQB 510 (parties Aboriginal); *R v Owjee*, 2008 ONCA 409 (parties Iranian); *R v Sandhu*, 2009 ONCA 102 (parties Indo-Canadian); *R v AR*, 2011 ONCJ 541 (parties Pakistani); *R v JSY*, 2011 BCSC 1280; 2013 BCCA 451 (parties South Korean).

[195] See eg Maneesha Deckha, 'Gender, Difference, and Anti-Essentialism: Towards a Feminist Response to Cultural Claims in Law' in Avigail Eisenberg (ed), *Diversity and Equality: The Changing Framework of Freedom in Canada* (Vancouver, UBC Press, 2006) 114; Colleen Sheppard, 'Constitutional Recognition of Diversity in Canada' (2005–06) 30 *Vermont Law Review* 463; Angela Campbell, 'Wives' Tales: Reflecting on Research in Bountiful' (2008) 23 *Canadian Journal of Law and Society* 121.

[196] See eg Deckha, ibid; Ayelet Shachar, 'The Paradox of Multicultural Vulnerability' in Christian Joppke and Steven Lukes (eds), *Multicultural Questions* (Oxford, Oxford University Press, 1999).

to international norms.[197] It is doubtful that these arguments could be used as direct defences against marital rape in Canada. For example, in *R v PB*, the victim's evidence indicated that in Greek culture 'it is customary for women to accommodate the wishes of their husbands whatever their individual preference'.[198] The Ontario Court of Justice rejected the suggestion that culture should mitigate sentence, commenting that: 'Cultural relativism cannot justify deviations from the social and legal norms expected under Canadian law.'[199] Rather, 'all cultural groups [must] appreciate that the law of sexual assault applies equally to them as well as others in our society'.[200] Nevertheless, the accused was sentenced to a relatively short jail term plus probation for forced sexual intercourse with his wife. In *R v VM*, the accused was Peruvian and there was some suggestion that his cultural background may have led him to believe that 'his wife is his property'; the sentencing judge responded that: 'Basically, and, fundamentally in this country, one must respect every other person.'[201] The accused was sentenced to 30 months jail for several offences against his estranged wife, including sexual assault.[202]

While so-called cultural defences are unacceptable, cultural considerations and biases may nevertheless creep into the analysis of issues in marital rape cases. One issue arising in several cases was the connection between culture, credibility and the victim's lack of timely or full disclosure of marital rape. In some cases, courts accepted evidence about the difficulty of reporting marital rape in a particular cultural context, and did not allow non-disclosure to adversely influence their credibility assessments. For example, in *R v HA*, the court accepted the complainant's explanation for why she had not fully disclosed the extent of the marital rape to the police: '[A]s a Muslim girl she could not discuss such matters.'[203]

However, there are other cases where courts made negative credibility findings that are problematic in light of the complainant's social location. In *R v TV*, the complainant NS's credibility was seen as negatively affected by the fact she did not leave or complain about the alleged rape, which occurred when her parents were visiting from India.[204] NS had testified that her parents would have taken the side of the accused if she had told them. The trial judge arguably engaged in problematic 'colour-blind' (or culture-blind) thinking by refusing to consider how

[197] See eg Report of the Special Rapporteur on violence against women, *Cultural Practices in the Family that Are Violent towards Women*, Doc No E/CN.4/2002/83, paras 62, 101.

[198] *R v PB*, 2009 ONCJ 303, para 17.

[199] ibid.

[200] ibid, para 20.

[201] *R v VM* [1999] OJ No 3905 (SCJ), para 8.

[202] See also *R v Agha*, 2010 ONSC 1540; 2011 ONCA 751 (affirming guilty plea of Syrian offender claiming not to have understood forced fellatio on ex-wife was criminal offence).

[203] *R v HA* [2007] OJ No 701, para 76 (OCJ). The accused was convicted at trial, but the Court of Appeal ordered a new trial based on the inadequacy of the trial judge's reasons. See *R v HA*, 2009 ONCA 438. For other cases where courts refer to the difficulty of reporting marital rape in particular cultural contexts, see *R v BSS* (n 8); *R v HSH* (n 34); *R v MG*, 2012 ONSC 5722 (all involving Indo-Canadian parties).

[204] *TV* (n 81).

the cultural context may have affected NS's lack of disclosure to her parents.[205] The judge also commented negatively on NS's adultery and had particular expectations about how she should perform as a witness: '[H]er strong demeanour in the witness stand [was] inconsistent with her evidence that she just lay there on the bed because she was fearful of the accused.'[206] *TV* is not an isolated case in terms of negative credibility findings courts have made against racialised women alleging marital rape.[207] In a strange twist on this theme, in *R v ED*, the Latin American complainant was called 'irritating' and therefore credible by the judge, who had 'little difficulty in accepting her evidence' that the accused assaulted her 'if she was as irritating in her arguments with him as she was on the witness stand'.[208]

On the other hand, courts sometimes mention culture and religion as creating vulnerabilities relevant to sentencing, recognising victims' isolation and value systems. For example, in *R v GR*, the parties were refugees from Sri Lanka; the offender was convicted of having forced sex with the victim approximately 200 times over a 5-year period together with other acts of domestic violence. The court accepted as aggravating the fact that the offender 'systematically created a situation where he was entirely responsible for his wife … where his wife had to come to him for food, for money, for clothing, for communication, for company, for anything'.[209] He was sentenced to 4 years in jail for the sexual assault charge and a total of 5 years overall. In *R v SH*, the court found it 'particularly egregious' that the offender committed repeated acts of sexual and physical assault against his wife when she was 'an extremely vulnerable, single mother without significant roots in the community or support in the community to which she could turn for assistance'.[210] The court sentenced him to 5½ years in jail, minus credit for time served. In *R v MC*, the court noted that the victim would not be 'viewed as an appropriate candidate for marriage' in her East Indian community after divorcing her husband for raping her. It was also seen as aggravating that the rape had such a 'colossal impact' on the victim, 'characterized by fear of loneliness … distrust of men generally and a fear of ever entering into another marriage relationship'.[211] The offender was sentenced to 4 years in jail.[212]

Another category of decisions involves cases where the victim's disability was seen as relevant to sentencing. In *R v RSM*, the Crown argued on appeal that the

[205] For a critique of colour blindness, see Carol Aylward, *Canadian Critical Race Theory: Racism and the Law* (Halifax, Fernwood Publishing, 1999).

[206] *R v TV* (n 81) (OCJ) para 165.

[207] See eg *R v GB* (n 102) (Fijian complainant's credibility affected by failure to make full disclosure to the police); *R v JS* [2004] OJ No 5637 (OCJ) (Indo-Canadian complainant's credibility undermined by failure to complain to family); *R v Singh*, 2009 ONCJ 78 (Indo-Canadian complainant's failure to fully disclose sexual assault to police fatal to credibility); *R v NR*, 2012 ONSC 6611(Pakistani complainant's credibility affected by failure to complain to 911 operator or first responders).

[208] *R v ED* [1999] OJ No 1502 (OCJ) para 13.

[209] *R v GR* [2000] OJ No 4096 (OCJ) para 66.

[210] *R v SH* [1999] OJ No 4728 (SCJ) para 3; varied on other grounds [2001] OJ No 118 (CA).

[211] *R v MC* [1994] OJ No 4348 (OCJ) paras 8, 10.

[212] See also *Cassels* (n 54) para 79 (offender 'deliberately and deeply offended' Hutterite victim's values; aggravating factor re: sentence).

trial court failed to take into account the victim's vulnerability and the gravity of the offence in handing down a sentence of 8 months' imprisonment for forced sexual intercourse and punching in the vaginal area. The Court of Appeal acknowledged that the sentence was very low, but because the accused had been released and his and the complainant's whereabouts were unknown, the court decided not to return him to jail.[213] In other cases, the vulnerability of victims with disabilities has been given more weight. For example, in *R v BT*, the fact that the accused had sexually assaulted his wife several times while she was unconscious from diabetic seizures was seen as aggravating. The court rejected the joint submission for a conditional sentence, which was supported by the victim because of her 'fears for her family's ability to sustain themselves financially'.[214] The accused was sentenced to 4 years imprisonment for a series of sexual assaults.[215] In *R v McPherson*, the victim's vulnerability as an elderly woman was noted.[216]

While it is positive that Canadian courts are willing to take the impact of marital rape on victims into account during sentencing, including impacts related to culture, religion, disability and age, judges' reasoning would be more compelling if the aggravating features were framed in terms of women's rights to equality, security of the person and sexual autonomy. Women's freedom from marital rape and the adverse impacts marital rape may have on them because of their social location are not always seen as rights-based entitlements imposing obligations on courts in interpreting and applying sexual assault laws.

III. Conclusion

This review of the judicial treatment of marital rape in Canada shows mixed success in terms of how the courts have applied sexual assault laws in spousal relationships. Some judges appear to understand the importance of interpreting these laws through the lens of women's rights to equality, security of the person and autonomy in the marital rape context. However, in other cases courts employ rhetoric that appears to take marital rape seriously, yet fail to do so in their actual application of the law. Worse still, some cases evidence the persistence of marital rape myths connected to assumptions about how women should react to spousal sexual violence.[217]

213 *R v RSM*, 1999 BCCA 376.

214 *R v BT* (n 32) para 42.

215 See also *R v FN* [2005] OJ Nos 3153, 3594, 2007 ONCA 276 (victim's physical disability aggravating).

216 *R v McPherson*, 2013 BCPC 250. The victim may also have been Aboriginal; she and the offender resided at the Sto:lo Elders' Lodge.

217 See Melanie Randall, 'Domestic Violence and the Construction of "Ideal Victims": Assaulted Women's "Image Problems" in Law' (2004) 23 *St Louis University Public Law Review* 107.

Myths around recent complaint, that wives are prone to fabricate where there is a family law dispute, that maintaining marital privacy and harmony are paramount, and that wives 'continuously consent'[218] to sex still influence defence strategies and persuade some judges.

An ideal victim of marital rape emerges from the case law.[219] While she must resist unwanted sex, she should not be too aggressive[220] and she should never agree to rough sex to maintain her credibility and to avoid buttressing a defence of mistaken belief in consent.[221] She should not engage in substance abuse[222] and should be faithful to her husband.[223] After she is sexually assaulted, she should separate from the accused and she should never again have consensual sex with him.[224] If she does, his sentence may be mitigated, particularly if he financially supports his family.[225] She must also complain about the sexual assault as soon as possible and properly present as a witness at trial.[226]

This review of the Canadian case law demonstrates that legislative abolition of the marital rape immunity alone is insufficient to provide women with legal recourse for sexual violence in spousal relationships free from the operation of discriminatory myths, stereotypes and rationalisations. Laws relating to consent, mistaken belief in consent, evidentiary rules and sentencing norms must be interpreted in light of principles that fully recognise women's rights under both domestic and international law and avoid marital rape myths. Training of lawyers, judges and other justice system personnel is critical in this effort, as are strong interpretations of their professional obligations to avoid discrimination.

Further research is crucially important on how the treatment of marital rape by legal actors is influenced by factors such as the race, religion, Aboriginality, disability, and class of the offender and victim. At the same time, it is clear that recognition of the equality rights of marital rape victims imposes a duty on judges to avoid the perpetuation of marital rape myths and stereotypes based on the parties' social locations. The case law analysed here indicates that that duty is not always fulfilled, however.

Another area for further research is the impact of domestic violence laws and policies in marital rape cases, including policies involving charging and prosecution of domestic violence cases, civil domestic violence legislation and domestic

[218] Randall (n 1).

[219] For a discussion of ideal sexual victims more broadly, see Melanie Randall, 'Sexual Assault Law, Credibility, and "Ideal Victims": Consent, Resistance, and Victim Blaming' (2010) 22 *Canadian Journal of Women and the Law* 397.

[220] See eg *R v JTD*, 2002 SKPC 59 (accused acquitted where complainant seen as aggressor).

[221] See discussion above, 262–264.

[222] See eg *R v CS* (n 163).

[223] See eg *R v TV* (n 81).

[224] See eg *R v Woods* (n 159).

[225] See eg *R v BJS* (n 166).

[226] See eg *R v TV* (n 81); *R v ED* (n 208); *R v CDH* (n 75).

violence courts.[227] That marital rape is a particularly egregious form of domestic violence cannot be questioned, however.[228]

In addition to the reform and implementation of laws concerning marital rape, public education and awareness are vital given the persistence of marital rape myths evidenced in the case law. Education is also essential to ensuring that women know what legal options are available to them. Victims' services and supports including advocates, legal aid, rape crisis centres, shelters and income support must also be made available to all women who experience sexual violence.

More fundamentally, structural factors contributing to women's social and economic inequality and their vulnerability to marital rape must also be addressed by courts and governments in accordance with their obligations under Canadian and international law. Until the systemic nature of marital rape is recognised and the underlying marital rape myths are rejected, spousal relationships will remain a location of women's inequality.

Appendix: List of Canadian Marital Rape Cases: 1983–2013

Supreme Court (cases included to end of March 2017)

1. *R v Sansregret* [1985] SCJ No 23 [1985] 1 SCR 570; affirming [1983] MJ No 225 (CA)
2. *R v W(G)* [1999] SCJ No. 37 [1999] 3 SCR 597; reversing [1998] NJ No 130 (CA)
3. *R v DGS* [2005] SCJ No 36 [2005] 1 SCR 914, 2005 SCC 36; affirming [2004] OJ No 3440 (CA); [2005] OJ No 3928
4. *FJ c R* [2007] QJ No 3027, 2007 QCCA 541, aff'd [2008] SCJ No 21 [2008] 1 SCR 723, 2008 SCC 21 (see *R v Mathieu*)
5. *R v JAA* [2011] SCJ No 17 [2011] 1 SCR 628, 2011 SCC 17; reversing [2010] OJ No 2902, 2010 ONCA 491
6. *R v JA* [2011] SCJ No 28 [2011] 2 SCR 440; 2011 SCC 28; reversing [2010] OJ No 1202, 2010 ONCA 226

[227] For an overview, see Jennifer Koshan, *The Legal Treatment of Marital Rape and Women's Equality: An Analysis of the Canadian Experience* (Equality Effect, 2010), theequalityeffect.org/pdfs/maritalrape-canadexperience.pdf, 25–27. See also *R v RT*, 2011 ONSC 1042 (discussing domestic violence policies); *R v JH*, 2012 NLTD(G) 32; 2014 NLCA 25 (refusing cross-examination of victim on emergency protection order against previous spouse).

[228] *R v AB*, 2013 NUCJ 15, para 28. See also Randall, chapter 2 in this volume.

7. *R v DC* [2012] SCJ No 48 [2012] 2 SCR 626, 2012 SCC 48; affirming [2010] QJ no 13599, 2010 QCCA 2289
8. *R v Hutchinson* [2014] SCJ No 19 [2014] 1 SCR 346, 2014 SCC 19; affirming [2013] NSJ No 1, 2013 NSCA 1
9. *R v Sipos* [2014] 2 SCR 423, 2014 SCC 47; affirming [2012] OJ No 5212, 2012 ONCA 751; [1998] OJ No 985
10. *R v SB*, 2017 SCC 16, reversing 2016 NLCA 20.

British Columbia

1. *R v NMR* [1985] BCJ No 2050 (CA)
2. *R v White* [1986] BCJ No 66 (CA)
3. *R v Harker* [1986] BCJ No 538 (CA)
4. *R v C(GC)* [1988] BCJ No 2153 (Co Ct)
5. *R v Nikal* [1986] BCJ No 2754 (Co Ct)
6. *R v MHC* [1988] BCJ No 2620 (CA)
7. *R v HLC* [1988] BCJ No 1299 (Co Ct)
8. *R v Lefebvre* [1991] BCJ No 2054 (SC)
9. *R v ASB* [1992] BCJ No 281 (CA)
10. *R v ED* [1992] BCJ No 1713 (CA)
11. *R v GAL* [1992] BCJ No 2529 (CA)
12. *R v Louis* [1993] BCJ No 2812 (CA)
13. *R v RF* [1994] BCJ No 2501 (CA)
14. *R v RG* [1994] BCJ No 3094 (CA)
15. *R v McDowell* [1995] BCJ No 929 (PC)
16. *R v MSW* [1995] BCJ No 1445 (CA)
17. *R v HSH* [1995] BCJ No 2855 (PC)
18. *R v JLA* [1995] BCJ No 2978 (PC)
19. *R v BA* [1996] BCJ No 268 (CA)
20. *R v DWK* [1996] BCJ No 1148 (CA)
21. *R v WJM* [1996] BCJ No 1661 (CA)
22. *R v TA* [1996] BCJ No 2492 (CA)
23. *R v JJC* [1997] BCJ No 1817 (CA)
24. *R v GPW* [1998] BCJ No 838 (CA)
25. *R v FGN* [1998] BCJ No. 2170 (CA)
26. *R v DNM* [1998] BCJ No 2810 (CA)
27. *R v NPR* [1998] BCJ No 2908 (CA)
28. *R v RSM* [1999] BCJ No 798, 1999 BCCA 218; [1999] BCJ No 1495, 1999 BCCA 376
29. *R v LSU* [1999] BCJ No 2618 (SC); [2001] BCJ No 1875, 2001 BCCA 529
30. *R v BJS* [2000] BCJ No 321, 2000 BCCA 117
31. *R v GOG* [2000] BCJ No 804, 2000 BCPC 10
32. *R v CK* [2001] BCJ No 1119, 2001 BCCA 379; [2002] BCJ No 735, 2002 BCCA 233

33. *R v DJS* [2002] BCJ No 1198, 2002 BCSC 612; 2002 BCSC 613; 2002 BCSC 614
34. *R v AMS* [2002] BCJ No 1443, 2002 BCSC 857
35. *R v RWV* [2003] BCJ No 2751, 2003 BCSC 1806
36. *R v TME* [2004] BCJ 844; [2005] BCJ No 1696, 2005 BCCA 388
37. *R v GEM* [2004] BCJ No 1856, 2004 BCSC 668
38. *R v Went* [2004] BCJ No 1900, 2004 BCSC 1205
39. *R v McIsaac* [2005] BCJ No 946, 2005 BCSC 385
40. *R v BSS* [2006] BCJ No 802, 2006 BCPC 135
41. *R v ASB* [2006] BCJ No 3447, 2006 BCPC 598
42. *R v DBM* [2006] BCJ No 3638, 2006 BCSC 208; [2007] BCJ 2903, 2007 BCSC 1937
43. *R v BT* [2007] BCJ No 1836, 2007 BCPC 268
44. *R v Dahlman* [2007] BCJ No 2822, 2007 BCSC 1912; [2007] BCJ No 2828, 2007 BCSC 1913
45. *R v MJT* [2008] BCJ No 900, 2008 BCPC 131
46. *R v Benham* [2008] BCJ No 2148, 2008 BCSC 1531
47. *R v Parsons* [2010] BCJ No 1824, 2010 BCCA 377
48. *Director of CFCS v DAJ* [2010] BCJ No 2449, 2010 BCPC 311
49. *R v JSY* [2011] BCJ No 1797, 2011 BCSC 1280; 2013 BCCA 451
50. *R v RNA* [2012] BCJ No 2147, 2012 BCSC 1527
51. *R v McPherson* [2013] BCJ No 2127, 2013 BCPC 250
52. *R v Drewes* [2013] BCJ No 236, 2013 BCSC 221
53. *R v Berry* [2013] BCJ No 2867, 2013 BCSC 307; [2013] BCJ No 2279, 2013 BCSC 1878; [2014] BCJ No 3, 2014 BCSC 3; [2014] BCJ No 306, 2014 BCSC 284; [2015] BCJ No 1038, 2015 BCCA 210
54. *R v JRS* [2013] BCJ No 2016, 2013 BCSC 1363; [2013] BCJ No 2881, 2013 BCSC 2413

Alberta

1. *R v RWF* [1992] AJ No 915 (PC)
2. *R v RH* [1994] AJ No 124 (CA)
3. *R v BGO* [1994] AJ No 604 (PC)
4. *R v Dutchek* [1995] AJ No 233 (CA)
5. *R v DPL* [1995] AJ No 1084 (PC)
6. *R v LWG* [1996] AJ No 653 (CA) [1996] SCCA No 410 (appeal to SCC abandoned)
7. *R v BHT* [1998] AJ No 223, 1998 ABPC 135
8. *R v DWG* [1999] AJ No 1123, 1999 ABCA 270
9. *R v GDM* [2000] AJ No 1456, 2000 ABCA 319
10. *R v MacFie* [2001] AJ No 152, 2001 ABCA 34
11. *R v GAM* [2001] AJ No 1711, 2001 ABPC 252
12. *R v AB* [2003] AJ No 1289, 2003 ABPC 180
13. *R v BJS* [2005] AJ No 883, 2005 ABPC 158

14. *R v GD* [2005] AJ No 1208, 2005 ABQB 163
15. *R v OFB* [2005] AJ No 1795, 2005 ABCA 451; [2006] AJ No 788, 2006 ABCA 207
16. *R v AFL* [2005] AJ No 1897, 2005 ABPC 367
17. *R v GEW* [2006] AJ No 476, 2006 ABQB 317
18. *R v McDonald* [2007] AJ No 186, 2007 ABCA 53
19. *R v CC* [2007] AJ No 1383, 2007 ABPC 337
20. *R v PPS* [2008] AJ No 662, 2008 ABQB 362
21. *R v LGP* [2008] AJ No 1488, 2009 ABCA 1
22. *R v DJD* [2009] AJ No 819, 2009 ABPC 216; [2010] AJ No 733, 2010 ABCA 207
23. *R v JW* [2009] AJ No 1534, 2009 ABQB 332; [2011] AJ No 1068, 2011 ABCA 285
24. *R v RPS* [2009] AJ No 1570, 2009 ABQB 235; [2010] AJ No 1535, 2010 ABQB 418
25. *R v KRD* [2010] AJ No 272, 2010 ABPC 56
26. *R v Brown* [2010] AJ No 998, 2010 ABPC 290
27. *R v Amaya* [2010] AJ No 1462, 2010 ABCA 398
28. *R v WAT* [2011] AJ No 547, 2011 ABQB 328
29. *R v Truong* [2012] AJ No 309, 2012 ABQB 181; [2012] AJ No 310, 2012 ABQB 182; [2012] AJ No 1125, 2012 ABQB 661; [2013] AJ No 1204, 2013 ABCA 373
30. *AM v Matthews* [2012] AJ No 628, 2012 ABQB 185
31. *R v QJK* [2013] AJ No 702, 2013 ABCA 244; leave to appeal denied [2013] SCCA No 361
32. *R v Volker* [2013] AJ No 992, 2013 ABCA 319
33. *R v NW* [2013] AJ No 1251, 2013 ABCA 393

Saskatchewan

1. *R v Boliantz* [1987] SJ No 189 (CA)
2. *R v WWB* [1991] SJ No 42 (CA)
3. *R v JK* [1993] SJ No 359 (CA)
4. *R v HKC* [1997] SJ No 577 (CA)
5. *R v WBT* [1997] SJ No 826 (CA)
6. *R v LEG* [1999] SJ No 318 (PC)
7. *R v CCB* [1999] SJ No 672 (PC); [2000] SJ No 423, 2000 SKCA 72
8. *R v Hetsler* [2000] SJ No 192, 2000 SKQB 126
9. *R v RDD* [2001] SJ No 354 (PC)
10. *R v DDH* [2002] SJ No 72, 2002 SKPC 7
11. *R v JTD* [2002] SJ No 525, 2002 SKPC 59
12. *R v Lemaigre* [2003] SJ No 686, 2003 SKPC 144
13. *R v SGB* [2005] SJ No 759, 2005 SKQB 510; [2009] SJ No 556, 2009 SKQB 360
14. *R v BU* [2006] SJ No 703, 2006 SKQB 477; [2006] SJ No 776, 2006 SKQB 476
15. *R v McAdam* [2006] SJ No 783, 2006 SKPC 109

16. *R v Woods* [2008] SJ No 200, 2008 SKCA 40
17. *R v TC* [2009] SJ No 665, 2009 SKCA 124
18. *R v Butz* [2009] SJ No 727, 2009 SKCA 142
19. *R v DS* [2012] SJ No 188, 2012 SKQB 118
20. *DG v RM* [2012] SJ No 464, 2012 SKQB 296
21. *R v MKK* [2012] SJ No 815, 2012 SKQB 531; [2014] SJ No 52, 2014 SKCA 15
22. *R v DGS* [2013] SJ No 31, 2013 SKCA 6

Manitoba

1. *R v Bodnar* [1990] MJ No 418 (PC)
2. *R v GBS* [1992] MJ No 162 (CA)
3. *R v ELD* [1992] MJ 445 (CA)
4. *R v Landry* [1992] MJ 473 (CA)
5. *R v CJC* [1994] MJ 155 (CA)
6. *R v CJK* [1994] MJ 166 (CA)
7. *R v SJM* [1995] MJ 514 (CA)
8. *R v ES* [1997] MJ 263 (CA)
9. *R v AWS* [1998] MJ No 26 (CA)
10. *R v MBM* [2002] MJ 455, 2002 MBCA 154
11. *R v Gibbons* [2007] MJ 254, 2007 MBPC 33
12. *R v Bone* [2007] MJ No 270, 2007 MBCA 95
13. *R v Brunen* [2007] MJ No 486, 2007 MBQB 320
14. *R v DLE* [2009] MJ 309, 2009 MBQB 218
15. *R v Allan* [2009] MJ No 427, 2009 MBQB 323; [2010] MJ No 183, 2010 MBQB 120
16. *R v WCD* [2012] MJ No 429, 2012 MBQB 128
17. *R v OEC* [2013] MJ No 208, 2013 MBCA 60
18. *R v Cassels* [2013] MJ No 380, 2013 MBPC 47

Ontario

1. *R v D* [1984] OJ 2594 (DC)
2. *R v KL* [1988] OJ 2973 (DC)
3. *R v DAL* [1991] OJ 2188 (OCJ)
4. *R v RP* [1991] OJ 2530 (OCJ)
5. *R v NB* [1992] OJ No 1802 (OCJ)
6. *R v SJD* [1992] OJ 3572 (CA)
7. *R v BW* [1992] OJ No 4011 (OCJ)
8. *R v GSG* [1993] OJ No 466 (CA)
9. *BW v PMM* [1994] OJ No 2241 (OCJ)
10. *R v Mielke* [1994] OJ No 2826 (GD)
11. *R v KL* [1994] OJ No 2875 (OCJ)
12. *R v JT* [1994] OJ No 3937 (OCJ)

13. *R v MC* [1994] OJ No 4029; [1994] OJ No 4348 (OCJ)
14. *R v TJ* [1994] OJ No 4167 (OCJ)
15. *R v Victoria* [1995] OJ 2139 (OCJ)
16. *R v EH* [1995] OJ No 3302 (GD)
17. *R v AV* [1995] OJ No 4012 (GD)
18. *R v DWC* [1995] OJ No 4360 (OCJ)
19. *R v AR* [1996] OJ No 367 (GD)
20. *R v SB* [1996] OJ No 1187; [1996] OJ No 5457 (OCJ)
21. *R v TS* [1996] OJ 3761 (OCJ)
22. *R v DJW* [1996] OJ 3836 (OCJ)
23. *R v DT* [1997] OJ 688 No (OCJ)
24. *R v AN* [1997] OJ 3439 No (OCJ)
25. *R v PDL* [1997] OJ No 3775 (OCJ)
26. *R v Green* [1997] OJ No 4082 (OCJ)
27. *R v DSF* [1997] OJ No 5628; [1999] OJ No 688 (CA)
28. *R v AA* [1997] OJ No 5758 (OCJ)
29. *R v SR* [1998] OJ 1439 (OCJ)
30. *R v JC* [1998] OJ No 1637 (OCJ)
31. *R v JCT* [1998] OJ No 1688 (CA)
32. *R v CPS* [1998] OJ No 2743 (OCJ)
33. *R v GWM* [1998] OJ No 3122 (OCJ)
34. *R v GS* [1998] OJ No 3552 (OCJ); [2001] OJ No 1963 (CA), leave to appeal dismissed [2002] SCCA No 21
35. *R v KB* [1998] OJ No 4146 (GD)
36. *R v HV* [1998] OJ No 4694 (OCJ)
37. *R v GDD* [1998] OJ No 4846 (CA)
38. *R v WF* [1998] OJ No 5424; [1998] OJ No 5604 (OCJ)
39. *R v SDD* [1998] OJ 5977 (OCJ)
40. *R v TT* [1998] OJ No 6369 (OCJ)
41. *R v LS* [1999] OJ No 309 (OCJ)
42. *R v WRB* [1999] OJ No 1394; [1999] OJ No 1470 (OCJ)
43. *R v ED* [1999] OJ No 1502 (OCJ)
44. *R v MT* [1999] OJ No 1561 (SCJ)
45. *R v CWR* [1999] OJ No 1583 (GD)
46. *R v MJB* [1999] OJ No 2235 (SCJ)
47. *R v KFL* [1999] OJ No 2623 (SCJ)
48. *R v EM* [1999] OJ No 3417 (PC)
49. *NC v WRB* [1999] OJ No 3633 (SCJ)
50. *R v VM* [1999] OJ No 3905 (SCJ)
51. *R. v. SH* [1999] OJ No 4728 (SCJ); [2001] OJ No 118 (CA)
52. *R v BSD* [1999] OJ No 5183 (OCJ)
53. *R v DGK* [1999] OJ No 5239 (SCJ)
54. *R v SF* [1999] OJ No 5807 (SCJ)
55. *R v GR* [2000] OJ No 4096; [2000] OJ No 4215 (OCJ)

56. *R v DB* [2000] OJ No 4699 (SCJ)
57. *R v GB* [2000] OJ No 5513 (SCJ)
58. *R v Samuel* [2001] OJ No 895 (OCJ)
59. *R v CG* [2001] OJ No 1243; [2002] OJ No 986 (CA)
60. *R v Nelson* [2001] OJ No 2353; [2001] OJ 2354; [2001] OJ 2355 (SCJ)
61. *R v SBG* [2001] OJ No 3785 (SCJ)
62. *R v RC* [2001] OJ No 4486 (CA); leave to appeal dismissed [2002] SCCA No 2
63. *R v RV* [2001] OJ No 5143 (OCJ); [2004] OJ No 849 (SCJ); [2004] OJ No 5136 (CA)
64. *R v JA* [2001] OJ No 5956 (OCJ)
65. *R v TEP* [2001] OJ No 6053; [2004] OJ No 1904 (CA)
66. *R v RC* [2002] OJ No 865 (CA)
67. *R v RR* [2002] OJ No 2162 (OCJ)
68. *R v TJD* [2002] OJ No 2992 (SCJ); [2004] OJ No 1444 (CA)
69. *R v CPK* [2002] OJ No 4929 (CA)
70. *R v DF* [2002] OJ No 5004 (SCJ); *R v FDJF* [2005] OJ No 2148 (CA), leave to appeal refused [2005] SCCA No 477
71. *R v ARC* [2002] OJ No 5364 (SCJ)
72. *R v DK* [2003] OJ No 562 (CA)
73. *R v WTV* [2003] OJ No 2272 (SCJ)
74. *R v JGC* [2003] OJ Nos 2274; 2275 (SCJ)
75. *R v DM* [2003] OJ No 2807 (OCJ)
76. *R v FD* [2003] OJ No 4320 (OCJ)
77. *R v RM* [2003] OJ No 5155 (CA)
78. *R v SDM* [2003] OJ No 5625 (SCJ)
79. *R v RB* [2003] OJ No 5627 (OCJ)
80. *R v QMJ* [2003] OJ No 6012 (OCJ)
81. *R v WRG* [2004] OJ No 399 (SCJ)
82. *R v TJD* [2004] OJ No 1444 (CA)
83. *R v DG* [2004] OJ No 3496 (OCJ)
84. *R v KEB* [2004] OJ No 3586; [2004] OJ No 3587 (SCJ)
85. *R v DJ* [2004] OJ No 4525 (CA)
86. *R v AAM* [2004] OJ No 5306 (SCJ)
87. *R v JS* [2004] OJ No 5637 (OCJ)
88. *R v MS* [2004] OJ No 5673, 2004 ONCJ 397
89. *R v BR* [2004] OJ No 5969; [2006] OJ No 3404 (CA)
90. *R v JM* [2004] OJ No 5976 (SCJ)
91. *R v OT* [2005] OJ No 1499 (CA)
92. *R v LB* [2005] OJ No 1798, 2005 ONCJ 143
93. *R v FN* [2005] OJ No 3153; [2005] OJ No 3594 (OCJ); [2007] OJ No 1391, 2007 ONCA 276
94. *R v CRG* [2005] OJ No 3764 (CA)
95. *R v CS* [2005] OJ No 3785, 2005 ONCJ 391
96. *R v TCJ* [2005] OJ No 4134; [2005] OJ No 5876 (OCJ)

97. *R v Latreille* [2005] OJ No 4845 (OCJ)
98. *R v Chapman* [2006] OJ No 185 (CA)
99. *R v DWH* [2006] OJ No 1009 (CA)
100. *Pilon v Nahri* [2006] OJ No 2640 (SCJ)
101. *R v McLeod* [2006] OJ No 3926 (SCJ)
102. *R v TV* [2006] OJ No 4089, 2006 ONCJ 338; [2007] OJ No 1300 (SCJ)
103. *R v Singh* [2006] OJ No 4415 (SCJ)
104. *R v EE* [2006] OJ No 4941 (CA)
105. *R v Hossain* [2006] OJ No 5061 (SCJ)
106. *R v Mitchell* [2007] OJ No 163 (SCJ)
107. *R v Ward* [2007] OJ No 444 (SCJ)
108. *R v HA* [2007] OJ No 701 (OCJ); [2009] OJ No 2146, 2009 ONCA 438
109. *R v RR* [2007] OJ No 1121; aff'd [2008] OJ No 2468 (CA)
110. *R v PS* [2007] OJ 1476, 2007 ONCA 299
111. *R v Douglas* [2007] OJ No 2156 (OCJ); [2007] OJ No 5032 (SCJ)
112. *R v Jackson* [2007] OJ No 3269 (SCJ); [2010] OJ No 4945, 2010 ONCJ 544
113. *R v SAT* [2007] OJ No 5059 (SCJ)
114. *R v VS* [2008] OJ No 513 (SCJ)
115. *R v Owjee* [2008] OJ No 2038, 2008 ONCA 409
116. *R v Wilson* [2008] OJ No 3583, 2008 ONCJ 418
117. *R v BM* [2008] OJ No 3653 (CA)
118. *R v KO* [2008] OJ No 4193 (SCJ)
119. *R v Tait* [2008] OJ No 4868, 2008 ONCJ 629
120. *R v RAG* [2008] OJ No 4925, 2008 ONCA 829 (CA)
121. *R v McGregor* [2008] OJ No 4939, 2008 ONCA 831
122. *R v Sandhu* [2009] OJ No 374, 2009 ONCA 102
123. *R v Enever* [2009] OJ No 648, 2009 ONCJ 49
124. *R v Singh* [2009] OJ No 840, 2009 ONCJ 78 (OCJ)
125. *R v BB* [2009] OJ No 862; [2009] OJ No 864 (SCJ)
126. *R v PB* [2009] OJ No 2707, 2009 ONCJ 303 (OCJ)
127. *R v Wigle* [2009] OJ No 3276, 2009 ONCA 604
128. *R v TT* [2009] OJ No 3388, 2009 ONCA 613
129. *R v Bain* [2009] OJ No 3516 (SCJ)
130. *R v Nolan* [2009] OJ No 4237, 2009 ONCA 727 (CA)
131. *R v TS* [2009] OJ No 4590, 2009 ONCA 770; [2012] OJ No 1962, 2012 ONCA 289
132. *R v RG* [2009] OJ No 4791, 2009 ONCA 796
133. *R v Ball* [2009] OJ No 5025 (SCJ)
134. *R v SR* [2009] OJ No 5470 (SCJ)
135. *R v MQ* [2010] OJ No 378, 2010 ONSC 61; [2012] OJ No 1584, 2012 ONCA 224
136. *R v SMH* [2010] OJ No 1047, 2010 ONSC 1635; [2011] OJ No 1187, 2011 ONCA 215; leave to appeal refused [2011] SCCA No 347

137. *R v Agha* [2010] OJ No 1170, 2010 ONSC 1540; [2011] OJ No 5321, 2011 ONCA 751
138. *R v CH* [2010] OJ No 1552, 2010 ONSC 1850
139. *R v EG* [2010] OJ No 2734, 2010 ONSC 3667
140. *R v Aysto* [2010] OJ No 3598, 2010 ONCJ 353
141. *SM v RM* [2010] OJ No 5710, 2010 ONSC 7069
142. *R v DJ* [2010] OJ No 5878, 2010 ONSC 3910
143. *R v LAM* [2010] OJ No 6100, 2010 ONCJ 742; [2011] OJ No 3488, 2011 ONCJ 387; [2013] OJ No 729, 2013 ONCA 113
144. *R v CA* [2011] OJ No 115, 2011 ONSC 291
145. *R v SJ* [2011] OJ No 405, 2011 ONCJ 26; [2011] OJ No 406, 2011 ONCJ 27
146. *R v NT* [2011] OJ No 551; 2011 ONCA 114
147. *R v RM* [2011] OJ No 690, 2011 ONCA 132
148. *R v RT* [2011] OJ No 1704, 2011 ONSC 1042
149. *R v JB* [2011] OJ No 2322, 2011 ONCA 404
150. *R v AP* [2011] OJ No 3320, 2011 ONSC 2716; [2013] OJ No 2291, 2013 ONCA 344
151. *R v Smith* [2011] OJ No 3832, 2011 ONCA 564
152. *R v MJ* [2011] OJ No 3981, 2011 ONCJ 412
153. *R v AR* [2011] OJ No 4939, 2011 ONCJ 541
154. *R v BJW* [2011] OJ No 6314, 2011 ONSC 5584
155. *R v SM* [2012] OJ No 1666, 2012 ONSC 2314
156. *R v LW1* [2012] OJ No 2018, 2012 ONCJ 270
157. *R v BS* [2012] OJ No 3268, 2012 ONCJ 447
158. *MDB v HLB* [2012] OJ No 3925, 2012 ONSC 4822
159. *R v MG* [2012] OJ No 4795, 2012 ONSC 5722
160. *R v RH* [2012] OJ No 5091, 2012 ONCJ 673; [2012] OJ No 5092, 2012 ONCJ 674; [2013] OJ No 5068, 2013 ONCA 676
161. *R v TS* [2012] OJ No 5341, 2012 ONSC 6244
162. *R v NR* [2012] OJ No 5454, 2012 ONSC 6611
163. *R v DR* [2013] OJ No 55, 2013 ONSC 161
164. *R v JS* [2013] OJ No 668, 2013 ONSC 1001
165. *R v RL* [2013] OJ No 917, 2013 ONSC 1247
166. *R v KM* [2013] OJ No 1479, 2013 ONSC 1271; [2015] OJ No 4524, 2015 ONCA 582
167. *R v DS* [2013] OJ No 1767, 2013 ONCA 244
168. *R v HAK* [2013] OJ No 3572, 2013 ONSC 4322
169. *R v JH* [2013] OJ No 5161, 2013 ONCA 693
170. *R v CDH* [2013] OJ No 5831, 2013 ONSC 7789; [2015] OJ No 672, 2015 ONCA 102
171. *R v CMW* [2013] OJ No 6251, 2013 ONSC 4713

Quebec

1. *R v WI* [1998] QJ 3560; [1998] QJ 3563 (SC)
2. *R c Richard* [2001] JQ 1516 (CA)
3. *Kolofsky v Freedman* [2001] QJ 3100 (SC)
4. *X (Dans la situation de)* [2001] QJ No 8159 (QCYD)
5. *R c J-MD* [2004] QJ No 13183; [2005] QJ No 6843 (CQ)
6. *R c Gorman* [2005] QJ 1319 (SC); [2006] QJ 2709; [2009] QJ 4376, 2009 QBCA 915; leave to appeal refused [2009] SCCA 288
7. *DIDuB c R* [2006] QJ No 2958, 2006 QCCA 460
8. *R c DD* [2006] JQ 11806 (CA)
9. *Cook c R* [2009] JQ 15641, 2009 QCCA 2423
10. *EA v LM* [2010] QJ No 9286, 2010 QCCS 4390
11. *Grey v R* [2010] QJ No 9725, 2010 QCCA 1776
12. *Vachon v R* [2011] QJ No 16650, 2011 QCCA 2103

New Brunswick

1. *R v KN* [1988] NBJ No 137 (QB); [1988] NBJ No 516 (CA)
2. *R v BJC* [1991] NBJ No 436 (CA)
3. *R v Munn* [1993] NBJ No 418 (QB)
4. *R v GJI* [1995] NBJ No 117 (CA)
5. *R v MIP* [1998] NBJ No 424 (QB)
6. *R v RKJ* [1998] NBJ No 483 (CA)
7. *R v DIA* [1999] NBJ No 303 (CA)
8. *R v LER* [2000] NBJ No 407 (QB)
9. *R v JF* [2001] NBJ No 286, 2001 NBCA 81
10. *R v NGB* [2002] NBJ No 147 (QB); [2002] NBJ No 357 (CA)
11. *LCM v BAC* [2010] NBJ No 107, 2010 NBQB 127
12. *R v EKM* [2012] NBJ No 261, 2012 NBCA 64
13. *R v NJD* [2013] NBJ No 151, 2013 NBQB 184
14. *Belong v Her Majesty the Queen in Right of the Attorney General of Canada et al* [2013] NBJ No 385, 2013 NBCA 68; leave to appeal refused [2013] SCCA No 367

Nova Scotia

1. *R v CBR* [1991] NSJ No 663 (Co Ct)
2. *R v Swinamer* [1992] NSJ No 57 (CA)
3. *R v RSR* [1993] NSJ No 42 (CA)
4. *R v DEB* [1993] NSJ No 46 (CA)
5. *R v TVG* [1994] NSJ No 348 (SC)
6. *R v SDM* [1995] NSJ No 236 (SC)
7. *R v DBC* [1995] NSJ No 413 (CA), leave to appeal dismissed [1995] SCCA No 225

8. *R v LDM* [2000] NSJ No 60 (SC); [2001] NSJ No 46, 2001 NSCA 19; [2000] NSJ No 189 (CA)
9. *R v CMM* [2002] NSJ No 197, 2002 NSPC 13
10. *R v SAW* [2002] NSJ No 533, 2002 NSPC 40
11. *R v GLJP* [2003] NSJ No 310, 2003 NSSC 168; [2003] NSJ No 348, 2003 NSSC 195; [2003] NSJ No 509, 2004 NSSC 8
12. *R v DSC* [2004] NSJ No 432, 2004 NSCA 135
13. *R v SEC* [2008] NSJ No 261, 2008 NSSC 161 (SC)
14. *R v OAP* [2008] NSJ No 534, 2008 NSSC 365
15. *R v RSDL* [2009] NSJ No 289, 2009 NSCA 74
16. *R v BRE* [2012] NSJ No 378, 2012 NSSC 253
17. *R v JJW* [2012] NSJ No 522, 2012 NSCA 96

PEI

1. *R v Beamish* [1996] PEIJ No 85 (SC)
2. *R v DARC* [2002] PEIJ No 91, 2002 PESCAD 22
3. *R v JMH* [2011] PEIJ No 14, 2011 PECA 8; [2012] PEIJ No 10, 2012 PECA 6

Newfoundland/Labrador

1. *R v Eisan* [1988] NJ No 241 (SC)
2. *R v Rowsell* [1990] NJ No 364 (CA)
3. *R v Gulliver* [1991] NJ No 145 (CA)
4. *R v Pastiwet* [1993] NJ No 130 (SC)
5. *R v JJ* [2002] NJ No 149; [2004] NJ No 422, 2004 NLCA 81
6. *R v DEDP* [2002] NJ No 174 (SC)
7. *R v RG* [2003] NJ No 82, 2003 NLSCTD 44; [2003] NJ No 336, 2003 NLCA 73
8. *R v GWP* [2006] NJ No 242, 2006 NLTD 136
9. *R v Squires* [2009] NJ No 9; [2009] NJ No 47; [2012] NJ No 101, 2012 NLCA 20
10. *LH v DH* [2009] NJ No 276, 2009 NLTD 153
11. *R v JH* [2012] NJ No 85, 2012 NLTD(G) 32; [2012] NJ No 307, 2012 NLTD(G) 122; [2012] NJ No 411, 2012 NLTD(G) 174; [2014] NJ No 159, 2014 NLCA 25

Yukon

1. *R v Atlin* [1986] YJ No 18 (CA)
2. *R v Schmidt* [1991] YJ No 84 (SC)
3. *R v SC* [1992] YJ No 93 (SC)
4. *R v JWK* [1993] YJ No 237 (TC); [1995] YJ No 9 (CA)
5. *R v BGD* [1997] YJ No 63 (SC)
6. *R v RF* [2000] YJ No 15, 2000 YTTC 507; [2000] YJ No 54, 2000 YTTC 27
7. *R v GPS* [2001] YJ No 95, 2001 YKCA 10
8. *R v DC* [2005] YJ No 54, 2005 YKSC 30

9. *R v Tronson* [2009] YJ No 150, 2009 YKTC 88
10. *R v WJA* [2010] YJ 118, 2010 YKTC 108
11. *R v DCR* [2011] YJ 17, 2011 YKTC 15
12. *R v Mantla* [2012] YJ No 57, 2012 YKTC 52; [2012] YJ No 132, 2012 YKSC 73

NWT

1. *R v KPR* [1989] NWTJ No 74 (SC)
2. *R v JJ* [1990] NWTJ No 41 (SC)
3. *R v MOM* [1991] NWTJ No 146 (SC)
4. *R v Maher* [1992] NWTJ No 148 (SC)
5. *R v CM* [1992] NWTJ No 236 (TC)
6. *R v RG* [1994] NWTJ No 20 (SC)
7. *R v BA* [1996] NWTJ No 7 (CA)
8. *R v Payne* [1996] NWTJ No 112 (SC)
9. *R v EPG* [1996] NWTJ No 119 (SC); [1997] NWTJ No 27 (CA); [1997] NWTJ No 160 (CA)
10. *R v LE* [1996] NWTJ No 137 (SC)
11. *R v Kalluk* [1997] NWTJ No 15 (CA)
12. *R v TG* [1997] NWTJ No 90 (SC)
13. *R v LRF* [1997] NWTJ No 103 (SC)
14. *R v LR* [1999] NWTJ No 68 (SC)
15. *R v MAL* [2000] NWTJ No 84, 2000 NWTSC 61
16. *R v DCM* [2003] NWTJ No 57, 2003 NWTSC 43
17. *R v Vermillion* [2003] NWTJ No 94, 2003 NWTSC 59
18. *R v PDC* [2005] NWTJ No 73, 2005 NWTSC 69
19. *R v DB* [2005] NWTJ No 93, 2005 NWTSC 89
20. *R v CM* [2005] NWTJ No 112; 2005 NWTSC 100
21. *R v Sunrise* [2006] NWTJ No 60; 2006 NWTSC
22. *R v Betsidea* [2007] NWTJ No 90, 2007 NWTSC 85
23. *R v TJM* [2010] NWTJ 64, 2011 NWTSC 70
24. *R v Nitsiza* [2010] NWTJ No 22, 2010 NWTSC 22

Nunavut

1. *R v JA* [2008] NuJ No 7, 2008 NUCJ 8; [2009] Nu.J No 2, 2009 NUCJ 3
2. *R v Ian* [2011] NuJ 11, 2011 NUCJ 09
3. *R v JA* [2013] NuJ No 11, 2013 NUCJ 7
4. *R v AB* [2013] NuJ No 19, 2013 NUCJ 15

INDEX

www.ingramcontent.com/pod-product-compliance
Lightning Source LLC
LaVergne TN
LVHW052248200926
848481LV00002B/313